Brewery Railways
of
Burton on Trent

Cliff Shepherd

INDUSTRIAL RAILWAY SOCIETY 1996

Brewery Railways of Burton on Trent

© Cliff Shepherd and Industrial Railway Society 1996

ISBN 0 901096 93 8

Published in 1996 by the Industrial Railway Society, 18 Osprey Close, Guisborough, Cleveland TS14 8HN

Available from IRS Publications,
1 Clifton Court, Oakham, Rutland LE15 6LT

Typesetting and artwork by the Industrial Railway Society
Printed by AB Printers Limited, 33 Cannock Street, Leicester LE4 9HR

CONTENTS

ANB   Allsopp's New Brewery
BB   Bindley Brewery
BEW   Baguley Engine Works
BLS   Midland Railway Burton Loco Shed
BMB   Bass Middle Brewery
BMY   Bass Middle Yard
LJS   Midland Railway Leicester Jnc. Sidings
RB   Robinson's Brewery
THB   Truman, Hanbury, Buxton Brewery
TW   Thornewill & Warham
WB   Worthington Brewery

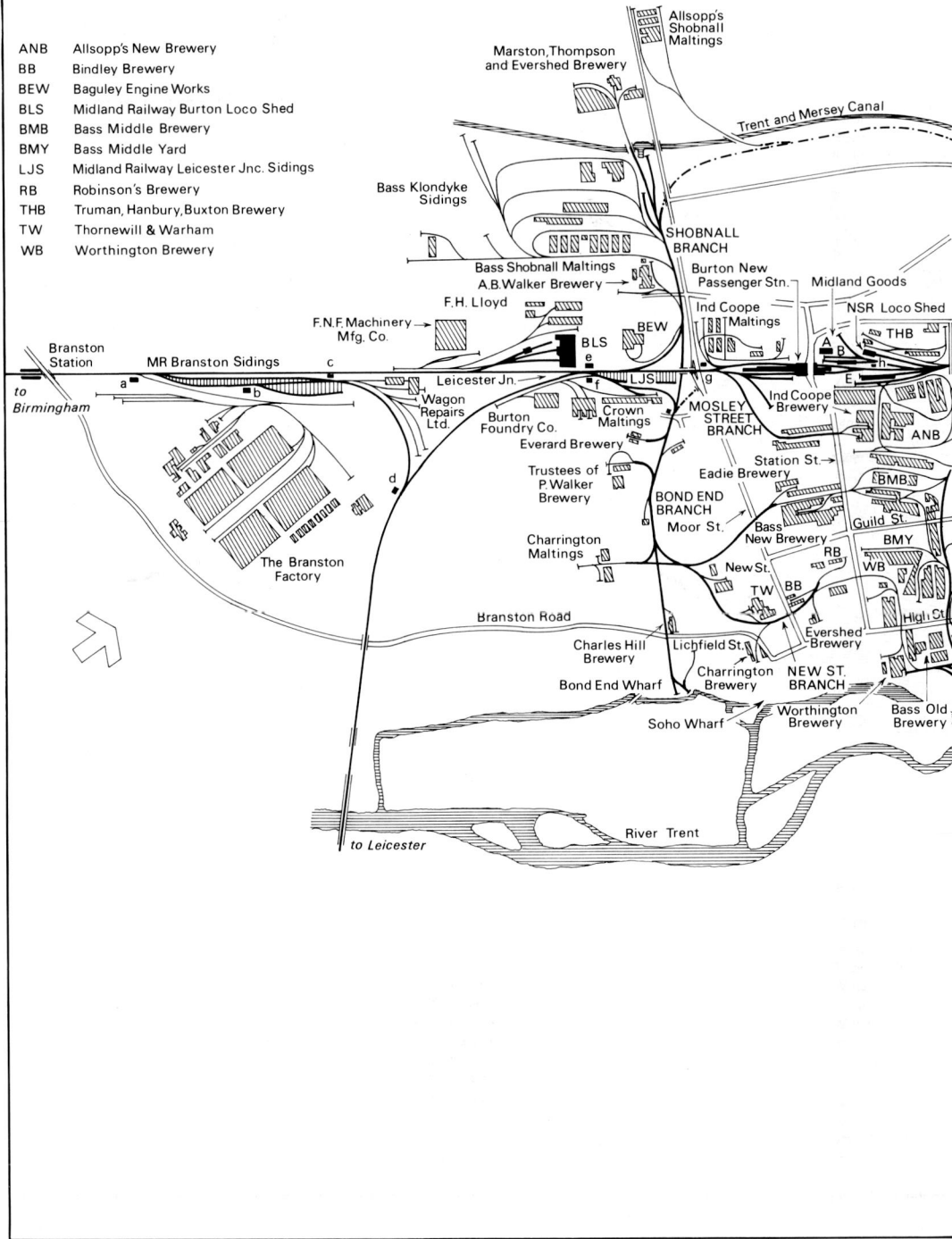

Allsopp's Shobnall Maltings

Marston, Thompson and Evershed Brewery

Trent and Mersey Canal

Bass Klondyke Sidings

SHOBNALL BRANCH

Bass Shobnall Maltings
A.B. Walker Brewery
Burton New Passenger Stn.
Midland Goods
NSR Loco Shed

F.H. Lloyd
Ind Coope Maltings
THB

F.N.F. Machinery Mfg. Co.
BEW
BLS
e
A B

Branston Station
MR Branston Sidings
c
Leicester Jn.
LJS
g
Ind Coope Brewery
E

to Birmingham
a
b
f
Wagon Repairs Ltd.
Burton Foundry Co.
Crown Maltings
MOSLEY STREET BRANCH
ANB

Everard Brewery
Station St.
BMB

Trustees of P. Walker Brewery
Eadie Brewery

d
BOND END BRANCH
Moor St.
Bass New Brewery
Guild St.

The Branston Factory
Charrington Maltings
New St.
RB
BMY
WB

Branston Road
TW
BB

Charles Hill Brewery
Lichfield St.
Evershed Brewery

Bond End Wharf
Charrington Brewery
NEW ST. BRANCH
High St.

Soho Wharf
Worthington Brewery
Bass Old Brewery

River Trent

to Leicester

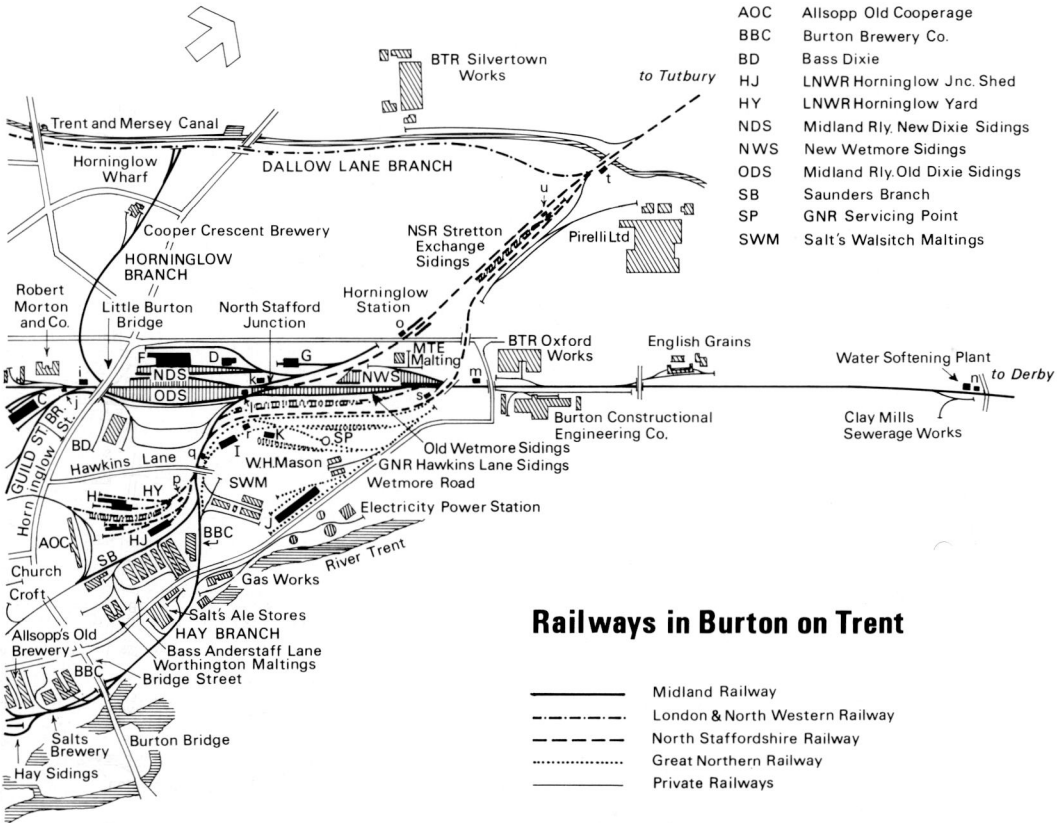

Railways in Burton on Trent

AOC	Allsopp Old Cooperage
BBC	Burton Brewery Co.
BD	Bass Dixie
HJ	LNWR Horninglow Jnc. Shed
HY	LNWR Horninglow Yard
NDS	Midland Rly. New Dixie Sidings
NWS	New Wetmore Sidings
ODS	Midland Rly. Old Dixie Sidings
SB	Saunders Branch
SP	GNR Servicing Point
SWM	Salt's Walsitch Maltings

Railway lines legend:

— Midland Railway
—·—·—·— London & North Western Railway
— — — North Staffordshire Railway
················· Great Northern Railway
— Private Railways

Railway premises on the mainline : see key for identity

Depots and warehouses ▬ B
Signal boxes ▪ a
Yards ▥

All sidings did not coexist

0 feet   1000   2000   3000   4000

Depots and Warehouses

- A MR Cheese & Corn Warehouse No.2
- B MR Goods Depot
- C MR Grain Warehouse No.1
- D MR Hydraulic Pumping Station
- E MR Grain Warehouse No.3
- F MR Bonded Stores & Grain Warehouse No.4
- G MR Wagon Repairs Depot
- H LNWR/NSR Horninglow Street Goods Depot
  (later named Burton Goods Depot)
- I GNR Hawkins Lane Goods Depot
- J GNR Wetmore Road Grain Warehouse
- K GNR Sugar Shed

Signal Boxes

- a Branston Junction
- b Branston Sidings No.2
- c Branston Sidings No.1
- d Birmingham Curve Junction
- e Leicester Junction (Burton)
- f Leicester Junction Sidings
- g Burton Station South
- h Burton Station North
- i Horninglow Bridge
- j Guild Street No.1
- k North Stafford Junction
- l Dixie Sidings
- m Wetmore Sidings
- n Clay Mills Junction
- o Horninglow
- p Horninglow Goods Yard
  (later named Burton Goods Yard)
- q Hawkins Lane
- r South Junction
  (later named Hawkins Lane Sdgs)
- s North Junction
- t Stretton Junction
- u Stretton Sidings

In the charter of incorporation granted in 1878, the town was called 'Burton upon Trent' but it is more usually referred to as 'Burton on Trent'.

3

INTRODUCTION

Burton on Trent could arguably claim to be unique, not only for the number of breweries dominating this Midlands town but also for the intricate network of railways which seemed to serve every ale bank and boiler, and cross its streets at frequent intervals.

For a settlement of about 50,000 population, Burton had a remarkable number of lines laid by four railway companies and various brewery firms. As late as the 1960s, the functional but substantial red brick buildings and forest of tall chimneys gave the town a distinctive character. Walking down its main streets was to experience the bustle of industry as gates opened to let locomotives puff by, to glance up yards where men rolled casks into railway wagons with practiced ease and steam seemed to escape from buildings and pipes in every direction. There was also the distinctive aroma which was not always to strangers' liking but signified to the town's residents that home was near, even with 4 miles to go before Burton Station was reached.

In the 1900s, most people worked for the brewery companies, in supporting industries or on the railways. Son and sometimes daughter followed father into the brewery. My relations were no exception with employees at Marston, Bass and Salt. We moved back to Burton in 1961, after Bass had closed its Sleaford Maltings, occupying a house behind the High Street on Worthington's Brewery premises. A railway passed within 20 feet of my front door and my bedroom had a view of the brewery copper hearth opposite! It was therefore not surprising that I should take an interest in Burton's brewery railways.

Thirty years have elapsed since then and during that time I have gained great pleasure from delving into its complicated history. Much of that enjoyment has come from talking to Burton people who have described what it was like to work in the breweries. This book not only sets down information on the brewery railways but gives an insight into the organisation of an industry and a way of life which has disappeared.

It is not possible to list everyone who has helped because there have been so many people over the years, some unfortunately no longer with us. I must, however, single out Ben Ward, to whom this book is dedicated. Ben has made an invaluable contribution and been a wonderful source of information. I should also mention the production team who helped me to put the book together - Trevor Lodge, Alan Bridges, Kath Bates and last but not least Ian Lloyd for his excellent maps. My thanks go to Ben, the team and all those other people who have assisted with this project over the years.

Cliff Shepherd January 1996

* * * * * *

This book is published by the Industrial Railway Society and any proceeds from its sale will go towards the costs of publishing other works which record the history of industrial railways and their locomotives, both in this country and abroad. Anyone requiring further information on the Society should write enclosing two first class stamps to Bernard Mettam, 27 Glenfield Crescent, Newbold, Chesterfield S41 8SF.

CHAPTER ONE

THE MERCHANT BREWERS

For much of its journey, the Trent is an old river meandering through the Midlands scenery accompanied by wide meadows frequently washed over by the river in times of flood. A succession of gravel terraces are to be found behind the meadows before the wide valley is lost in the surrounding countryside. At Burton on Trent, the valley is more obviously defined by the higher ground to the west and east so that the flat terraces were actively sought by the Roman Ryknield Street, the canal, and the first railway which came to the town. The location was also an appropriate crossing point of the river and the thirty six arches of the old Burton Bridge swept round in a great curve across the various channels of the Trent.

In the middle of the eighteenth century, the properties of the town mainly faced on to High Street which lay parallel with the river. Here the frontages were comprised of ordinary tenements and these properties extended towards the river, until terminating at the Hay ditch. On the other side of the street, the rear gardens were bounded by open fields. Horninglow Street and Cat Street (later to become Station Street) headed westwards across a broad continuous tract of common land. There was scarcely a house on them beyond the boundary of the High Street gardens.

With the dissolution of the monasteries in the 16th Century, Burton Abbey and most of the surrounding land passed to Sir William Paget. The seventh Lord became the Earl of Uxbridge in 1714. When his grandson died unmarried in 1769, the two titles together with the extensive land holdings at Burton passed to Henry Bayley via his mother, a Paget. His eldest son commanded the cavalry at Waterloo and was created the Marquis of Anglesey. As the principal land owner, the Marquis was to figure prominently in the subsequent development of the town.

Some of the inns in Burton carried on the local tradition of brewing; an activity which had become established at the abbey. The ale was of sufficiently good quality to have been sold in 1630 at the Peacock in Grays Inn Lane, London but this was the exception. Amounts of ale brewed were small and most sales were made in the immediately locality, because of the expense of carting the bulky casks over the poor roads. The distinction between 'ale' and 'beer' could be very arbitrary. In the 1790s, Bass referred contemptuously to low gravity cheap brews as beer, and when ale began to go off, it was said to have 'a beerish taste'. Later on, the word 'beer' came to be used for all brews, including lager. Thus Burton pale ale was a high quality bitter beer!

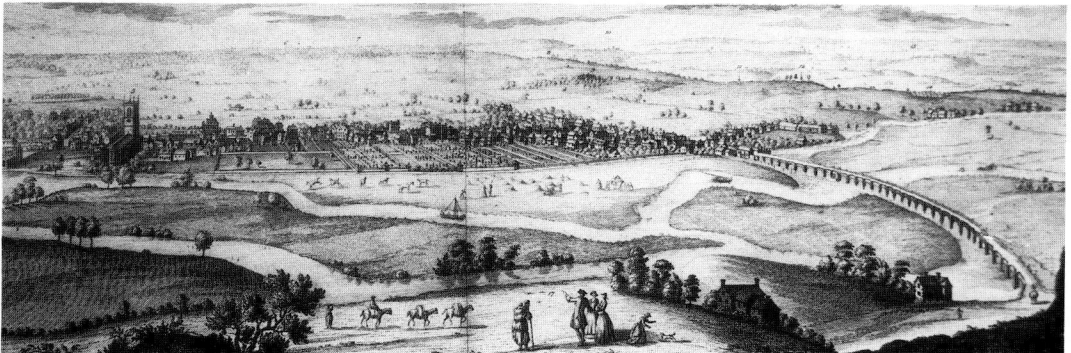

In 1732, the curve of the old Burton Bridge sweeps across the winding River Trent to the houses and inns on the High Street at Burton on Trent.   *(B. Ward Collection)*

At one end of the High Street lay Bond End with its few straggling cottages, and a wharf and small warehouse for the barges on the river. The extension of the Trent Navigation from Wilden Ferry over the nineteen miles to Soho Wharf at Bond End, authorised in 1699 and opened in 1712, allowed ale to be carried by water for export via Hull to the Baltic countries and to London. Unfortunately, there were many limitations to the river as a form of transport. Twenty shallows existed between Wilden Ferry and Burton and this, together with the monopolistic control of the wharves, discouraged further improvement. Turnpike Trusts were also having a gradual, if sporadic, beneficial impact on the condition of the main roads. The Burton to Lichfield road along the Trent valley was turnpiked in 1729 and others followed in the decades after 1750. They included the Tutbury to Ashby Turnpike, which passed along Horninglow Street and crossed Burton Bridge, before climbing steeply out of the valley to reach the countryside with its small collieries around Swadlincote. By this time, William Bass was a carrier in Burton. His wagons shared the Manchester to London service with Pickfords and ran twice weekly. During the 1762-63 season, Bass' slow lumbering wagons took a total of 100 barrels of Burton ale from several brewers to London but it was certainly not practicable to convey any larger amounts over long distances by road. The brewers continued to have a vested interest in the condition of the roads and both Samuel Allsopp and William Worthington 2 later became trustees of the Burton to Derby Turnpike.

These modest improvements encouraged merchant brewers to establish businesses in Burton. The town was proving to be a useful distribution point at the head of the Trent Navigation for the Baltic timber trade and ale could provide a good return cargo. The first record of a specialised brewery was that belonging to Benjamin Printon, who was reputed to have employed three men in 1708. Benjamin Wilson was one of the foremost brewers of this period. He had a brewery on the east side of High Street by 1742 and built up a large trade with the Baltic countries. His son, also called Benjamin, had assumed sole charge by 1778 and he subsequently purchased additional premises on the north side of Horninglow Street. Annual output in 1800 was about 4,500 barrels, but the Napoleonic blockade of Baltic ports restricted exports and he sold the business to his nephew, Samuel Allsopp, on 26th September 1807 for £7,000. The plant and stock were valued at an additional £3,000. The firm traded as Wilson & Allsopp, but Samuel Allsopp had trouble in reducing his mortgage debt, and so another agreement was drawn up on 15th April 1818 for a reduced sum of £6,507. It became Samuel Allsopp & Company when he had settled the debt, soon changing to '& Son' after Charles James (1805-44) came of age in 1826. The title was altered to '& Sons' when the other surviving son, Henry, reached 21 years of age. After Charles' death, Henry ran the business and three of his sons became directors—Samuel Charles, George Higginson and Alfred Percy.

The other most important eighteenth century brewer in Burton was Henry Evans who started brewing in 1754 and later became involved in many commercial undertakings, including the Burton Boat Company. His brewery stood on the west side of High Street. Across the road, William Worthington, who had come to Burton as a cooper in 1744, purchased an inn and small brewhouse in 1760. His two sons married Mary and Sarah Evans in 1791 and this brought under Worthington's control the brewery previously operated by John Walker Wilson. One of Worthington's sons, William 2, also had a son (William 3) and it was he who purchased Evans' brewery in 1819, transferring his brewing operations to it.

The inadequacies of the Navigation were becoming more and more frustrating. Brindley was quoted as saying in 1755 that 'no tract of land in the kingdom was naturally better adapted for the purpose of inland navigation, that none stood in more need of it.' Following pressure from the pottery and salt manufacturers to the north, together with the attraction of exporting ale via Liverpool, the Trent & Mersey Canal was authorised in 1766 between Wilden Ferry and Runcorn Gap. The section passing by Burton was opened in 1770 and completed throughout in 1777. The Trent & Mersey soon fitted into a whole network of canals and the domestic market for ale expanded to include the growing towns of Liverpool and Manchester, but proximity to the canal was still essential. Pilferage was a considerable problem which deterred sending small loads to scattered locations; indeed Samuel Allsopp had to abandon his West Bromwich agency because of pilfering. The canals were

Rowland Hilder produced some paintings based on old photographs which Bass used for a series of Christmas cards. This view of Soho Wharf showing a horse drawn dray laden with casks of beer is probably very representative of the Trent Navigation at the end of the eighteenth century. *(C. Shepherd Collection)*

important to the continued growth of the breweries because they could carry bulky low value cargoes more cheaply than road transport.

The Burton Boat Company had leased the Upper Trent Navigation since 1762 and was obviously unhappy about the prospect of a competing canal. It acquired some land from the Earl of Uxbridge in 1769 at a yearly rent of £20 and constructed a short canal from the river at Bond End to the Trent & Mersey at Shobnall, so that its barges could use both the river and canal. The Bond End or Burton Canal was completed in the following year but approval for the connection to the Trent & Mersey was not received until 1795. The proximity of Soho Wharf to the breweries, and some of the brewers' interests in the Burton Boat Company, allowed the Upper Trent Navigation to continue for some years but most of it closed in 1805.

It was an opportune time for William Bass to become involved in the local industry and he began brewing at a small brewhouse on the east side of High Street in 1777, later to develop into the Old Brewery. Following his death ten years later, his son Michael Thomas (the elder) continued the brewery whilst the other son, William took over the carrying business. Production at this time was only about 700 barrels of ale each year. Michael Thomas Bass (the elder) was determined to displace Benjamin Wilson as the premier brewer in Burton. He joined with James Wood Musgrave in 1791 and this enabled him to gain a strong representation in the Baltic trade. The partnership broke up in 1797, Bass having been joined by John Ratcliff, who had previously been responsible for the accounts and commercial correspondence. A new brewhouse was constructed in High Street to make up for the loss of Musgrave's premises. Annual output had reached about 10,000 barrels, but the health of Bass was declining, and his eldest son Michael Thomas (the younger) increasingly took over, finally succeeding following the death of his father in March 1827. On 1st July 1835, the company was reorganised to become Bass, Ratcliff & Gretton with the shares apportioned to Michael Thomas Bass (13/16), Samuel Ratcliff (2/16), and John Gretton (1/16); the latter having been brought in to run the brewing operations. These three, under Bass' dynamic leadership, would turn the company into the world's largest ale brewing business. The partners were joined by Charles Walter Lyon between 1847 and 1859 and Joseph Spender Clay in 1854, although the title of the company remained the same.

7

Other individuals, who were to be associated with the railways, had also begun to brew in the town. Thomas Salt had taken over the management of Joseph Clay's breweries, when Clay had become a partner in a commercial bank. Salt went on to establish his own brewery on the east side of High Street between 1807 and 1812 and later acquired most of Clay's brewery property. We know about the founding of the brewery because in a mortgage agreement dated 18th July 1807, there was a house leased to Thomas Salt situated on the north side of some property in High Street. On 21st July 1818, the same property was bounded on the north side by a brewery belonging to and occupied by Mrs Salt; Thomas Salt had died on 15th April 1813 aged 35. Along Horninglow Street, John Thompson could be found at the Bear Inn brewhouse and in 1849, he purchased the nearby small brewery previously run by John Mason and his son-in-law, Robert Gilbertson. The canal era, therefore, saw the establishment or consolidation of many of the brewing companies which were to be such a feature of Burton's growth in the railway age.

Burton brewers in 1835

Samuel Allsopp & Sons	High Street
Bass, Ratcliff & Gretton	High Street
Charles Hill	Lichfield Street
John Marston	Horninglow
John Mason	Horninglow Street
Jonathan Meakin	High Street
Lewis Meakin	Lichfield Street
Thomas Salt	High Street
John Thompson	Horninglow Street
William Worthington	High Street
John Yeomans	High Street

Whilst the last twenty years of the eighteenth century had been prosperous for the brewers, the arrival of the new century brought depression. The valuable export trade was halted when the Baltic ports were temporarily closed in 1806 and this market declined rapidly after 1822, following the imposition of a final prohibitory tariff. Fortunately, there were the beginnings of a new export trade with the colonies. An 'East India Pale Ale' had been produced in London and its good keeping qualities enabled it to arrive in a hot distant country as a clear sparkling drink. Water taken from the wells at Burton was impregnated with calcium sulphate from the gypsum beds underlying the town and this proved ideally suited to producing pale ales. Bass and Allsopp dominated the East India trade. Of the 12,000 barrels of ale reaching Bengal in 1832-33, Bass sent 5,200 barrels and Allsopp forwarded 1,400. As P. Mathias stated in *The Brewing Industry in England 1700-1830,* 'Considering the high relative costs of transporting beer. . . there is irony in the fact that the fame of the product which the railway enabled at last to be deployed in the home market should have been born and nurtured in places as far distant as the Baltic and India.'

Burton was still a small town and, even with the surrounding villages of Horninglow, Stapenhill and Winshill, there were only about 7,000 inhabitants in the 1830s. The breweries were well established but in no way could they match the scale of the great London porter brewers, who had the advantage of a large easily accessible market and were already making extensive use of steam power for grinding, mashing and pumping. There had been no significant improvements in transport since the arrival of the Trent & Mersey Canal fifty years before. True, there had been efforts to construct other canals, such as the abortive proposed link to the Coventry Canal in 1781. There had even been talk of a horse worked tramway, and Oswald Mosley had written to the Earl of Uxbridge in 1809 that it was 'the general wish of the inhabitants of Burton upon Trent and its neighbourhood to have a Rail Road made from the collieries of Newhall and Swadlincote to Burton,' but nothing came of it. So the brewers' carts, or floaters as they were popularly known, continued to make their laborious way up the road to the Trent & Mersey's Horninglow Wharf. Floaters were made from two long planks balanced between two high wheels and could be loaded with about a dozen casks from an ale bank. Later, and certainly before 1860, they developed into a low slung two-wheeled platform balanced about a foot off the ground and drawn by a single horse.

This activity connected with the brewers was not reflected in Burton's other industries which were in decline. Small iron working firms, such as Thomas Thornewill, were suffering as the focus of activity moved to the local coal and iron ores of the Black Country. Cotton spinning, which at its peak had employed 500 people, declined almost as rapidly as it had grown, with the last mill closing in 1841. It is a good commentary on the significance of the age when it is realised that there were still house gardens running down to the Hay ditch from High Street, the location of most of the breweries. It was left to a brewer to sum up the dependence of the Burton breweries on good cheap transport. 'If we lived only a few miles nearer. . .' wrote Allsopp to Arthur Heywood of Liverpool on 13th April 1808, 'we could sell our malt liquor upon the same terms as the Liverpool brewers do and would soon acquire a fortune' (Mathias).

CHAPTER TWO

THE ARRIVAL OF THE RAILWAY

The First Railways Reach Burton

On Monday 5th August 1839, a special train conveying 150 people comprising the directors, shareholders, and the company's officers pulled into Burton Station behind the locomotive TAMWORTH on its way to Derby and a banquet for the travellers at the Kings Arms Hotel. It was a momentous day for the town. The Birmingham & Derby Junction Railway had been formally opened and public traffic was to start a week later. As the Bass 1897 *Trip Handbook* was later to confirm, from that day 'the rapid advancement of the Town and Trade commenced.' The railway eliminated the difference in costs between water and land transport and gave Burton's brewers a national rather than a local market for their products.

The idea of a railway had not originated in the town but in Birmingham where influential men were attracted by the possibility of a railway from Derby. George Stephenson was commissioned to carry out a survey, and in April 1835, he proposed a route for the new railway from Derby through Burton and Tamworth to Stechford, Birmingham, where it would join the London & Birmingham Railway which was then under construction. There was also to be a branch from Whitacre to Hampton, again on the London & Birmingham Railway. Meetings were held in places along the route to gather support, including Burton where representatives were appointed to the provisional committee. Most of the financial backing came from outside, particularly from London and the Liverpool/Manchester party which was a significant force in early railway promotions. Thomas Webb, Samuel Allsopp, and William Worthington from Burton all subscribed £2,000 each, whilst Michael Thomas Bass put his name down for £4,000 of shares.

The Birmingham & Derby Junction Railway was not an isolated proposal but was deeply involved in the early competition to provide a route between the north of England and London. Its rival, the Midland Counties Railway, intended to construct a line from Derby and Nottingham through Leicester to the London & Birmingham Railway at Rugby. Both aimed to connect at Derby with the proposed North Midland Railway. The Midland Counties Railway also desired an extension up the Erewash valley to the North Midland Railway at Clay Cross. This was regarded with considerable apprehension by the North Midland Railway because it would provide an alternative route to its own. The Midland Counties Railway was itself unhappy about the Birmingham & Derby Junction Railway's Hampton Branch which offered another route to London. It was agreed that the companies would drop their respective proposals for the Erewash Valley line and the Hampton Branch but when the Midland Counties Railway Bill was published, it was found to contain the Erewash Valley line. The Birmingham & Derby Junction Railway had already submitted its own Bill and it therefore sought additional powers for a 'Stonebridge Railway' from Whitacre to Hampton. This was consolidated with the main Bill during its passage through Parliament. The three companies were all authorised in the same session of 1836.

The Birmingham & Derby Junction Railway decided to concentrate on the Derby to Hampton line in order to establish a through route to London before the Midland Counties Railway. Construction started in August 1837 and the work was divided into eighteen contracts under the direction of George Stephenson's son, Robert, who appointed his resident assistant, John Cass Birkinshaw, to superintend the works. The topography was generally favourable and only a few major engineering works were required. Even so, the shareholders were slow in meeting their 'calls' and the contract for the 4¾ miles Burton section was not let until 7th March 1838. The rails, provided by Bradley & Company of Stourbridge, were set in chairs secured to cross sleepers but the ballast was generally only 'small gravel'.

The new railway passed to the north west of Burton and a small station was provided at the end of Cat Street with Thomas Evans as the first station master. Initially there were three trains each way

Railways serving Burton on Trent

to Macclesfield   to Buxton   to Sheffield

North Rode

Clay Cross

0 miles   10   20

to Lincoln

to Crewe   Leek   to Matlock

Erewash Valley

Ambergate

Churnet Valley

STOKE   Ashbourne

DERBY
Friargate   Midland

2

Victoria   Colwick

Midland
NOTTINGHAM   Grantham

Egginton
Tutbury
Uttoxeter

7

Trent →

4
3

to Stafford

BURTON
ON TRENT   Bretby

Castle
Donnington

Swadlincote
Woodville

1

5   Ashby   Coalville

West Bridge

LEICESTER
London Road

Desford

6

Lichfield

Tamworth

Ashby and
Nuneaton Joint

to Rugby and London

Sutton
Coldfield

WOLVERHAMPTON   Walsall

Whitacre   Nuneaton

Dudley   Aston
New Street
BIRMINGHAM

to Rugby
and London

Hampton

to Bristol   to Rugby
and London

1	Wichnor Junction
2	Awsworth Junction
3	Willington Junction
4	Stenson Junction
5	Overseal
6	Knighton Junction
7	Bromshall Junction

—————— Midland Railway
—·—·—·— London & North Western Railway
– – – – – North Staffordshire Railway
············· Great Northern Railway
++++++++ Great Central Railway

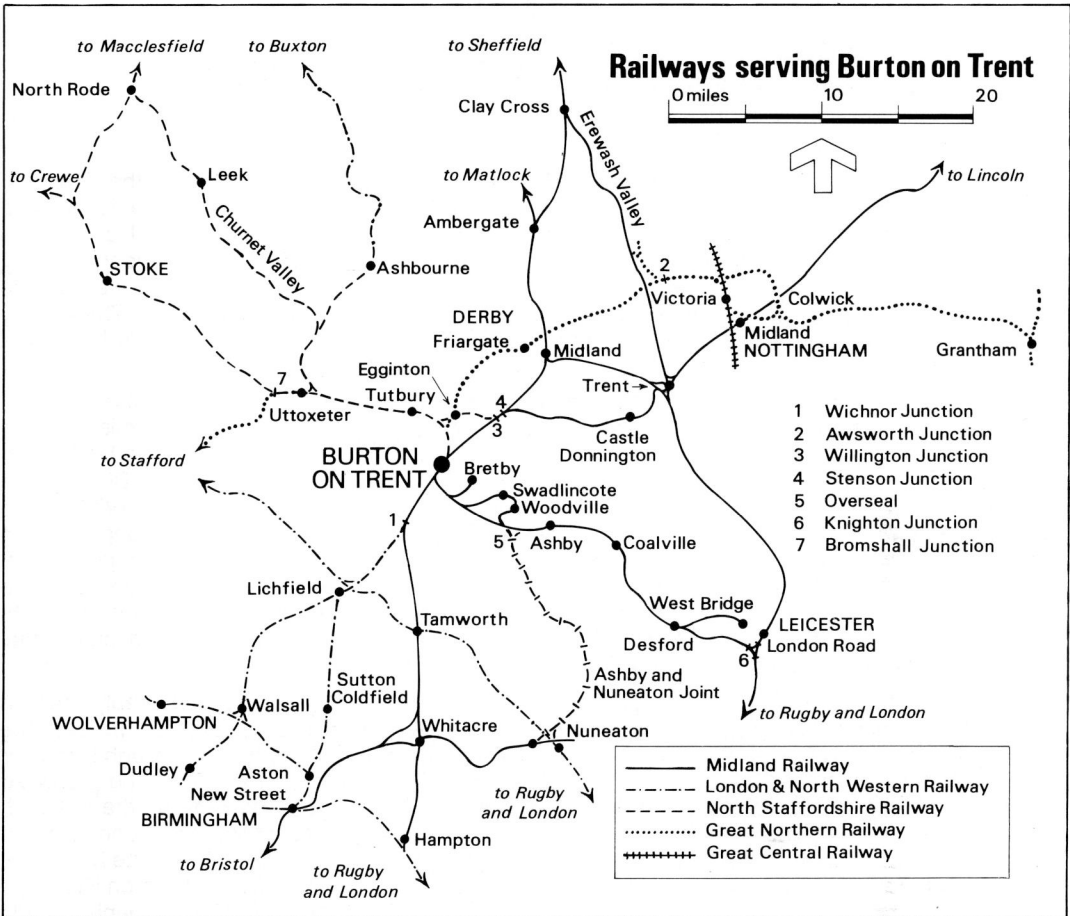

daily, with the through carriages to Euston being attached to the London & Birmingham trains at Hampton. The Birmingham & Derby Junction Railway purchased twelve 2-2-2 tender locomotives to work its traffic. Loads were often mixed. BURTON, a Tayleur & Company product, was noted in 1839 pulling two first class carriages, one closed second and two open second class carriages, a horse box, a coke wagon, and three other wagons. A mail train began operating on 5th April 1840, following a directive issued by the Postmaster General. Excursions also ran from an early date, such as a special in 1842 from Birmingham and Burton to Ambergate.

Much emphasis has been placed on the difficulties of developing these early railways, but in the case of the Birmingham & Derby Junction Railway, they were to be overshadowed by events after it opened. The benefits to trade and industry took some time to filter through and goods traffic was less than initially expected. By the time that through traffic became available from the north in July 1840, the Midland Counties Railway with its shorter route to London had also opened. The result was intense competition and fare cutting for the London traffic. Operating the new railway proved to be more expensive than previously thought. Efforts were made to cut costs by reducing the number of employees and by seeking alternative sources of revenue. Although Michael Thomas Bass continued to increase his financial stake in the Birmingham & Derby Junction Railway,

11

purchasing another 50 shares at a cost of £2,027 in April 1843, he had to write to a Mr Hodgkins two months later saying that he would be unable to get him a job with the company because 'all railways are now economising and most of them dismissing clerks.' Greater attention was given by the Railway Company to attracting more traffic from the breweries at Burton, and two 0-4-2 locomotives were obtained about 1841, reputedly from Thompson & Cole of the Hope Foundry, Bolton, to work the goods trains. The Birmingham & Derby Junction Railway undertook, in conjunction with the London & Birmingham Railway, to run full train loads of 26 wagons with casks of ale intact to London twice a week at an all-in contract price and Bass later had stores and stables at Camden Town for this traffic. The problem of high tolls on its trains over the London & Birmingham Railway to Birmingham was overcome when the Birmingham & Derby Junction Railway opened its own line from Whitacre to a new terminus in the city at Lawley Street on 10th February 1842, replacing the original proposal for a railway to Stechford. As a result, the Whitacre to Hampton line was singled in 1842-43. Relations with customers were not always good, and Bass had cause to write to Mr Allport of the Birmingham & Derby Junction Railway in 1844 because Bass' agent had 'complained to me last Thursday that on arriving at Burton station with a drove of beasts, your porter refused to discharge them unless he had a drink given him'!

Some of the shareholders had interests in more than one of the competing railway companies and there were numerous attempts to end the severe rivalry which was reducing the returns on their investment. Moves to finally amalgamate the Birmingham & Derby Junction Railway, Midland Counties Railway and North Midland Railway began in July 1843 and the Midland Railway Consolidation Bill received the royal assent on 10th May 1844. The Midland Railway began operating from 1st July 1844, with George Hudson as Chairman.

It was not long into the life of the new company before an unfortunate accident occurred at Burton on Saturday 31st October 1846. The 8am train had set off from Derby as usual. There was a 'drawbridge' carrying the railway over the Bond End Canal with a railway porter on duty, who had orders not to allow any boats to pass within a quarter of an hour of the arrival of any train. About 9 o'clock, a train went by from Birmingham and a boat then appeared on the canal. The railway porter, knowing that a train had just passed, opened the bridge to let the boat through forgetting about the imminent arrival of the train from Derby. No sooner had he done so than he became aware of the approaching train. There was no possibility of replacing the bridge in time and so he ran furiously up the line for about fifty yards 'using all his signals of danger.' The driver braked but was unable to stop. Although the locomotive passed over the gap, the tender and an adjoining second class carriage fell into it. Fortunately the carriage was empty and no passengers were hurt by the derailment of the rest of the train, the only injury being a minor one to the driver. The MR had already decided to replace the drawbridge by a permanent structure. This involved lifting the track

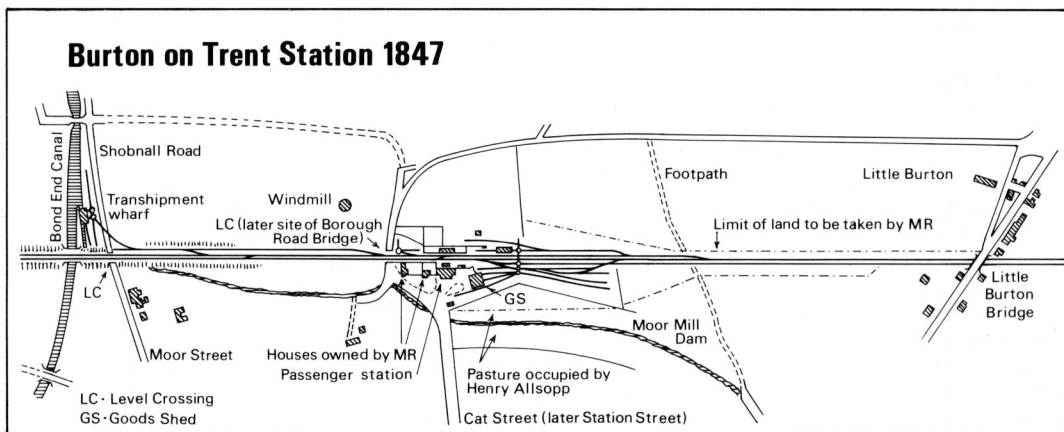

Burton on Trent Station 1847

Bond End Canal
Shobnall Road
Footpath
Little Burton
Transhipment wharf
Windmill
LC (later site of Borough Road Bridge)
Limit of land to be taken by MR
LC
GS
Little Burton Bridge
Moor Mill Dam
Moor Street
Houses owned by MR
Passenger station
Pasture occupied by Henry Allsopp
LC · Level Crossing
GS · Goods Shed
Cat Street (later Station Street)

on both sides of the bridge to give adequate clearance for the canal. Plans dated November 1847 for extensions at the station show that the main line had been raised on to an embankment on both sides of the new bridge to give fifteen feet clearance over the water. The resulting gradients were to pose problems for the Midland drivers attempting to restart heavy trains from the station with their small locomotives. Gradients were 1 in 112 up from the Burton station direction and 1 in 163 from Leicester Junction, although these were later modified to 1 in 143 and 1 in 155 respectively.

Despite some setbacks, the early railways were mostly successful. This, together with the growing wealth in the country led to investors speculating wildly in a multitude of schemes during what came to be known as the Railway Mania of 1845-46. The Burton brewers were not to be left out of this activity and yet ironically out of the chaos of the Mania, there evolved the basis of a railway network around Burton which was sufficiently resilient to last for over a century.

The area to the north west of Burton was still practically devoid of railways. There was no shortage of projected schemes eager to tap both the rich potential of the Potteries and to establish a more direct route between Manchester and the south. The proposed Churnet Valley Railway aimed to link Macclesfield with the MR between Tamworth and Hampton, missing Burton as a result. Michael Thomas Bass was against the scheme and he wrote to Sir Henry Every of Egginton Hall on 9th January 1845 congratulating Sir Henry on his opposition to it. Bass, for his part, could see no advantage to it because Manchester already had excellent communications to the south. Although Bass assured Sir Henry that he had no interest in any competing railway, this did not last for long and he was soon on the board of Remington's Direct Independent Manchester & London line. (Macclesfield–Burton–Leicester–Kings Cross)! No doubt Bass hoped for a good return on his speculation but the scheme also offered the prospect of a new north–south trunk line passing through Burton and serving the town's breweries. This view was encouraged by developments taking place on other railways because the MR was under the direction of the unscrupulous George Hudson, whilst the infant North Staffordshire Railway had already shown signs of coming under the influence of what was to become the LNWR. On 30th March 1846 Bass wrote to W.H. Ashurst of 48 Moorgate Street, London:-

> 'My dear Sir,
>
> It has occurred to me that we ought to get before the Amalgamating Committee an order stating that the North Stafford is prospectively only another branch of the London & Birmingham and Grand Junction which, if it is passed will certainly serve to extend and close the more lines against the public (and that in like manner the lines from Burton to Leicester and hence to Bedford would have a similar centring) and that moreover it is in close confederacy with the London and Birmingham.
>
> The North Stafford has bought the Grand Trunk Canal and proposes to shut up an important branch of it. Hudson has bought the Swannington Railway and the Ashby Canal. If these projects succeed, the public are injured by closing present communications and since, by making bad lines which will ultimately exclude good ones. Can you bring this subject before your committee?
>
> My dear Sir, very faithfully yours
>
> M.T. Bass

Unfortunately for Bass, Remington's line was already a lost cause and although he attempted to help by visiting landowners along the projected route, he found that the engineers had badly neglected seeking their support. Other landowners, such as Lord Vernon whose coal mines at Poynton were 'one of the most valuable properties in the kingdom yielding £30,000 to £35,000 clear revenue' were better served by the line of the North Staffordshire Railway. As the likelihood of the Remington line being approved diminished, so the haggling over the apportionment of the expenses increased. Bass complained that he had devoted many weeks of his time to the company and incurred a degree of animosity which he would not be tempted to hazard in any similar undertaking. It was not until January 1853 that Bass was finally able to settle his account for £12,526 with the company.

Meanwhile, the local interests in the Potteries had formed the North Staffordshire Railway. In November 1845, they took over the rival Derby & Crewe Junction Railway, amending their own proposed network to give a revised line from Crewe to Derby with a branch from Tutbury to Burton. The NSR was officially authorised on 26th June 1846, although the extension towards Derby was delayed by an objection from Sir Henry Every. Michael Thomas and Abraham Bass took up their preference shares in the new railway in January 1847 and Messrs Earle & Combe began construction of the 12½ miles from Uttoxeter to Burton Junction (later known as North Stafford Junction) in the summer. The NSR, or the Knotty as it was more familiarly known, established its presence in the town with the start of passenger trains on 11th September 1848, making use of running powers over ¾ mile of the MR from North Stafford Junction to reach Burton Station. A service operated between Burton and Tutbury, where connections could be made for Stoke and Crewe. The little passenger train which shuttled between the two stations was called the Tutbury Jenny (pronounced Jinny) and ran for almost 112 years. Its name was probably derived from the word 'engine'; old horse gins were once referred to as 'Jinney Rings'. The intermediate stations at Horninglow, Stretton and Claymills, and Rolleston-on-Dove did not open until much later when the population of the district had increased. Goods trains also began running through to Burton but they initially had to use the MR's sidings. This practice was consolidated by an agreement between the companies on 1st January 1851 when running powers were granted over the MR lines in the town.

Other railway developments had been taking place in the small coalfield to the east of Burton. The nearest colliery was only 3 miles away and in the pre-railway era, both Bass and Benjamin Wilson had been supplied with coal by Fletcher Bullivant at Swadlincote and William Nadin at Newhall. This had to be hauled over the difficult terrain traversed by the Ashby–Tutbury and Stapenhill turnpikes. The colliery proprietors were most interested in the lucrative Leicester market but could not compete with the Erewash Valley coal being carried by canal boat to that town. An answer to this problem was the Leicester & Swannington Railway, a typical early Stephenson line making use of two inclined planes which opened throughout from Swannington via Long Lane (Coalville) to West Bridge, Leicester in 1833. The effect on the price of coal was dramatic and the West Leicestershire collieries could now sell their coal in Leicester at 10 shillings (50p) per ton (7s 6d pithead price plus 2s 6d carriage). Although the Leicester & Swannington Railway enjoyed a fairly prosperous existence, its future prospects were threatened by new railways aiming to tap the coal traffic. These mostly favoured a route between Ashby and Nuneaton following the course of the Ashby Canal. Amongst them was the proposed Nottingham, Birmingham & Coventry Junction Railway supported by Michael Thomas Bass, John Gretton, and Robert Collings Gilbertson of Burton. Gilbertson was a friend of Bass who eventually sold his business to Bass, including the Plough property in Horninglow Street. Bass again had trouble with his railway speculation, writing to a Mr Gillon on 15th April 1846:-

'Dear Sir,

I am extremely sorry to learn there is a dispute between you and the Nottingham & Coventry Railway, with which I am connected. For some time past I have been unable to attend the Board: the Board exists for the most part of men of business of highly responsible character and more than average ability and I am persuaded their only object is to do what is right. . . If, however, you think it desirable to proceed at law, may I request you will do me the favour not to select me. I have already one action against me by the Engineer for £1,300 and I have no doubt I shall be able to answer you at the proper time. . .

I remain, dear Sir, faithfully yours,

M.T. Bass'

The MR responded by offering to purchase the Leicester & Swannington Railway on very favourable terms and this was accepted by the shareholders in August 1845. Following completion of the sale in 1846, another Act was obtained to improve the line and extend it to Burton. The existing railway was doubled between Coalville and Desford, by-passing the Bagworth Incline, and extensions were built from Coalville to Leicester Junction, Burton, and from Desford to Knighton Junction at Leicester. The Marquis of Anglesey was paid £6.641 for 39 strips of land between the Bond End Canal and the boundary between Stapenhill and Stanton so that the MR could construct the railway in Burton. A notable feature was the series of viaducts which carried the line over the River Trent and the adjoining water meadows. A signalman was appointed at Leicester Junction in July 1847, two years before the line opened throughout. John Hill was one of the main contractors on the Coalville–Burton section. The line was inspected by Captain George Wynn on behalf of the Government on 13th February 1849 and, following attention to various minor items, it was formally opened on Wednesday 1st August 1849, when the MR 2-4-0 No.42 worked the first passenger train between Burton and Leicester Campbell Street Station. Two goods trains had been running each way daily since 2nd October 1848.

The South Staffordshire Railway was the last railway company to enter Burton in this period. It was formed in 1846 from two separate concerns, the South Staffordshire Junction and the Trent Valley, Midland & Grand Junction Railways. Michael Thomas Bass was not to be left out, writing to H. Wyatt 'what do you think about the Trent Valley?' and complaining bitterly that Anson was holding up the amalgamation by arguing which of the two railways in the merger was to be in control. These railways aimed to provide a cross country route to compete with the MR but finally became established in the heart of the Black Country; an area eagerly fought over by the MR and LNWR. The line ran from Dudley, through Walsall to join the MR at Wichnor Forge (later called Wichnor Junction). This was a lonely place set in the middle of the river meadows at the confluence of the Rivers Trent and Tame and two miles from the nearest village. The South Staffordshire Railway also gained running powers to Burton Station and a service of four passenger trains each way was inaugurated from the opening of the line on 9th April 1849. Trains were timed so as to avoid the need for any servicing to be done by the MR at Burton. Involvement with the LNWR grew closer, and from 5th May 1852, the LNWR's Northern Division began to operate the line and maintain the locomotives, although the latter remained South Staffordshire Railway property. In contrast, the worsening relations with the MR led to restrictions being imposed on the running powers to Burton. By 1855, South Staffordshire locomotives were banned from going to Burton and its carriages had to be attached to the MR trains at Wichnor Junction where a small booking office and platform were constructed, together with sidings for the exchange of goods traffic. This resulted in long delays for the South Staffordshire Railway's passengers, particularly as the MR local trains were not very punctual.

As a result of all the Railway Mania nationally, there were nearly 7,500 miles of railway in use in the country by 1852 and it was possible to travel by railway from Burton to London, Liverpool, Newcastle, Glasgow and Plymouth. Five passenger trains ran each way between Derby and Birmingham covering the 41¼ miles in a best time of 1 hour 50 minutes with stops at Burton, Tamworth, and Whitacre. Six goods and empty wagons trains, together with a mail train in each direction, completed the service. Rail traffic was increasing rapidly and the economic limitations of the previous forms of transport had truly been shattered. Peter Mathias in *The Brewing Industry in England 1700–1830* concluded 'For centuries a great industrial potential had lain imprisoned in a narrow overland marketing area by high transport costs until freed by the railway to Derby in 1839.'

At last, the Burton brewers were able to reap the benefits of large scale production. During the 1840s, beer output increased from 70,000 to 300,000 barrels per annum and the number of employees rose from 350 to nearly 1,000. The growth in production was matched by an increase in the number of brewery companies. Henry and Thomas Wilders founded the Burton Brewery Company in High Street. William Middleton came from London and opened a small brewery in High Street in 1846 later moving to Station Street and beginning work on a new brewery. This was uncompleted when health and financial resources failed the unfortunate gentleman and it came on the market. Ind Coope purchased the premises, completed the work, and began brewing in 1858. Edward Ind had entered the brewing business at Romford in 1799 and was joined by the brothers O.E. and George Coope to form Ind Coope Company in October 1845. Worthington & Company was owned by William Worthington 3 at this time but Thomas Robinson was the practical brewer until he left in 1862. Wyllie had a small brewery nearby, which later became Clement & Berry's Star Brewery, then Dobson's Brewery, before being absorbed into Worthington's premises in 1879.

No.			BURTON,			186		No.			BURTON,			186
Midland Railway Company,								Midland Railway Company,						
Received as under in good condition.								Receive as under in good condition,						
From WORTHINGTON & ROBINSON.								From WORTHINGTON & ROBINSON.						
			Carter											
Mark.	Hhds.	Barls.	¼Hhds.	Klns.	Firks.	Destination.		Mark.	Hhds.	Barls.	½Hhds.	Klns.	Firks.	Destination.
Signature,														

Form for receipts of beer dated 16th October 1863.   *(R. Farman Collection)*

Much of the expansion was due to the continued growth of the two leading firms. Allsopp had already extensively enlarged his original brewery (later called the Old Brewery) in High Street. In 1859, Henry Allsopp began to erect the huge New Brewery in Station Street next to the main line. The company produced 270,000 barrels of beer in 1861 and, following further extensions to the New Brewery approved in 1865, output was raised to 500,000 barrels. Henry Allsopp eventually became the first Baron Hindlip in 1886 and, when he died in the following year, Samuel Charles succeeded him as the second Lord Hindlip. Allsopp became a public limited liability company on 2nd February 1887 with Samuel Charles Allsopp as chairman, but he gave up the chair in 1892 after five very stormy years and died in July 1897.

Bass, Ratcliff & Gretton was transformed by the driving force of Michael Thomas Bass from a minor provincial concern to a major company eventually turning out a million barrels of quality beers each year which carried his name to all parts of the world. Output in 1827 was only about 10,000 barrels. This rose to 40,000 barrels in 1842 and 148,000 barrels in 1853, when a second brewery was commenced in Guild Street. Bass' net profits for the two years 1862 and 1863 came to £423,000. The Company was also building a third brewery so that production totalled 911,000 barrels in the year 1880-81 (Old Brewery 281,000 barrels, Middle Brewery 272,000 barrels, New Brewery 358,000 barrels). It was not for nothing that the London & South Western Railway ordered on 26th April 1882 that 'it is essential in the interests of the travelling public that Messrs Bass' and Allsopp's beers should be supplied at all refreshment rooms.' During the nineteenth century, Bass came to be regarded by many of the other local brewers as a highly efficient organisation and one to be emulated rather than competed with; a view not shared by the ruthless W.P. Manners at Worthington who believed in all out competition.

The relationship between Bass and the MR grew closer after the downfall of George Hudson and much of the company's beer was sent out over its tracks. Michael Thomas Bass became a substantial investor in the MR, writing on the 12th April 1849 'I am only very recently become a proprietor in the Midland which I consider a fair objection to me'. A year later, he received a dividend payment of £245 15s (£245.75p) on his £21,000 worth of consolidated stock. His association with the MR broadened even further when he was elected Member of Parliament for Derby in September 1848.

Brewery Companies in Burton on Trent in 1857

Company	Number of employees in 1861 (a)	
Samuel Allsopp & Sons	889	(b)
Bass, Ratcliff & Gretton	1,167	
John Bell, Lichfield Street	15	
Burton Brewery Company, High Street	297	
James Eadie, Cross Street	15	
Evershed & Malleson, Bank Square	18	
Charles Hill, Lichfield Street	30	
Ind Coope, Station Street	50	
John Marston, Horninglow	10	
Meakin, Lichfield Street	35	
Joseph Nunneley, Bridge Street	16	
W.S. & John Perks, Horninglow Street	30	(c)
Thomas Salt, High Street	194	
William Saunders, Horninglow Street	-	(d)
John Thompson, Horninglow Street	35	
Tooth, Victoria Crescent	80	
Worthington & Robinson, High Street	191	
Wyllie, High Street	-	
John Yeomans, High Street	6	

Notes. List excludes small inn brewhouses
(a)   Excludes clerical staff
(b)   In 1869, the total of all employees was about 1,260
(c)   T.M. Carter in 1861
(d)   Ceased brewing

The Struggle for the Brewery Railways

In contrast to the expansion of the national network, the railway in Burton remained fairly simple in the 1850s. A few sidings had been laid alongside the main line near the station and the Midland Goods Yard has been established but there were only two private sidings. One ran past the ends of Allsopp's maltings from the main line and the other was a separate horse worked line from Tooth's Brewery in Victoria Crescent to the Trent & Mersey Canal.

Traffic was increasing rapidly and James Allport had cause to comment in 1860 'when the station was originally laid out, the trade of Burton was comparatively very small indeed. I remember some 15 years ago, the brewers had very great difficulty in making up their minds to guarantee. . . . to the London & Birmingham 10,000 tons per annum. Now the trade from Burton; the beer business alone is about 200,000 tons per annum, the entire trade in and out of Burton I should think would not be at all short of any of 300,000 tons a year.'

Most of the casks of beer had to be laboriously carried by horse drawn carts and floaters along the streets for loading into railway wagons standing on sidings near the station. Cat Street had been widened and renamed Station Street but road congestion was considerable with long lines of floaters waiting to gain access into the station yard. The *Burton on Trent Times* of May 1858 recorded that 'the quantity of ale sent out of Burton during the present season far exceeds anything previously done. In fact, the streets have been literally crowded with floaters from morning till night wending their way to the Railway Station and back again.' The MR was forced to ask the brewers not to send ale to the station after midday because its facilities were totally inadequate to deal with it.

A solution was already under active consideration. In November 1857, a Burton upon Trent

Railway Bill had been proposed by the MR and the brewers for a railway along the route later taken by the Guild Street Branch from the main line to the High Street breweries, together with a line across Allsopp's land at Church Croft and Horninglow Street to Salt's cooperage and ale stores. The Bill was dropped in 1858 reputedly because it was not possible for the MR to pay for the line and the brewers to have powers to make it. The LNWR was also determined to secure a greater share of the lucrative traffic. Back in 1852, the LNWR had arranged contracts with both Bass and Allsopp giving them preferential rates in return for guaranteed consignments. It therefore supported a nominally independent Burton upon Trent Railway Bill in 1859 which would have given it access to most parts of the town. The proposed railway was intended to begin at Wichnor Junction, crossing the MR by a flyover, and following a separate but parallel route to Burton. After passing under the Leicester line, it would have cut across the river meadows before eventually swinging round the north east of the town to join the NSR at Stretton. Branches would have served Bond End, Saunders' Maltings, and Allsopp's, Ind Coope's and Bass's Breweries. Naturally, the MR was completely opposed to this attack on its interests and its Erewash Valley Extension and other New Branches Bill in 1859 contained proposals for its own railway branches in Burton. The rival projects both involved the straightening of one of the river channels, and the construction of a new road bridge across the Trent because the old Burton Bridge blocked the railway's access to the numerous breweries along High Street.

The LNWR and MR were not the only parties with an interest in that first session of 1859 because the Marquis of Anglesey had also petitioned Parliament to introduce a Burton on Trent Bridge Bill for the replacement of the old bridge; the quarter of a mile long bridge was in a state of dilapidation. It was still only 15 feet wide in places with pedestrian refuges, although some widening to 26 feet had taken place at the Winshill end in 1831. There had been many accidents. One involved a farmer who dismounted from his horse on the bridge and was crushed to death by the horse pushing against him as a carriage passed by. The Marquis of Anglesey was responsible for the maintenance of the bridge, with a contribution being made by the Ashby to Tutbury Turnpike.

The conflict between the various parties was resolved at a meeting between the MR and the LNWR on 1st June 1859. It was agreed that only the MR Bill would proceed, excluding the Burton provisions, and that the MR should obtain a new Act to authorise the construction of two railway branches in Burton, the new road bridge over the Trent and the alterations to the adjoining water channels. The Midland Railway and Burton upon Trent Bridge Act was approved in August 1859. This specified that the new Burton Bridge was to be constructed by the MR and the LNWR at their equal expense, consequent upon the Marquis of Anglesey paying £10,000 towards the cost as a release from his maintenance liability. The responsibility would then be transferred to the counties of Staffordshire and Derbyshire; the boundary between them followed the course of the river at that time. Provision was made for the NSR to be included in the agreement, if required, upon payment of one third of the excess beyond the Marquis' contribution up to a maximum of £3,000 and a similar proportion of any other liabilities incurred by the LNWR. All other costs were to be borne by the MR which had authority to raise an additional £60,000 capital for the various works. The Marquis of Anglesey received £26,029 for the land taken under the Act, from which £10,000 was deducted for his contribution. He did quite well out of the deal!

Both Guild Street and Hay Branches began near North Stafford Junction; the Guild Street Branch initially ran parallel with the main line until, after passing under the Little Burton Bridge, it headed off to terminate on the south east side of Guild Street. The first section later became an additional running line for the main line and the branch junction was then situated near the bridge, although access could still be gained under the bridge to Dixie. Allsopp objected to the alignment of part of the proposed railway because of the proximity to its maltings, the company already having a siding from the MR. Both Allsopp and the MR put forward competing proposals but eventually a compromise was reached, albeit reluctantly by Allsopp. The necessary powers for the deviation were obtained in 1860 in the Midland Railway (Burton Branches) Act, and the line of the branch was moved slightly eastwards to traverse through Allsopp's residential property. Nor was the railway allowed to cross Brook Street and it had to pass immediately to the west of it, although a road

Main line

Little Burton Bridge

Mount Pleasant Bridge

Horninglow Street

Hawkins Lane

Carter & Sons Brewery

Line authorised by 1859 Act

LNWR Goods Depot

Saunders' Branch

Gas Works

Bass Malthouses

Anderstaff Lane

Guild Street Branch

Brook Street

Malthouses

Allsopp's Old Cooperage

Allsopp New Brewery

Allsopp Engine Shed

Allsopp's connecting railway

Bass Engine Shed

Wm. Saunders C.

M

M

Salt's Cooperage

Store Room

BBCo. Cooperage

M

Street

M

Thompson's Brewery

Stables

Hay Branch

Bass Middle Brewery

M

Guild

Trinity Church
Church Croft

Line in November 1857 Burton upon Trent Railway Bill

Old Bridge

Barley Store

Nunneley Brewery
Burton Brewery Co.

Bass Steam Cooperage

Allsopp's connecting railway

New Bridge

Cask washing shed

Salt Brewery

Allsopp Old Brewery

Store

High Street

Sidings

River Trent

Bass Middle Yard

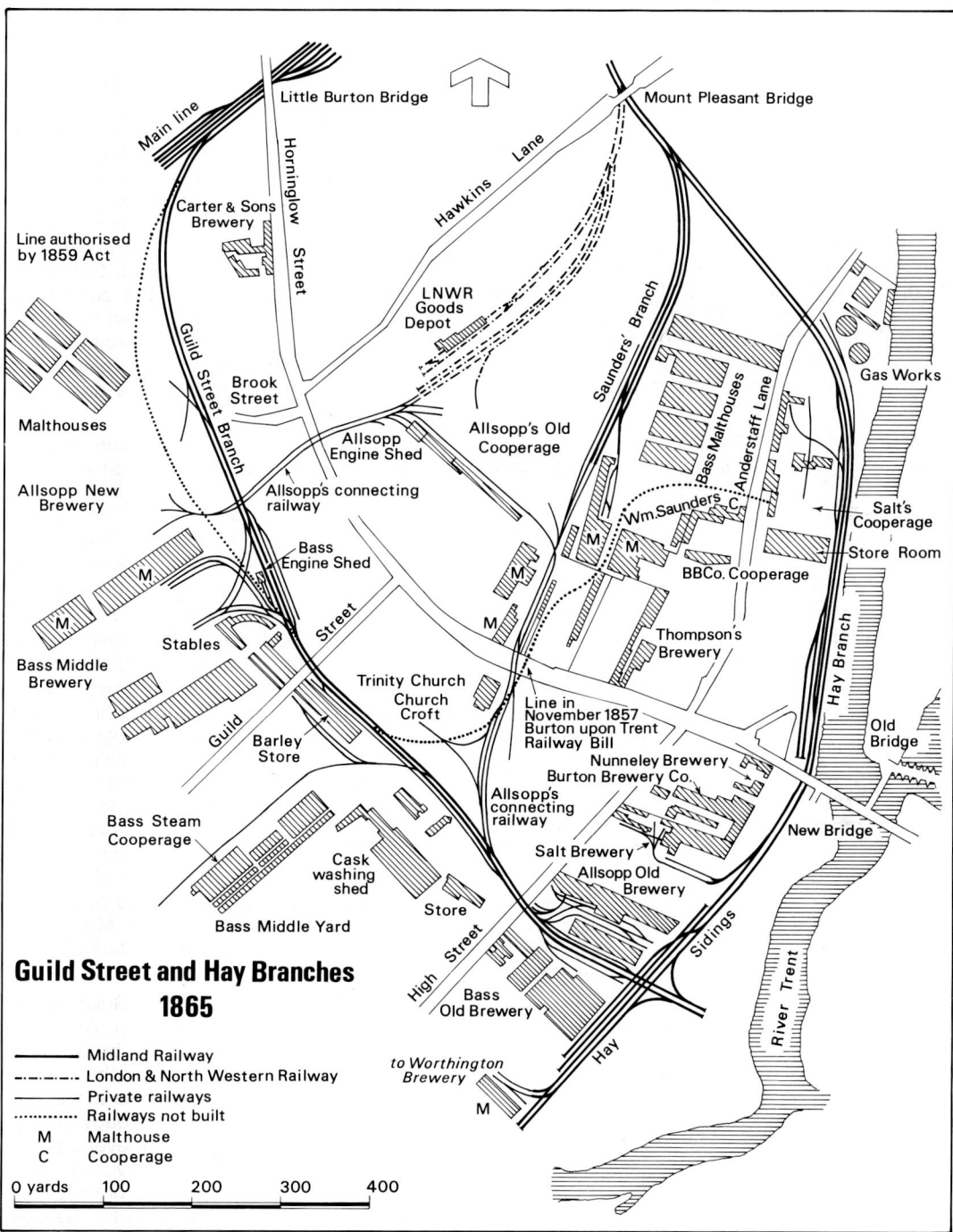

Guild Street and Hay Branches
1865

———— Midland Railway
–·–·–·– London & North Western Railway
———— Private railways
·········· Railways not built
M   Malthouse
C   Cooperage

Bass Old Brewery

to Worthington Brewery

Hay

M

0 yards   100   200   300   400

A group of MR platelayers stand near the Brook Street Crossing Box on the Guild Street Branch. The sidings on the right lead into Allsopp's New Brewery. The box was probably downgraded to a ground frame between 1937 and 1945 merely controlling the road crossing. *(R. Farman Collection)*

crossing of the branch was later provided. The MR also received powers to extend the Guild Street Branch to join up with the recently authorised Hay Branch. The branches were built as follows:

MR GUILD STREET BRANCH. It ran south eastwards away from the main line past Allsopp's New Brewery and Bass' New Brewery (later Middle Brewery) to cross Guild Street, continuing on between Bass' Middle Yard and Allsopp's land at Church Croft before crossing High Street where access could be gained to the Old Breweries of Bass and Allsopp and the Hay Sidings.

MR HAY BRANCH. This curved from near North Stafford Junction under Hawkins Lane, which was carried across on a new bridge (sometimes known as Mount Pleasant Bridge). The short **SAUNDERS BRANCH** trailed off to the right terminating at Allsopp's Old Cooperage Yard. Meanwhile, the Hay Branch continued on to the river, which it ran alongside, before passing under the new Burton Bridge to reach the High Street breweries at the Hay.

The 1860 Act authorised a widening of the main line from Leicester Junction to immediately north of Moor Street by the provision of a third line. No change in gradient was necessary but the bridge over the Bond End Canal had to be widened by 12 feet. A curve was constructed between the Leicester and Birmingham lines at Branston (Birmingham Curve Junction to Branston Junction) to enable coal traffic from Leicestershire to reach Birmingham. This had opened by 1st January 1863. The 1860 Act also allowed Allsopp to build its own private railways to connect some of its premises with the first line going from its New Brewery at right angles across the Guild Street Branch and Horninglow Street to its Old Cooperage. From there, it ran back across Horninglow Street to join the Guild Street Branch near the High Street level crossing, thus enabling Allsopp to reach its Old

Allsopp's level crossing over Horninglow Street with the adjacent Holy Trinity Church. *(A. Moss Collection)*

Brewery. Taken together, these private lines would have meant that Allsopp could have avoided using most of the Guild Street Branch. The MR insisted on a restriction on through traffic being inserted in the Act. Allsopp's rail traffic between its Old and New Breweries was forced to travel along the Guild Street Branch, the MR receiving payment for the use of its line.

There had been much opposition from the people of the town to the level crossings proposed in the 1860 Act because it was considered that they would constantly interrupt road traffic and that they were not for the general benefit of the public. People complained that 'our two main streets and thoroughfares are to be crossed in three different places, and at a cost of perhaps £150,000 *(sic)* incurred, for no other purpose than to give Messrs Allsopp an advantage over their neighbours.' (*Burton Weekly News* 16th March 1860). The House of Lords Select Committee which investigated the complaint in May 1860 found that there was already considerable inconvenience caused by floaters being taken to the station. A constant flow of wagons monopolised the traffic and the carts pulled by two horses blocked the street whilst turning. James Allport told the Committee 'I have seen the streets completely crowded with these floaters. I have seen them in line towards the afternoons and evenings, when they were waiting to unload beer and could not perhaps get into the station.' The road surfaces had become so rutted that 6in wide wheels had to be fitted to the floaters. A railway truck could carry twice as much as a floater and it was concluded that the railways would relieve the road congestion to the benefit of the public.

The problems of the level crossings did not end there; the MR naturally wanting to work its branches with locomotives but, because of the outcry from the town, the Board of Trade proposed that horses should be used. It was specified in the 1859 and 1860 Acts that the level crossings at Guild Street, High Street, and the two over Horninglow Street could not be crossed by locomotives worked by steam or 'atmospheric agency'. Wagons could not be pulled across by ropes using a stationary engine and the MR was also not allowed to shunt wagons over or permit them to stand on these level crossings.

Work pressed ahead on the construction of the new railways. The responsibility for the design of Allsopp's two private lines was given to the company's consultant engineer, John Fowler, and they were opened in 1862. Traffic also began to travel along the Guild Street Branch from the 4th October 1862, with horses hauling the wagons between Guild Street and the Hay. Bass' inward rail traffic of barley and coal started from this date with the first outward consignment of beer leaving on 7th November 1862. Much of the land required was not conveyed to the MR until after the opening.

Trains began to work along the Hay Branch as far as Anderstaff Lane and on the Saunders Branch to Allsopp's Old Cooperage in November 1861, but progress on the remainder was held up by work on the new Burton Bridge; local people more usually referred to it as the Trent Bridge. The first stone of the bridge was laid on 23rd February 1863. It was built of millstone grit from the Whatstandwell Quarries in Derbyshire and was formally opened by the Marquis of Anglesey on 22nd June 1864 having cost £22,000, of which £12,000 had been provided by the MR, LNWR, and NSR. A banquet was held to celebrate the event and a large gathering assembled in one of the brewery buildings. According to that partial observer George Potter Neele, then Superintendent of the LNWR Central Division, the Chairman of the MR made a long speech in so low a tone that was quite lost in the vast space. In contrast, Mr Bancroft who was a director of the LNWR is reported to have replied on behalf of his company by standing on a chair and leading off in a voice audible throughout the whole place. Vociferous applause greeted the energy displayed. The MR became the owners of the old bridge and quickly pulled part of it down to permit the completion of the Hay Branch. With the opening of the railway on 6th November 1864, MR locomotives began to work over Anderstaff Lane and down to the Hay. At this time, Anderstaff Lane was only a minor road leading to the Gasworks and the fields beyond. Signals began to be used at Anderstaff Lane on 14th October 1867 when the box opened and new level crossing gates were erected on 15th February 1868. The remains of the old bridge stood for some years until there was a complaint at the Quarter Sessions that it constituted a nuisance and the MR was ordered to remove it. Virtually all of the bridge was taken away in 1870, a solitary arch remaining in the cellar of the former Meadow Road Brewery. The new bridge was widened from thirty to fifty feet in 1924-26.

With the principle of the railway branches now firmly established, both Bass and Worthington & Robinson lost no time in seeking parliamentary powers to link more of their premises to the new railway system. The Burton upon Trent Railways Act of 1862 specifically drew attention to the reduction in traffic on the streets which had taken place. This would be further decreased when the MR branches were completed. As a result, Bass was able to construct a private railway from its first mechanised steam cooperage (soon to be the site of the New Brewery), through its Middle Brewery premises, to the Guild Street Branch. Worthington & Company, as they had now become, also laid a private line from the Hay Branch across High Street to its brewery and this line opened in 1863. Significantly, the restrictions on locomotives working over the level crossings were omitted from the Act.

Allsopp's horses had begun to take railway wagons along the Guild Street Branch from its Old Brewery but problems occurred almost immediately. Traffic was increasing rapidly and the location of the maltings and ale stores at Allsopp's New Brewery meant that there was substantial interchange working between the two breweries. The Guild Street Branch also formed an integral part of the railway network which linked together Bass's premises in the centre of the town. Allsopp soon had cause to write to Mr Harrison at Burton Station on 20th October 1862 and this was followed up by another letter two days later:

'Dear Sir,

We are sorry to find that notwithstanding our letter the main line to our Old and New Breweries was impassible yesterday and the down line is again today. In consequence of this, we have been obliged to use our own lines to the New Brewery of which we wish you to take note.'

Minutes of Select Committee of House of Lords dated 25th May 1864. House of Lords Records Office.

This was the first time that Allsopp had resorted to taking through traffic over its own railway and it was of course in contravention of the 1860 Act, hence the specific reference. Allsopp continued to complain to the MR about the blockages on the Guild Street Branch but to little effect.

'Dear Sir,

We are again compelled to complain of the great inconvenience we suffer by the line from our New to Old Brewery being blocked with waggons this evening. In addition to a large number of empty cask waggons being unloaded, there is also on the line a number of trucks loaded with grains. The inconvenience we sustain daily is so serious that we must request an alteration.'

28th November 1862

W. Richard Dilworth, Allsopp's manager, told the Parliamentary Select Committee enquiring into the MR's 1864 Bill that the hinderance to its traffic had continued up to then. Allsopp had been obliged to use its private railway for through traffic for nearly two years and the MR had neither voiced objection nor taken steps to stop the practice. Allsopp had only used the Guild Street Branch a little and most of the traffic on it belonged to Bass.

The MR Bill of 1864 was intended to relieve the congestion on the branch by repealing the restriction against locomotives. In particular, it aimed to reduce the delays resulting from the exchange of traffic between the horse worked part of the line and that used by locomotives. The horses could only pull one or two wagons and so these wagons were collected together on the south east side of Guild Street crossing until a sufficient number were present for a locomotive to come along and pick them up. The locomotive was not allowed to run over the road and so, rather than continually opening and shutting the gates for the horses, the locomotive would bring about another five wagons. These would remain attached to it so that the waiting wagons could be picked up from

Bass' Station Street crossing controlled by two signal arms fitted to a single slotted post and worked by the original signal box. The tram lines along Station Street are also visible. *(R. Farman Collection)*

the opposite side of Guild Street without the locomotive crossing the road. Allsopp objected to this arguing that it contravened the 1860 Act and that the waiting wagons often blocked the line stopping Allsopp from working through with its horses.

According to John Bockett Hall, Allsopp's Superintendent Cooper, it was an everyday occurrence to shunt wagons across the road to act as a reacher. The locomotives mainly belonged to the MR but occasionally Bass was also responsible. He wrote to Allsopp's manager:

'I beg to inform you on Saturday morning December 19th 1863, Messrs Bass & Co's locomotive engine pushed a short train of railway trucks 7 or 8 in number across the street, and again on the 30th, another train of 18 trucks. On both these occasions, the engines stopped without crossing the public way. It has been very common to have the road blocked up by the Midland engine's train being shunted down across the road to meet another train on the other side and then all come out together, all the above I have witnessed.'

Allsopp complained to James Allport at the MR drawing his attention to a method of working which was 'fraught with danger to the servants and horses of ourselves and other brewers using the lines south of Guild Street.' The railway company simply replied that no locomotives were taken across Guild Street.

Allsopp strongly opposed the 1864 Bill, no doubt fearing with the more efficient working that it might lose the excuse for using its own lines in preference to the Guild Street Branch. It was not prepared to agree to the repeal of the prohibition against locomotives unless it was freed of the restriction on through working over its own lines. This was a difficult case to argue because the use of locomotives would relieve some of the congestion which was the apparent basis of Allsopp's complaints. The brewery company stated that to allow locomotives to work over Guild Street would simply transfer the problem to High Street which would make matters worse because of the proximity to its Old Brewery. In answer to the suggestion of allowing locomotives to run over High Street as well, it retorted that this would make it impossible for it to work over the line with horses. In its own premises, Allsopp had prohibited the use of horses on lines working by locomotives. Allsopp admitted that the Hay Branch under Burton Bridge was not yet complete but pointed out that this would not significantly affect the congestion because two thirds of the traffic was beer taken from Bass' and Allsopp's Old Breweries to stores located along the Guild Street Branch. The Committee was reluctant to come to a decision preferring to ask the two parties to try to reach some agreement. The MR was ready to release Allsopp from the restriction if it received compensation for the loss of potential revenue but Allsopp thought this should only be considered if a diminution in traffic took place, an unlikely event in view of the increasing output of beer. Therefore, the MR was unsuccessful and the Act in 1864 only included powers for the construction of the Mosley Street Branch.

MR MOSLEY STREET BRANCH. This ran from the main line near Moor Street, over Mosley Street and Station Street, into Ind Coope's Brewery. Ironically, it allowed for a double line of rails to be carried across both streets with no restrictions against locomotives.

Battle was soon rejoined in November 1864 with the MR, Bass and Allsopp all depositing new bills. Even the MR recognised the pressures caused by the increasing traffic and tried to duplicate parts of the Guild Street Branch, whilst the brewers attempted to secure their own independent lines. The railway company's proposals were for a third line across Guild Street on the south side of the branch and another line across High Street on the north side. The MR again failed to achieve all it wanted and its New Lines & Additional Powers Act of 1865 contained neither of these items, although the restriction against locomotives working over the Guild Street and High Street level crossings was finally removed. In contrast, the brewers mostly got their own way despite the MR's objections. Bass built a private single line over Guild Street between the Middle Brewery and its cask washing plant in the Middle Yard. Attention was again drawn to the reduction in road traffic which would result from another railway crossing Guild Street. No limitations were placed on locomotive working.

Allsopp was already able to take locomotives over its Horninglow Street crossings following the removal of the restriction in a LNWR Act of 1862. The Act obtained by Allsopp in 1865 finally allowed it to work through traffic along its private railway, subject to it paying compensation to the MR for the loss of revenue on the Guild Street Branch; the sum to be decided by arbitration. Allsopp also received approval to make its connecting railways totally independent of the MR by constructing a replacement line between the New Brewery and Horninglow Street on a straighter alignment. This would have dived under the Guild Street Branch in spectacular fashion with gradients as steep as 1 in 22 and a clearance of twelve feet. It would have been a difficult line to operate and then there was the risk of flooding, because this had once been the site of the old western arm of the Trent, and only a quarter of a century before it had been a withy bed. Brook Street was always one of the first areas to flood in Burton. Allsopp was allowed to extend its Old Cooperage–Church Croft railway by a double line of rails over High Street a little to the north of the existing crossing to reach its Old Brewery. Some demolition of property would have been necessary. Allsopp's Executive Committee approved finance for a railway to the Old Brewery on 10th April 1866. Neither of these railways was built; the crossing on the level of the Guild Street Branch proved to be perfectly adequate and an alternative arrangement was made at High Street. In 1867, Allsopp purchased some land at High Street from Bass and this was then exchanged with the MR for a strip of land occupied by the northern running line of the Guild Street Branch, which became Allsopp's private line across High Street. The railway company laid out a replacement running line on the land which it had received in exchange on the south side. Despite these works, Allsopp paid an annual sum of £400 in 1905 for its use of the Hay and Guild Street Branches. Bass was charged £400 for working over the Hay Branch and £400 for the Bond End and Shobnall Branches. The other MR branch authorised in the town at this time was the Horninglow Branch.

MR HORNINGLOW BRANCH. This was approved in 1867 and ran from the main line at the Little Burton Bridge to the Horninglow coal wharf, near the Trent & Mersey Canal. The branch opened on 27th February 1873 and the LNWR received running powers in the Act.

The Competing Railway Companies

The 1859 Agreement had confirmed the MR as the dominant railway company in Burton but the LNWR had gained some significant concessions. These included the right to use the main line to Burton so that it could reach its own goods station. Exchange of traffic with the NSR at Burton was excluded and it could not use the MR's other sidings and depots. The LNWR remained deeply suspicious and it went so far as to obtain duplicate powers in 1861 for the branches from North Stafford Junction to Allsopp's Old Cooperage 'near William Saunders' malthouse then occupied by Bass & Co', and from the main line to the south east side of Guild Street. Neither was built because the MR completed its own branches.

The LNWR did lay out a railway from the main line at Wetmore, across the Hay Branch at Hawkins Lane, to its new Horninglow Goods Depot. Charles Mason, Assistant General Manager of the LNWR, and G.P. Neele came up in the autumn of 1861 to inspect the new works at Burton. The LNWR had only recently leased the South Staffordshire Railway in the previous February and was subsequently to absorb the company in 1867. Naturally, the LNWR was keen to exercise its running powers over the MR. It announced that it intended to work goods trains to Burton and submitted the proposed times to the MR. Relations between the two companies were still far from good, and early on 1st November 1861 when the first LNWR train arrived at Wichnor Junction, a large force of MR platelayers and two or three locomotives stood by to stop it. One of the locomotives had the V crossing of the junction attached to its tender. When the LNWR train drew forward and G.P. Neele claimed the right to proceed, the request was refused by Mr Needham, the MR's Superintendent, who appeared to have spent all night in a saloon carriage stabled in the sidings. When asked the reason for the force of men, Mr Needham said that they had heard reports that the LNWR would attempt to make its way to Burton with the aid of 300 men and three locomotives. The LNWR had no alternative but to withdraw. It tried again in the afternoon when wiser counsels had prevailed and it was allowed to proceed. The train made its triumphal journey to Burton with repeated whistling from the locomotive and LNWR goods services to the town began on 4th December 1861.

The LNWR also tried to work over the Burton branches on 7th March 1865 but did not succeed until 2nd October 1865. This was formalised in the following year when the LNWR received running powers over the Guild Street, Hay and Saunders Branches, paying interest of £5% each year on half of the MR's outlay, together with a proportion of the annual maintenance costs. In 1867, it obtained permanent running powers at specified tolls over the MR to Derby, and access to the MR's Burton goods depots in 1868. The LNWR first ran regular trains between Wichnor and Derby on 1st July 1871 but was prohibited from taking Burton goods traffic to Derby. The running powers over the three Burton branches were not used very much by the LNWR but the ready availability of the MR main line and associated sidings was an essential complement to its Horninglow Street Goods facilities. The LNWR built up a reasonable share of the Burton beer trade particularly from Allsopp and Ind Coope. Allsopp had sole use of the basement of a LNWR warehouse in London for storing nearly 70,000 barrels; there were also stores at Richmond and Poplar. Other traffic came from Worthington and Salt, but the LNWR was never able to match the MR's importance in Burton, mainly due to the latter's close relationship with Bass. Regular LNWR passenger trains began to run from Walsall on the same day as the incident at Wichnor and were extended to Derby on 1st March 1872. They were often worked by elderly rebuilt Trevithick Singles and McConnell Small Bloomer locomotives. After the completion of the Sutton Coldfield–Lichfield route, the LNWR was able to introduce a passenger service between Birmingham and Derby on 1st May 1885 which competed with the MR. About half of the trains continued to follow the original line via Walsall, where connections could be made for Dudley and Wolverhampton. Various 2-4-0 locomotives hauled these trains for many years.

The NSR had been running to Burton for some years and was urgently in need of a depot to handle the increasing traffic. It ultimately employed three goods agents in the town which was more than any other on the NSR system. As the company was closely involved with the LNWR, it was not surprising when it agreed to become joint owners of an enlarged Horninglow Street Goods Depot. The first priority for the NSR was to construct a new railway from its existing line at Stretton Junction round to Hawkins Lane and authorisation was received in 1863. Although only short, it was quite an expensive project requiring long embankments with bridges over the Derby Road and the main line. The resultant 1 in 76 bank from Hawkins Lane to the bridge posed a severe test for locomotives and trains were allowed to be assisted in both directions between Stretton Junction and Horninglow Goods Yard. Up to 20 wagons could be propelled in clear weather from Stretton Junction to Burton South Junction but two wagons' brakes had to be pinned down near the brake van before leaving Stretton Junction. The Act specified that the railway had to be built within five years and it was completed as a single track on 1st April 1868, when NSR goods trains began running to the goods depot, and double track from 4th November 1873.

The LNWR and NSR exchanged reciprocal running powers over similar mileages of their networks in 1867. Most of the LNWR local goods traffic continued to go out via Wichnor and the ex South Staffordshire route, but some trains for the northern part of its system used the NSR to Crewe. The Horninglow Street Goods Depot was also increased in size in 1867, approval being obtained to acquire additional land and to divert Hawkins Lane through the National Schools site. Some land appears to have been taken but no alteration was made to Hawkins Lane. In the following year, the two companies agreed on a fixed division of the competitive traffic to and from Burton.

In those hectic years, the railway companies could scarcely keep pace with the growth of traffic. The MR began to introduce block signalling over much of the Derby to Bristol main line; the Willington to Wichnor section becoming operational at 9am on 18th March 1872. Despite its success in building many of the branches in Burton, the MR was hamstrung by the lack of an independent route to the important London market. It had to rely on its running powers over the GNR from Hitchin to Kings Cross or send goods over the LNWR from Rugby to Camden Town.

Increasing delays to its trains forced the MR into action and it planned an independent line from

Bedford to London. A start had already been made on the construction of its own goods depot at Agar Town in the parish of St Pancras in 1860 to cater for the growing volume of East Midlands coal and Burton beer. The MR had also begun to erect a large ale warehouse for Bass' traffic to the north of St Pancras Station. Within six weeks of the Agar Town Goods Depot coming into use, James Allport was writing to Michael Thomas Bass promising occupation of the new warehouse by 31st August 1865 in time for the Burton brewing season. In fact, storage of beer had already begun in March. When completed, the warehouse was said to accommodate 100,000 barrels of Burton beer. Bass rented these extensive stores from the MR and the offices of Bass' premier agency controlling the London trade were located there for a century.

The line to St Pancras opened for goods traffic in the autumn of 1867 but the passenger station was not ready for another year. Its platforms had to be erected on a deck twenty feet about ground level because of the crossing of the Regent's Canal. Barlow, the MR's Engineer, made use of the space underneath by laying it out as a large beer store. The supporting columns were spaced at 29ft 4in centres, which was a multiple of the girth of a beer barrel, and the store had the benefits of a constant temperature and a central location. Both Marston, Thompson & Evershed and Salt used it and the frontage facing on to St Pancras road behind the hotel bore the prominent legend 'Salt & Company East India Pale & Burton Ale Stores.'

The 1860s had been a decade of major expansion in railway traffic, particularly for an ambitious company like the MR. Bass sent over 90% of its rail traffic by the MR and in 1866 had paid nearly £17,000 to the railway company in a single month. There was much over-working of locomotives and men to the chagrin of Michael Thomas Bass. Despite his obvious commercial interests, Bass was a liberal who had a genuine concern for his constituents. He took up the subject of excessive working hours with the MR management.

'To: James Allport, Esq.,   Burton-on-Trent,
Manager,   10th March 1870.
Midland Railway.

My dear Sir,

Since I received your letter assuring me that your "engine drivers" were never worked to an unreasonable excess except in cases of accidents or unforeseen pressure, I have received communications on this important subject which I do not feel at liberty to pass over and which leave no doubt in my mind that your men have, since you wrote to me, been kept on their engines a length of time which makes it impossible for them to perform their duties properly, and that their intervals of rest have been quite inadequate to restore their strength. Moreover the increased weight of your trains and your stringent regulations with regard to the consumption of coal, greatly aggravate the toil and pressure on your men.

No man can better appreciate the dangers incident, to be inattentive of such things I have described, than you can. I write not less in the interest of your drivers and the safety of the public than for the benefit of the Midland proprietors, for should I since find that accidents are the result of a stinting and unwise economy, I will not be sparing of doing as I am urged - to publish our correspondence.

In the hope that your reply may remove apprehensions which are very extensively entertained,

I remain,
Very truly yours,
(Sgd.) M.T. BASS.'

A reply that 'there was no ground for complaint' forced Bass to raise the issue both in the House of Commons and at the half yearly shareholders' meeting in February 1871. The absence of adequate line and sidings capacity meant that the duration of train journeys were extended. A particular example was that of John Walker, a MR goods driver who had worked more than 15 hours at a time on 36 occasions during 1870-71. One day, when Walker had worked 30 hours out of the last 34 hours, he and his fireman fell asleep whilst travelling through Burton at 35mph on their return from Dudley to Derby. The signalman directed them into a siding where they ploughed through the buffers; Walker was instantly dismissed. Despite Bass' protestations at the shareholders' meeting that he also had some interest in the MR, having 'between £70,000 and £80,000 of its stock', his views did not gain the support of the people present. By July 1871, Michael Thomas Bass was employing a full time agent to help form a trade union for the railwaymen, and from February 1872, he subsidised a weekly newspaper to put the case for a trade union. As a result, a number of railwaymen banded together to form the Amalgamated Society of Railway Servants, the forerunner of the National Union of Railwaymen.

When Michael Thomas Bass died in 1884, his fortune was worth nearly £2 million. He was succeeded by his son, Michael Arthur (1837-1909) who had married Harriet Thornewill, and was created Lord Burton in 1886. Michael Thomas Bass had declined to join the Board of the MR but Lord Burton eventually became a director until he took on a similar role with the South Eastern Railway. When he died in 1909, the *Railway Magazine* described him as an ardent railwayist and a regular reader of the magazine.

The combination of heavy traffic on the MR in the 1870s and the use of wagons, particularly those owned by private firms, which were not always up to the required standard meant that minor mishaps were frequent. Thomas Ryder was the District Locomotive Superintendent at Burton with responsibility for dealing with breakdowns. His assistant was Robert Weatherburn, who had come from Kitson and was to later record his reminiscences in the *Railway Magazine* for March 1914; 'Mr Ryder was the best man at breakdowns I had met with since leaving South Wales. . . . At that time the vast sidings at Burton and the neighbourhood were prolific of derailments of both engines and wagons, and although the great majority could be promptly dealt with, there were at times some of a very irritating character caused by barrels being flung out of low-sided wagons and getting under the vehicle, the result of rough shunting. One would hardly think that such objects would be capable of supporting impact and weight under these conditions, but when one considers the shape and form as being very resistant, there was no wonder that light wagons were canted and pitched into awkward positions which rendered their extraction, if not a difficult, at all events an irritating task. But Mr Ryder was the right man: he simply revelled in a big accident and nothing pleased him more than a good smash-up. His acerbity of temper, coupled with an uncompromising sense of duty, made him somewhat unpopular, but by those who knew his many good qualities he was held in esteem.'

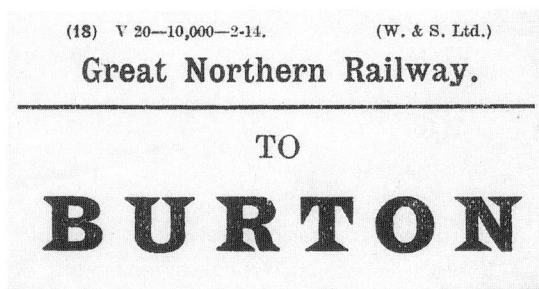

(18) V 20—10,000—2-14.   (W. & S. Ltd.)
Great Northern Railway.

TO

BURTON

The final railway company to arrive in Burton was the Great Northern. An idea for a Burton & Nottingham Railway had been put forward in 1865 as a nominally independent proposal by J.C. Forsyth who had close connections with the NSR. It was not built but would have started from near Anderstaff Lane crossing, and run alongside the Hay Branch and the NSR at Hawkins Lane, before heading off to Nottingham via Repton and Kegworth. Although the project came to nothing, the GNR began to investigate the possibility of a railway between the two towns in 1871, following the breakdown of an agreement with the MR concerning rates for the carriage of coal from Derbyshire and South Yorkshire to London. To counter opposition, the GNR offered running powers to the LNWR from Burton to the East Midlands collieries. As a result, it gained the support of the coal owners who had been inclined to view the GNR as the champion of the South Yorkshire collieries. In 1872, the GNR received approval to construct the railway from Colwick, near Nottingham, to Derby and Burton. In the next year, Samuel Charles Allsopp was elected to the GNR Board becoming Deputy Chairman in 1884.

The GNR line from Derby met the NSR Derby–Crewe railway at Egginton East Junction, diverging a short distance beyond at the West Junction to sweep round to join the NSR Tutbury–Burton Branch at Dove Junction. This latter curve, although only a mile in length, was slow in completion. It crossed a marshy inaccessible area which was prone to flooding and changes had to be made to the design of bridges to accommodate the water. The East and West Junctions at Egginton had been passed for traffic by Captain Tyler of the Board of Trade as early as 22nd February 1877 but the line to Dove Junction was far from complete. The GNR ran a first special between Grantham and Egginton on 24th January 1878 and goods trains began four days later but were still unable to reach Burton directly. They were taken to Tutbury where a NSR locomotive was attached to work them to Burton. The Egginton West Junction–Dove Junction section finally opened on 11th February 1878, although the NSR still hauled the trains from Egginton until 1st May 1878 when the GNR took over.

The first official passenger train ran on 1st April 1878 but it did not reach Burton, travelling instead to Tutbury, where refreshments were taken, before returning to Derby. Passenger services continued to operate to Tutbury until 1st July 1878 when they began to run via Dove Junction to Burton. The GNR had aspirations of providing its own passenger station in the town but then decided to work its passenger trains through to the MR station. There were seven passenger trains each way and this had increased to 9-10 each way by 1897.

The GNR sidings at Hawkins Lane were not ready to receive the first goods traffic and so the Company had to rely on MR sidings at Wetmore as a temporary measure until April 1878. Even then, it was not until 1st July 1878 that the goods depot was officially opened at Hawkins Lane. Access was over the NSR from Stretton Junction until after crossing the main line, the GNR had its own separate single line running parallel to the NSR down to Hawkins Lane at gradients of 1 in 100 and 1 in 276. There were NSR signal boxes at both ends of this single line. Burton North Junction near the bridge was a 15 lever frame box dating from 1878 and similar to, but smaller than, Stretton Junction. Burton South Junction box at the bottom of the bank was replaced by another standard structure on the same site with 46 levers possibly about 1892-93. The GNR also built a substantial grain warehouse alongside Wetmore Road reached by a double reversal.

The Battle Renewed Over Shobnall

With the central and eastern parts of Burton well served by railways, attention turned to the more undeveloped western areas. The brewery companies were attracted by the larger unconstrained sites and the expanding railway system was expected to reduce any problems resulting from the spread of their activities. As Molyneux correctly forecast in 1869, 'there is every reason to conclude that in a short time the town which is now but partly, will be wholly encircled by railway communications.' Again the MR and LNWR were in competition.

In 1871-72, Bass began to erect an extensive range of maltings at Shobnall, which was said in 1887 to be the largest group of maltings in the world belonging to one brewery company. In anticipation of this event, the MR gained parliamentary powers in 1872 to acquire, by agreement with the Marquis of Anglesey and other owners, land comprising the 'disused Burton or Bond End Canal' together with adjoining property. As a temporary measure, part of the canal was quickly filled in and the siding from the main line to the former transhipment wharf was extended to the maltings.

Both the MR and LNWR put forward conflicting proposals to permanently link Shobnall with the town's railway network. The MR wanted to provide a line from Bass's New Brewery along the course of the Bond End Canal. Although the LNWR countered with a similar idea, its railway would have

Bass's Shobnall Maltings as seen from the cask washing shed about 1880 before the new ale stores were built. The straw hurdles on the bank behind the Bass locomotive were used for covering the casks of ale. *(Bass Museum Collection)*

started from the Hay Sidings and initially run along the river meadows to Bond End where it would have joined the route of the canal. It was the LNWR's intention to pass under the main line to the south west of the canal. This would have required the main line to be raised by 2ft 9in, consequently extending the length of the adverse gradient from the station. Two lines then in existence at the Leicester Junction Sidings would also have had to be cut back. This was vigorously opposed by the MR. Both companies received approval to make the Bond End line in 1874 but the MR was given the first option which it immediately took up. In recompense, the LNWR had running powers over the new line and could provide goods facilities in connection with it. The LNWR's suspended powers had also included approval for the section of line from the Hay Sidings to Bond End which would have been a difficult and expensive railway to construct with 625 yards having to be laid on a viaduct raised on piles to allow a clear headway of 5ft 6in for water below the viaduct and above the ordinary level of the Trent. In accordance with its prior option, the MR obtained the necessary powers for the line over the river meadows and purchased the land in 1875 but that section was never built. The railway company sold some of the land to the brewers in the 1930s, with Bass acquiring land and half of the river bed at the Andressey meadows and Worthington making a similar purchase at the Hay. Railways built comprised:-

MR BOND END BRANCH. It started from the Bond End Wharf and followed the course of the former canal to Wellington Street Junction at Shobnall. En route, it descended at 1 in 100 from Anglesey Road under the main line before climbing more steeply at 1 in 55 to Wellington Street where it levelled out. These gradients were necessary to obtain sufficient clearance at the site of the canal bridge or 'Bridge Hole'. The level of the main line remained unaltered.

MR DUKE STREET BRANCH. A second line sometimes known as the Duke Street Branch diverged at Uxbridge Street and ran across numerous level crossings to link up with Bass's New Brewery railway.

MR SHOBNALL BRANCH. The connection from the main line to Shobnall was

Worthington's Brewery in 1887-88 with one of the firm's locomotives shunting railway company wagons. The extensive use of single plank wagons to carry casks was mainly a feature of the nineteenth century.

(R. Keene)

replaced by a new curve from Leicester Junction to Wellington Street Junction where it joined up with the existing line. This was then extended to the Trent & Mersey Canal where access was to be gained to Mann, Crossman & Paulin's Brewery.

An approach to Shobnall from Stretton had been partly anticipated by the NSR which had unsuccessfully applied in 1867 for a railway from Stretton Junction to Horninglow Wharf running parallel to the Trent & Mersey Canal. The LNWR took up the idea of this line, extending it on to Shobnall with two short branches to Shobnall Wharf and Mann, Crossman, & Paulin's Brewery. The MR put forward its own optimistic proposals with two lines curving round in broad arcs from the Horninglow Branch to Shobnall. These ambitious plans came to nothing and it was the LNWR which this time proved successful. Its England & Ireland Act authorised construction of the Dallow Lane Branch in 1874, although the two short lines to Shobnall Wharf and Mann, Crossman, & Paulin's Brewery were omitted, because the running powers over the MR's Shobnall Branch gave the LNWR access to these properties.

LNWR DALLOW LANE BRANCH. The LNWR branch ran from Stretton Junction to Shobnall alongside the Trent & Mersey Canal, with a half mile line heading off westwards over the canal to Allsopp's Shobnall Maltings. The branch was opened throughout in 1881-82 and the MR and NSR received running powers over the new railway.

The MR quadrupled much of its main line through Burton between 1873 and 1876 by the addition of goods lines. Those by the station were not opened until 1882 as part of the works to provide a new station. The MR obtained powers in 1878 for the New Street Branch and in the following year, short lengths of railway were authorised off the Bond End Branch to Charrington's Maltings and from the Duke Street Branch into Eadie's Brewery yard. In 1881, Worthington obtain approval for a railway across Station Street to connect its brewery to the cooperage and provide an outlet along the New Street Branch; reference continued to be made to the beneficial effects of reducing road traffic!

MR NEW STREET BRANCH. This ran from James Street Junction on the Duke Street Branch to serve the breweries in the area behind Station Street and High Street and was opened on 26th April 1880.

CHAPTER THREE

A CONGERIES OF BREWERIES

The London Brewers

The increasing numbers of people in the towns and cities led a hard life and beer drinking was one of the few pleasures available to them. With the rise in beer consumption, the number of companies in Burton grew dramatically. Competition between the breweries revolved around the quality of their beers and the local firms were well placed to compete because of the suitability of the brewing water. Burton pale ales became renowned for their strength, flavour, and light clear sparkling appearance. As a result, in the forty years from 1839, most of the land between the river and the main line was occupied by brewery premises, railways, and workers' terraced houses giving the town a unique character.

The Victorian love of statistics about the new enterprises knew no bounds. In 1869, the twenty six breweries in Burton covered a total of 174 acres and produced 1,755,000 barrels of beer. To process the barley, brew the ale, and make the casks so that it could be despatched required 5,000 employees; 189 horses; 282 floats, carts and wagons; 8 private locomotives; and 67 fixed engines. In 1872-73, Bass used 250,000 quarters of malt, 34,000 hundredweights of hops and 40,000 tons of coal to produce 837,000 barrels of beer. It paid nearly £170,000 to the railway companies to transport the beer.

Above. Looking across the River Trent to the brewery chimneys of Burton in 1870. The contrast with the earlier 1732 view is most striking, although the remains of the old Burton Bridge can still be seen.   *(B. Ward Collection)*

TRUMAN, HANBURY, BUXTON & CO.
LONDON.
1 NOV. 1877.

ESTABLISHED AT BURTON ON TRENT 1873.
THE BREWERY ENLARGED & FITTED
WITH ENTIRELY NEW PLANT. 1874-6.

TRUMAN, HANBURY, BUXTON & CO HAVE NOW COMPLETED
THEIR BREWERY AT BURTON ON TRENT. AND THE WHOLE OF
THE NEW & EXTENSIVE PLANT IS IN FULL WORKING ORDER.
EAST INDIA PALE & STRONG BURTON ALES
ARE NOW SUPPLIED FROM THE BREWERY TO ANY RAILWAY STAT'N
IN ENGLAND, CARRIAGE FREE IN LARGE OR SMALL QUANTITIES.
SEASON BREWED PALE ALES
FOR EXPORT & PALE & MILD ALES FOR BOTTLING
FROM 1ST NOV. TO END OF MARCH.

PRICE LIST & TERMS ON APPLICATION.

'One no sooner enters the town of Burton than he begins to be oppressed by a sense of brewery on the brain. There is no escape from the brewery incubus. There are breweries to right, to left, in front and in rear. Huge piles of casks, arranged as we see shot and shell in an arsenal rise high above the walls flanking the streets. You meet a locomotive coming serenely down *(sic)* the street drawing a long tail of trucks loaded with barrels full of beer, or with grains on their way to the dairies. A scent of brewing ever floats upon the air. . . . It is impossible to realise that Burton is a town with breweries in it; the inevitable impression is that Burton consists of a congeries of breweries.'
Daily News 22nd October 1872.

The big London porter brewers were forced to establish themselves in Burton in order to compete. In 1871 Charrington, Head & Company bought Lewis Meakin's old Abbey Brewery on the corner of Lichfield Street and erected a new brewery on the site in the following year. Lewis Meakin had owned the Abbey Brewery, since taking it over from Sherratt in 1823, and had traded as the London & Burton Brewery Company from 1860.

Phillips Brothers had constructed a small brewery near the station in 1865 and began to load their own ale on the railway on the 16th November 1865. Although Truman, Hanbury, Buxton & Company could produce pale ales at its Brick Lane Brewery in London, it found that the soft water of the Thames basin could not give sparkling ales of the same quality as the Burton brewers. Truman unsuccessfully sought agency agreements with two large brewers in Burton to produce pale ales and bitter beers for it but finally took over the brewery of Phillips Brothers on 1st October 1873. This was substantially enlarged to become the Black Eagle Brewery and was fitted with new plant and machinery. Mann, Crossman, & Paulin also came from London to build the Albion Brewery up at Shobnall in 1875.

Peter Walker had originally been a brewer in Ayr. He was persuaded by his son, Andrew Barclay Walker, to come south in 1846 and develop a brewery at Warrington. In 1877, A.B. Walker erected the Shobnall Brewery in Burton with the intention of producing pale ales for transit by railway to the Liverpool and Warrington stores. His father died two years later and he became the sole proprietor until 1881 when he was joined by his three sons. In 1883, Peter Walker & Company built the Clarence Street Brewery alongside the Bond End Branch. On 16th April 1890, Peter Walker & Son (Warrington & Burton) Limited was formed to purchase from the late Sir A.B. Walker, the brewery previously carried on as Peter Walker & Son at Warrington and A.B. Walker & Sons' Brewery at Shobnall. The brewery in Clarence Street remained under the control of the Trustees of the late Peter Walker; a complicated story!

The growth of the town's breweries reached its peak in the 1880s, although it was not until 1901 that the population of Burton exceeded 50,000 and it could become a County Borough. About 70%

Breweries in Burton on Trent in 1884

Company	Location	Barrels April 1883-March 1884	Notes
Bass, Ratcliff & Gretton	High Street, Guild St, Station St	959,345	
Samuel Allsopp & Sons	Station St, High St	853,281	
Ind Coope	Station Street	213,305	
Worthington	High Street	188,365	
Thos Salt	High Street	162,667	
Truman, Hanbury, Buxton	Derby Street	126,727	
Burton Brewery Company	High Street	122,548	
Charrington	Abbey Street	66,386	
John Thompson & Son	Horninglow Street	58,238	
Mann, Crossman & Paulin	Shobnall Road	53,196	
T. Cooper	Victoria Crescent	45,664	
Dawson	Moor Street	41,186	a
Trustees of P. Walker	Clarence Street	38,840	
Walker A.B. & Sons	Shobnall Road	33,576	
T. Robinson	Union Street	29,495	
Sydney Evershed	Bank Square	25,781	
James Eadie	Cross Street	23,103	
Joseph Nunneley	Bridge Street	18,108	
J.A. Bindley	New Street	15,753	
Charles Hill & Son	Lichfield Street	15,513	
H. Boddington	Burton Bridge	14,693	b
John Marston & Son	Horninglow	13,323	
John Bell	Lichfield Street	12,250	
Green & Clarkson	Victoria Street	10,437	
J. Porter & Son	Dale Street	5,959	
Cooper G & W.F.	?	5,405	
Thos Sykes	Kimmersitch Street	5,447	
J. & T. Bowler	New Street	3,129	c
Thos Yeomans	?	1,835	
John Yeomans	High Street	1,624	
F. Heape	Victoria Street	1,429	
Cliff	?	1,028	d
Samuel Carter	Victoria Street	167	
Clayton	Horninglow Road	-	e

Notes

a   Built 1863 and owned by John Dickenson of Wolverhampton; it had passed to Nichols & Stone by 1869 and was purchased by Edwin Popplewell Dawson of Leeds in 1872. Dawson sold it to the Burton & Lincoln Brewery Co in 1890, which was registered in December 1889 to acquire Dawson's brewery at Burton and Henry Buckmaster's at Lincoln. It was followed by the Albion Brewery (Burton on Trent) Ltd. In October 1899, the premises were finally acquired by S. Briggs. Dawson built up a good trade from 18,600 barrels produced in 1875 to 45,049 barrels in 1882 but did not have his own railway siding.

b   Whitbread was brewing at the old Burton Boat Company's warehouse off the Burton Bridge in 1869. Ten years later, H. Boddington was in occupation before it was taken over by Everard & Welldon in 1885.

c   A brewhouse at the Anchor Inn. The business was acquired by Marston in 1891.

d   No further records given for this brewery.

e   At the Dingo Brewery. Last shown in 1882-83 when output was 411 barrels.

the number of railway lines, but where Burton gained its unique character was the way in which the railway penetrated most parts of the town. Tracks ran into firm's premises serving bank and boiler, the locomotive and its wagons were rarely absent from the scene.

At times, it seemed that there was a level crossing every few yards. Going from Winshill by tramcar to catch a train at the railway station could be exciting. There were five level crossings to negotiate and it was almost certain that at least one would be closed if people were in a hurry. Of course, trains were missed and complaints were made to the Tramways Office. To maintain a check on the times that cars reached the bridge at the station, a Bundy's pendulum recording clock with a dial visible to passers-by, was fixed on each side of the road. The conductor of every Corporation car running over the bridge had to jump off and turn his key in the clock; not that it would bring the train back to comfort the latecomer! Yet the level crossings were accepted as a necessary feature of the town and serious incidents were rare. There were still 29 level crossings in use as late as 1962. The frequent opening of some of the gates was accompanied by the ringing of a bell and the familiar sight of pedestrians running to get through before the gates closed. Strangers were advised by a notice attached to the signal box although the priority of trains was clearly implied.

CAUTION
WHEN THE BELL RINGS THESE
GATES WILL BE OPENED

Worthington's High Street Signal Box carried a complementary warning on the opposite side of the swinging board for workers leaving the brewery yard.

DANGER
Beware
of the
Cars

There were two tramway systems serving Burton. The MR was the surprising owner of one, the Burton & Ashby Light Railways which opened throughout on 2nd July 1906. Although a normal street electric tramway, it ran from the town along country roads, including a mile long trip across the fields, to Swadlincote, Ashby, and Gresley. The idea had originally been put forward in 1901 by a group of local businessmen to cater for the expanding population in the thriving coal and stoneware districts in South Derbyshire. Naturally, the MR was strongly opposed to the proposal; its answer was to eventually obtain the Order for the line. The Light Railway connected with the Burton upon Trent Corporation Tramways system at the Borough boundary in Winshill and its trams ran over the Corporation track past the station forecourt to the Town Hall.

At the level crossings, the railways and tram lines were at first only bolted together and there was much clattering as the trams passed over them. Later the crossovers were cast in one piece and this reduced the noise. A major cause of tram breakdowns was a broken axle due to the crossings; there were eighteen in 1920. It was Car 22, one of four new English Electric trams with covered in top decks recently purchased by the Corporation, which fractured its axle on Worthington's Station Street Crossing on 3rd November 1921. It overturned near the Staffordshire Knot public house and twenty eight people were injured, the landlady bringing out tots of brandy to revive the driver and conductor. Six Corporation trams were fitted with the Pringle Emergency Brake. When operated, the rear wheels mounted partly on to the brake shoes giving extra weight on the shoes. Incidents between tramcars and level crossings were not always one sided, and on one occasion, operation of the brake lifted a piece of brewery railway line completely out of the ground.

The Passenger Station

Writing in 1869, Molyneux had suggested that there was a probability of the LNWR opening its Horninglow Goods Depot for passenger traffic and that the NSR might join in. Nothing came of the proposal; nor was use ever made by the NSR of powers obtained under the Light Railways Act of 1896 to work the Stretton Junction–Horninglow line as a passenger light railway. There was certainly dissatisfaction with the original passenger station and the adjacent level crossing had earned an

Mr J.M. Jacques was the MR Station Master at Burton in 1909.   (C. Shepherd Collection)

Warning notice for users of Wetmore Road at Anderstaff Lane Signal Box.   (C. Shepherd)

unenviable reputation for the number of fatalities which had occurred there. The level crossing was finally replaced by the Borough Road Bridge and road traffic began to use this on 5th December 1881. Construction of the bridge also resulted in the demolition of the Bowling Green public house, adjacent to the crossing, and Salt's Station Hotel was provided as a replacement.

The new station constructed by Cox of Leicester was laid out 7 chains south west of the old station and was located partly underneath the Borough Road Bridge, with the approach roads and forecourt actually on the bridge. It comprised a substantial island platform, with the NSR and GNR using a bay at the north end, and the MR and LNWR another bay at the south end. The parts of the platforms under the bridge were gloomy places which had to be permanently lit by gas lights. Gordon Biddle described the new station as 'an incredible place with a vast brick and timber patterned entrance, canopied, cab drive, and an odd open fronted balcony overlooking the long island platform, along much of which ran a narrow black and white pseudo half timbered building frivolously decorated with fancy gables. The platform was roofed by hipped iron and glass awnings of the standard type.' The new station opened and the old one closed on 29th April 1883; it becoming a 'closed' station for ticket collection purposes on 1st October 1899.

In their heyday, the four railway companies provided Burton with an excellent service and 110 passenger trains left the station daily. On the main line, the MR expresses ran between the north and west of England, their graceful locomotives and trains of substantial carriages all clad in an immaculate crimson lake livery making an impressive sight. In the latter part of the nineteenth century, various types of Kirtley and Johnson 2-4-0 locomotives were on these trains. They were followed by the handsome Midland 'Spinners', which were well suited to the easy gradients along

The 1883 station at Burton was a place full of character. A Johnson 2-4-0 locomotive is about to depart with a Leicester train about 1910. MR wagons loaded with casks stand next to the goods line, whilst the wagons coated with whitewash are at the cattle dock siding.

(Historical Model Railway Society Ibbotson Collection)

the Trent valley, but the rails at the south end of Burton Station required frequent replacement as a result of MR drivers' attempts to restart their trains up the gradient over the Bridge Hole. The Class 3 4-4-0s succeeded the Spinners on the expresses.In addition to the Derby–Birmingham and Walsall locals, the LNWR also ran a few long distance passenger trains through Burton. There was one working each way between Nuneaton and Ashbourne in 1890 and there were two Euston–Buxton through carriage workings each way in the years immediately before World War 1.

Half of the MR passenger trains on the Burton–Leicester Branch ran round the Swadlincote–Woodville Loop before terminating at Ashby. The rebuilt 6ft 2in 2-4-0s of the old MR 156 Class worked the trains and 7, 8, 9 and 13 from Burton shed were still on them in 1920, by which time they were the oldest passenger locomotives on the MR. Ben Ward can still remember 7 in its crimson lake livery and gleaming brass work, with coupling rods sometimes clanking, running down to exchange the tablet at Darklands Signal Box on the Loop. After the 2-4-0s came Leicester's Deeley 0-6-4 tanks (2005/06/11/13) and Burton's Class 2 4-4-0s. The 'Flatiron' 0-6-4 tanks were prone to derailments and 2011 came to grief between Moira West Junction and Woodville Junction, fortunately without serious injury. Shortly after, the class was taken off passenger work and the Class 2 4-4-0s generally worked the trains to Leicester.

The Tutbury Jenny was a frequent sight at the north end of Burton Station. Back in 1851, two Hick locomotives numbers 7 and 8 had been rebuilt as 2-2-2 well tanks to work the service and it was 8 which crashed down an embankment when crossing the Dove Valley with the 7.05pm to Tutbury on 21st June 1861. The well tank locomotives were replaced by two rebuilt Little Sharp 2-2-2 saddle tanks in 1881. There were no intermediate stations at the opening but a NSR poster (dated July 1883) states that Horninglow Passenger Station was to open on 1st August 1883. The Public Record Office gives November 1883 according to Higginson. Other stations were later provided at Rolleston-on-Dove (1st November 1894) and Stretton and Claymills (1st August 1901). NSR Class B locomotives usually worked the Jenny from 1890-91. The GNR added another colour to the railway scene and, particularly after the turn of the century, its apple green Stirling singles and teak carriages made a memorable sight at the north end of Burton Station on the passenger service to Derby, Nottingham and Grantham, with nine or ten passenger trains each way before World War 1.

The Brewery Trips

Although the brewers prospered on the proceeds from the boom in brewing, several of them took a genuine interest in the welfare of their workers. Some such as Ind Coope, the Burton Brewery Company, and Mann, Crossman, & Paulin organised free Christmas dinners and also ran annual excursions for their workers. The *Burton Weekly News* recorded that on 20th July 1865, Salt's employees left by a special train to Crystal Palace, whilst workers from Allsopp's Brewery went to Llandudno. Ind Coope celebrated its centenary in 1899 by taking four special trains to the Crystal Palace and 3000 excursionists went from Allsopp to Blackpool in the same year. The most ambitious series of trips was run by Bass. The first took place on 19th August 1865 when two trains travelled to Liverpool. On arrival, the workers formed a procession to the Pier Head where two tugs made trips to Eastham and the Northwest Lighthouse, to be followed by a dinner with long speeches at the Corn Exchange. That first trip was organised by Captain Anderson from the Engineers' Office; he had previously been in the army in India before becoming police superintendent at Burton and then moving to Bass.

The responsibility for the next trip on 24th August 1867 was transferred to the Railway Department which ran them until the last one to Scarborough in 1914. Arrangements had been made in 1881 for an excursion to London, but an outbreak of smallpox in the capital caused a change of mind, and Scarborough was visited instead. The 1881 trip was also of interest because the six trains left from the 'ale bank at the Midland Station'. Presumably special arrangements were required because of the construction work proceeding at this time. M.T. Bass' interest in the Coton Park Colliery is demonstrated by the fact that the men from the colliery were conveyed to Burton by special train and their carriages were attached to the No.2 train departing at 4.10am. From 1883, the Bass trips became an annual event; previously they had run every other year. Five trains were needed in 1884 for an afternoon outing to the Fine Arts exhibition at Wolverhampton, and next year eight trains went to Blackpool starting from the 'NEW RAILWAY STATION'. Ten trains made the journey to Brighton in 1888 but the day was very wet and the visit was not a success. In future the Bass trips alternated between Blackpool, Liverpool, Great Yarmouth and Scarborough where there was ample covered accommodation. All of Bass' employees, together with the staff at the agencies, could go and tickets could be purchased to allow wives and children to also travel. For the 1894 trip to Scarborough, the 8,000 Burton people were joined by 250 London Agency employees who travelled in a special train from St Pancras. Into the new century and there were usually 15 to 16 trains conveying 9,000 to 10,000 passengers; the highest number was 17 trains carrying 11, 241 passengers to Blackpool in 1900. At least 24 newspapers were said to have reported the 1909 trip with headlines such as 'Yarmouth invaded by Messrs Bass' army.' Once at the resort, the railway ticket gave free admittance to many of the attractions and each employee received his full day's pay and some pocket money as well.

Such an event required considerable organisation and the trips were meticulously planned by the Railway Department headed by the redoubtable William Walters. A handbook was given to each employee with all the necessary travel details, rules to be observed, points of interest en route and information on places to visit. These became important publications in their own right; the handbook for the 1909 trip ran to 135 pages! William Walters left the passengers in no doubt as to how they should behave.

'The Great Eastern Railway **are most particular about you travelling by your own train,** and there will be trouble in store for any persons who do not do so.'

Requests to wait until the train stopped before entering the compartment were backed up by extracts from cuttings which explained in graphic detail what might happen if they were ignored. To allay any fears back at 'good old Burton', a telegram was sent on arrival at the destination and this was displayed on the Old Brewery gates; a similar telegram was sent to Burton Station.

CHAPTER FOUR

THE VICTORIAN LEGACY

The Railway Companies' Premises

The involvement of four railway companies in Burton and the steady expansion of the MR resulted in a complicated network of railway yards and warehouses. When combined with the spread of brewery premises, it meant that wagons were having to be continually sorted and moved around the town according to their load and destination. For a town of its size, Burton had an amazingly intricate network of yards and sidings. Despite the decline in traffic, most of this system was to remain intact until the 1960s; a true Victorian legacy. The old patterns of working continued, although the LNWR staff had moved over to the MR Goods Office in Mosley Street within a year of the railway companies grouping in 1923 and the MR agent Mr H.G. Waggett had taken over responsibility for the previous LNWR and NSR interests.

Even with nationalisation in 1948 when all of the yards came under one owner, trains continued to use their respective former railway company sidings. Whilst the system increasingly became outdated, it nevertheless provided a fascinating insight into the Victorian railway, as R.C. Riley recorded forty years after the decline in rail traffic had begun. 'Walking northwards from Burton station the first yard I reached was Horninglow Bridge, where a Class 3F 0-6-0 was busily marshalling the 6.50pm train for St Pancras. The engine for the St Pancras beer train was a Fowler 'Crab' 2-6-0 which left a few minutes before time with a load of thirty four wagons. At Hawkins Lane another Class 3F 0-6-0 was preparing the three evening departures over the GN line so keenly that the trains were ready well before time. The 6.15pm York train left at 5.56pm and the 6.55pm Colwick at 6.29pm, both with Class K3 2-6-0s in charge. . . . . A diesel was shunting Old Dixie Yard, while 0-6-0 tank 47643 was forming up a train for a transfer trip to Wetmore Sidings. At 6.15pm No.5, one of the sturdy little Bagnall tanks in the Worthington fleet, emerged from the brewery sidings past Horninglow Shed and Hawkins Lane to deposit a load of twenty two wagons in Old Dixie Sidings. As soon as it returned to the brewery a bevy of BR engines arrived to divide its load among them, No.43679 taking some wagons to Hawkins Lane for GN destinations and No.44420 moving others away to Horninglow Bridge, while No.47643 added the remainder to its rake of wagons for Wetmore Sidings. Soon after 7pm Class 4F 0-6-0 No.44245 passed by on the main line with a load of nine wagons and a brake from Shobnall, bound for Wetmore Sidings; there it would form the 8.25pm train to Carlisle. . . . It was followed by Class 3F 0-6-0T No.47643 with fifteen wagons on a transfer trip from Old Dixie to Wetmore.' *(Trains Illustrated Annual 1962)*

The first facilities for railway goods traffic in Burton were provided near the original passenger station at the end of Cat Street. By 1847, a small goods shed faced on to the station forecourt and there was much use made of wagon turntables to manoeuvre rolling stock about. A single siding also left the main line, immediately beyond the adjacent level crossing, and ran alongside to the Bond End Canal where a transhipment wharf with warehousing space was available for the exchange of traffic between the railway and the canal.

The goods shed was clearly becoming inadequate and powers were obtained in the following year to enlarge the passenger station and acquire land for the establishment of the Midland Goods Yard, including widening the main line between the Little Burton Bridge and passenger station. The Birmingham & Derby Junction Railway had previously bought the field behind the station from Edward Phillips on 7th August 1838. The MR completed the purchase of an additional two acres at a cost of £2,000 from the Marquis of Anglesey for the approach lines to the yard on the 31st August 1850. A three storey Cheese and Corn Warehouse and goods depot were erected by the MR. The warehouse was originally planned to be two bays in length but it was either built with a third bay or this was added almost immediately, the signed contract drawings being dated 1854. A century later, the warehouse was still in use offering temporary storage for a wide range of animal feedstuffs.

The Co-operative Society, based at the Midland Goods, was the biggest local supplier of domestic coal. (Historical Model Railway Society Collection)

Sacks came in railway vans and were stowed away until required when they were loaded on to lorries for delivery to local farms. Human beings were not neglected and the light weight variation to this work was the similar handling of Kelloggs cornflakes. Much of the adjacent yard was a large coal depot operated by a number of local merchants and the Goods and Coal Yard could accommodate 223 wagons. There was also a very small shed with its own siding which in 1941-42 was used exclusively by J. Lyons for storing tea. Peter Williams recalls that it was a regular Friday evening job to help Uncle Les unload the tea ready for the next week's delivery; he even parked his Lyons van in the shed. The goods depot contained three 30cwt cranes and there was a larger crane of 10 tons capacity in the yard. Soon after Grouping, the Midland Goods was renamed the 'Station Street Goods' but it was often referred to by its former name up until rail traffic ceased. The depot closed on 2nd July 1979, but the Cheese and Corn Warehouse was converted into offices and associated uses.

Locomotives were also serviced at Burton and a coke stage and pit had been provided near the station in 1849. The shed building was erected not long after probably to accommodate two tracks, its outline being indicated on the 1855 Town Improvement Map. Its foreman was Thomas Ryder in June 1859. Various alterations were made to the shed and in October 1863, the MR's Way and Works Committee ordered 'that the shear-legs at Burton be lengthened, and the sand furnace be rebuilt and a roof erected between the shed and the Tank House.' The turntable was enlarged in the following year, so that by 1865, the shed had assumed its ultimate form of a straight shed with four lines, a rudimentary coal stage, a water tank and 42 feet diameter turntable.

Over the years, the MR laid out more and more sets of sidings on either side of the main line in Burton. A start was made on the Leicester Junction Sidings as early as 1860 and further lines were added in the 1870s (there is a reference to additional sidings opened at 'Leicester Old Junction on 1st October 1874'). The capacity of the yard was doubled towards the end of the nineteenth century so it could accommodate 387 wagons. It was mainly concerned with exchanging goods traffic with the breweries particularly situated on the Bond End Branch. Wagons were also 'tripped' round from Shobnall Exchange Sidings by the Shobnall 'Jacko' for distribution to other yards or for attachment to southbound trains, a few of which started from the sidings. North bound traffic from Shobnall was taken to Wetmore Yard.

By 1864, the Old Dixie Sidings had come into operation and were increased in size towards the end of the 1870s. Another fan of sidings was provided on the opposite side of the main line called New Dixie. The Goods Agent notebook records that the MR opened new sidings between North Stafford Junction and Horninglow Bridge on 30th October 1874. Old Dixie was a popular starting

Where it all began! A fascinating photograph taken from the Iron Bridge looking towards Burton Station on 16th October 1965. From left to right, the line on the far left marks the approximate position of the first private siding in Burton which ran past the ends of Allsopp's Maltings and later served its New Brewery. The dark single storey building beyond is the MR No.3 Grain Warehouse, whilst further back, the 1883 Passenger Station building on the Borough Road Bridge dominates the skyline. The original station was situated between these two buildings but most traces of it were obliterated by the widening of the main line. Class 4F 0-6-0 43953 is running round the carriages of the RCTS Midland Locomotives Requiem special.

Behind is the Midland Goods Yard and the MR Cheese and Corn Warehouse No.2 with its substantial external timber hoists. The row of wagons, vans, and carriages stand on one of the lines which were used for the exchange of traffic with Truman's Brewery. These lines once formed the approach to the old MR Locomotive Shed, later occupied by the NSR. At the far end of the row is the distinctive shape of Truman's No.1 Malting, built by Joseph Chamberlain of Burton in 1879-80. On the right is part of Truman's Brewery still with some railway vans on its sidings. The scene is completed by Burton's 3F tank 47643 chuffing steadily along the Down goods with a coal wagons trip.

(C. More)

point for southbound trains carrying traffic for Birmingham, Bristol, and London. Wagons were brought from the breweries via the Guild Street and Hay Branches and exchanged with the MR at the sidings. Old Dixie could hold 716 wagons and New Dixie 231. Later on, operations at the yard were reorganised and that part near the Little Burton Bridge became known as the Horninglow Bridge Yard with responsibility for train departures. The north end continued to be referred to as Old Dixie but was mostly used for sorting wagons. New Dixie despatched trains to Stoke and Liverpool, with some Irish traffic travelling via Holyhead also starting from here.

Further along the main line, Wetmore Down (or Old Wetmore) Sidings were laid out by the MR in the early 1860s. They could hold 245 wagons and some trains stopped here to take water. There was a bank called the Empty Cask Sorting Depot, Wetmore Bank, which was used for breaking down the incoming loads of casks according to the different breweries. The railway companies offered a delivery to cellar and return service, making sure that the beer reached its destination generally within 48 hours and often in 24 hours. Some public houses wanted three or four casks at a time and these would only fill part of a wagon. They had to be amalgamated into wagon loads and all the railway companies had 'checkers' in the breweries to help organise the consignments. Some of the returning wagons were labelled 'mixed empties' and had to go to the Wetmore Bank for sorting into loads for each of the breweries. Bass and Worthington fetched their wagons, as did the shunting locomotives from the 'North Western' at Horninglow Street and the 'Eastern' at Hawkins Lane. The Old Wetmore locomotive propelled wagons through Old Dixie and Horninglow Bridge to Ind Coope & Allsopp. Sometimes, British Railways sent a man by road round all of the breweries collecting surplus wagon sheets. They were loaded into a railway wagon and despatched to the Sheet Stores at Trent Junction. It was not a job for the faint hearted because the man was expected to accept the generous hospitality offered at each establishment! A subsidiary duty of Wetmore Bank was cleaning wagons before they entered back into beer traffic.

Wetmore on 26th May 1959. A trip working behind 3F tank 47464 runs along the Up goods line. New Wetmore Sidings are to the right with the Wagon Repairs Depot beyond. On the other side of the main line are the Old Wetmore Sidings, the ex-NSR bank and Hawkins Lane with its water tower. (R.C. Riley)

Burton on Trent Wetmore Sidings 1933

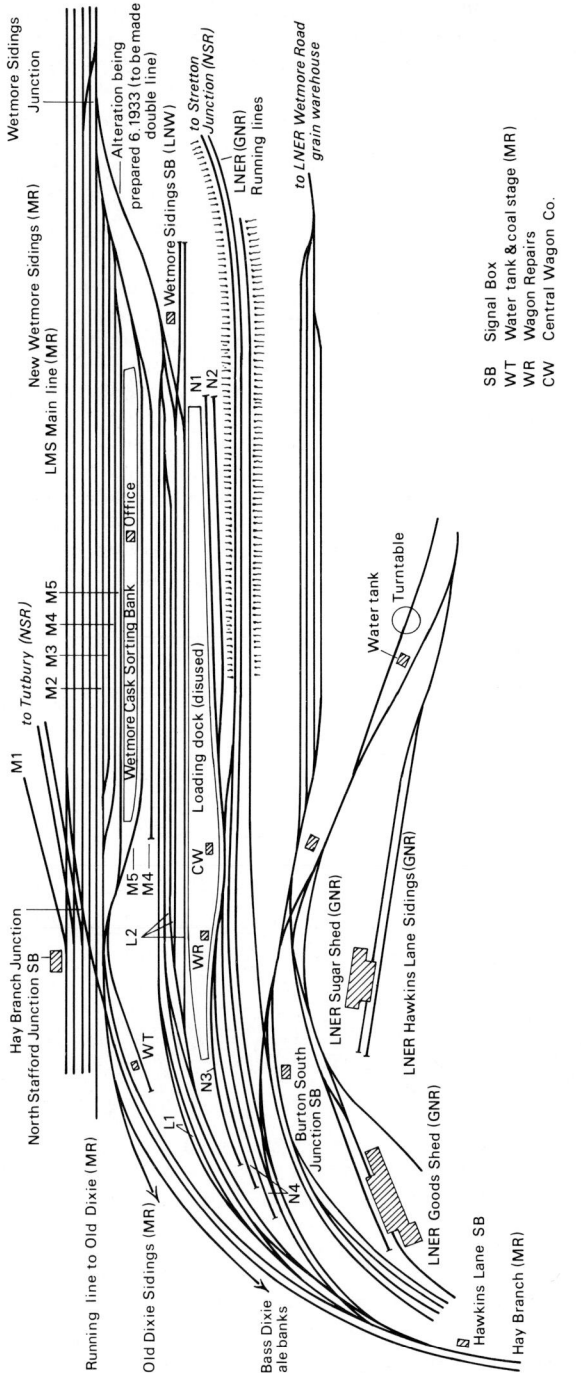

Wetmore Sidings Junction

New Wetmore Sidings (MR)

LMS Main line (MR)

Alteration being prepared 6.1933 (to be made double line)

to Stretton Junction (NSR)

Wetmore Sidings SB (LNW)

LNER (GNR) Running lines

to LNER Wetmore Road grain warehouse

M1

to Tutbury (NSR)

M2 M3 M4 M5

Wetmore Cask Sorting Bank

Office

Loading dock (disused)

M5

M4

CW

WR

N1

N2

N3

Water tank

Turntable

Hay Branch Junction

North Stafford Junction SB

Running line to Old Dixie (MR)

Old Dixie Sidings (MR)

L2

WT

L1

N4

Bass Dixie ale banks

LNER Sugar Shed (GNR)

Burton South Junction SB

LNER Hawkins Lane Sidings (GNR)

LNER Goods Shed (GNR)

Hawkins Lane SB

Hay Branch (MR)

SB   Signal Box
WT   Water tank & coal stage (MR)
WR   Wagon Repairs
CW   Central Wagon Co.

Use of LMS Sidings at Wetmore

M   Ex Midland Railway
M1   Spur to Wagon Repair Shed
M2   Empty sorted barrels for Bass removed by LMS at own convenience
M3   Empty sorted barrels for Worthington removed by LMS at own convenience
M4   Empty barrels to be sorted awaiting accommodation at Sorting Bank
M5   Empty barrels sorting by LMS employees

L   Ex London & North Western Railway
L1   Outwards traffic from Horninglow Street wharf removed daily
L2   Inwards coal traffic for Burton Gas Works awaiting orders

N   Ex North Staffordshire Railway
N1   Outwards coke traffic from Gas Works awaiting orders
N2   Inwards coal traffic for Burton Gas Works awaiting orders
N3   Wagon repairing
N4   Crippled wagons

46

The more extensive Up sidings at Wetmore, usually known as New Wetmore, are thought to have been constructed about 1879-82 and could accommodate 486 wagons. They were the starting point for many northbound trains. Some through workings also called here to pick up and set down traffic. At dinnertime, there was a train from Wetmore to Nottingham and the three wagons next to the locomotive would be filled with spent hops destined for John Player's factory where they were incorporated into the tobacco mixtures. The Up sidings were rather isolated from the breweries and this necessitated frequent trips from the other yards where traffic could be more easily exchanged. The LMS insisted that any brewery company locomotive which did proceed from Hawkins Lane Junction towards Wetmore Sidings Signal Box had to be accompanied by the shunter or foreman in charge of Horninglow Yard.

The MR also had sidings at Branston, enlarged on 3rd November 1875, which were mainly concerned with coal traffic and later with wagons destined for the Ordnance Depot. There were no fewer than three signal boxes at the sidings. At the southern end was Branston Junction Signal Box; replacement structures were provided for it in 1874, 1889 and on 28th January 1923. This latter box was the first to be erected by the LMS on Midland territory and not surprisingly, it was identical to the MR boxes built immediately prior to the Grouping. At the other end of the sidings was another signal box which had opened before 1877. It was named Branston Sidings No.1 about 1889-93 and replaced by a new structure on 6th April 1908. In the midst of the sidings was the appropriately named Centre of Branston Sidings Signal Box. This was replaced on 14th January 1889 and renamed Branston Sidings No.2 Signal Box. It closed on 8th January 1939 which allowed the No.1 Box to simply become 'Branston Sidings Signal Box' until 13th October 1963 when a ground frame was provided instead. Branston Sidings was divided into two main groups of lines, the Down sidings holding 813 wagons.

The MR owned three more grain warehouses in the town. It built the Brook Street Warehouse (MR Grain Warehouse No.1) in the early 1890s which was leased by Bass by 1900 and probably from its erection. It contained Bass' plant inside which was powered by a Robey gas engine before electrification in the 1930s. Outside, capstans were available to move the wagons and Bass made successive payments to the MR, LMS, and BR for pressure from the Hydraulic Pumping Station at New Dixie. The lines on either side of the warehouse and the three sidings between the building and the Guild Street Branch were used by Bass for its grain traffic, with shunting being performed by its locomotives. A final siding nearest the branch was also worked by Bass and coal wagons were kept on it. Eventually Bass took the screens out of its Burton maltings and all barley was then screened at Brook Street. After the bulk handling of barley commenced at Bass in 1939-40, as much barley as possible was taken from the growing areas via Klondyke to Brook Street in railway company vans. The barley was dropped into elevator boots for lifting into store, ready for several stages of screening. On completion, the two van Boby pump was brought by Bass' No.5 diesel and set at the north end of the warehouse. Screened barley was then transferred by suction from the store to a line of Bass internal grain (lettered 'malt') vans which carried the barley to the maltings. On arrival there, the barley was dropped in to elevator boots and lifted to the garners. Sometimes barley arrived from the growing areas and could not be immediately handled at Brook Street. This had to be taken to one of the maltings which had a fourth floor above the three working floors, such as Nos.1 to 8 Shobnall and Nos.18 to 21 Anderstaff Lane. As this barley had not been screened, it had to be later fetched out by the mobile Boby pump, put into internal grain vans, and moved to Brook Street. Bass's locomotives were kept busy working up and down the Guild Street Branch to Brook Street, particularly in the malting season. After floor malting ceased and with railway closures in mind, Bass built a barley drying and screening plant at Shobnall where the mobile Boby pumping plant ended its working days. Paradoxically, Bass bought the defunct Brook Street Warehouse, together with the Guild Street Branch (Dixie to High Street) in 1968, but soon sold the warehouse to Allied Breweries, which demolished it and stored metal casks on the site.

The MR Grain Warehouse No.3 was located at the Station Street Wharf near the station. It was a single storey building, but nevertheless quite extensive, and was mainly used by the Co-operative Society. The wharf had a horse and carriage siding and the circus used to unload here on its visits.

Five sidings between No.3 Warehouse and the main line had been in existence for a long time, being shown on the 1865 Spooner map. In Chapter 3, it was noted that the 1881 Bass' trip had left from 'the ale bank at the station'. This was a time of change with the Borough Road Bridge under construction – its ironwork shows 'MR 1881' – and the station being replaced. It is likely that the trip trains in that year left from these sidings because there was access for passengers through the old gateway at the end of Station Street.

The MR Bonded Stores and Grain Warehouse No.4 at Derby Road was an impressive structure measuring 305ft x 170ft. Part of the site had previously been Burton Wanders' ground until they failed to get re-elected to the English Football League in 1897. The grain warehouse opened on 21st September 1901 and the bonded stores on the following 4th December. Barley was stored on the top three storeys which could be reached by hoists inside the building. Wagons came in alongside the 'docks' (banks), which could run the length of both sides of the warehouse, and they could be manoeuvred by hydraulic capstans; there was a 30cwt hydraulic crane which could swing out from each dock. In the old days, the railway companies turned and rebagged the barley and even as late as the 1950s, railway men still occasionally had to 'bushel' barley and put it into sacks for deliveries to the breweries. It was not an attractive task because the dust could be very irritating. The bonded stores occupied the whole of the ground floor and these contained mostly wines and spirits belonging to Grants of St James, with the Customs and Excise officers checking all movements. Casks were carried under bond roped down in open wagons. During a hot spell, an accidental rough shunt would leave port or sherry dripping through the wagon floor, for the benefit of all those working in the immediate vicinity. The railway line next to the Derby Road was used for crippled wagons awaiting removal to the nearby MR Wagon Repairs Depot. In 1969, a replacement depot was constructed by McAlpine at a cost of £200,000 to maintain merry-go-round coal wagons.

With this level of provision for goods traffic, the locomotive shed at the Midland Goods soon proved far too small. In February 1868, the MR decided to acquire eight acres of land near Leicester Junction from the Marquis of Anglesey at £500 per acre. An estimate was obtained for a roundhouse in March 1869 and this was opened, together with a coal stage, in the following year on 29th April 1870. Some of the earliest designs for sheds had been roundhouses and the MR continued to rely on this style for many of its establishments, despite the problems sometimes caused by the gradual introduction of larger locomotives. The roundhouse was of standard design based on a turntable with 24 radiating spurs, all enclosed within a square building. This type of roundhouse was rather attractive with plenty of ornamentation and two sets of gables with the roof pitches at 90° to one another. A typical MR high level coal stage was provided where wagons were shunted up a ramp and the coal transferred to locomotive tenders in small barrows. The MR added another roundhouse in 1892 on the spare land between the original building and the main line. This again had 24 spurs but was built to a more austere design with three large parallel roof pitches resting on lattice girders supported by cast iron columns. It was therefore possible at Burton to see the two standard designs of MR roundhouse side by side. MR locomotive sheds were allocated codes 1 to 33; Burton was 2 after Derby (1). The code was first displayed on an oval tablet in the cabs of the locomotives in 1898, but from 1908-09 was repositioned to the lower part of the smokebox door.

The LNWR and NSR joint property in Burton comprised the Horninglow Street Goods Depot and its associated yard with a capacity of 615 wagons, together with an ale bank between the two companies' respective sidings at Wetmore. Horninglow Street Goods Depot had been opened by the LNWR in 1861 and was reached by a line from the MR at Wetmore. By November of the following year, the LNWR also had a group of sidings operational alongside the MR down yard at Wetmore, together with a connection across the Hay Branch to the Old Dixie Sidings. When the NSR became joint owner of the enlarged goods depot, it paid half the salaries of the employees. In 1914, there were 57 clerical and administrative staff employed there compared with 28 at the GNR depot, and the MR's 120. The joint goods agent was Mr G. Padmore who had come from Dundalk, Newry & Greenore Railway in Ireland after absorption by the LNWR. H. Burchell was the Chief Clerk and the Chief Accountant was Ralph Tweed who subsequently became Allsopp's traffic manager.

The depot was shunted by LNWR locomotives from the adjacent shed and by horses; the LNWR had about 6 horses for shunting in Burton, compared with the MR's 14 or 15. General merchandise was also handled at the depot and so there was a considerable transfer of goods to road vehicles for deliveries to shops and business premises. The depot also contained bonded stores and another floor was turned over to this use in the late 1950s. Much of the traffic belonged to Grants because Ind Coope & Allsopp was deeply involved in the wine and spirits business. The depot was latterly known as Burton Goods and it closed on 1st January 1968. In addition to the sidings associated with the depot, Burnett & Company had a wagon repair works nearby which became part of Wagon Repairs Limited's operations about 1958.

Growing beer traffic had convinced the LNWR's Locomotive Committee of the need for a 'Locomotive Steam Shed' (as most LNWR employees called them) at Burton and approval was given in December 1868. This contained four roads and no doubt took over some of the duties of the old South Staffordshire Railway shed at Wichnor Junction. The LNWR introduced shed codes about 1862 but Burton Shed initially came under Walsall. In 1873, Webb created a new district comprising Derby, Burton, and Coalville which was altered in 1878 to Derby, Burton, Colwick, and Doncaster. It was not long before the original shed had to be extended but even this soon proved inadequate. A replacement was provided on the site of the old shed in 1882-83. Constructed to Webb's 'New Standard Steam Shed' design, it was a single ended brick structure with six roads and a saw teeth pattern roof with northern lights. The accompanying sidings were modified to include a coal stage which was of typical LNWR design and supported a massive iron water tank. A 42 feet turntable was provided near the entrance to the yard. As a result, Burton LNWR Shed was allocated code 12 with the shed at Derby becoming its subshed. The slackening in the growth of brewery traffic was becoming noticeable though, and in February 1887, the foreman at Burton and Derby was sent to Bushbury, 'Burton and Derby sheds being placed under the charge of Mr Stilton, foreman at Walsall, as the work had not increased as expected.' Nevertheless, twenty two locomotives were allocated to the shed by 1912 and this rose to thirty one at the Grouping. The shed serviced visiting freight locomotives but many of its own duties were concerned with local trip workings and shunting in the yards. This was reflected in the monthly mileage by locomotives at the shed which only totally 9,000 miles in 1888. It still had almost the lowest monthly mileage of the main LNWR sheds in 1914, but by then this had increased to 43,000 miles.

The NSR was by no means totally reliant on its agreement with the LNWR; it owned the Stretton Sidings near Stretton Junction where drivers engaged in shunting were assisted by signals from a mechanical gong worked from the sidings stage. Trains leaving here for the Potteries often comprised many different loads. As driver Frank Holmes said 'If ever you were there, say you had got 50 wagons, you could reckon that you would have 80 or 90 shunts to make. They were doing that up until the time they closed Stretton Junction Sidings down. It was claimed that the head shunters there came up to the age of 65 practically all together, and they closed it down sooner than make anybody else headshunters.' No doubt, the decline in traffic also had a significant impact! Stretton Junction Signal Box, closed on 29th January 1967, dated from the opening of the Dallow Lane Branch in 1882, although after a fire in the 1950s it had been rebuilt with new windows and a flat roof.

After the MR moved to its new locomotive shed, the NSR occupied half of the old shed and had the coal stage at the Midland Goods. They were included in the agreement between the NSR and MR for the continuation of running powers from North Stafford Junction to Burton Station at a cost of £250 each year. The MR used the remaining part of the shed as a warehouse. On 11th August 1914, the MR agreed that all of the old locomotive shed should be taken over by the NSR. A new coaling crane was erected at the north east end of the coal stage, together with alterations to the stage itself. An additional rent of £50 per annum was paid by the NSR for the extra capacity at the shed, plus 5% of the actual cost of the altered coal stage each year and the cost to the MR of maintenance and renewal. In November, the NSR asked for the scheme to be modified and the ordinary rails for the short pit were extended and replaced by flat bottomed rails. On the night of 31st January 1916, there was a raid on Burton by three Zeppelins which were under the mistaken

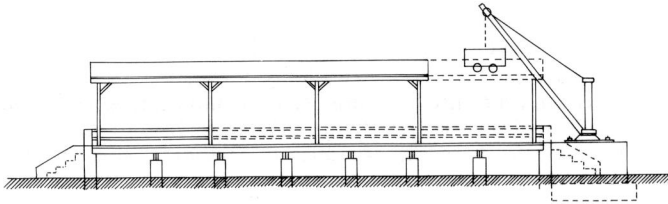

ELEVATION TOWARDS MAIN LINE

SECTION A.B

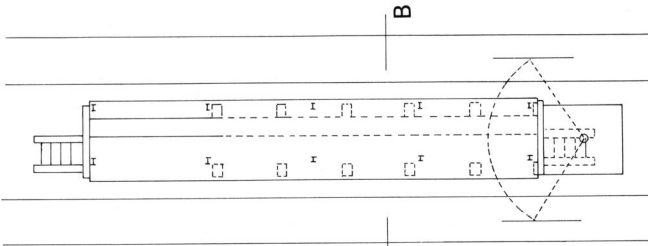

PLAN

0 feet   10   20

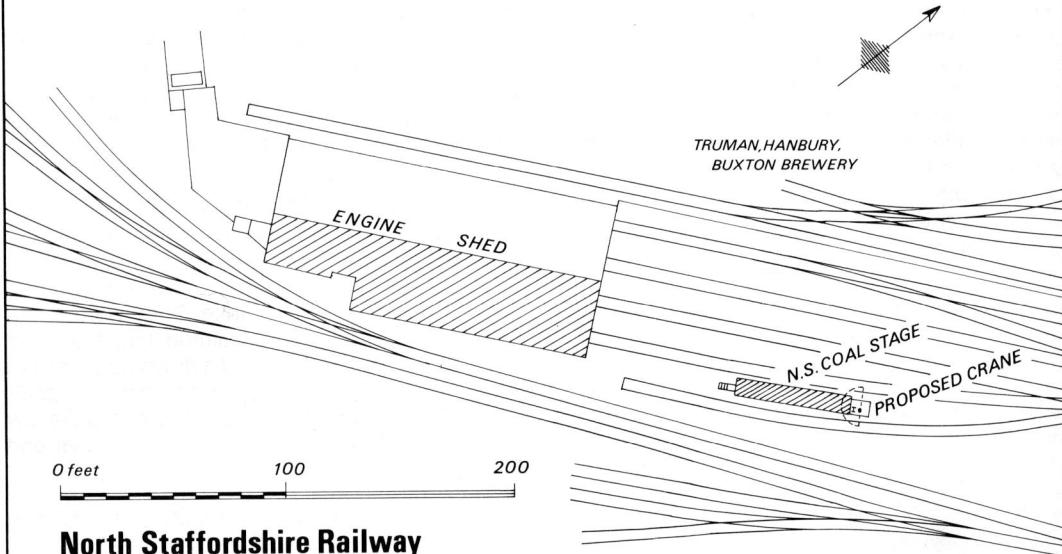

TRUMAN, HANBURY, BUXTON BREWERY

ENGINE SHED

N.S. COAL STAGE

PROPOSED CRANE

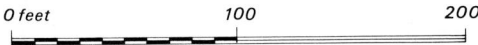

0 feet   100   200

North Staffordshire Railway
Engine Shed, Burton

An agreement on 9th September 1874 gave the NSR running powers from North Stafford Junction to Burton over the MR and use of half of the MR Engine Shed (hatched). The two companies extended this Agreement on 11th August 1914 when the NSR was permitted to occupy the remainder of the shed building, and the MR erected a coaling crane and altered the coal stage for the NSR.

impression that they were over Liverpool or Sheffield. About 25 high explosive and 20 to 25 incendiary bombs fell on the town and fifteen people were killed. The NSR Locomotive Shed was badly damaged and John Lees Finney was killed at the nearby Midland Goods Depot.

The GNR's sidings in Burton were at Hawkins Lane but there had been a delay in opening because of the marshy nature of the area, which had previously been used as a gravel pit. Fill to raise the level of the site was brought by the contractor Firbank from Stretton and a siding was put in north of the later position of Stretton and Claymills station to collect it. The first four sidings at Hawkins Lane were opened in 1878, another six sidings capable of accommodating 156 wagons were sanctioned in 1883 and new stables were provided three years later. A small timber built warehouse known as the Sugar Shed was erected in 1905; inside it was quite attractive with a lovely aroma of wood! The Hawkins Lane Goods Depot had been opened on 1st July 1878 adjacent to Hawkins Lane Junction, a favourable location because of its proximity to the MR Hay Branch which gave access to the major breweries. This Depot was also a timber structure and had a crane with a maximum capacity of 5 tons. According to a letter dated 5th February 1904, the brewery companies were not allowed to hand over their traffic to the GNR Goods Depot using their own locomotives. Wagons had to be left at agreed locations, from where the MR locomotives would take them to the GNR Depot.

In its 1873 Bill the GNR had originally intended to cross Hawkins Lane 100 yards away from the Mount Pleasant Bridge, but this would have required stopping up the road, so the line was laid alongside the MR Hay Branch underneath Mount Pleasant Bridge before making its final connection with the branch. The GNR purchased land here at Walsitch from the Marquis of Anglesey for a new grain warehouse but did not proceed with the proposal. Instead, it constructed the single storey Wetmore Road Grain Warehouse in 1880 on the large area of land which it had acquired at Wetmore. Anderstaff Lane and various public footpaths were diverted and extended by the GNR; the previously unmade part of the lane being reformed as a 'straight carriageway road 36 feet wide at the expense of the company', and so Wetmore Road came into existence. A 3 storey extension costing £15,000 was added to the warehouse six years later more than doubling it in size. The ground floor was retained by the GNR for general trade but the other floors were leased to Allsopp and Ind Coope at £50 a year for barley stores; a modest income but presumably the attraction of barley traffic to the GNR was worth it. Part of the adjoining land was let to Messrs Redfern and Mason for a timber yard in 1898 and further land was rented for a saw mill in 1902. Railway sidings ran into both yards. By the time that W.H. Mason & Son had become the owning company, the yards contained sawing, planing and moulding mills. Access to the GNR was convenient for taking delivery of soft woods imported from Scandinavia via Hull.

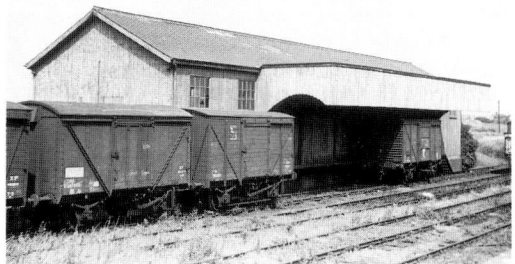

Ex-GNR warehouses at Burton. The more substantial 3 storey building is the Wetmore Road Grain Warehouse, with part of Mason's timber yard on 29th December 1963; the Warehouse closing on 6th June 1966. The other photograph shows the wooden Sugar Shed on 4th August 1964.

(C. Shepherd)

Class K3 61870 begins the climb past Hawkins Lane Sdgs Signal Box up the bank over the main line on 26th May 1959. The box had received a replacement 35 lever frame and lost its original 'Burton South Junction' name when the separate ex GNR line on the bank and Burton North Junction Box had closed on 9th May 1954. *(R.C. Riley)*

There was no GNR locomotive shed at Burton and crews had to use the ash pit, 44ft 7in diameter turntable and water tower at Hawkins Lane Sidings to prepare their locomotive for its return. The water tower had been added in 1888, a temporary structure being relied on before then. A solitary GNR locomotive was stabled at the LNWR Shed to deal with any shunting. Incoming BR Eastern Region locomotives still continued to use the facilities at Hawkins Lane up to the 1960s before heading the 6.15pm to York and the 6.55pm to Colwick away up the bank over the main line.

The NSR's Locomotive Shed at Burton on the extremity of that company's system was an obvious candidate for closure after the Grouping of the railways. It is difficult to identify when this took place because the years following the Grouping were confusing, even for the staff of the new LMS! Burton NSR Shed was supposed to have officially closed on 6th July 1923, with servicing and stabling being moved to the LNWR Horninglow shed, but the locomotives and men were still listed separately by the Chief Mechanical Engineer at the end of 1925. The sheds in the North Stafford section included Burton (12 locomotives, 52 men) and Burton LNW Horninglow (19 locomotives, 77 men). Horninglow shed seems to have retained its Western A Division code of 12 until 1925 and the Running Shed Foreman was W. Walklate. It then lost its separate designation and became part of the Stoke district under code 40. Logic finally prevailed and the shed was renamed Horninglow, coming under the control of the town's ex MR shed. Burton NSR Shed probably ceased to exist as a separate concern in 1926 and the building was demolished in 1930. A few former NSR locomotives were still to be found at either of the remaining sheds until 1936. For example, there were five ex-NSR locomotives on Horninglow Shed in August 1931 (Class B 2-4-0 tanks 1441, 1442, and 1444 and Class 159 0-6-0s 8673 and 8674). They spent their last days on local trip work, for example 1444 was seen on 19th April 1932 shunting Allsopp's Sidings on the Dallow Lane Branch.

MR designs came to dominate the allocation at the Horninglow Shed, despite the seven LNWR 18in Class 0-6-0s present in 1938. The shed continued in use because of its convenient position for incoming locomotives; it was nearer to many of the yards and the men could sign on there, thus reducing the time spent walking to their place of work. Old patterns of activity persisted and, even in the 1950s, there was a daily freight from South Wales which travelled over the former LNWR

52

Central Wales route, resulting in the regular sighting of a Swansea 2-8-0 locomotive on Horninglow Shed. The roofs of LNWR sheds had a poor reputation for succumbing to the corrosive effects of the atmosphere inside compared with the high more airy MR roundhouses. By 1944, the Horninglow Shed roof had been removed and in 1946, the LMS fitted its standard more robust louvre pattern roof and provided some increased shelter at the coal stage. It was a surprising move in view of the rundown of the allocation which only totalled nine locomotives in 1953. Horninglow shed closed on 12th September 1960 and the remaining men and locomotives were transferred to the ex MR shed, although occasional locomotives were stabled in the yard for some time afterwards.

The principal locomotive shed at Burton, the MR's establishment at Leicester Junction, was something of an anachronism. Despite sometimes having an allocation of over 100 steam locomotives, there was very little glamour about the duties. Its main purpose was to serve the needs of the coal and brewing industries which required a regular and dependable delivery; much reliance being placed on a long tradition of MR and LMS 0-6-0s. When these became too antiquated to earn their keep on the main line, they spent their last days drifting backwards and forwards between the various yards in the town.

There had once been grander plans. In 1934, there was an abortive proposal to make Burton a large repair depot for most freight locomotives allocated to the Derby–Bristol line with some 235 locomotives. Nothing came of the idea and, in the following year, it became a 'garage' depot classified as 17B with the sheds at Horninglow and Overseal as its subsheds. Under the LMS scheme, garage depots were theoretically only intended to carry out preparation, disposal, and minor repairs. All boiler washouts and major repairs would be done at the main or 'concentration' depot, in this case Derby (17A). Much depended on the number of fitters at the garage depot, however, and many carried out additional work. Burton had a properly equipped machine shop including a wheel lathe. As a result, the shed performed boiler washouts, major repairs and mileage examinations up to and including 20,000-24,000 miles, piston and valve examinations, and the repair of hot boxes. The MR had relied almost exclusively on shear legs for lifting locomotives to carry out hot box repairs and bogie and driving axle examinations. Burton had shear legs but the LMS later provided a wheel drop housed in a corrugated iron building in the shed yard. The shear legs at Derby shed had gone

For much of its existence, Burton shed was home to a multitude of 0-6-0 locomotives, although by the 1950s old 2F locomotives such as 58130, seen here by the coaling plant on 28th September 1957, were mainly restricted to trip working. *(R.C. Riley)*

by 1944, leaving Burton as the only shed in the district with such facilities and it was kept busy with axle box repairs, with locomotives larger than a 2-6-4 tank having to be sent from Derby! Other improvements helped accommodate larger locomotives; the 42 feet turntable in the original No.1 roundhouse was replaced by a 57 feet table and the 50 feet Cowans Sheldon turntable in the newer No.2 roundhouse was increased to 55 feet. Turning locomotives was not a serious problem because of the proximity of the Branston triangle. Other elements of work at the shed continued unchanged and in 1948, the steam breakdown crane was a 15 tons machine built for the Caledonian Railway in 1886. Burton Shed also had a hostel or barracks which provided 32 beds for men on lodging turns; a two storey extension being added to the hostel in 1939. Even by the middle of the 1950s, there were still 96 locomotives based at Burton, of which over half were 0-6-0s.

Trip Work

Various of the railway company locomotives occupied their time at Burton on trip work. Wagons could be hauled without a brakevan between Wetmore Sidings and Leicester Junction provided that they used the goods lines. There was simply a lamp swinging from the last wagon as then required by Rule 153. Up to 35 wagons could also be propelled in clear weather along the down goods between Horninglow Bridge and Leicester Junction. The trip numbers varied according to the particular administration area under which Burton came. It changed from Birmingham to Stoke and finally Nottingham. This led to inconsistencies and, in the early 1960s, the locomotives carried an old set of trip numbers which differed from those in the working timetable. Although the same locomotive might turn up on a trip on successive days, there was little regular allocation of locomotives and they were moved about the various rosters haphazardly. One exception was the Dixie link where they had a regular locomotive for a week. It used to go to the Horninglow Shed to attend to its shunting requirements every day and one of the trip locomotives took over at the yard until it returned.

The arrangement of trips varied according to the amount of traffic and line occupation. Those running along the main line picked up wagons in the different yards at scheduled times in order to make up a train for departure. Others shunted a particular branch, but then the arrangements were very flexible as long as the wagons were delivered to a particular yard by a specified time. Trip 74 moved traffic between the Midland Goods, Horninglow Bridge, and New Dixie. When not required, it kept the Midland Goods supplied with wagons and did any necessary shunting. Trip 90 was another main line duty; it began at midnight working between Horninglow Bridge and Leicester Junction Sidings. At half past seven in the morning, Trip 92 took over whilst Trip 90 spent the remainder of the day visiting other yards, including Branston and a Monday/Wednesday/Friday outing to deliver coal to the Clay Mills Sewage Works. Other trips followed more complicated rosters. There was a regular working (121 in 1955, 86 in 1962) which began the day by servicing the Cask Sorting Bank at Wetmore. It then took a load of empty casks or 'Bass Tubs' round the Dallow Lane Branch to Shobnall in the late morning, sometimes going on to Klondyke Sidings before returning to 'Old Wetmore' via the main line for more empty casks. The locomotive was then at Shobnall until four o'clock when it took a train over the Dallow Lane Branch to Horninglow Yard. Coal was brought to Shobnall by Trip 128. It returned to the Midland Goods and New Dixie but later reappeared at Shobnall with empty casks before going on to the locomotive shed.

This pattern of working was all very well in fine weather but fog could bring problems. The prevailing smells of malt and brewing helped to give some identify to locations in poor visibility. Nevertheless, with the many varied movements and the additional presence of the brewery companies' locomotives, great caution had to be exercised and strings of wagons still had an uncanny knack of appearing out of the gloom with little or no warning.

The 0-6-0 type of locomotive was ideal for trip work with both tender and tank versions being used, although the former tended to be found in and between the yards. These were mostly ex MR designs of classes 2F, 3F, and 4F. If Burton Shed was short of suitable locomotives, more unlikely power might turn up in the shape of one of the Jenny locomotives or a 2P 4-4-0 which had strayed from its regular duties on the Leicester locals. As more modern locomotives became available and traffic declined, the older classes were relegated to trip working. A solitary elderly Kirtley double frame 0-6-0 (22822) soldiered on at Burton and was not withdrawn until 1947. Just over a decade later, the remaining Belpaire boiler 2Fs (58148, 58160, 58165, 58186, 58305) were taken off the trips and placed in store, leaving the survivors of the 3F class at Burton (43574, 43608, 43709) soon to be confined to these menial tasks.

Former MR well tank 1607 in front of Allsopp's New Brewery.
(C. Shepherd Collection)

The tank locomotives worked over much of the Burton railway system and, just like the brewery companies' locomotives, were very much part of the local scene. Smaller locomotives with four wheels could usually be found hidden away amongst the buildings of the town busily shunting around the tight curves of some firm's sidings, although they did work along the main line to Ind Coope's Bottling Stores near the station. They were particularly associated with Bond End and are described in Chapter 8. The mixed remnants of a class of MR 0-6-0 well tank locomotives lingered on at Burton long after other members had gone for scrap. Four of the type had been built new as well tanks for banking on the Lickey Incline, but the remainder were supposedly rebuilds from 0-6-0s and old 'Jenny Lind' singles. This was more of an accountancy exercise and there was little if anything left of the original locomotives. Most of the well tanks were withdrawn about the turn of the century, but the last locomotives survived into the LMS, and as Ahrons noted 'some of the oldest MR shunting engines are kept at Burton to attend to the beer.' The first standard MR 1F 0-6-0 tank locomotive

Use of 1839, later 41839, at Burton

	Miles	Heavy/light repairs	Weekdays out of service Running repairs and examinations	Not required
1945	21,926	-	50	8
1946	22,074	-	14	7
1947	15,344	54	58	4
1948	20,722	-	29	9
1949	19,394	28 (Heavy general)	23	7
1950	18,159	-	30	20
1951	20,114	-	15	8
1952	16,922	18 (Light intermediate)	21	11
1953	18,894	-	13	5
1954	14,375	-	37	7
1955	15,542	-	12	11
1956	6,803	-	9	6

Locomotive withdrawn from stock week ending 17th June 1956.

Breweries in Burton in 1914

Company	Number of breweries
Samuel Allsopp & Sons Ltd	Two (one lager)
Bass, Ratcliff & Gretton Ltd	Three
Bindley & Co Ltd	One
Charrington & Co Ltd	One
T. Cooper & Co	One
James Eadie Ltd	One
W. Everard & Co	One
Ind Coope & Co (1912) Ltd	One
Marston, Thompson, & Evershed Ltd	One
North East Breweries Ltd *	One
Robinson's Brewery Ltd	One
Thomas Salt & Co Ltd	One
Truman, Hanbury, Buxton & Co Ltd	One
Trustees of Peter Walker & Co Ltd	One
Peter Walker & Son (Warrington & Burton) Ltd	One
Worthington & Co Ltd	Two (one operational)

* The 'Broadway' belonged to North Eastern Breweries Ltd of Sunderland which wished to be able to say that they brewed in Burton. Only small quantities of beer were produced.

was more than matched by a drop in the gravity of beer from an average of 1055 in 1900 to 1040 in 1918 and the higher prices meant that the brewers' profits recovered. This era of weaker beers was not particularly helpful to the Burton brewers, who had traditionally relied on the strength and quality of their beers to compete in the free trade. The recession in the early 1930s also meant that beer consumption in the United Kingdom fell from 25 million bulk barrels in 1930 to 17.9 million three years later, although there was a recovery back to the original figure by 1939. The process of takeovers and closures continued as companies sought to increase their market share. Both Charrington and Walker ceased to brew in the town. Ind Coope particularly responded to the challenge by buying controlling interests in other breweries and it prospered in the 1920s, taking over both Bindley and Robinson and closing their breweries. Allsopp had always financially struggled and it finally merged with Ind Coope in 1934 to become Ind Coope & Allsopp Ltd. Although Bass' net profits improved in the 1920s, its sales declined to 836,708 barrels in 1930-31. It did not get involved in many company acquisitions, amalgamating instead with its great rival Worthington on 1st January 1927, when Bass, Ratcliff & Gretton Ltd became the holding company for the Worthington ordinary shares. Surprisingly, the opportunity to cut costs by rationalising plant and equipment was not generally taken. In many respects, Bass and Worthington continued to function as two separate companies with little reduction in the feelings of animosity between them. The founding families of Bass gradually withdrew and the Manners supplied most of the directors of both companies. Bass took over Eadie's brewery in 1933, so that by World War 2, the number of brewing companies had been reduced to five – Bass & Worthington; Everard; Ind Coope & Allsopp; Marston, Thompson & Evershed; and Truman, Hanbury, Buxton.

The Beer Trains

During the first half of the twentieth century, the amount of goods traffic remained at a high level. The MR operated many of the trains before the Grouping but the other companies contributed their share. In 1900, the GNR ran 11 goods trains from Burton on most weekdays, and apart from a through working to Doncaster, all were destined for Colwick or Nottingham where traffic could be sorted for further movement. In LNER days one of the beer trains was extended to York and larger types of locomotives appeared, including ex North Eastern Railway 4-6-0s (LNER Class B16) and these remained regular performers until 1963. After nationalisation a few goods workings over the ex GNR line were extended to Wichnor Sidings, some travelling via the Dallow Lane Branch. As late as 1954, there were still about 10 goods trains booked to travel over the Burton to Derby Friargate route.

The NSR sent beer trains as far afield as Liverpool and Manchester; indeed the NSR shed at Burton loaned locomotives to the LNWR sheds at Edge Hill (two) and Longsight (one). A return train from Liverpool Edge Hill arrived at Burton (Horninglow) at 9am and Station Street at 9.55am, whilst the 11.17pm from Manchester Ducie Street was booked to reach Horninglow at 6am and set off back from Station Street at 9.35pm. The NSR wagon labels referred to 'Burton Station St Station'. There was also one train each way between Alsager and Wellingborough daily, which called at Burton between 12.35pm and 1.50pm, before departing on its leisurely southbound journey via the Swadlincote Loop.

Principle goods trains carrying beer from Burton in 1962

Departures	Class	Destination	Traffic for
4.0pm SO	D	St Pancras	London
4.20pm SX	C	Bristol	Cheltenham, Gloucester, Bristol
6.15pm	C	York	York and beyond
6.50pm SX	C	St Pancras	London
6.55pm	E	Colwick	Hull, Boston, Doncaster, East Anglia
7.55pm*	D	Rowsley	Rowsley, Manchester
8.25pm SX	C	Carlisle	Heysham, Barrow, Lancaster, Scotland
8.45pm SX	E	Crewe	Macclesfield, Chester, North Wales
9.10pm MO	C	Niddrie	Scotland East Coast
9.30pm SX	D	Swansea	Brecon, Wellington, Shrewsbury, South Wales
9.33pm*	E	Nuneaton	Rugby, Leamington, Bletchley
10.40pm*	C	Nottingham	Nottingham, Lincoln
10.54pm*	C	Leeds	North Eastern Region
11.10pm SX	D	Wigston	London, Leicester, Eastern Counties
2.0am MX*	E	Sheffield	Chesterfield, Sheffield
2.53am MX	D	Derby	Derby

* Trains did not start at Burton

Source R.C. Riley Trains Illustrated Annual 1962

A publicity photograph taken on 11th December 1929 of LMS 4F 4432 at Leicester Junction, with some of the 100 ale vans built specially at Derby for the important Burton to London beer traffic. The signal box on the right is Leicester Junction Sidings which controlled access to that yard.

(Derby Collection, National Railway Museum. DY 15986)

Examination of the 1951 goods service in Burton reveals just how busy the railways still were and workings passed by on the main line every few minutes. Most trains stopped somewhere in Burton, partly due to the business originating from its breweries, but also because of its strategic position and siding capacity, which allowed water to be taken without holding up the flow of traffic. There were some Class C through freights which sped along the main line, their vans banging behind them despite the speed restriction at the station. These contrasted with the far more numerous slow moving coal trains originating from the East Midlands collieries, and yards such as Toton, Colwick, Beeston, and Chaddesden. They headed for the series of sidings on the Birmingham line, starting with Branston and going on to Wichnor, Water Orton, and Washwood Heath. The complexity of yards at Burton meant that, in addition to the trip workings, there was much movement of light locomotives to and from the sheds.

By the end of the 1950s, the reduction in rail traffic through Burton was beginning to be noticeable. Even so, there were still numerous workings which conveyed beer to different parts of the country.

The most notable beer trains were those to and from St Pancras. In 1922, they set off back on the return journey from the Somers Town Depot at 10.55pm and 1.55am calling at St Pancras shortly after the start. Wagons on the 10.55 were marshalled in the following order (1) Saffron Lane (Coalville Line Traffic) (2) Rough Burtons (3) Burton Shed Goods, Trumans' Empty Casks, Crosse & Blackwells, and Trent Cold Storage traffic (4) NSR line. There was a strange arrangement on the London link in the 1950s. One week, the driver would be on the 6.50pm Horninglow Bridge to London job but in the following week he could be on a little 4-coupled shunter working round the Bond End Branch. The 6.50pm called at Leicester Junction Sidings to pick up traffic and then it was right away to London. The other London train was the 4.40pm and its crew used to be on this for a week, before going on the 8.50am Horninglow Bridge shunt for the following week, a 'soft little job' picking up traffic brought to the yard and sorting it on to the different lines usually with a Class 3F tender locomotive.

The most powerful locomotives at Burton Shed for working the beer trains during the 1930s and 1940s were five Hughes-Fowler 2-6-0s. They were well liked, although their ungainly appearance earned them the nickname of 'Crabs'. Numbers 42818/22/24/25/29 had Lentz RC poppet valves but

The Horninglow Bridge end of Old Dixie Sidings with Hughes-Fowler 42763 departing on the 6.50pm beer train to London, 26th May 1959. (R.C. Riley)

were rebuilt with Reidinger rotary poppet valves in 1953. They all came to Burton from Saltley because the latter's men were not keen on them. As a Burton man admitted "they weren't as strong as the ordinary Walschaerts valve, and when you started away, you never knew whether you was going forwards or backwards for a start!". In the 1950s, some Stanier Class 5 and later 8Fs took over, although the number of 2-6-0s increased as well. The most spectacular development was the transfer of 18 Jubilee class 4-6-0s in November 1961, following their displacement from the expresses by diesels. It was the largest ever migration of the class to one shed and several were kept busy working beer and coal trains until 1964 when the final two at Burton were stored in the cattle dock siding before going to Cashmore's Yard at Great Bridge for scrap early in 1965.

A typical scene on one of the brewery banks at Burton. Butts are probably being loaded into the MR open wagon, in view of the presence of a cooper in the group. The nearest labourer holds a lever, or 'throwing stick' used for tipping casks to stand on end. *(C. Shepherd Collection)*

The railway companies supplied the wagons for the casks of beer. There was nothing very special about them and usually traditional open wooden wagons and old cattle trucks would do, because good ventilation was the essential requirement if the beer was to remain in its best condition. Some were labelled ALE WAGON. The LMS did bring out a batch of 100 ale vans in 1929, each of which could carry 12 tons (Diagram D1817 numbers 189331-189430). These were usually kept on specific routes and that between Burton and St Pancras was the most well known. Later, some open wagons were designed so as to be shock absorbing and a stock of about 700 was allocated to Burton and solely employed on beer traffic.

The transport of beer was not solely confined to casks, nor was the movement one way. Ind Coope & Allsopp received a considerable number of rail tank wagons bringing lager to its bottling stores. Other brewers hired wagons off British Railways to send beer to Ireland, Belgium, and the

An Allsopp rail tank wagon built by Charles Roberts & Co Ltd in 1929.
(Charles Roberts Collection, National Railway Museum. ROB 1876)

Channel Islands. Although the wagons were owned by the railway company, the cylindrical tanks belonged to the brewers. They were painted in the individual firms' liveries and could be lifted off by crane to finish their journey by road.

In addition to beer, there was the important barley trade particularly from East Anglia with the barley initially coming in sacks but later transported in bulk grain vans. Other items requiring urgent handling included spent hops and wet grains for use as fertiliser and cattle feed. The MR even put twelve yeast vans into service in 1896, looking very much like cattle wagons with additional louvres, and a surviving photograph shows that they bore the legend 'To be returned to Burton'. Later improvements in technology meant that the brewers were able to culture their own yeast. There were also wagons of timber for the stave yards and the cooperages, the engineers' stores, and the coal which once fed the boilers powering the industry. In 1902, it was recorded that Bass's boilers and engines consumed 65,000 tons of coal annually and its malting kilns used another 10,000 tons. A supply of wagons was usually available from those which had brought back the empty casks. In the early 1960s, sidings were set aside for stabling 200 wagons to meet any additional day to day requirements. When this total fell below a certain level, another train of empties would be requested, often coming from Chaddesden Sidings at Derby.

Road Transport Begins to Take Over

The railway companies continued reliance on a system of working set up in Victorian times was to prove increasingly outdated as the new century developed with changes in the structure of the brewing industry and the adoption of road transport. After World War 1, motor vehicles became increasingly reliable and were often more convenient. Some of the new firms attracted by the town's Commercial Development Committee set up in 1907 relied on road transport from the start. Even the railway companies' previous virtual monopoly of beer traffic beyond the immediate surroundings of Burton was being challenged.

In 1914, the amount of beer sent out from the town in casks by rail was probably nearly 600,000 tons. Nine years later, it was down to 450,000 tons, but then it stayed fairly constant throughout the 1920s.

Beer despatched in casks from Burton by railway (tons)

	1914 (1)	1923 (1)	1926 (1)	1929 (2)
Bass	234,379	200,674	193,578	175,966)
Worthington	86,678	60,810	84,451	98,001)
Allsopp	67,441	32, 304	28,916	38,570
Ind Coope	61,251	46,634	51,306	49,659
Marston, Thompson & Evershed	(3)	22,350	27,488	22,510
Truman, Hanbury & Buxton	(3)	26,682	29,933	31,247
Salt	(3)	25,115	24,501	Finished Dec 1927
Burton Brewery Company	(3)	5,215	4,676	Finished Dec 1927
Charrington	(3)	9,149	8,079	Finished July 1926
Eadie	(3)	8,414	7,598	7,809
P. Walker & Co (Clarence Street)	(3)	4,509	3,462	Finished Sept 1926
P. Walker & Sons (Shobnall)	(3)	4,330	Nothing forwarded after February 1923	
Robinson	(3)	2,864	2,816	2,039(4)
Everard	(3)	109	No casks sent by rail after 1924	
Totals	–	449,159	466.804	425,981

Notes
(1) Year ending 30th June
(2) Year ending 30th September
(3) No information available
(4) Finished June 1929

Ind Coope & Allsopp put a lot of goods on the roads and by 1946 it had 52 lorries based at Burton covering 970,000 miles in a year. Its high speed bottling plant allowed smaller stores elsewhere to be closed and it was preferable to transport bottles by road,thereby avoiding breakages previously caused by shunting. Ind Coope & Allsopp had also developed a network of strategically placed warehouses again mostly dependent on road transport. The company changed its name to Ind Coope Ltd from 1st January 1959 and became part of the Ind Coope, Tetley and Ansells group in 1961. Two years later, the group was renamed Allied Breweries Ltd.

In contrast, Bass and Worthington continued to depend on the railway and this helped to sustain the rail traffic, although Bass had acquired a fleet of ten 3 tons platform motor lorries as early as 1919 for working to the agencies and stores at Stoke, Leicester and Nottingham. They made an impressive sight lined up in their Winchester green livery but were disposed of by the end of 1920 because the railway companies offered more economical terms. Many of Bass' outside agencies were rented from the railway companies which carried most of the local deliveries from them. After the Bass Worthington merger, Shepherd & Hough's petrol lorries became responsible for most of the local deliveries in the Burton area. Starting in 1928, Bass began to use tractors for moving materials around the breweries and eight had been acquired by 1939. Their replacements included two adapted for shunting. As a result, by 1931 there were only 36 horses left at Bass. The last horse, MONTY, shunted railway wagons at Sleaford Maltings. A grey Shire born in 1942, MONTY was bought in 1948 for £100 and following his retirement in 1951, spent his final years in a field at Shobnall until his death in 1967. For external carriage to bottlers, the company had just three tank lorries (30 barrels capacity each) in 1939. Ten years later, it had only eleven platform and four tank lorries. Virtually all of Bass Worthington's traffic beyond a 30 miles radius still went by rail, the continuing attraction being the low rates for carriage. It was only from the mid 1950s that the company began to make increasing use of road vehicles and the days of the railway's brewery traffic were numbered.

As rail traffic declined, the heavy costs of maintaining the town's railway network with its multiplicity of level crossings and many individually manned signal boxes became increasingly apparent to BR. The legacy of pregrouping practices remained and BR began to press for increased charges, which hastened the move to road transport. This trend was encouraged by the 1955 railway strike which lasted for 17 days, and by 1968 Bass had expanded its fleet to 127 platform lorries, 40 tank lorries (1,900 barrels each) and 24 tank trailers (1,650 barrels each). Coal had come by road from the Derbyshire collieries since 1960 because it was easier to distribute to the various boiler plants and hops ceased to be brought by rail from 1964. Radical changes were also taking place in brewing technology. The introduction of drum malting at Shobnall made many traditional floor maltings redundant, and the use of metal casks meant that there was little need for the trades associated with the cooperages. New breweries could produce far more beer than their predecessors on a smaller site area. During the 1950s, Bass had tended to be left behind by the more progressive Ind Coope & Allsopp which recognised the importance of marketing. The positions prior to World War 1 had been reversed and it was Ind Coope & Allsopp which doubled its total capital to £63 million and increased its gross profits from £2.6 million to £7.2 million between 1954 and 1960. In contrast, Bass could only manage a growth in profits from £2.4 million to £3.5 million. On 1st April 1961, it merged with Mitchells & Butlers to become Bass, Mitchells, & Butlers Ltd, going on to form part of the largest brewing group in the country when Bass Charrington Ltd was established on 17th August 1967.

Railway Closures

The tramways were the first to suffer from the competition with motor vehicles; the Burton & Ashby Light Railways closed on 19th February 1927 and the Burton upon Trent Corporation Tramways finished on 31st December 1929. Branston Station, opened in October 1889 following local requests for a service, closed on 22nd September 1930. There was also a steady withdrawal of secondary passenger services particularly in the 1960s. Regular LNER passenger services from Burton to Derby Friargate ended on 4th December 1939, although excursions and Saturdays only trains continued to run over these routes for many more years. The intermediate stations between Burton and Tutbury closed to passengers on 1st January 1949 and the Tutbury Jenny was given an emotional farewell on Saturday 11th June 1960. The era of the Beeching cuts had the most impact and regular passenger trains ceased to run between Burton and Leicester on 6th September 1964 and Burton and Wolverhampton on 18th January 1965. A number of the local stations between Birmingham and Derby also closed on 4th March 1968.

Bass' traffic in 1966

Inward	Source	Means of transport
Barley	East Anglia	Rail
Malt	East Anglia, Berkshire, & Lincolnshire	Road 50%, rail 50%
Hops	Kent, Worcestershire	Road
Coal (malting)	South Wales	Rail
Coal (boilers)	Derbyshire	Road

Outward	Destination	
Spent grains	Local	Road
Bulk ale	England, Wales, Belgium	Road 97%, rail 3%
Cask ale	British Isles, small amount to Europe & America	Road 70%, rail 30%
Bottled ale	Midlands	Road

At the beginning of 1966, the yards at Horninglow Bridge, Old Dixie and Old Wetmore were remodelled, resulting in the closure of a section of the Hay Branch between the main line at North Stafford Junction and Hawkins Lane Junction on 23rd January 1966. These new arrangements comprised a West Yard, replacing Horninglow Bridge and Old Dixie, served by two reception lines with a 'Run Round road' on the site of Old Wetmore. The entrance to the West reception lines was via a new connection from the down main Goods line and controlled from Wetmore Sidings Signal Box. A new single line was opened on 26th January 1966 between Horninglow Bridge and Hawkins Lane Sidings, known as the 'Up and Down' goods line, under the control of these two signal boxes. This gave a route to the ex NSR flyover line to Stretton Junction, thus allowing the closure of the railway between North Stafford Junction and Stretton Junction, and the abolition of North Stafford Junction Signal Box (renewed 1907) on 17th April 1966. A new connecting line was laid from

Removing the rails at Bond End between the coal wharf and Midland Joinery on 23rd May 1964. This had once been the course of the Bond End Canal before the MR filled it in to build the railway.

(C. Shepherd)

Wetmore Sidings and Hawkins Lane Sidings bounding the East Yard. All movements from the 'Up and Down' goods line towards the remainder of the Hay Branch, Saunders Branch, Engine Shed Sidings and Horninglow Street Goods Yard were controlled by Hawkins Lane Sdgs Signal Box. Hawkins Lane Box had closed on 2nd February 1966.

Railway lines which had once witnessed the steady rattle of goods trains taking beer away from Burton became quieter, with fewer trains and less loads. Tracks which had weaved their way in and out of the brewery premises in Burton began to fall into disuse and return to nature. The late 1960s saw the removal of virtually all of them. Bass built pipe carrying bridges across High Street and Station Street to link its breweries to a new central racking room. There was no longer any need for the private railway and it closed in March 1967. Marston's railway had finished shortly before and Allied Breweries closed all but a few sidings some months later. The sundries traffic in Burton was transferred to Derby and this was followed soon after by the parcels business. In 1914, there had been twelve railway bonded stores and warehouses in Burton; by 1974, there were none. Most of the extensive railway yards lay empty, with only New Dixie being used mainly for coal wagons waiting attention at the BR Wagon Maintenance Depot.

Burton Locomotive Shed had become part of the Nottingham district and was recoded 16F in September 1963. A large new diesel depot was contemplated on the site of the roundhouses but the dwindling traffic ruled this out. Instead, part of No.2 roundhouse was demolished to make way for the approach lines to a new two track diesel fuelling and light servicing shed constructed on the old coal stocking ground and opened on 18th April 1966. The first main line diesels had arrived in February 1965 and the shed closed to steam locomotives from 5th September 1966. Diesel shunters were kept in the remaining roundhouse but this was eventually sold to Lloyds (Burton) Ltd which used it for storing wooden patterns. With a subsequent reorganisation of locomotive sheds, Burton lost its allocation of main line diesels, becoming a stabling point for Toton and the code was changed to BU in 1973. Burton no longer has a locomotive shed; the fuel and inspection depot closing from 3rd October 1981. Shunting is now confined to the Wagon Maintenance Depot, a far cry from the busy scenes of just 25 years ago.

Most signal boxes in Burton became redundant when railway lines closed. Others were replaced in 1969 when 243 route miles between Nottingham, Derby and Birmingham came under the control of three power boxes. The last signal box in the town was Wetmore Sidings which was abolished on Sunday 13th October 1985 when the points and signals became the responsibility of Derby power box. Wetmore Sidings Signal Box had opened about February 1873 and replacement structures commenced operation on 12th July 1891 and 12th June 1949 before it was made a shunting frame on 15th June 1969.

The main line continues to carry expresses between Newcastle, Leeds and the south west but the frequency is much reduced. Today, High Speed Trains rush along the Trent Valley, contrasting with the Stanier Class 5 and Jubilee locomotives which formed the mainstay of the service up to the 1960s and the Class 45/46 diesels which took over from them. The 1883 station buildings at Burton were demolished in 1970 and replaced by a small building dwarfed by its setting on the Borough Road Bridge. Lines from the North Stafford Junction, and Hawkins Lane over the Derby Road bridge,

The last train passes over Derby Road level crossing behind D3773 on a wet 2nd April 1966. A signal box was erected here in 1888 and it was initially open to the elements, walls and roof of standard NSR design being added in 1896. Behind it is the Horninglow passenger station which was closed to regular services on 1st January 1949 but the building was not demolished until 23rd March 1989. *(P. Waterfield)*

to Tutbury and Derby Friargate closed in sections, although a stretch near Mickleover was retained for research purposes. Closure dates were North Stafford Junction to Horninglow 4th April 1966; Dove Junction to Marston Junction 30th October 1966; Horninglow to Stretton Junction 29th January 1967 and Stretton Junction to Egginton Junction 6th May 1968; although July 1968 has been suggested for Hawkins Lane to Stretton. In fact, the railway network has returned to more like its form in 1850 with the main line from Birmingham to Derby and goods only branches to Leicester, Walsall and Trent via Stenson Junction. The ever changing balance of transport was symbolised by the sight of the redundant railway embankment on the Dallow Lane Branch being removed over a Bailey bridge across the Trent & Mersey Canal to provide fill for the new A38 Burton bypass road.

'The industrial history of the town has been set by the stages in which the problems of transporting the commodity, which its breweries could produce pre-eminently well, have been overcome.' P. Mathias

CHAPTER SIX

GUILD STREET AND THE HAY

The Bass Breweries

The Guild Street and Hay Branches lay at the very heart of Burton's internal railways linking together the breweries of Bass, Ratcliff & Gretton and providing outlets to the railway companies' sidings on the main line. Bass had two breweries in 1859 – the much enlarged original Old Brewery in High Street and the New Brewery. The latter had opened in 1853 on land between Guild Street and Station Street; it was renamed the Middle Brewery from 1864. A malting erected next to it was subsequently demolished to make way for the No.2 Union and Racking Rooms, when the copper hearth in the brewery was extended about 1873-74. A short distance away, John Gretton's Scutari Malting was also acquired by the Company.

The area between the Old and the Middle Breweries was occupied by Bass's Middle Yard. Much of this land had been purchased by Bass from William Worthington between 1842 and 1851 and it was used for the cask washing sheds. There was also a large barley store with a ground floor for the storage of 5,000 barrels of ale and two upper floors for barley. The ground floor later became a bonded store where strong ales were locked up so that the excise duty could be levied after maturing. In the 1890s, the two upper floors were altered by Couchman to hold malt only and it was

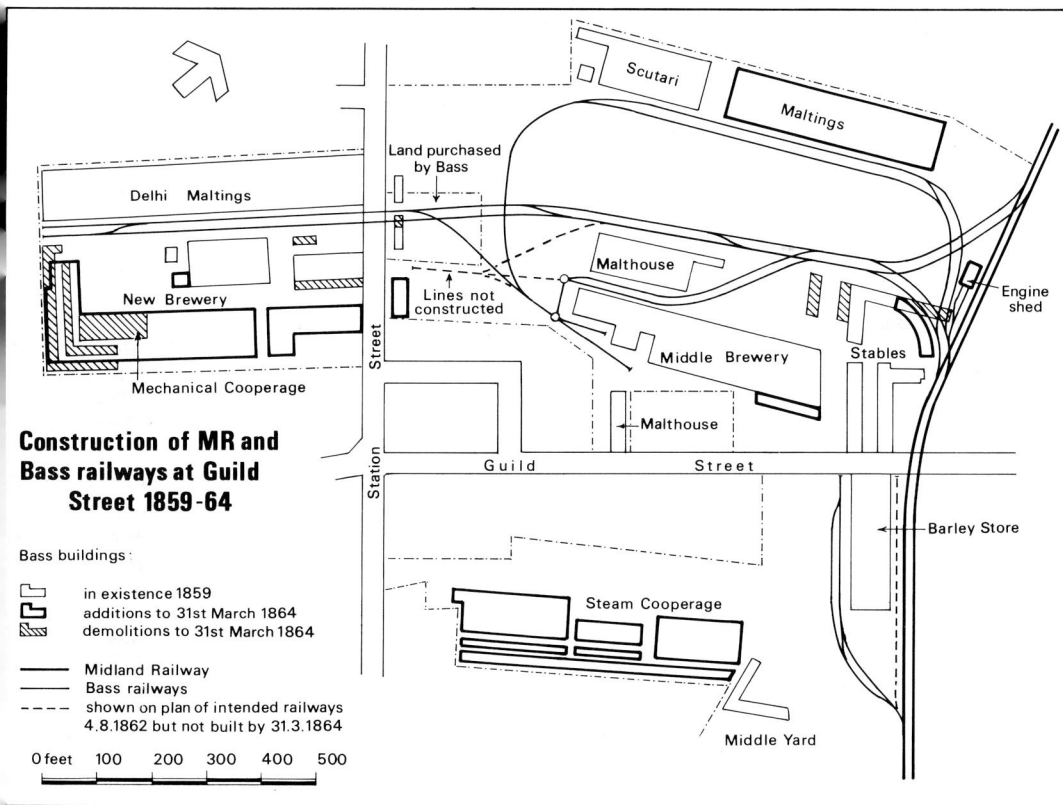

Construction of MR and Bass railways at Guild Street 1859-64

Bass buildings:
- in existence 1859
- additions to 31st March 1864
- demolitions to 31st March 1864

—— Midland Railway
—— Bass railways
- - - shown on plan of intended railways 4.8.1862 but not built by 31.3.1864

0 feet 100 200 300 400 500

The Middle Brewery and No.2 Union Room with the ale and hop stores on the right about 1925. The watchman operated the ground frame with its crossbar signal and also attended to the centralised control of fire alarms in the adjacent building.
(Railway Magazine)

then called the Middle Yard Store Room. Bass had also begun to develop land on the south side of Station Street with the construction of the handsome Delhi Maltings block and the first mechanical cooperage.

Dates of construction of some of Bass' premises

1852	Scutari Malting (later numbered 27) built by John Gretton
1853	Middle Brewery, No.1 Union and Racking Rooms, and stables
1853	Barley Store (later called Middle Yard Store Room)
c1855	Malting, later replaced by No.2 Union and Racking Rooms about 1874
1858-59	Delhi Maltings (later Nos.28-30)
1861-62	Additional maltings at Scutari (later Nos.31 and 32)
1863-64	New Brewery
1863-64	Steam Cooperage
1865	Ale and Hop Stores, Middle Brewery
1866	Joiners' Shop (now the Bass Museum)

This was the position when work began on the new railways and the next five years were to present a scene of hectic activity. The MR was soon busy laying the double track of the Guild Street Branch along the side of Bass' premises. Fortunately, only a limited amount of demolition was required and the houses occupied by Edward Allcock and Samuel Lovatt near the Little Burton Bridge and three small buildings in the Middle Yard had to be knocked down. Bass also began constructing its own railway into the Middle Brewery, one of the lines requiring the removal of part of the stables. The curved wall of the replacement block dictated by the alignment of the new railway was to be a prominent feature in subsequent photographs taken at the locomotive sheds. Continuing on through the Middle Brewery premises, Bass' railway served additional maltings at Scutari, the vast ale and hop stores, and numerous ale banks. The stores had platforms along both sides at the same level as the ground floor which allowed casks to be rolled directly from the stores into the waiting railway wagons. Beer was also kept in the cellar and these casks were raised to the bank level, originally by steam hoists. The railway also brought in 'pockets' of hops which were broken up and blended on the top floor. When required, the hops were despatched in bags down slides and taken to the brewery coppers by floaters. Loading ale on to the railway at the Middle Brewery started on 7th November 1862.

The ale banks were a common feature of the breweries. They were used for storing casks of 'running ale', which were covered with straw hurdles and sprayed with water if necessary, prior to being sent out. The brewers had originally made mostly strong high gravity 'stock ales' between

October and March, which were kept in the ale stores for maturing, but production increasingly changed to running ales brewed all year for almost immediate consumption. As far back as 1883, Michael Arthur Bass had written that "practically all our pale ales now, except that brewed in January, February, and March may be said to be running beer." The job of loading casks into railway wagons probably remained unaltered since the opening of the brewery railways, and the ale loader was ever present with his bobbing stick propelling casks from the bank up the gauntries to the wagons. The practice of coupling up wagons from the ale banks was discontinued because of the danger and the shunters had to connect wagons at rail level. Some of the banks were given names such as the Half Moon and Sun Banks.

Bass' Faery locomotive No.4 at the Station Street end of the Middle Brewery. (F. Jones Collection)

The railway to Scutari Maltings had some sharp curves as it passed round these banks. It was the usual practice to propel the grain vans at some speed to avoid the perennial problem of locked buffers. Fred Ollis, the much respected head maltster, nearly came to grief here. Joe Slater's locomotive was pulling the vans on this occasion and a brisk speed was being maintained to keep the couplings stretched when Fred Ollis stepped out of Scutari just as the locomotive was coming up to the doorway. He instinctively threw his arms out and fortunately fastened them round the shank of the nearer locomotive buffer. Hanging on tightly, he was carried as far as the gap near No.27 Malting where the boilers and engine house were situated. Joe Slater had not seen the incident and only pulled up in obedience to the leading shunter's whistle. When Fred Ollis returned later to talk to Joe, he remarked that Joe was travelling very fast. The driver pointed out that they had to or the buffers might become locked and Fred Ollis replied that he quite understood. As a result, red lights were installed inside those doorways which led directly on to a railway line. These had to be switched on by the shunter before the locomotive could work past. Incidentally, Joe Slater's grandfather was said to have been killed at the old passenger station whilst coupling stock by hand at the time of the first issue of the *Burton Chronicle* (18th October 1860).

The railway line continued past Scutari Maltings to enter the bricklayers' yard and supplies of bricks were brought in by rail for a long time. They included Staffordshire blues from Aldridge, red bricks from the Erewash Valley and London Brick Company and firebricks from Knowles of Woodville. Used fire bricks were sent back to Knowles for milling into 'grog' to form a constituent of new bricks. The carriage of bricks by rail is exemplified by Couchman's letter to Messrs Edward Barnett on 15th December 1898 stating that we 'Have at our Shobnall Sidings two trucks of Best

Blue Facing Bricks which are very badly fire flawed.' Some of the platelayers' tools and rail keys were stored on the nearby Allen's Bank, the name probably coming from Edward Allen who sold some cottages in Station Street to Bass in 1880. The brewhouse at the Middle Brewery had a separate railway siding underneath the coppers and furnaces for coal wagons, and the walls of the brewery had to be continually shored up because of the tremendous vibration which resulted during the boiling process. For example, Bass No.1 Old Strong Ale had to be boiled for twelve hours. There was a bay near the No.2 Union Room, and a siding later put in here was known as Page's End reputedly after the name of the shunter who had taken the first wagon in.

Bass' original proposals for its new railway envisaged that the main part of the layout would be concentrated on the Middle Brewery, with a simple double line spur crossing Station Street to serve the Delhi Maltings and the mechanical cooperage. The foundation stone of the New Brewery, however, was laid on 18th May 1863 on the site of this cooperage which was mostly demolished. As a result, the layout in the Middle Brewery was modified to its later form in anticipation of the greater amount of traffic which would be passing through to the New Brewery. Various lines at the Middle Brewery joined near Station Street, where there was the curious sight of one signal post carrying two semaphore arms with red faces on the same side, one pointing to the left and the other to the right. In order to cross Station Street, Bass had to purchase the leases of seven houses and two were demolished to make way for the new railway. The private signal box which controlled the

Whilst the premises near the tall chimneys are Ind Coope's Brewery, the stacks of casks are situated in Allsopp's New Cooperage Yard and the railway wagons are at the Station Street end of Bass's Middle Brewery. The wagons are a mixture including five GNR and some MR open wagons, two LNWR covered vans with half roof access for vertical lifting and probably a Bass wagon with rounded ends and dust covers to the axle boxes. Stacks of bricks can be seen at the bricklayers' stores.

(J.A. Peden Collection)

No.3 pulls out of Bass' Middle Brewery, past the old signal box, and across Station Street about 1925. *(Railway Magazine)*

level crossing was replaced by a new box in 1937. Wilf Birkin was latterly in the new box; he had the unfortunate experience to be gassed in World War 1 and had a weak chest. Jack Royle who followed him worked the box until the end. When propelling wagons across Station Street, locomotives had to stop immediately inside the Middle Brewery gate, so that the shunter could go ahead and check that all was clear before signalling the driver to proceed slowly round the curve.

Over 1,300 workers were employed to construct the massive eastern range of the New Brewery in a period of ten months. Some of the walls were three feet thick. The New Brewery began work on 25th January 1864 and additional sidings were laid off the original spur by the following year to serve the new buildings. Wagon turntables had to be used in some places because of the constricted nature of the site. Malt was brought in railway wagons and large carts to the Station Street end of the brewhouse block where the bags were lifted up to the two (after 1875) malt receiving rooms. The malt was screened and crushed before being infused with hot water in the mash tuns. After the resultant 'sweet' wort had been moved to the coppers, the spent grains were thrown out of the tuns into grain squares by 'grainers', dressed in flannel trousers and clogs, for later collection by farmers' carts. Alternatively they were sent down wooden square chutes into the railway wagons waiting in the passage below. Space was very restricted and the wagons nearest Station Street were securely braked when a locomotive was approaching them. There had obviously been earlier incidents because even the relief shunters were to be 'advised of the great importance of this rule, and tell the men to use the utmost care in guarding against the Iron Columns which are in such close proximity to the wagons so as to avoid injury.'

There were eleven wort coppers at the New Brewery, compared with nine at the Middle Brewery and eight at the Old Brewery. The New Brewery coppers were 42 feet above the ground and heated by large furnaces. Coal for them was brought in railway wagons along the line, running underneath the brewhouse in a lofty arched passage, and lifted up to the furnaces in wooden iron-bound boxes. The wort was boiled with hops in the coppers. When ready, the liquid was 'cast' (emptied) through the hopbacks, which allowed the spent hops to be taken off and pressed before being sent away for use as cattle feed or manures. Yeast was added to the wort in the wooden fermenting squares to

Len Haywood, Bass' Traffic Manager, stands by the Delhi Maltings as No.11 passes the New Brewery ale bank. *(Ivo Peters)*

break down the malt sugar into alcohol and carbon dioxide. Finishing off was completed in special cleansing vessels known as Burton Union Sets which allowed the yeast to be removed. There were 2,548 union sets in the 'room' and these were fitted with 'swan necks' which syphoned off the yeast into wooden troughs as fermentation was completed. The Union Room formed the upper floor of a long two storey building and was of such a size that Barnard reported that it could have seated 2,000 people on one floor! From here, the beer was let down into the racking vats below, before being run into casks. These were taken outside to the ale bank for loading into railway wagons; the bank at the New Brewery was unusual in being roofed over. There were three railway lines between the ale bank and Delhi Maltings. The far line served the maltings, whilst the middle line was under signal box control and carried through traffic in either direction between Shobnall and Bass's breweries.

The buildings for the new steam cooperage were constructed in the Middle Yard on land recently received in exchange from Worthington and the plant was transferred from the New Brewery site for it to open in 1864. These were early days for the application of machinery to the traditional craft of making casks. Michael Thomas Bass, commenting on the ability of such plant, wrote that he would not say yet that it was cheaper to make a cask by machine although Mr Creasy had told him that it was "but he has yet to prove it". Bass was sure that the machine-made casks were superior in quality. Much of the early machinery was manufactured by Burton engineering companies, such as Buxton & Thornley. The buildings became the Electric Cooperage in 1916 when British Thomson-Houston electric motors were fitted. The oak slabs were seasoned up at Shobnall and originally they had come from Shobnall to the Middle Yard where they were sawn to the required lengths, submerged in steeping tanks to extract the tannin from the wood, before returning in railway wagons to the stave yard at Shobnall. Later the steeping tanks were dispensed with and the slabs simply travelled from Shobnall. Following manufacture, the completed casks were filled with a common salt solution and allowed to steep in the brine for 3 to 4 days. After washing out they were then ready for use. In later years, Bass borrowed a Planet petrol locomotive from Worthington to shunt the stave yard, thereby reducing the number of horses required, and this brought down a load

Guild Street Branch and Bass' Breweries 1904

────	Midland Railway
──	Private Railways

B	Bank
E	Engineers
GF	Ground Frame
L	Loco Shed
S	Stables
SB	Signal Box
SM	Saw Mill
U	Union and Racking Room

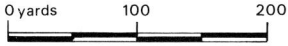

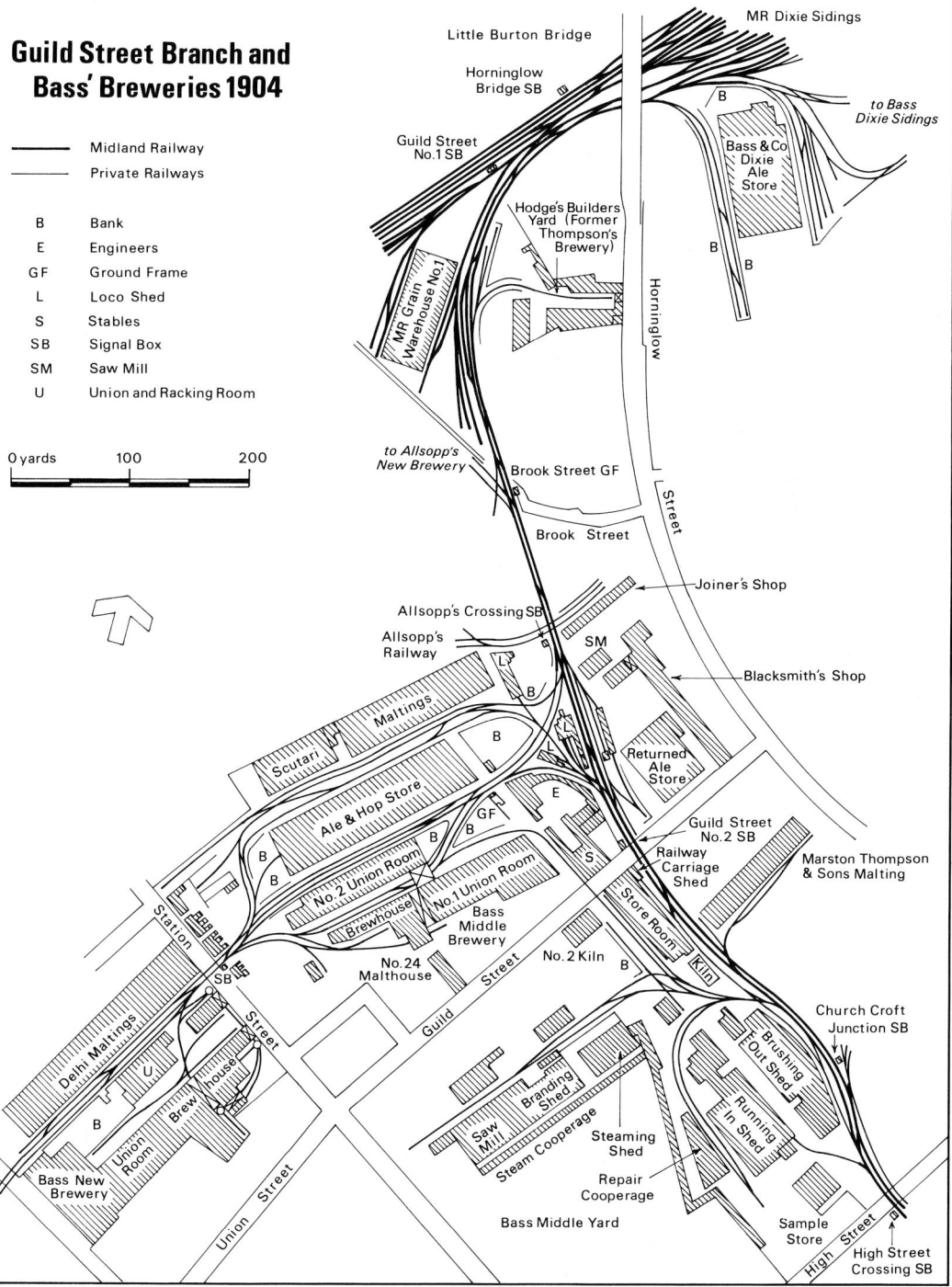

0 yards   100   200

Little Burton Bridge

MR Dixie Sidings

Horninglow Bridge SB

to Bass Dixie Sidings

Guild Street No.1 SB

Bass & Co Dixie Ale Store

B

B

B

Hodge's Builders Yard (Former Thompson's Brewery)

MR Grain Warehouse No.1

Horninglow Street

to Allsopp's New Brewery

Brook Street GF

Brook Street

Joiner's Shop

Allsopp's Crossing SB

Allsopp's Railway

SM

Blacksmith's Shop

B

Maltings

Scutari

B

Returned Ale Store

Ale & Hop Store

B

B

GF

E

Guild Street No.2 SB

No.2 Union Room

B

B

S

Railway Carriage Shed

Marston Thompson & Sons Malting

B

B

Brewhouse

No.1 Union Room

Bass Middle Brewery

Station Street

No.24 Malthouse

Guild Street

No.2 Kiln

Store Room

Kiln

Church Croft Junction SB

Delhi Maltings

SB

U

Union Room

Brewhouse

B

Bass New Brewery

Saw Mill

Steam Cooperage

Branding Shed

Steaming Shed

Repair Cooperage

Brushing Out Shed

Running In Shed

Sample Store

High Street

High Street Crossing SB

Union Street

Bass Middle Yard

of slabs to the Electric Cooperage each night on its way back to Worthington's Shed. The slabs were taken into the cooperage on a hand worked narrow gauge railway. They were shaped into staves in the saw mill and a constant stream of wood chippings was projected by fans out of the building into a hopper. Here the chippings were stored, prior to being loaded into railway vans which carried them away to the East Coast for use in smoking fish.

Much of the remainder of the Middle Yard was devoted to cleaning and repairing casks and again, a railway line was usually close at hand. The Brushing Out Shed was an extensive open sided structure with a corrugated iron roof. A private siding ran along one side of it next to the Guild Street Branch and this was used each day by scores of wagons laden with returned empty casks. In former times the incoming casks were unheaded and 'brushed out' by hand. After reheading, the hoops were 'driven' (tightened) by the coopers. The casks were tested with steam for leaks and then rolled across the granite setted roadway to the Running In Shed where they were filled with boiling water and, after standing sufficiently to be sterilised, they were turned over and allowed to drain. When cask washing machines replaced brushing out, the shed became known as the Washing Out Shed. 'Running in' continued as before, although much later steam sterilised the casks. When ready, the casks were loaded back into railway wagons standing on a siding which also served the Repair Cooperage.

In 1865, the railway line on one side of the Middle Yard Barley Store was extended across Guild Street, by the stables and into the Middle Brewery. This was a private level crossing and there was no signal box, the gates being worked by hand. The line was used to bring clean casks from the Middle Yard to the racking wharves at the Middle Brewery. A locomotive would place half its load at the No.1 Racking Room and the remainder at the No.2 Racking Room. The casks ran down gauntries from the side doors of the railway wagons and there was a 'smeller' at each door of the racking rooms who put his nose to the bung hole of every cask. Occasionally, he would tip one out which meant that it was a 'stinker' and would have to go back to the Cask Cleansing department for special treatment. The defect was usually caused by the previous customer not corking the tap hole when the cask had been emptied. There was an admonition on invoices to do so and that is why a clean cork held in a wire hoop was sent out on the head of every full cask.

Bass' No.7 was a popular locomotive for this working and it would make the journey across Guild Street several times a day. Old Bob Hartshorne was on No.7 and he is well remembered leaning out of his cab by those workmen who squeezed between the locomotive and the stable wall; there was just enough room! Bob Hartshorne had 14 children and the joiners once made him a board with fourteen brass checks on, each with the initials of one of his children. After the clean

The new signal box at Bass' Station Street level crossing with the ale and hop stores and former Middle Brewery behind. 12th April 1958.

(R.C. Riley)

casks had been filled, it was necessary to set up gauntries over the railway to reach the ale stores. They were supported on trestles where there was a wide gap between the banks. It had to be done over two sets of lines from the No.1 Racking Room. A locomotive would often come along whistling for the gauntries to be removed so that it could continue on its way.

In 1935, the Middle Brewery ceased continuous operations because the amalgamation of Bass and Worthington had meant that the company had five breweries and some rationalisation was possible. From then on, the Middle Brewery only brewed for twelve weeks every year. This was when the New and Old Breweries were stopped for their general overhauls, each of which lasted for six weeks. After World War 2, Bass considered reopening the Middle Brewery and closing Worthington's No.1 Brewery, which was in poor condition, but eventually it was decided to refurbish the latter. Following early experiments with carbonated beers at Shobnall, Bass had erected some chilling plant at the Town Ale Stores in the New Brewery in 1930 and at the Middle Brewery in 1934. When the new Redox process came along with only one tank being required for conditioning and chilling, the union and racking rooms at the Middle Brewery were converted to hold Redox tanks. The decision had been taken to stop brewing at the Middle Brewery in January 1957 and plant was removed in 1958; the brewhouse being demolished in 1960 and the Keg Beer Plant erected on its site.

Dixie

The Guild Street Branch was a major outlet, not only to the MR's sidings and the Brook Street Warehouse, but also to Bass' own property at Dixie. In 1870 Bass leased 11 acres of land from the Marquis of Anglesey to the north west of Hawkins Lane and it laid out some sidings on the site which opened on 20th October 1871. Previously the MR had exchanged traffic with Bass at the Old Dixie Yard. Now Bass' own sidings could handle this exchange, thus relieving the lines at the station and Old Dixie. Between the leased 11 acres and Horninglow Street stood the Burton Poor Law *Union* Workhouse. Seemingly the MR took that as the designation for the whole of the Bass site; the Goods Agent recording that 'Bass & Co's new Union premises opened on October 1st 1872' and the new lines leading from these premises under the Little Burton Bridge to the Guild Street Branch were brought into use on 24th December 1873. Bass eventually adopted the MR term 'Dixie' for its property.

William Canning constructed two spacious banks at Dixie next to the exchange sidings and much material must have been brought in to raise the banks to wagon floor height. The banks were separated by two railway lines, with another track following their outer edges. There were ultimately three miles of private sidings at Dixie shunted by Bass' locomotives and horses. The central lines were crossed by a steel footbridge, arched to permit the passage of railway vans. A splendid building was provided for about 10 or 12 horses. Simple plant was installed on the banks for cleansing returned casks.

The original rush to provided bank space at Dixie and Shobnall was prompted by a tremendous increase in the sales of high gravity beers which at that time were approaching 900,000 barrels a year. In January 1874 M.B. Foster & Sons placed a single order for 38,600 barrels of Bass pale ale, original gravity 1063⅓ at £3 a barrel. All of the export trade and the bulk of domestic sales were 'stock' ales brewed between October and April. Producing a year's trade requirements in six months meant that a lot of space had to be found for storage. The ale stores alone could not cope so the remainder lay out on the banks; there was not an ale store at Dixie for another 20 years. Ale in the open could withstand frost but not heat and so when the warmer weather brought seasonal malting to an end, the remaining stacks of ale were moved to the ground floors of the maltings out of the direct sunlight. Theft was presumably not a significant problem; Victorian thieves would have lacked the transport to silently shift 7cwt hogsheads and 12cwt butts! This pattern of brewing also meant that a large reserve of unemployed casks had to be kept. Returned empty casks received from the MR were unheaded, hand brushed out and stacked in vast truncated pyramids on the banks until seasonal demands brought them back into use. The photographs of the piles of casks were usually taken at Dixie although similar stacks could be seen at Shobnall. In June 1877, Bass had over 170,000 casks in storage (68,000 at Shobnall, 64,000 at Dixie and 25,000 in the Middle Yard).

Casks stored unheaded at Dixie waiting for the October to April brewings of the heavier gravity beers. The cask washing plant had two sets of boilers which stood out in the open.

On 18th June 1891 Bass purchased the 10,588 square yards of land and buildings at the Burton Poor Law Union Workhouse from the Guardians for £4,000 freehold. The workhouse was pulled down and Couchman built some ale stores on the site. 'Docks' (banks) were provided on the north and south sides of the building served by railway tracks. Broadbent electric capstans were installed about 1922 to assist with shunting wagons. The filled casks came in railway wagons from the Old Brewery which did not have any stores.

Paradoxically at the very time that Canning's layout at Dixie was put to use in the 1870s, a process was being developed which ultimately contributed to the disuse of the banks almost 50 years later. That was the application of Lindt's ammonia compressor to the control of wort and barm temperatures in summer, so permitting continuous brewing all year. The consequence was that much 'stock' ale was replaced by 'running' ales, casks could be used all year and there was less need to have casks filled with beer lying on the banks or in store.

During World War 1 the banks were used for storing shell and sea mine cases awaiting despatch to factories where they would be filled with explosives. There is a photograph in H.N. Twell's book *Railways in Burton and the Trent Valley through 145 years* looking over the site towards the No.4 Warehouse taken from the vicinity of Mount Pleasant Bridge and showing the banks crammed with war supplies. After the War, exports of beer dwindled as a result of national tariff barriers. By 1922 Dixie Banks had run their course and were devoid of casks, full or empty; ale stores could handle the trade which had become virtually 'immediate' – in and out of store within 3 weeks. The new cask washing machines installed at Dixie in 1923 to replace manual brushing out did not last long and were soon finished; the Middle Yard and Shobnall being able to cope with all of the cask cleansing demands. For many years the banks remained large open tracts devoid of buildings but with the dock walls and railways maintained in good condition.

From 1943 Bass and Worthington's Wetmore Road Maltings were requisitioned to billet United States Army troops massing for D day. The Dixie Banks were used for their stores; it must have been a spectacular sight. Amongst the stores delivered to the US Army at Burton were some Wickham Type 17A railcars (maker's numbers 3487-3501 in December 1943, 3502-10 in February 1944 and 3511-41 in June 1944). At least ten were sold back to their makers after World War 2.

Coal was in short supply after the War and it was a case of accepting any fuel that was offered. Bass managed to buy a lot of slack and small coal which was delivered to Dixie and piled in great mounds on the banks, from whence it was loaded out by mechanical shovels for delivery to the numerous boiler houses. This resulted in some bewilderment in 1955 when fuel charges began to drop despite an expansion in brewing. The explanation was revealed after a spell of heavy rain when two vast lakes appeared on the Dixie banks where the mechanical shovels had loaded out bank infill with slack. No wonder there had been periodic complaints by boiler firemen about the burning quality of the fuel supplied to them! The infill was not distinguishable in colour from the slack. It was not marl or sand or gravel, and it did not put out the boiler fires, so had Canning built his banks of material brought from colliery waste tips? The ground was eventually restored to its pre 1870 level when the banks were removed for the new A38 Burton bypass. Dixie Ale Stores remained in use until the closure of Bass' railway.

Guild Street Branch

The Guild Street Branch commenced at Guild Street No.1 Signal box. Originally there had been a cabin called Top of Guild Street Signal Box but this closed and appears to have been replaced by the No.1 Box on 6th August 1893. The latter was fitted with a new frame and renamed Horninglow Bridge in 1933, when the box on the far side of the main line shut. As the branch curved away from the main line past the Brook Street Warehouse, a siding joined it from one of Thompson's breweries

View underneath an awning of the Brook Street Warehouse on 14th April 1968, with the Guild Street Branch alongside. Horninglow Bridge Signal Box stands by the main line and behind is Yeomans, Cherry & Curtis's grain store on the Horninglow Branch. *(C. Shepherd)*

on the opposite side of the tracks. This brewery had originally been established by John Perks in 1846 and was still identified as such in 1859. Thomas Mark Carter & Sons were in possession in 1861 and John Thompson had taken it over by 1869. The brewery was a very small affair with one siding entering the yard almost up to the Horninglow Street entrance and another serving an ale bank. According to the Goods Agent's notebook, Thompson's Guild Street siding opened on 23rd August 1869 and ale loading began on 1st November 1869, the LNWR also enjoying running powers. It is assumed that this statement refers to this particular siding. George Hodges, the builder, was using the site in 1902.

Bass' No.1 pulls past Guild Street No.2 Signal Box on 30th May 1960. The company's locomotive sheds are on the left with the Returned Ale Stores behind No.1. (R.C. Riley)

The branch continued on, crossing over Allsopp's private railway where the movement of trains was controlled by an old MR crossbar signal, past Bass' locomotive sheds to reach Guild Street, where the later Guild Street No.2 Signal Box dating from 1889 had ten levers and a 3ft 6in diameter wheel for operating the gates over Guild Street. This box had a tradition of signal women and Mrs Riley was in charge during World War 2. Cecil Welch, Bass' Traffic Manager, once presented her with a bottle of King's Ale for her prompt action in opening the gates when a moving string of wagons suddenly appeared without a locomotive. After the War, Mrs Sheffield and Mrs Appleby worked the box. Doris Sheffield used to open the gates at Clay Mills, but BR put a wheel in that box in 1952, and so she went to Birmingham to train as a signal woman before going to Guild Street. The branch continued on past the Middle Yard Store Room where Bass' Engineer, Herbert Couchman, had built the No.2 Barley Drying Kiln by carefully picking out the best of the delivered bricks and rejecting the rest. Thompson had a malting on the opposite side of the branch which was provided with two short sidings which began to be used on 19th December 1874. The lines into the Middle Yard and a connection to Allsopp's railway over Horninglow Street were controlled by the Church Croft Junction Signal Box until it closed from 1st April 1963; the points for the Middle Yard then being hand operated. This particular box had been opened on 8th March 1892 by the MR and was later classified as an example of what is now called the Type 2a with the separate 3ft 6in windows at the door end. A signalman called Bird was in charge of it at the finish.

Yet more signal boxes were encountered at High Street and the junction with the Hay. The latter was not surprisingly named Hay Signal Box and was finally operated until its closure on 27th October 1930 by a man called Palmer who had only one good arm. This box had been relocated on 20th May

Top. *Guild Street Branch on 26th December 1965 with the Middle Yard Store Room, Marston, Thompson & Evershed's tower and the Midland Cooperage's tall chimney and black shed visible.* Below. *Bass' No.3 shunts wagons by Church Croft Junction Box on 30th May 1960.* (C. Shepherd, R.C. Riley)

1889 and a new structure provided on 22nd October 1905. Although this last short section of the Guild Street Branch had the appearance of double track, only the up line initially connected with the Hay Branch, and this was controlled by High Street Crossing Signal Box. It was necessary for the shunter to walk to the box to collect the round black staff and hand it to the driver, before the locomotive could proceed from the Hay round to High Street. No locomotive could run along this line without the staff. This arrangement had commenced on 2nd July 1893. With the closure of the line to Salt's Brewery, it was possible to make a second connection with the Hay Branch, and the use of the train staff was no longer required. Before leaving the down line, the shunter had to make sure that no conflicting movements were being made in the Hay Sidings. New level crossing gates had been erected at High Street in October 1866 and at Guild Street in March 1867. The signals and boxes at Church Croft and High Street first came into operation on 14th October 1867.

Allsopp's Church Croft Property

Holy Trinity Church

Guild Street Branch

Allsopp & Son's Old Cooperage

SB

Church Croft Junction SB

M

M

Railway constructed later

Worthington Wetmore Rd. Maltings

Horninglow

Allsopp

Marston Thompson and Son

M

High Street Crossing SB

Allsopp's Railway

Former Brewery

No. 3

No. 4

Bass' Old Brewery

Offices

High Street

Burton Brewery Co's Brewery

to Worthington's Brewery

Old Dock

and Tunnery

Allsopp's Old Brewery

Tower

B

B

Salt & Co's Brewery

B

Former Nunneley's Brewery (Disused)

Salt's Ale Stores (later No.3)

Burton Brewery Co. Malthouse

Wetmore Road

Street

Bridge

Hay Walk

Hay Sidings

B

Street

Hay Wharf

Hay SB

B

Hay Branch

Burton Corporation Baths

River Trent

Continued opposite

Trent Bridge SB

Burton Bridge

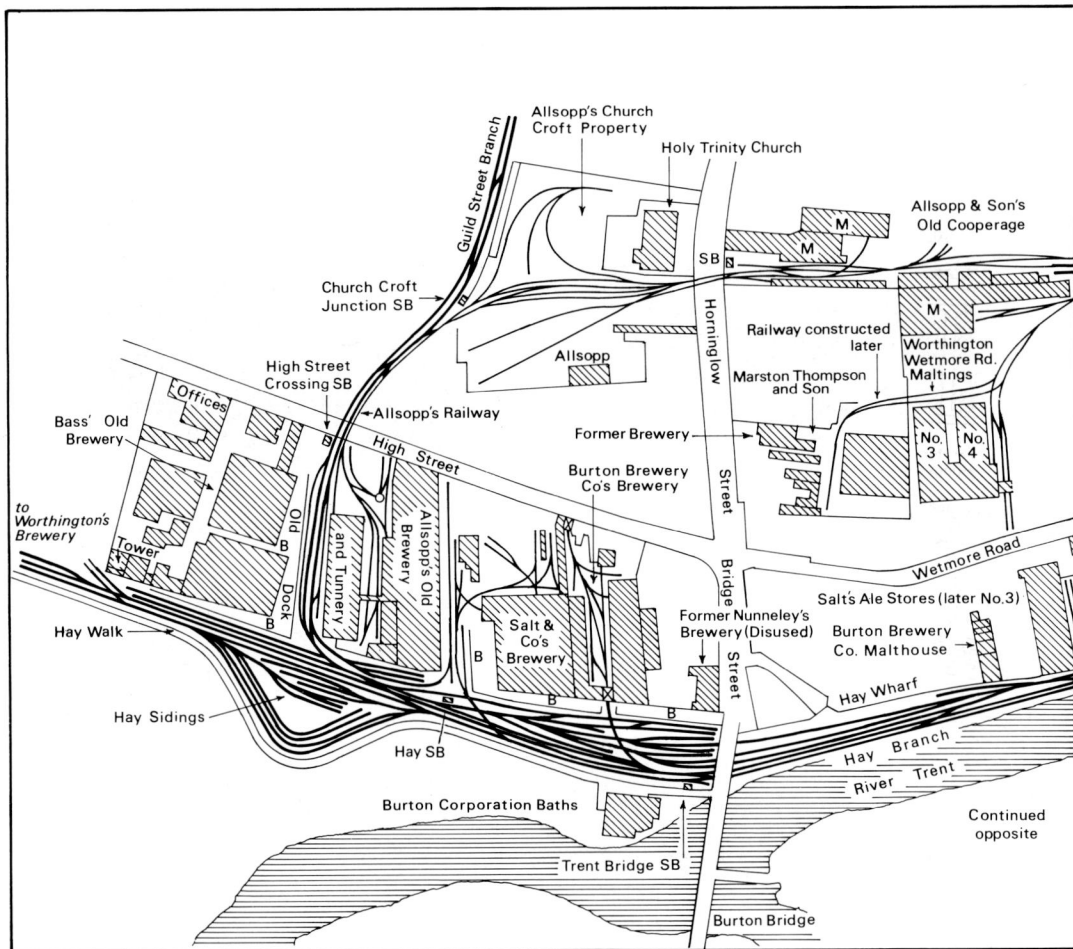

Traffic on the Guild Street Branch was predominantly worked by Bass, with Worthington's locomotives also appearing after the two fleets merged in 1960. Allsopp's locomotives rarely ventured along the branch and the few occasions when it did happen were probably due to its own private railway via Horninglow Street being blocked. In later years, the railway company visited the branch twice a day to shunt Marston, Thompson & Evershed's malting. If it was a six-coupled locomotive, the wagons had to be given a good push to flyshunt them round to the building. The little four-coupled shunters could work right round the tight curve into the premises. One day in the 1920s, a special party was due to arrive at Burton and the suggestion was made that a Bass locomotive should pick up the railway company's carriage at Dixie and bring it along the Guild Street Branch to the 'Old Dock' at the Old Brewery. The railway company did not consider this to be necessary and a relatively large ex NSR 0-6-4 tank locomotive was entrusted to the task, with unfortunate results because it spread the track and the carriage had to be rescued by one of Bass' locomotives!

Bass' Old Brewery was situated on land between the Guild Street Branch and the Hay Sidings. In 1876-78, at the time of the Bass centenary celebrations, the original Old Brewery was pulled down to make way for a larger and more modern plant. Despite being the newest of Bass' three breweries,

Map

Hawkins Lane

Hawkins Lane SB

to LNWR
Horninglow Yard

GNR Sidings

Saunders
Branch

Ale Store (later No.2)

Mount Pleasant

No.
9

No.
17

B

Salt's
Maltings SB

Salt's Walsitch Maltings

B

No.
17

No.
16

No.
21

No.
20

No.
19

No.
18

Cooperage

Bass Anderstaff Lane
Maltings

No.
16

Burton Brewery Co.

Anderstaff Lane SB

Burton Corporation
Electricity Works

Wetmore Road

Hay Branch

Salt's
Cooperage

B

B

Burton Corporation Gas Works

River Trent

Salt's Engine Shed SB
Salt's Engine Shed

Continued
opposite

———————	Midland Railway
—·—·—·—·—	London & North Western Railway
··················	Great Northern Railway
———————	Private Railways

Hay and Saunders Branches 1904

0 yards   100   200

B	Bank
M	Maltings
SB	Signal Box

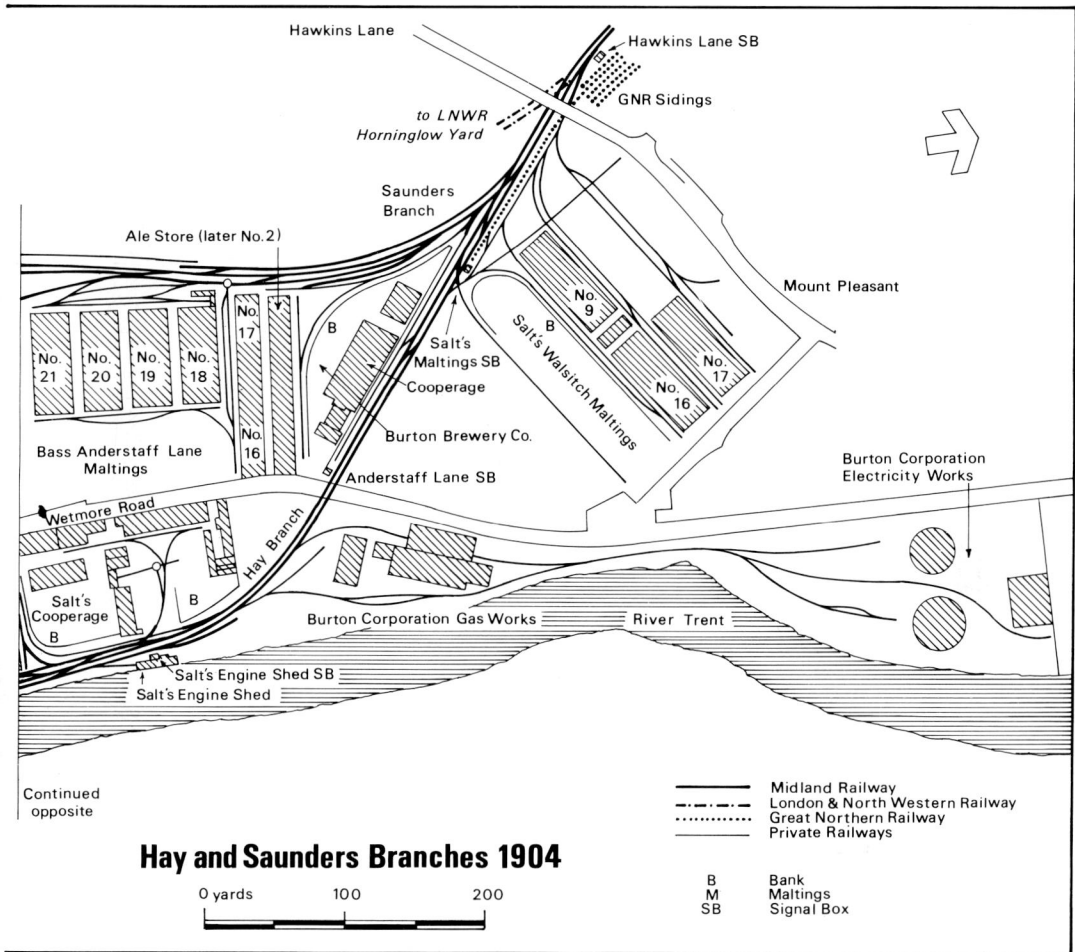

it was still known as the Old Brewery. Looking across the flat river meadows, it formed an impressive spectacle particularly enhanced by the 120 feet high tower erected back in 1866.

The siding off the Guild Street Branch to the 'Old Dock' was used to unload clean empty casks for filling. There was a small detached building at the end of the bank used by Bass' Railway Department ale loaders and number takers as messrooms and the foreman's office. The Old Brewery ale loading bank faced on to the Hay. All the banks on the eastern side of the High Street breweries were on the route of the old Hay ditch and so belonged to the MR. In 1859, it had been proposed to construct the Hay Branch immediately past the ends of these breweries, diverting the Hay Walk in a straight line on the river side of the railway. The situation was complicated, however, by the opening of the Guild Street Branch which crossed the Hay Branch at right angles and reverse curves gave access to it. This curious arrangement worked whilst horses were used for pulling wagons, but must have proved increasingly impractical for longer locomotive hauled trains, and it was replaced by a more normal direct curve at the end of the 1870s. A bulge had been inserted in the alignment of the Hay Walk to accommodate the end of the Guild Street Branch; the bend in the boundary wall remaining long after the reason for its formation had largely been forgotten. The MR took advantage of the extra space by laying out more sidings.

83

Bass' No.7 at the Hay Sidings on a frosty 27th December 1965. The buildings behind the train once formed part of Allsopp's Old Brewery. Further along are Bass' Old Brewery and Worthington's maltings. (C. Shepherd)

Despite the rebuilding of the Old Brewery, no railway track was laid into the centre of the premises and as a result, some of the materials had to be brought in by horse drawn transport. The Old Brewery coppers were always heated by coal fired furnaces because it was considered that strong ales were better for more vigorous 'rousing' in the coppers. Coal wagons were positioned on a siding in the Middle Yard near High Street and the coal was transferred into huge two wheeled carts which were taken to the copper hearth and boilers. Sacks of malt came in high sided road wagons sheeted over with tarpaulins. A small amount of spent grains was removed by local farmers for feeding livestock but most was dropped into large close sided wagons and taken by road to a

No.8 propels a grain van through the Hay Bank into Bass' Old Brewery yard on 5th April 1965. (C. Shepherd)

siding opposite the Middle Yard Store Room where the grains were thrown into railway wagons. When the horses were replaced by tractors, a bank was built to stand above the railway wagons so that a hydraulically equipped trailer could shoot the wet grains directly into them. These inconvenient methods of handling materials at the Old Brewery lasted for many years and a possible explanation for them may have been fear of flooding because the Trent quite often overflowed its banks and the water occasionally extended up to the High Street level crossing, with the Hay Sidings taking on the appearance of a river. The Old Brewery was protected by its two ale banks and Worthington's adjoining buildings. Flood prevention measures were only slowly introduced by the Town Commissioners, and later the Corporation, so that the existence of a gap in the Old Brewery ale bank could have led to the inundation of the brewery. The dangers were reduced in more recent times and a railway siding was required into the brewery to allow for the use of bulk grain vans, so a way was cut through the Hay Bank and a single line laid into the brewery yard alongside the brewhouse in 1955. Nothing was left to chance and a water tight wooden barrier could be built up to bank level to protect the brewery if flooding did occur. There was a system of red lights and loud electric bells which were switched on by the leading shunter when a locomotive worked into the yard. Coal was never brought into the brewery by railway because it had become more economical to deliver it by lorries direct from the collieries to the boilers.

Anderstaff Lane

The route to Anderstaff Lane, or 'A Lane' as it was known, was over the Hay and Saunders Branches. Bass had built three small maltings and laid out a cask washing plant and cask yard at Anderstaff Lane on land which had been purchased from John Mason in 1845. Mason and Gilbertson also owned the Plough Malting in Horninglow Street which Bass later acquired and replaced in 1899-1902 by a new building, designed by Couchman, although it did not have a railway siding. Gilbertson was the man involved in the projected Nottingham, Birmingham & Coventry Junction Railway. Bass sold 464 square yards of land at Anderstaff Lane to the MR which opened its Saunders Branch in November 1861, the name coming from William Saunders' property at the end of the branch. Part of this was subsequently incorporated into Allsopp's Old Cooperage premises. Bass had leased Saunders' six maltings in 1854.

In 1862, Bass decided to devote its land at Anderstaff Lane to malting and it demolished the buildings on its freehold property, erecting a single three storey malting a year later. Nos.16 and 17 Maltings had the barley intake in the centre separating the two sets of working floors. Early in 1864,

Nos.16-17 Maltings on the right at Anderstaff Lane were double maltings, in which barley was hoisted at the centre of the building and worked to each end. In contrast, the Nos.18-21 block on the left set the pattern for future multi-storey floor maltings. There were hoists at each end of the building; one for barley to enter and the other for malt to exit. The barley was processed as it moved through the building. 28th March 1966. (C. Shepherd)

Worthington's No.5 emerges from under the Mount Pleasant Bridge on the Hay Branch on 26th May 1959. The latest Hawkins Lane Signal Box visible here was opened on 8th December 1929. *(R.C. Riley)*

Bass purchased the adjoining site from the Feoffees of Burton Town Lands and immediately built four 200 quarter maltings (Nos.18-21). These became the prototype for all future Bass floor maltings, including Shobnall and Sleaford, with the barley stores provided over the top of the working floors. Private sidings were taken off the Saunders Branch to serve the barley intake at the north end of the maltings, whilst a wagon turntable allowed another line to run between Nos.16-17 and 18 blocks to the barley intake of Nos.16-17 and the south end of Nos.18-21 Maltings. When these were in full production, Bass had no further use for Saunders' Maltings and they were then leased by the Burton Brewery Company. After Bass' merger with Worthington, a curve was constructed to link up with the siding at the south end of Nos.18-21. This meant that the wagon turntable could be avoided and bulk grain vans shunted round to the malt outlet. In addition to working traffic to and from the maltings, Bass' locomotives also went along the Hay Branch to gain access to the LNWR yard at Horninglow and to take wagons for the GNR at Hawkins Lane. In LNER days, some of the Newcastle traffic went to Hawkins Lane.

Locomotive whistle code approaching Hawkins Lane Junction
from the Anderstaff Lane direction in 1921

On to MR lines	1
On to LNWR branch	2
Over junction to return to any lines on the Anderstaff Lane side	3
On to NSR branch	4
To the GNR goods station	5

Thomas Salt & Company

The brewery was located in High Street to the north of Allsopp's Old Brewery. Salt always enjoyed a good reputation as brewers of quality beers but was never particularly prosperous. In fact, the premises were at one time conveyed to the Burton, Uttoxeter & Ashbourne Union Bank to secure the company's bank account. The brewery was renewed in the 1880s and Barnard described it as a noble and lofty structure with seven large coppers. Production worked down from the High Street end of the premises to the union and racking rooms which faced on to the Hay.

With the opening of the Guild Street Branch, no time was lost and Salt began loading beer into railway wagons on 30th November 1862, following the construction of a line from the Hay into the brewery yard by the side of the racking room. Horses worked the trains initially. The MR also provided a siding for the Hay bank at the end of Salt's, the Burton Brewery Company's and Nunneley's Breweries and this was used extensively for loading casks into wagons.

The lack of space at High Street had forced Salt to build its ale stores beyond the Burton Bridge between Anderstaff Lane and the river. When the MR came along to lay the Hay Branch, it had to fill in part of the river to provide enough ground for the line to pass by the building. Salt kept its strong ale called 'October Brew' maturing in casks here for twelve months before delivery. There was none for sale in early 1917 because there had been a serious fire in the stores and thousands of gallons of strong ale had flowed into the Trent. The cask washing facilities were situated adjacent to the ale stores and there were the usual buildings, with casks being rolled out of railway wagons into the unheading shed for washing out by hand to be followed by the steaming and examining sheds. The completion of the Hay Branch meant that wagon loads of casks could be moved over the railway to and from the brewery. MR locomotives also worked traffic away from the stores along the Hay Branch to Old Dixie Sidings. Casks were repaired at Anderstaff Lane and there were stacks of Baltic timber waiting to be cut into staves at the nearby sawmill. When the staves, heads and hoops were ready, they were loaded into wagons and taken from the staveyard siding up to Walsitch prior to being made into new casks at the cooperage there.

Salt's Brewery yard at High Street. There are various forms of conveyance present, including two private open wagons labelled 'SALT & CO BURTON ON TRENT', and presumably used for coal; a MR Van under the hoist and a horse drawn floater lettered 'SALT & CO BURTON STOUT'.
(Bass Museum Collection)

knowledge of its capabilities close at hand because Worthington had purchased a similar locomotive just fifteen months before. One of the Thornewill & Warham locomotives could now be disposed of and an advertisement was placed in *The Engineer* on 3rd April 1885 for the sale of a 'four wheels coupled tank engine **with cab** by Thornewill & Warham.' It was unusual for a Thornewill & Warham locomotive working at Burton to have a cab at this time and certainly Salt's other locomotives up to this point did not possess such a feature. The locomotive for sale was quoted as having 12in x 15in cylinders and 3ft 2½in diameter wheels. Salt was again left with three locomotives and the Thornewill & Warham and Hudswell Clarke were photographed for Alfred Barnard probably in 1887, so that an illustration could appear with a description of his visit to the brewery. The second Thornewill & Warham locomotive was probably disposed of in the following year, an advertisement appearing in *The Engineer* dated 24th February 1888 offering a 12in x 16in Thornewill & Warham locomotive for sale.

Nothing is known about the disposal of the Fowler locomotive apart from the fact that it later passed through the hands of the Middlesbrough engineers Thomas Ridley. Salt ordered another Hudswell Clarke locomotive (maker's number 576) on 22nd May 1900. Delivery was promised for the following October but the locomotive did not emerge from the works until 14th December 1900. The new acquisition was generally similar to the earlier Hudswell Clarke but was fitted with steel boiler tubes and tyres; the position of the brake was altered and the brake connecting rod was in two parts; the dome was put as high as possible and there was a manhole under the boiler barrel for maintenance. Two sets of water gauges were fitted. The new locomotive weighed 20 tons 19cwts and cost £1,550.

Salt's locomotives were painted in a dull maroon livery which was not as bright as the MR colour. About the time of World War 1, William Charles Harvey was the senior driver at Salt's Brewery. He was a very conscientious man working for eighteen years without a day off. He received

The Fowler locomotive purchased by Salt was presumably bought from stock as the order was dated 16th January 1873, only six days before delivery. Salt's locomotive, maker's number 1573, appears in Fowler's register as part of a batch starting with 1567. It is therefore likely to have been similar to 1567 seen here and destined for the Calder Vale Iron Works in Wakefield.
(Courtesy Institute of Agricultural History and Museum of English Rural Life, University of Reading)

£1 4s 0d (£1.20) for a 54 hour week and also worked at weekends to earn extra money. Very few people could afford to buy their own house then but he managed to save enough money and bought one in West Street, Winshill for £100. At the end of the War, Salt must have been short of working locomotives because a second hand Hudswell Clarke (maker's number 724 built in 1905) was hired from the manufacturer in May 1919. It had once worked for the Swansea Harbour Trust, hence its name SWANSEA. The loan lasted until Salt purchased a third locomotive in February 1920 and the hired locomotive was then returned to Hudswell Clarke in the following month.

E. E. BAGULEY LIMITED, Engineers, BURTON-ON-TRENT

Tank Locomotive. 6" to 13" cylinders. Any gauge.

A Baguley postcard showing Salt's locomotive, the only standard gauge steam locomotive built by the manufacturer. *(E.E. Baguley Ltd, courtesy Staffordshire County Record Office)*

The new locomotive was of interest because it was the only standard gauge steam locomotive built by the local firm of Baguley (maker's number 2001). Strangely it had not started out in that form. In early 1914, Baguley had begun to build a 0-4-0 petrol hydraulic locomotive (maker's number 621) for McEwan, Pratt & Co Ltd which was intended for the Lacombe & Blindman Valley Electric Railway in Canada. Had it been completed, it would have been the first locomotive in the world with hydraulic transmission. Unfortunately, the Electric Railway was in financial difficulties and the advent of World War 1 made it difficult for Baguley to find another customer. The locomotive was to have been powered by a White & Poppe 150hp 6-cylinder engine linked to a Hele-Shaw hydrostatic transmission. Only the underframe and the testing of the transmission were completed. Locomotives were needed desperately for the war effort in 1917 and so Baguley decided to make the chassis and wheels the basis for a steam locomotive. A fairly traditional 4-coupled saddle tank emerged with two 13in x 18in cylinders and 3ft 5in diameter wheels, although its peculiar ancestry could be detected in its rather long 7ft coupled wheelbase. Another unusual feature was the adoption of Baguley radial valve gear and the locomotive had sanding by gravity only. Length was 22ft 7½in and height was 10ft 7½in.

The locomotive does not appear to have been completed until the end of 1919 so it must have been a spare time occupation for Baguley; no doubt materials were hard to come by and there was a full order book with war work for the military railways. Initially Bass was offered the locomotive and

A.H. Roberts, Bass' plant draughtsman in the Drawing Office, prepared an assessment of it dated 3rd January 1920. Comparing the main dimensions with a Bass' Class A locomotive, it was clear that the Baguley product was slightly smaller and less powerful. Roberts also noted that the 'steam chests on top of cylinders protruding in part through foot plate and thus exposed to weather. Steps leading to cab are weak and require staying to frame. Back of cab is closed except for a small rectangular opening to allow of hand brake operating. The tilting into cab of standard to this handle restricts the movement of driver and impedes his look out over side of cab. This could be remedied largely if cab back was open and brake standard fixed vertically. Lamp brackets should be fixed to suit our lamps and in positions to agree with our engines. In point of finish, the Baguley does not agreeably approach the finish of our engines.' Bass which did not require another locomotive anyway, rejected the offer.

As the senior driver at Salt, William Harvey took over the new locomotive but it was not very popular and he complained that he was nearly "roasted alive" with the heat. A.H. Roberts had obviously been correct in his assessment of the cab! Children had used to wave to the driver as he worked along the Hay, but it was difficult to see him when he received the Baguley because of the cab. The locomotive would sound its hooter as it came under the Burton Bridge; it was the only locomotive in the town with a hooter at that time. When William Harvey had not arrived home after work at the expected time, his family always knew that he was working late because they could hear the hooter of the Baguley in the distance. Harvey was a burly fellow who fell out with Palmer, the signalman at Hay Box. One day, the latter had a long handled brush gripped in his one good hand and was busy tarring the adjacent platelayers' hut which was constructed of old sleepers. William Harvey called him "Wingy" whereupon Palmer swung the brush round and deposited a dollop of warm tar on the side of Harvey's face and neck!

The arrival of the Baguley allowed No.1 to be sent to Hudswell Clarke in 1923 for a major overhaul. No.3, the Baguley locomotive, soon followed it in 1925 which was surprising because it was then barely five years old. It is difficult to believe that there were serious faults in it, certainly not in the chassis if it was built like the contemporary petrol locomotives, and improbably in the boiler considering Baguley's experience. Admittedly it was fitted with a boiler enclosing 113 steel tubes of 1¾in external diameter and a steel firebox, presumably as an economy measure, and British builders took a long time to master the techniques of steel fireboxes. It may have been involved in an accident but why send it to Leeds when Baguley's fully equipped works was still in operation?

A railway van stands next to the former Salt's covered bank at Anderstaff Lane, while across the Hay Branch is the company's disused locomotive shed. 28th March 1966.

(C. Shepherd)

Perhaps it had something to do with Baguley's agreement with the Yorkshire Engine Company, in which standard gauge steam locomotive work was to be passed on to the Yorkshire Engine Company. In those circumstances, Salt may have preferred to deal directly with an outside firm of its own choice.

The Thomas Salt Company failed in 1903 and a new set of directors had come in with the reconstruction. Frederick J. Roe, the only one concerned with brewing, had been chairman and manager of Bell's Brewery which Salt had taken over in 1902. The business did not recover fully until after World War 1 but was sufficiently attractive for Bass to agree to buy it on 11th October 1927 by the issue of £2½ million worth of debenture stock. The machinery was removed from the brewery in 1928-29 and Joe Slater was sent from Bass to collect the tools from Salt's Locomotive Shed. No.1 (Hudswell Clarke 272) was still in good condition following its visit to Leeds and it was included in Worthington's locomotive stock in February 1928. The other locomotives were disposed of in 1928 as surplus to requirements; No.2 (Hudswell Clarke 576) was sold to the Wellingborough Iron Co Ltd and No.3 (Baguley 2001) went to Greaves, Bull & Lakin's Harbury Cement Works.

Burton Brewery Company

Henry and Thomas Wilders founded their brewery on part of an old tanyard next to Salt's establishment in High Street. According to Owen quoting from some 1844 deeds, it consisted of a 'newly-erected Brewery, cooperage, stores, malt office, and kilns.' In 1858, it was incorporated as the Burton Brewery Company Ltd and by then, was the third largest brewer in the town. It remained an important concern for much of the nineteenth century, although the *Brewers Guardian* in 1872 recorded that the company had lost £109,000 in the previous twelve years. A modest revival in its fortunes then took place.

Rail traffic began to be loaded at the brewery on the 3rd February 1863 and it was initially worked by horses until MR locomotives took over. Four years later on 30th October 1867, a railway line was laid across four of the sidings on the Hay through a narrow archway underneath an office with a bay window, the gap forming one of the arches which decorated the facade of the building. On entering the brewery yard, the railway served various buildings and ale banks. The Trent Bridge Signal Box controlled both the curve into the brewery and a nearby short siding which enabled coal to be delivered to the Corporation swimming baths; a replacement box was provided on 24th February 1908. Tenders were accepted by the Council in 1964 for the replacement of the coal fired boiler at the baths, thus bringing the siding's function to an end. There was not much space between the Hay Branch and the wall bordering the Hay Walk which rose up to the Burton Bridge. As a result, the box was very narrow and fastened to the wall. It had a chimney shaped like a letter 'T' and occasionally, some mischievous individual would stand on the wall and block up both ends of the chimney. The annoyed and spluttering signalman would soon emerge much to the amusement of the well hidden onlookers. At one time, the box was operated by a MR signalman named Cooke who worked a single shift between 8.30am and 5pm. The railway company did away with the box on 18th June 1934.

There was a small brewery owned by Joseph Nunneley at the end of the Hay bank between the Burton Brewery Company and Bridge Street. Nunneley had built the brewery on the site of some leased houses which he had obtained in 1848 although he was already described as a 'common brewer' at the time of the transaction. The MR started to collect and deliver his traffic on 5th June 1865 and the LNWR also began to run on to the siding in December 1870. W.M. Pegge sold Nunneley's business for £77,500 to a group, including his son J.V. Pegge, on 30th July 1888. The new owners floated J. Nunneley & Co Ltd with J.V. Pegge as secretary, but on 6th October 1896, the Burton Brewery Company took it over. Nunneley ceased brewing and the buildings were used by a firm manufacturing feeding stuffs from brewery byproducts in 1899. The brewery buildings were demolished about 1926.

The Burton Brewery Company's other production property was mainly located along the Hay Branch in a similar pattern to Salt. It included some land at Anderstaff Lane next to Salt's Ale Stores and this was later extended to include the small malting previously occupied by Nunneley and served by a siding off the Hay Branch. Ale stores and a cask washing plant on a semi-circular bank were erected in the angle between the Hay and Saunders Branches, with sidings off both lines. The Burton Brewery Co began to use the cooperage siding off the Saunders Branch on 22nd January 1868. Malt came from the former Saunders Maltings although it presumably had to be purchased from outside suppliers after 1896.

In October 1867, the *Burton Weekly News* carried an advertisement announcing that the Burton Brewery Company was selling off horses and drays because it had purchased a locomotive from a Leeds firm. The new acquisition was built by Manning Wardle (maker's number 228) and was ex works on 30th September 1867. It began to work the brewery traffic between the various premises and up to the exchange sidings near the main line on the 3rd October 1867. This locomotive was the first of Manning Wardle's original Class D design; a typical four-coupled saddle tank with 12in x 18in outside cylinders and the firebox crown raised above the outline of the boiler to give a large steam space over the inner firebox and to keep the regulator valve well clear of the water level to avoid priming. It was fitted with Naylor's patent safety valves. The 3ft diameter wheels were on a wheelbase of 5ft 3in, but all subsequent locomotives of this type had the wheelbase increased by one inch, the various rods being lengthened to suit. One of a pair constructed to the same order, presumably for stock because some time elapsed between the first steaming of the locomotive on 19th June 1867 and its despatch to Burton, Manning Wardle 228 was allocated Burton Brewery's No.1 and carried 'Trade Mark and Brass Plates'.

Very little is known about the Burton Brewery Company's next locomotive which began work on 3rd September 1872. We can only surmise that it did not prove particularly successful because Manning Wardle sold another locomotive to the brewery company in 1877. By this time Manning Wardle had revised its standard class designations, with the old Class D becoming Class H. Consequently, the new locomotive (maker's number 593) was a Class H – one of four laid down for stock in February 1876. It was steamed in November 1877 and despatched a few days before Christmas. Obviously clearances at the brewery were fairly critical because it was specified that the

Manning Wardle 1427 had once been the Burton Brewery Company's No.4 before ending its days at the Beckton Gasworks in London, where it was photographed on 12th April 1958. The locomotive has lost its cab because of the restricted clearances at Beckton, but still displays the large buffers of plated oak which were necessary to avoid locking buffers at the brewery.
(J.A. Peden)

height of the locomotive should not exceed 3ft 8in from the top of the smokebox, although a 3ft 9in replacement chimney was fitted in 1893. The railway curves around the premises were also tight and No.3 was fitted with special buffer beams. The locomotive carried engraved brass plates which read 'THE BURTON BREWERY COMPANY LIMITED, BURTON UPON TRENT, No.3'. There was a local tradition among the brewery firms in the town that the title of each should be proudly displayed on their locomotives, not merely painted on but shown on a brass plate. In contrast, names for locomotives were uncommon and most just had a number.

Unfortunately, the Burton Brewery Company was not enjoying prosperous times. It had 'gone public' in 1888 but was in financial difficulties in 1894-95 when a fifth of the capital had to be written off. By the end of the century, No.3 was badly in need of repair and so a new locomotive was ordered, again from Manning Wardle, in September 1898. Delivery was specified in five months and this was almost achieved, the locomotive being steamed on 8th February 1899 and despatched to Burton on the same day. A more powerful Class P locomotive with 14in cylinders, No.4 (maker's number 1427) had several special features including the frames, buffer beams, a cab with wrought iron pillars and steam brakes. The builder elaborated that 'the outer buffer beams are of wood, plated with steel plates having large buffers of oak (plated)'. Overall height of the locomotive was 10ft 3¾in and brass owner plates were carried in the established tradition. The purchase of a new locomotive allowed the Burton Brewery Company to dispose of one of its existing stock. No.1 had received a new boiler in 1890 and so No.3 was sold. It went to Manning Wardle and was thoroughly overhauled by them in January 1899, being fitted with a new boiler, firebox, and a different braking arrangement, prior to being sold to J.D. Nowell & Sons for its GNR Harringay contract.

After unsuccessful attempts were made to merge with Allsopp and Salt, the Burton Brewery Company went into voluntary liquidation in 1906 and a receiver was appointed but it did not cease brewing until 1911. It still had many licensed outlets and these were then supplied with beer made by Salt. No doubt, the latter's locomotives worked the resultant traffic. The Burton Brewery Company's production plant and equipment fell into disuse and were acquired by Worthington on 23rd November 1914, together with the cooperage and ale stores at Wetmore Road and No.4 locomotive. What had happened to the original locomotive? It had been repaired at regular intervals, receiving another new boiler in 1902. The fact that it had a new copper firebox in July 1913 suggests that it outlasted the Burton Brewery Company, but when it passed out of the latter's ownership is not known. Fred Shorthose and a man named Clamp had been drivers for the Burton Brewery Company.

Worthington & Company

Worthington was one of the oldest brewing concerns in Burton and was to become amongst its most important. On 24th October 1862, the management of the company was taken over by William Worthington 3 and two of his sons, William Henry and Calvert. A third son, Albert Octavius was later included in the firm. William Worthington 3 died in 1871, to be followed by Calvert only a month later. In 1862, the brewery was located on the west side of High Street; the original establishment behind William Worthington 1's former house on the opposite side of the street being used as a wine and spirit vault. Mr Bindley was head brewer at that time.

Approval for the private railway from the Hay Branch to the brewery was secured on 30th June 1862. The railway was originally intended to pass through the wine vault's yard but would have involved the demolition of the Worthington house, so the line was built between the wine vaults and Miss Pratt's house on land which was then occupied by a coach house, stables, and domestic offices. Land was conveyed to Worthington on 10th July 1863, and on the 24th Worthington paid £1,300 to the Marquis of Anglesey for the enfranchisement of the lease so that it became the company's freehold property. Less than a month later, Worthington purchased the house formerly occupied by Miss Pratt who had died, and ultimately converted it into the firm's offices. Meanwhile, Worthington pressed ahead with the new railway. On the 14th November 1862, Thomas Lowe advised the company on 'getting ballast' out of Mr Wright's garden and the likely cost. Mr Wright lived in the original Worthington house and his garden extended down towards the Hay ditch. The ballast would have comprised river gravels. A week later, it was agreed that Thomas Lowe would

New Street Branch

B

Boilers

B
Cooperage

B

SB

Street

No. 5 Ale Store

New Loco

Hop and Ale Store

Cat Street Malthouse

Old
Loco

B

B

Station

B

B

Y

New
Racking
Room

Saw Mill

Water
Tank

Brewery

Old
Racking
Room

High

B

SB

Offices

Worthington's Original House

Street

Boilers

Friars Walk

B

B

Ale Store

Wine and Spirit Vaults

No. 15 Malt and Barley Store

No. 14 Malting

No. 12 Malting

River
Trent

Hay Branch

Worthington Brewery 1920

Midland Railway
Worthington's Private Railway

B   Bank
S B   Signal Box
Y   Yard Office

0 yards   100

Worthington's High Street crossing when it was still protected by manually operated wooden slatted gates probably in the 1880s. The prominent building is the old Worthington family house with the original Worthington Brewery behind which became the wine and spirit store and closed about 1900. *(R. Keene)*

obtain 500 cubic yards of ballast at not more than 11d per cubic yard measured in the heap and this was to come from Mr Wright's garden.

By 1865, two railway lines entered Worthington's premises from a conventional junction with the Hay Branch. One ran by the side of the vaults and over the High Street level crossing. The other terminated at the offices, with a siding serving a malting (later No.12) which then rejoined the Hay Branch at right angles via a wagon turntable. This had been the original junction for the private railway and the turntable was removed in the 1870s. Once across High Street, the other line continued on to the brewery and the Cat Street Malting. The latter was reputed to have been one of the oldest recently worked maltings in Burton when it was demolished in 1954. It had been built with extra large Jumbo bricks at a time when there was a duty on bricks.

There were small additions to the railway over the years, but in 1880-82, a new brewery was erected on the site of the existing brewery and some remnants of the old building were incorporated in it. The design was by Evans & Jolly of Nottingham and all of the engineering work, including 600 tons of ironwork, was carried out by Thornewill & Warham. The brewhouse bore the inscription 'WHW 1880 AOW'. Much of the original railway was retained. East of High Street, sidings were added to connect the No.14 Malting (erected 1876) and an ale store (erected 1912) to the system, requiring the diversion of Friars Walk. A Planet petrol locomotive was regularly employed shunting these lines and it often became derailed on the tight curves; before that, horses were used. One of them was quite a character and certainly intelligent. It would come round the curve by No.14 Malting just in answer to a whistle from its master. If two wagons were coupled up, it looked round as if to say that it was one too many. Billy Gray was the blacksmith, he was so gentle that the horse would pick up its own hoof so that he could shoe it. Another siding ran alongside the No.15 Malt and Barley Store, which was built at the same time as the brewery; it had a barley drying kiln at the Hay end and bore an identical inscription to that on the brewery.

The crossing over High Street was initially protected by manually operated vertically slatted wooden gates certainly up to the late 1880s. A set of more conventional crossing gates was then provided, together with a signal box painted in a buff colour. Frank Pretty once said that the box was put up in 1886. It was MR in style, and basically Type 1 in outline, but nothing is known about its origin. The box used to be manned to midnight to allow for workings over the crossing by the Yard Engine. On the last trip of the day, the gateman leant out, checked that they were going in, and asked the shunter to bring up the lamps. George Gilson was in the box in later years; he was 15

Worthington's Brewery in 1887 with men on the Old Racking Room ale bank pausing from their labours while the photograph is taken. *(R. Keene)*

when he lost an arm in the Zeppelin raid on Burton during World War 1. An old MR wooden signal protected the crossing. This type had been generally introduced on the MR in the late 1870s, had a white roundel on the red side of the arm, and was white with a black roundel on the reverse side. After 1906, this type of roundel began to be replaced by the more familiar stripe on the MR although a few could still be seen as late as 1911. Some of the signals on Worthington's railway remained in the old form until removal in 1967! If the gates on the General Office side of High Street had to be opened for any other purpose, than for the admission of rail traffic into the brewery yard, the gateman had to make sure that the distant signal was set at danger before opening the gates. Whenever possible, the locomotive was attached to the front of the train if it was working over the crossing. The shunter also went ahead to check that the line was clear before signalling to the driver to proceed.

West of High Street, there were two lines by the Old Racking Room and this allowed trains to pass a string of wagons being loaded at the bank. Beyond, a siding curved round behind the small two storey Yard Office to the New Racking Room and Old Engine Shed. Clearances were often minimal in the brewery premises and the Company's regulations stated that:

'In working round the Curve at the back of the Yard Offices, the Whistle must be blown, and a Shunter must walk at least six yards in front of the advancing Train, to ensure the Line being clear. This Rule also applies to the Curve round the Hop Room, and to all curves on the Brewery Premises.'

Despite this rule, an accident occurred here when the shunter whistled for Planet No.12 to move a load out of the bank. He then stepped through the narrow space between the locomotive and the Yard Office wall, caught his foot in the points, and fell in front of the locomotive. Sidings under the brewhouse allowed spent grains to be removed by being run off from the mash tuns into the waiting railway wagons below. Coal could also be brought in for the boilers. The trackwork near the Yard Office was very complicated and the cutting and trimming of the sleepers was a work of art. In the centre of the yard was an ale bank covered with a five spanned corrugated iron roof. It was used for storing racked casks until they could be loaded into railway wagons on either side of the bank for the journey to the ale stores. At the end of the yard, sidings were provided to the coopers' sawmill, engineers' shops, No.5 Ale Stores, the New Engine Shed and a bank for storing timber. At the finish, the railchairs on the branch were a typically varied collection with MR 1914 and 1919, LNER, and GWR chairs of 1904 to be seen.

In 1881, the Burton upon Trent (Station Street Extension) Railway Bill was placed before Parliament. Worthington was intent on linking its new cooperage and cask washing plant to the brewery and this required a railway to be constructed across Station Street. The Marklews held land and a right of way behind the Mayor's Arms which blocked Worthington's access to Station Street and, on the 6th December 1881, the following agreement was reached:

> 'Received from Messrs Worthington & Co, the sum of £100, the amount of compensation agreed to be paid by them to the late Miss Sarah Marklew for right of way in Station Street, Burton on Trent given up for the purposes of Messrs Worthington & Co's railway.
>
> Signed Henry Goodger, executor of the will of Miss Marklew.'

There was only a narrow space for the single track railway on the Mayor's Arms side of Station Street. Two short gates of equal length were provided there but were not overlapped because of the difficulty of opening them. Consequently, one (A) folded back through 180° along the wall of the public house and the other (B) closed the gap between the brewery yard and Station Street. On the wheel mechanism in the box, there was a separate gear for (A) giving twice the speed of that for (B) and the two gates on the cooperage side. The latter were both long overlapping gates but did not reach from post to post, and so were not difficult to open. The MR sent a man to organise the arrangement. Frank Pretty told of a shunting horse which worked in the cooperage yard. To clear

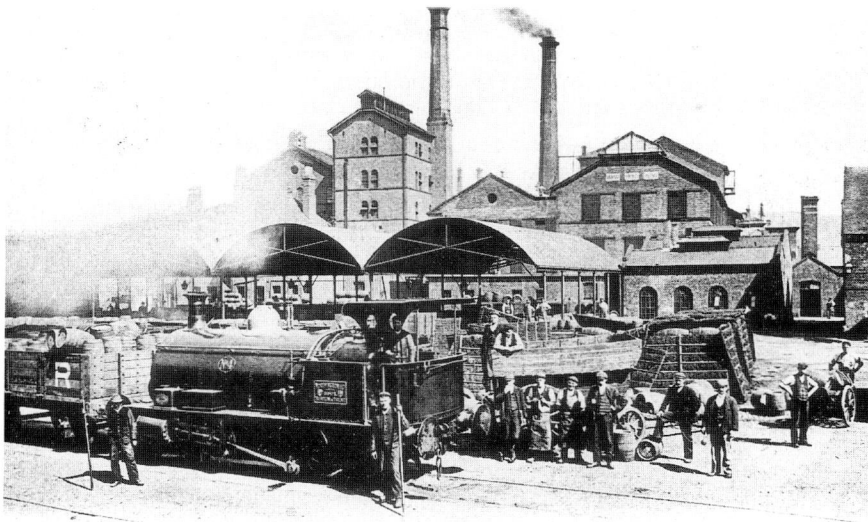

Worthington's Brewery, Burton-on-Trent

The other side of the brewery in 1909, with Worthington's No.4 locomotive next to the covered ale bank. On the right is the Old Locomotive Shed and the higher ridge of the roof over two of the lines is clearly visible.   (J.A. Peden Collection)

No.22 propels wagons between the Yard Office and the covered ale bank to Worthington's New Racking Room bank on 12th June 1964.   (C. Shepherd)

the points, the horse would come right up to the gates and whilst standing there, bit the top rail of the inner gate. Frank said its liking for the resin in the pitch pine was such that he had to eventually fit a mild steel plate to protect the rail in order to reduce the frequency of repairs. A tall private signal box was provided to control the crossing and it used to be operated by an old man with a huge beard. When Worthington's locomotives were approaching, they had to give three whistles to warn the signalman that they wanted to cross Station Street and two whistles for the High Street level crossing. Two railway lines ran through to the end of the cooperage; one provided an outlet to the New Street Branch (connection opened 20th May 1881), although it latterly stabled wagons waiting for accommodation on the other line which served the cask washing bank. The siding at the end nearest Station Street was known as 'the Little Dustpast'. A short siding was also provided for coal wagons being taken to the boilers. In World War 1, the company had to screen the boilers and lights at the cooperage with old hop sacks.

In the late nineteenth century, the business of Worthington & Company flourished based on the excellence of its malting and beers under the guidance of Horace Tabberer Brown and with the forceful direction of William Posnette Manners, who rose from a position of junior clerk to become managing director. By 1900, Worthington produced 369,719 barrels of beer and had a considerable London trade, a train being despatched to Broad Street every weekday.

From 1st December 1894, Worthington took over the lease of the former Saunders Maltings from the Burton Brewery Company and in the following year paid £40 per annum to the MR so that it could work over the Saunders Branch. It demolished the maltings and on their site, Thomas Lowe began to erect two new maltings in 1899 (Nos.3 and 4 Wetmore Road) for Worthington. They were connected to the Saunders Branch from 15th January 1902, only minor modifications being required to the sidings. Demolition also allowed a line to be extended into Thompson's former brewery premises in Horninglow Street. Thompson had begun loading ale on the railway on the 22nd May 1865 but it is not known where. Marston, Thompson & Evershed later used some of these buildings as a cold store. Worthington did not begin production immediately at the former Burton Brewery Company's plant in High Street. A lot of renewal and some additions were required and the intervention of the War meant that essential equipment could not be obtained. Brewing did not start until the early 1920s when it became the company's No.2 Brewery. It had been reported to be unlikely to be ready by mid summer 1921 because Morton was still installing plant.

Amalgamations and closures naturally led to some reduction in the variety and colour of locomotives seen chuffing back and forth along the Hay Branch, but it nevertheless continued to present an interesting spectacle. The railway company had to visit the branch to shunt those sidings not belonging to the brewery firms and, in fact, its locomotives were the last to use the branch. Their main duty was keeping the Corporation Gasworks supplied with coal. The Works was erected in 1853-54 and a siding was provided when the branch opened. Additional lines entered the premises by 1882 and these were extended to the Corporation Electricity Works when it began operating in 1894. At the beginning of the twentieth century, about 33,000 tons of coal were being carbonised and 11,000 tons of coke were being produced at the gasworks each year. Both concerns were nationalised after World War 2, the gasworks passing to the East Midlands Gas Board on 1st May 1949. The MR Hay Wharf was located at the foot of the Burton Bridge and there were always a few wagons in the siding. Sam Tilley collected his coal from here by horse and cart for delivery to houses in Winshill.

The most frequent visitors from the railway company were 6-coupled tank locomotives, but occasionally one of the MR 0-4-0s, the 'Coffee Pots', would put in an appearance. They had a very rudimentary cab which was open at the back. One day during World War 2, a 'Coffee Pot' had brought some empties to the Hay Sidings and was preparing to run back. Ernest Chapman was on a Worthington locomotive and his mate commented 'Here's Coffee coming'. It had begun to rain and the little four-wheeler stopped near the Baths whilst the shunter began to drape an old tarpaulin over the back to give some shelter. There was a detachment of soldiers waiting at the Baths and one of them shouted "You needn't cover the bloody thing up, we've seen it!" The 0-6-0 tank locomotive

A Worthington Hudswell Clarke locomotive rushes the floods at the Hay Sidings about 1912. Most of the wagons belong to the MR but the two wagons full of wet grains are NSR. The impressive building facade belongs to Salt's and the Burton Brewery Company's breweries, with Allsopp's Old Brewery and the Hay Signal Box further away amongst the steam and smoke.   (J.S. Simnett)

shunting the gasworks was a nuisance for the brewery companies' drivers because of the long line of wagons it left on the branch.

The Hay Branch and some of its associated sidings passed under the Burton Bridge through two openings formed by iron girders, which contrasted with the remaining brick and stone arches. This ground was always prone to flooding and, as the *Burton Mail* of the 9th January 1900 reported, 'the locomotives had to get up steam and rush the flood.' It was particularly difficult during the dark winter evenings because the only light came from the lamps on the bridge. One night about 8 or 9 o'clock, a Planet locomotive stuck in the flood water. Fortunately, a Hudswell Clarke steam locomotive was still up at Dixie and it was summoned to the rescue. The shunter had to be issued with thigh boots for these conditions. He would make his way gingerly up the track ahead of the train feeling with his shunting pole for the point levers. In the dark and with the water, it often seemed that the wagons on the next road were moving. He then had to roll his sleeves up so that he could reach down into the water and change the points. With the route set, he waved his green lamp for the driver who sounded his whistle and put on all steam so as to keep moving through the floodwater. Even in normal circumstances, the visibility under the bridge was not very good and drivers had to take care to ascertain that the way was clear. After sunset, and during fog or falling snow, the driver had to bring his locomotive to a stand whilst the shunter checked that all was well on the other side of the bridge.

After Salt closed, the only private locomotives working along the Hay Branch belonged to Worthington and Bass, with the former being particularly prominent. The Hay Branch was the main outlet for its traffic and the company had taken over responsibility for operating most of the ex Burton Brewery Company's and Salt's premises. There was also little space available at Worthington's Breweries and it made considerable use of the Hay Sidings for storing and marshalling wagons. Of the sidings to the north east of Burton Bridge, one brought coal to the Hay Wharf; the next was a through line under the bridge which could stabled 50 to 60 empty wagons; and the last, terminating at the bridge, held wagons with filled casks from the ale stores eventually destined for the exchange sidings. Worthington also operated the Walsitch Maltings, and the nearby old coopers' buildings at the Mount Pleasant end of the property, were adapted by Shepherd & Hough for maintaining their petrol lorries. They were responsible for Bass's and Worthington's local deliveries until Bass, Mitchells, & Butlers own lorry fleet rendered them unnecessary about 1962-63. The ale stores on either side of Wetmore Road became Worthington's No.2 or Newton Ale Stores (ex Burton Brewery Company) and the No.3 Remote Ale Stores (ex Salt). 'Newton' was a reference to a long forgotten previous owner of the land.

It was here that Alfred Hill, Worthington's Chief Engineer, was inspecting the ale stores when the floods were up. He was walking along the line by the bank making sure to step on the sleepers because of the depth of water. Suddenly, he disappeared from view and only his hat could be seen on top of the water. Unknown to him, a deep hole had been excavated to reach some pipework! The usually immaculate Chief Engineer was unhurt if a little bedraggled. Harry Pretty was in charge of the ale stores and he was talking to Percy Thornell, the Bass Engineer's chauffeur, on the bank when it happened. Percy was sent post haste to Hill's home at 27 Ashby Road for a change of clothing "Don't worry ma'am – he's all right" he assured Hill's wife and the Chief Engineer was seen later in the day apparently none the worse for his ordeal.

Worthington's steam locomotives shunted the breweries and took traffic up to the main line sidings. The Planets, or 'Petrols' as they were often known, spent much of their time around the ale stores and maltings. One was specifically allocated to the duties at No.2 Ale Stores and another was at the No.3 Stores, and they alternated each week. The Brewery Engine would leave wagons at the sidings and a Planet then moved a few at a time to the Ale Stores' banks. Sometimes, if the Planet was blocked in by wagons still being loaded, the waiting steam locomotive would clear the other ale bank siding. The drivers on the Planets were Ernest Chapman and either Harry Toplis or Jim Barton on the other; Ernest had joined Worthington sometime after the end of World War 1, beginning by working in the maltings in the winter at both High Street and No.9 Walsitch, and ale loading in the summer. It was not long before he agreed to become a shunter and, as part of his training, a number of wagons were buffered up on a line in the Hay Sidings and he spent the next three days running up one side uncoupling them and back down the other side coupling them up again. The three link couplings were difficult enough for the inexperienced but the later screw couplings were to prove very heavy to lift. Shunting poles were made of hickory and the shunters had to oil them once a week to stop them splitting. Both men booked on at No.3 Ale Stores at 6am and then went to fetch the Planets out of Salt's shed, which was handily placed for these duties. Ernest Chapman occasionally had No.7 but his regular Planet was No.12 which he preferred because of its taller cab. Generally, the newer Planets were used on the two jobs because, despite appearances, there was a difficult gradient working round the curve to No.2 Ale Stores. It was sometimes necessary to pass a rope round a capstan to give some assistance to the locomotive. No.2 Ale Stores closed about 1962-63 and it was sold with Nos.16 and 17 Maltings to the Clarke organisation about 1967-68. Ernest Chapman then shunted at the No.3 Ale Stores every week and the operator of the other Planet went driving at Bass. With the

An old MR signal at Worthington's Brewery with an internal ash wagon. 3rd March 1963. (C. Shepherd)

declining traffic, the points to these stores were hand operated from 1st April 1963 following the closure of Salt's Engine Shed Signal Box; the latter dated from 21st April 1907. Eventually, Ernest Chapman was put on the Yard job at the High Street Brewery which, with the run down, could easily be done by a Planet. The No.3 Ale Stores finally closed in 1972 but rail traffic had finished some years before.

The Closure of the Branches

The shutdown of premises was nothing new. Following the merger with Bass, some of Worthington's beers began to be produced at Bass' Old Brewery and Worthington's No.2 Brewery was stopped in 1933-34. Indeed, Bass had brewed for Worthington since October 1926 even before the formal merger had taken place. The plant was removed over the next four years but most of the derelict building stood until the Bargates shopping development was started in the early 1960s. Up to then, it had still been possible to look down an entry off High Street and see the end of one of the former Burton Brewery Company's sidings. The introduction of cask washing machines meant that the Middle Yard and Shobnall could cope with all Worthington's requirements for cleaning casks. Both Salt's former cooperage in Wetmore Road and Worthington's No.1 Cooperage at Station Street closed, the latter in 1936. The Station Street level crossing gates were padlocked but the lines were left so that they could be used in an emergency. A shunter then had to go across and operate the gates. If flooding blocked the normal outlet to the Hay, it was possible to open up this alternative route with Worthington's locomotives running through the cooperage yard and along the New Street and Bond End Branches to hand traffic over to the railway company at Shobnall. A pilotman would

George Gilson opening Worthington's High Street gates by hand on 4th July 1966. No.4 is bringing in an empty wagon to be filled with scrap from the demolition of the brewery.

(C. Shepherd)

ride on the footplate, presumably to operate the railway company's gates and points where necessary. It only happened once in the three years to World War 2. Most of the cooperage buildings and associated sidings were not removed until 1968.

After World War 2, Worthington's No.1 Brewery at High Street was refurbished with new coppers, Burton Unions, and another boiler house. It was transformed into a reasonable unit although was fairly expensive to operate. The Worthington beer brewed at the Old Brewery was said to have a different character to that coming from the No.1 Brewery, despite the use of identical materials and water. This was possibly because the wort and beer received a great deal of agitation with the frequent pumping between levels at the No.1 Brewery.

Both Bass and Worthington steam locomotives shunted the No.1 Brewery in 1961. The change to diesels took place in the following year and it was one of the first lines on the Bass Worthington system to be consistently worked by diesels. They were either the Baguley 204hp or Sentinel 207hp locomotives. In February 1963, there was a reduction in brewing and the Old Racking Room ale bank was taken out of use, leaving just the New Racking Room bank. A few months later, the Baguley 107hp diesels appeared and No.11 especially became a frequent performer on the Brewery job, working with either Planet No.17 or No.22. Bass's No.5 also put in a brief spell in January 1964 before going for overhaul. The amounts of rail traffic in beer, malt, and spent grains were small in those last years of operation but the unfortunate George Gilson still had to open the level crossing gates eighteen times during the day across one of Burton's busiest main streets. Nos.8 and 22 were working into the brewery on the 29th December 1964 and No.19 and a newly painted No.18 were also seen during the first half of 1965. By late June, the number of trains running into Worthington's Brewery had been reduced to a morning and afternoon working with grain vans. These were brought in by No.6 as part of its job on the Hay and Old Brewery shunt. In early 1966, the demolition of the brewery began and the High Street gates were disconnected from the signal box to aid quicker entry in case of fire. The last rail traffic consisted of the occasional wagon taking away scrap; a story which had started in 1754 had ended.

All floor malting ceased at Bass and Worthington by 1965-66. Sleaford closed after the 1958-59 season, to be followed by Nos.16 and 17 Maltings at Anderstaff Lane, and later Nos.18-21 and Walsitch. There were still a few grain vans to be seen on the siding by No.15 Malting at Worthington's premises in June 1964, but the network of lines at the back of No.14 Malting was rusty and the surrounding buildings disused. Wetmore Road Nos.3 and 4 had been made into refined floor maltings, pneumatic and mechanised for all year working, but they were not as efficient as the drum maltings at Shobnall. They were later serviced by road transport until gutted by fire on 4th January

Train working at Worthington's High Street Brewery on 2nd June 1964

Time	Locomotive	Direction	Activity
7.30am	22	-	Shunts wagons
8.40am	22	out	Light engine
8.51am	22	in	8 wagons, 2 shunted *
9.10am	22	-	Shunts wagons
9.20am	22	out	5 wagons loaded with casks
9.30am	22	in	Light engine
10.00am	11	in	Light engine
10.43am	11	out	Light engine
11.00am	22	-	Shunts wagons
11.06am	22	out	4 empty grain vans
11.07am	22	in	Light engine
11.16am	22	-	Shunts wagons
11.23am	22	out	5 wagons loaded with casks
12.30pm	11	in	Light engine
2.12pm	11	out	6 wagons loaded with casks
2.13pm	22	out	Light engine
2.24pm	22	in	8 wagons *
2.25pm	22	out	Light engine
2.40pm	22	in	9 wagons *
2.41pm	22	-	Shunts wagons
3.17pm	22	-	Shunts wagons
3.27pm	22	out	3 wagons of spent grains
3.28pm	22	in	Light engine
3.33pm	22	out	5 wagons loaded with casks
3.54pm	22	in	6 wagons *
4.30pm	22	-	Shunts wagons
4.58pm	22	-	Shunts wagons
5.00pm	22	out	10 loaded wagons
5.19pm	22	in	Light engine
6.15pm	11	in	4 loaded grain vans

Notes
* Most incoming wagons contained empty casks.

1978, by which time they were due for closure, once the new tower plant had been installed at Shobnall.

Racking stopped at Bass' Old and New Breweries as soon as bridges were erected over High Street and Station Street to carry pipelines from the breweries to a new racking plant near the ale stores at the Middle Brewery site. All beer was piped to the new plant allowing much of the railway to be closed at the end of March 1967. After some final clearing up, the last train of ten wagons driven by Reginald Brooks passed over the High Street and Guild Street level crossings on the Monday afternoon of 8th May 1967. At the High Street Crossing Signal Box, Bill Foxall of Woodville opened the gates for the last time and the line from Guild Street to the Hay and the Burton Bridge was lifted soon after. High Street Crossing Box, demolished on 9th October 1968, was a most unusual box tapering from half the normal width at the street end to a quarter of the normal width at the other end where the door was situated. In fact, the doorway was virtually the end! This abnormality also meant that a sloping hipped roof had to be used. The box had been erected in 1889 and its dimensions were dictated by the proximity of the house and its outbuildings at 132 High Street occupied by the Head Brewer at Bass' Old Brewery. No doubt, the box caused many a visitor to look twice, particularly if they had not long emerged from the allowance room! The name of the signal box was displayed on a MR enamelled iron plate with white letters on an ultramarine background, in contrast to the more customary wooden board with raised iron letters found on many of the boxes in the town.

A new loading bay was provided at the Middle Brewery site to continue allowing some beer to

Last days of steam on the Hay Branch. Top shows where the MR had straightened the River Trent and infilled behind the retaining wall. The locomotive is working past the former Burton Brewery Company malting and Salt's ale stores on 22nd July 1966. Middle. Anderstaff Lane Signal Box seen from the cab of an unlikely trip locomotive, Class 8F 2-8-0 48681, on 27th July 1967. Bottom. 47643 crosses Wetmore Road on 22nd July 1966. The original Anderstaff Lane Signal Box had opened on 14th October 1867. Replacements were provided in 1881 and 1904, and the box closed on 1st March 1969.

Bass' No.7 has the honour of working the last train over the High Street level crossing on the Guild Street Branch. 8th May 1967.   *(Burton Mail)*

be sent out by rail and Bass bought the Guild Street Branch between Dixie and High Street from BR on 19th November 1968 to secure access along part of it to Horninglow Bridge. The resultant siding was shunted by one of British Railway's 350hp diesels, but amounts of traffic were small, and the track was finally closed on 31st March 1973 and lifted the same year. Horninglow Bridge Signal Box had been reduced in status to a shunting frame on 15th June 1969 and closed on 2nd December 1973. Closure of the Old Brewery took place in January 1969 because there was no longer the demand for high gravity beers, and anyway, a new brewery had been erected by Bass on the site of the Delhi Maltings; the Old Brewery was held in reserve for about two years before it was mostly demolished in 1971. The Electric Cooperage finished in 1970 after Bass stopped using wooden casks and the buildings were converted to a maintenance depot for the lorry fleet. The New Brewery, opened back in 1864, remained hard at work sending out non carbonated beers but its days were also numbered. It closed in 1982 and was demolished in 1985-86.

The last rail traffic along the remnants of the Hay Branch had been coal for the gasworks but this finally ceased and the line up to the Mount Pleasant Bridge was downgraded to a siding on 1st March 1969 and abandoned shortly afterwards.

CHAPTER SEVEN

THE RAILWAYS AT SHOBNALL

Bass' Shobnall Maltings

Bass first acquired land at Shobnall in 1871-72 and soon erected a substantial range of seven maltings designed by the Chief Engineer William Canning. Numbers 1 to 4 were completed by Lowe in 1873, 5 and 6 in 1874, and 7 in 1875. Construction then had to stop because of problems with the foundations due to the presence of running sands. When Barnard visited Shobnall in 1887, he was able to take in 'the noble proportion of this splendid range of maltings which are said to be the largest belonging to any one firm in the world.' They were built of brick with roofs covered by Bangor slates and gables coped with Hollington stone. Each block was almost identical with 190 quarter steeping cisterns and consisted of four storeys. Barley was stored on the top floor until required when it was then spread out on the remaining floors for processing by germination and carefully controlled growth. When ready, the grain was taken to the kilns where it was dried and cured to become malt. In the middle of the group of maltings was the engine house occupied by two 40hp steam engines, manufactured by Abell of Derby, to operate the shafting, machinery and six sets of pumps for raising water up to the tower.

Use of a railway to reach the new construction site was an urgent requirement. The temporary expedient was adopted of filling in part of the Bond End Canal and extending the existing siding from the main line along the course of the canal to the maltings. After this railway opened on 28th April 1873, it is presumed that horses were initially employed because the MR locomotives only shunted the maltings from 9th November 1874 to 10th April 1875. Bass then had sufficient of its own locomotives available, but was unable to reach Shobnall directly until the Bond End Branch was laid from the New Brewery. This became available on 1st December 1875. In the meantime, Bass' locomotives were allowed to run along the main line through the passenger station between Shobnall

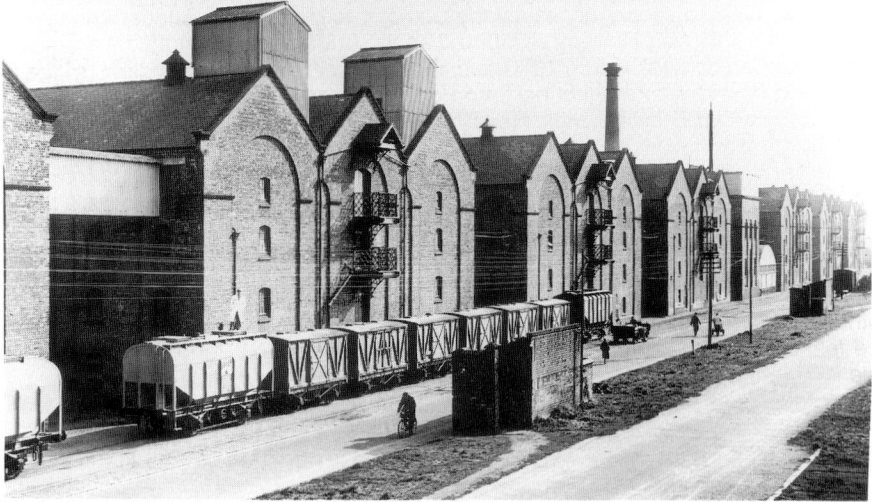

Nos.1-7 Maltings at Shobnall, together with some of Bass' metal bulk grain vans and ex MR wooden vans.   *(Bass Museum Collection)*

and Dixie accompanied by a MR pilotman. No other information has been found concerning this arrangement, but it would seem likely that the MR handled much of the traffic to and from Shobnall, with Bass' locomotives assuming responsibility for shunting the maltings. A return along the main line to Bass' Guild Street shed would be required when servicing became due.

The original connection with the main line was soon replaced by the Shobnall Branch which swept round from Leicester Junction to Wellington Street Junction, the new curve opening on 27th November 1876 when the former connection closed. Wagons awaiting entry to Sharp Bros & Knight's works were subsequently stored on the remaining spur of this connection. The signal box at Leicester Junction was replaced on 3 occasions, the last opening on 9th February 1902 and continuing in use until 15th June 1969. At Wellington Street Junction, the branch joined the original railway which ran over an unadopted field lane, later widened into a modern road called Wellington Street Extension. When the original line swung away towards Bass' maltings, the branch continued on to serve the MR Shobnall Exchange Sidings (190 wagons capacity). An extension to the Trent & Mersey Canal had opened for traffic on 2nd November 1874. Nearby was the MR's Shobnall Wharf situated alongside a basin comprising the last remnant of the Bond End Canal. The MR shunted the wharf and its attendant coal depot which had opened on 28th April 1878. Both Staton & Newton and Mann, Crossman & Paulin began to use these facilities from the opening of the line. The junction with Bass' lines was controlled by Shobnall Junction Signal Box. Records state that the MR provided a gateman for the 'Shobnall level crossing leading to Bass & Co's maltings' on 23rd January 1878.

Bass' railways at Shobnall were carefully designed from the beginning to permit efficient working. They consisted of a series of loops with each encircling a particular part of the premises and giving access to both sides of the buildings. Wagons passed directly under hoists or chutes and alongside the raised banks. For example, a Bass locomotive could leave wagons laden with sacks of barley under the hoists on one end of the maltings and run round the block to be ready for the return, possibly picking up wagons with sacks of malt en route. The Old Ale Stores and a cask washing plant had been established at Shobnall by 1882 and another part of the area had been laid out as a stave yard. The latter was used for storing oak slabs, from which the cask staves were made, and for seasoning timber. It was said that the ideal length of time for seasoning was one year per inch of thickness. As much as 25 acres could be covered with timber and this might spread on to the cask washing bank. Some of it had to be moved if the cask cleansing department needed more space. When ready, the staves were taken in railway wagons to the steam cooperage.

William Canning, the man responsible for the fine set of maltings, retired after twenty five years as Bass' Chief Engineer. He was born in 1823 and had first come to Burton on the 1st November 1846 as a surveyor and engineer on the construction of the railway from Leicester. Old hands in Bass' Engineers' Office used to tell how he had narrowly missed death or serious injury when driving Gresley Tunnel. When the MR was involved with the construction of the Burton Bridge, he was the site engineer responsible for the infill, revetment, and layout of the Hay Branch. This remarkable man became Bass' Chief Engineer in 1867 and was best remembered for his embankment which eased the dire effects of perennial flooding in the town; well might people who had suffered in the past say God bless Alderman Canning."

The authoritarian Herbert A. Couchman came as assistant to Canning in 1891, and soon made his presence felt, although Canning remained as Chief Engineer until June 1892. Couchman's first work was the No.8 Malting and engine house at Shobnall. These were built in 1891 and were sited away from the other maltings on firmer ground. Bass' railway was extended to serve both ends of the new malting. Far more structural steelwork was used in the building and it was to be the forerunner of the magnificent range of eight maltings erected in 1901-06 at Sleaford in Lincolnshire. Couchman marked his accession to office by introducing a number of stringent regulations upon employees in his department. He was not in favour of the men drinking their allowance beer during working hours and suggested that oat meal and water would be a more refreshing alternative! He also tried to stop the concession of the men being allowed fifteen minutes to walk from the outlying

Railways at Shobnall 1900
with subsequent changes

Key (lines):
- ——— Midland Railway
- –·–·– London & North Western Railway
- ········ Private Railways
- +++++++ Railways added after 1900

- B Bank
- C Cairo Well Pumphouse
- E Engine House
- L Boilers
- M Maltings
- N Nile Well Pumphouse
- R Running in Shed
- S Shed
- T Water Tank
- W Washing out Shed

Key to Signal Boxes
1 Shobnall Crossing
2 Shobnall Junction
3 Wellington Street Junction
4 Shobnall Maltings
■ Later positions of Signal Box

Map labels:
Marston, Thompson & Son Albion Brewery
Shobnall Road
Crossman Street
Shobnall Wharf
Dallow Lane Branch
Shobnall Exchange Sidings
Bass Cottages
Stables
No. 1
No. 2
No. 3
No. 4
No. 5
No. 6
No. 7
Walker (Peter) & Son Warrington & Burton Brewery
The Tablet Road
New Ale Stores
Footbridge
Bottling Stores, erected c.1913
Old Ale Cellar
Cask Washing Plant
Bass, Ratcliff and Gretton Ltd.
Stave Yard
Trent and Mersey Canal
Platelayers' Storage
Platelayers' Materials
Signal Box (removed by 1922)
Klondyke Sidings
Coal Yard (sidings added pre 1922)
Ash Tip (siding added c. 1940)
No. 8 Malting
Added post 1937
PH

Scale: 0 yards 100 200 300 400

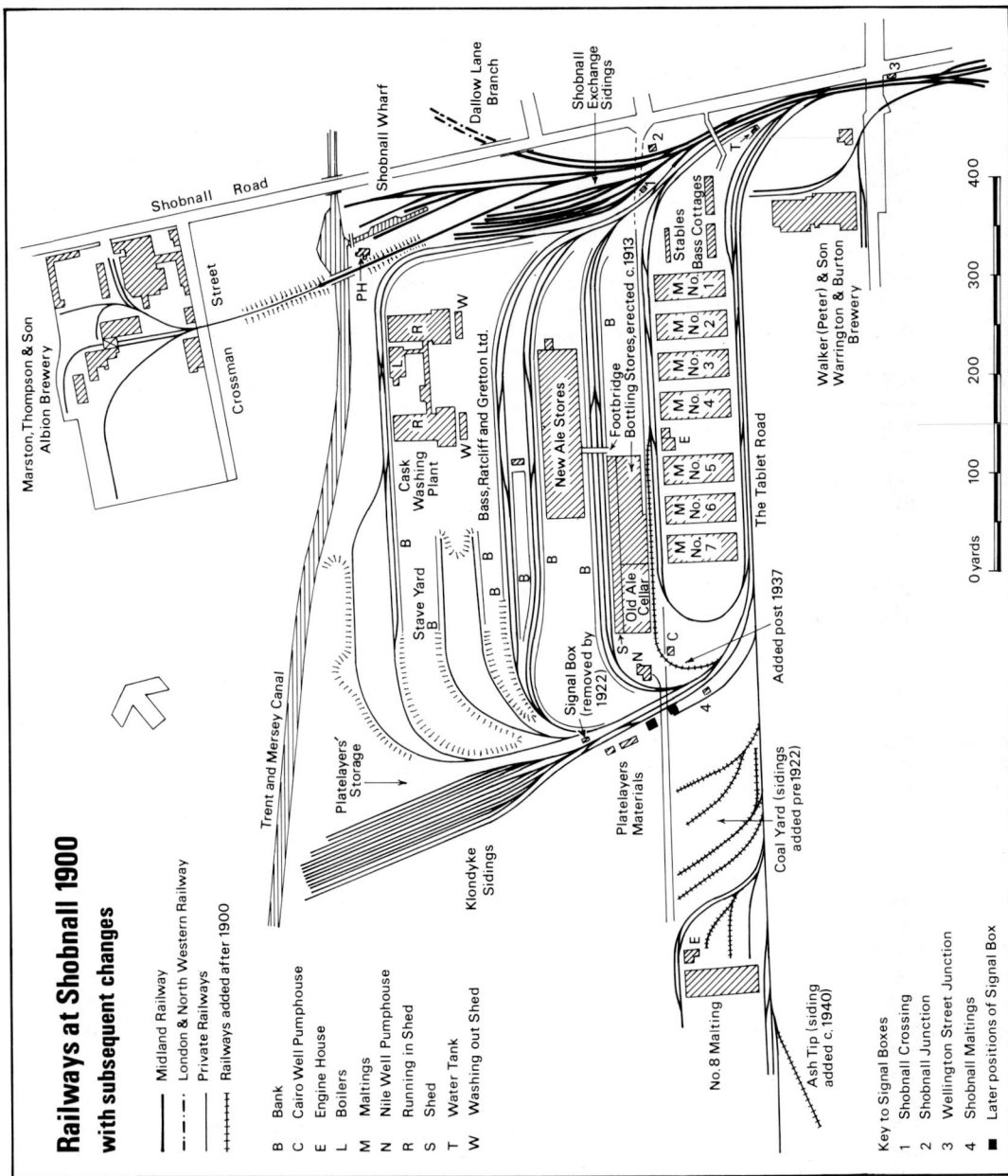

premises, such as Shobnall, to clock off at the time offices. He insisted that they must work until the bull (buzzer) blew and walk in their own time. By early November 1892, the whole department was out on strike and the directors ordered Couchman to withdraw his regulations.

Most of the beer from the New Brewery came by rail to the ale stores at Shobnall. These were augmented in 1895 when Couchman constructed the New Ale Stores over the new ale cellar. They

Bass' No.10 waits to depart from the New Ale Stores at Shobnall on a sunny 12th April 1963.
(C. Shepherd)

were enlarged by 50% around the turn of the century. The casks could be loaded directly into the waiting railway wagons ready for despatch to different parts of the country. In warm weather, a Bass locomotive would collect the waiting wagons and haul them slowly away from the bank underneath a cold water spray; a process known as 'sparging' which helped to ensure that the beer left in the best possible condition. The following notes prepared in 1925 describe the scene:

'Imagine yourself standing in any one of the Ale Loading Stores on a week day morning. The first person you meet is the Head Storekeeper. In his hands are the orders for the day dealing with consignments for delivery at destinations reached by every Railway Co. in the Kingdom, and at the ports for export to countries all over the world. According to the area and the destination, the times at which the consignments must be ready are printed on his "slips". Not far away from him you will find his men getting the casks ready, filling up those which require it; the Cooper tightening the hoops and closing the casks; the man with the Company's seal; the Number Takers, and lastly the labeller. The casks are now ready, and the Railway Dept. Foreman, at the head of a gang of ale loaders, appears on the scene. Stepping out on to the platform, we see the casks being rolled into a long line of wagons ready for despatch. Then the engine arrives, and on a signal from the Foreman, the Shunter in charge of the train gives the "right away" and off she goes to make her connection with the departures of the Railway Co. concerned.'

In 1895, Couchman was replaced as Chief Engineer by William Baker Ollis, possibly because his brusque dictatorial way of dealing with his workers was alien to the traditional Bass approach. Ollis administered the department, leaving Couchman free to build, invent, and perfect his works much as before. He was scrupulous about standards of workmanship and always used the best materials. Shortly after 1900, the cask washing sheds at Shobnall were being extended. The bank

111

tapered at the end and the men had erected the columns slightly out of line. Luckily Couchman had not noticed and he went to Sleaford on Mondays. A man was posted to see him leave Shobnall Grange and, having heard the whistle of the GNR train departing, they set to work to remedy the fault. Unfortunately, Couchman had missed the train and he came up to Shobnall to start the day's work, catching them redhanded. He preferred red and brindle bricks from Hall, Nadin and Stanton of South Derbyshire and special egg shaped sewer pipes for Sleaford from Knowles and Wraggs. Couchman retired in 1917, leaving behind him some memorable buildings, but the name of W.B. Ollis has largely been forgotten.

The Tablet Road

In the mid 1890s, Bass decided that additional siding capacity was required for the exchange of traffic with the MR. A site was initially considered alongside the MR main line on the opposite side to the Branston sidings and plans were prepared for a yard with a capacity of 500 wagons. This proposal was eventually dropped, and instead, Bass opened its Klondyke exchange sidings at Shobnall in December 1897. There were thirteen lines, plus the extension of the Tablet Road which was kept empty unless some special requirement arose. Klondyke was capable of holding 400 wagons. Back in the 1870s, Bass had considered an abortive scheme for a canal basin on the site of Klondyke, together with proposals for steam boats on the canal. If it had come to fruition, the steam machine cooperage would have been built in line with, and not far from, the canal.

The MR had to work over Bass' private railway to reach the new sidings and it insisted on proper safeguards to avoid two trains meeting head on. As a result, the railway lines to the east of Nos.1 to 7 Maltings were remodelled to create a single line separate from the other sidings. The four

About the last decade of the nineteenth century, the MR introduced what is now identified as the Type 3 signal box, which could be either 10ft or 12ft wide. The previous Type 2 had generally been 10ft wide, although a few were made 12ft 10in by the addition of another section. Wellington Street Junction was an example of the wide Type 2 box and was amongst the last to be built when opened on 24th February 1901. Seen here on 26th December 1965, it was designated as a 'gate box only' on 17th March 1968 and was taken out of use on 10th June 1968. (C. Shepherd)

lines approaching the north east end of the maltings became, in order, the Tablet Road/Bass running line/malting line/short machine line. There was a weighbridge on the latter and the accompanying small cabin was eventually used by the drivers and shunters as a messroom. The driver would walk down to it, whilst the locomotive was being coaled and watered. A rivetted water tank supported on brick piers, together with a small water softening plant, was located near the metal footbridge which gave access to the Bass cottages. The footbridge was erected in 1883 and the MR paid half of the cost. When there was flooding at the Bridge Hole, a Bass locomotive would be stabled overnight by the water tank and a man had to be sent up from the shed to attend to the fire.

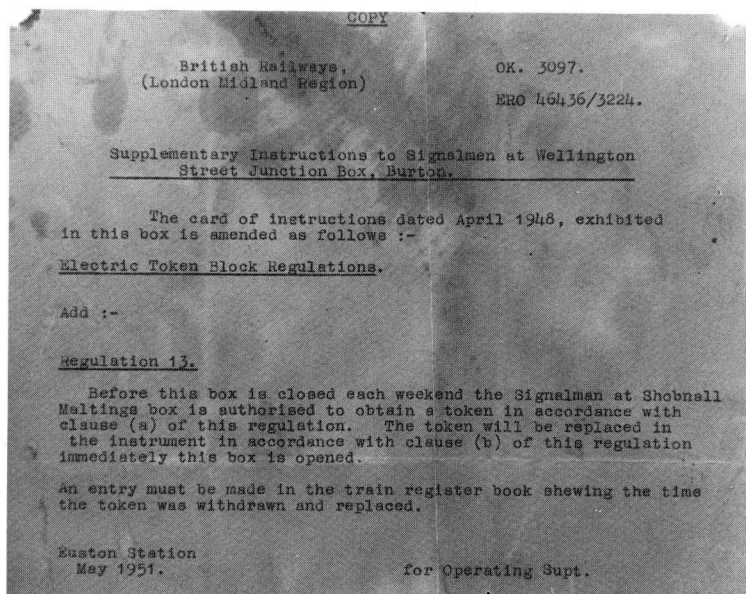

COPY

British Railways,
(London Midland Region)

OK. 3097.

ERO 46436/3224.

Supplementary Instructions to Signalmen at Wellington
Street Junction Box, Burton.

The card of instructions dated April 1948, exhibited in this box is amended as follows :-

Electric Token Block Regulations.

Add :-

Regulation 13.

Before this box is closed each weekend the Signalman at Shobnall Maltings box is authorised to obtain a token in accordance with clause (a) of this regulation. The token will be replaced in the instrument in accordance with clause (b) of this regulation immediately this box is opened.

An entry must be made in the train register book shewing the time the token was withdrawn and replaced.

Euston Station
May 1951.

for Operating Supt.

The MR carried out the alterations to the lines and installed the electric token system. Wellington Street Junction Signal Box and Shobnall Maltings Signal Box at either end of the single line were equipped with the Tyers tablet instruments which were electrically interlocked; the instrument in Shobnall Malting Box being purchased by Bass from the MR. If a tablet was removed from either instrument, it was impossible to take another tablet out unless the first had been replaced in one or the other instrument. The speed of trains on the single line was restricted to 10mph and the MR also insisted that all wagons worked from Leicester Junction to Shobnall Maltings should be positioned in front of the locomotive and that a guards van should be attached at the head of the train. Loads were limited to 30 wagons. In BR days, it was specified that trains were only to be propelled in clear weather during daylight. Later relaxations included increasing the maximum load to 35 wagons and not requiring the use of a brakevan. The exit from the Tablet Road towards Wellington Street was controlled by a bracket signal, the taller arm being for trains following the curve round to the main line and the other for trains heading towards the Bond End Branch. Joe Slater reckoned that when they were coming off the machine line line, "we whistled to indicate whether we were going to Burton or under the footbridge to Shobnall. Wellington Street Junction Box called us on by flag before we passed the signal post."

The signalbox controlling the Klondyke end of the Tablet Road had a chequered career. It was a two storey MR type box originally positioned near the junction with the line to No.8 Malting and opened in 1897. When it had been erected, Bass' traffic manager, William Walters, wrote to

Operating the Tyers tablet instrument inside Shobnall Sidings Signal Box about 1926. *(Bass Museum Collection)*

Couchman enquiring what the new box was to be called. Couchman replied to the effect that he did not care and Walters could call it what he liked! On 8th January 1923, the box was moved to the west side of the vehicular road leading to No.8 Malting. This allowed the signalman to hang a flag out of the box to stop the road traffic because there were no crossing gates. The box was renamed Shobnall Sidings and it was later cut down to a single storey structure. In 1952, it was replaced and Bass paid BR £200 for the signal box from Swadlincote Station. This was erected on the opposite side of the road and was named Shobnall Maltings. Sergeant Billy Garnham, who had fought in World War 1, was the regular signalman for many years. He was followed by Norman Littlewood.

Special bellcode at Shobnall Maltings Signal Box

Signals exchanged with Wellington Street Junction Signal Box.

Midland		Midland	
Engine in front	3-7	Engine in front	3-1
Engine in rear	4-7	Engine in rear	4-1
Light engine	5-7	Light engine	5-1
Bass		**Bass**	
Engine in front	1-3-7	Engine in front	1-3
Engine in rear	1-4-7	Engine in rear	1-4
Light engine	1-5-7	Light engine	1-5
Train entering section	2	Train out of section	2-1

Cancelling signal	3-5
Opening signal	5-5-5
Closing signal	7-5-5

The Director's Saloon with No.10 during an enthusiast's tour of the Bass railway system on 27th May 1961. Shobnall Maltings Signal Box is in the background.
(R.K. Hateley)

The line to No.8 Malting continued straight on from the Tablet Road, as the latter began to curve round to Shobnall Maltings Signal Box. Only Bass' locomotives went up to No.8 Malting and they always propelled the wagons. Near the junction with the Tablet Road was a small hut which sheltered an ancillary receiver for a Tyers tablet which interlocked electrically with Wellington Street Junction Signal Box. When the tablet was inserted, the points were freed for the locomotive to run up to No.8 Malting. If only a brief period was to be spent on the line, the access to the Tablet Road was left open, but if more considerable time was required, the shunter informed the Bass signalman and reset the Tablet Road towards Klondyke Sidings. Wellington Street Junction Box then released the tablet, which the shunter held up for the Bass signalman to fetch and insert in the Shobnall Maltings Box, thus clearing the Tablet Road. When the points on the Tablet Road were switched towards Klondyke, the same action isolated the line to No.8 Malting, opened the catch points on that line a short distance from the Junction, and locked its signal on. The catch points were to throw off any wagons which might run down the slight gradient towards the junction and foul the Tablet Road. It had been known to happen! Before the locomotive could return to Wellington Street, it was necessary for the shunter to collect the tablet from the Shobnall Maltings Signal Box. It was inserted in the ancillary receiver so that the points could be set for No.8 Malting, the catch points closed, the signal pulled off, and the train could pass on to the Tablet Road. The shunter then had to reset the Tablet Road to Klondyke Sidings. Wellington Street Junction Box released the tablet which the driver gave up to the railway company signalman on his return. When a train had passed Shobnall Maltings Box towards Klondyke and handed back the tablet, more trains could follow one at a time. Bass' locomotives were able to enter and leave Klondyke Sidings to the remainder of the private system at Shobnall without using the Tablet Road.

After 1900, the land next to No.8 Malting was laid out by Bass as a coal stockyard with railway sidings for use should there be any disruption to normal supplies. The original proposal had been to locate the coal stocks in the Middle Yard but the area available was too restricted. In 1940, Alan Shipley built a mobile ash screening plant, incorporating a Lister diesel engine, on the chassis of a railway van. A wagon was attached at each end, one for the dust and the other for the unburnt

115

material. The locomotive changing the wagons had to have a low 'reacher' wagon coupled next to it in order to avoid hitting the chutes. This ash screening plant was initially shunted round Bass' railway system but eventually it was stationed on a siding which had been extended from No.8 Malting 100 yards into the next field. The anthracite ashes were then brought to it from all of the kiln furnaces in Bass' own wagons and the screened waste was deposited into the nearby gravel pits. Unburnt coal was reused and it was said that it dried all the barley at the Middle Yard storeroom kilns producing a good saving.

Bass' No.8 Malting at Shobnall on 2nd August 1964. The internal high sided wagon is standing on the coal stock yard sidings.   (C. Shepherd)

There is no documentary evidence to confirm where Bass obtained its supplies of gravel from, but it may have been somewhere at Shobnall. In 1896, however, Bass purchased four acres of land at Wichnor abutting on to the MR main line and next to the railway company's extensive ballast pits. From then onwards, Bass quarried its own sand and gravel at Wichnor, loaded them into railway wagons on its own sidings and had them delivered to locations in Burton as directed. Bass generally used gravel supplemented by boiler ash for railway ballast, although limestone chippings from Breedon on the Hill were later put down in some places. The crossings for horses and carts were paved with Mountsorrel granite setts. Where the railways were set flush in the roads, they were paved inside and along the outside edges with setts.

The last major addition to the railway layout at Shobnall was the provision of another loop to serve the east bank of the new experimental bottling stores. These had been built over the Old Ale Cellar in 1913. All of the early work on chilled and filtered beers was carried out here although the bulk of Bass' bottling continued to be done by outside firms. In 1877, none of Burton's 28 brewing companies had bottled beer for general consumption on a large scale, although Worthington is known to have bottled some at least between 1862 and 1870 for Australia, the West Indies, and South America. Most of the large Burton brewers used numerous outside bottlers sending the beer to them in butts and hogsheads. Up to 1918, Burton bottled beers were only naturally conditioned in the bottle (secondary fermentation) and it was not until the 1920s that carbonated beers were taken up by the Burton brewers. Bass had experimented with such beers before World War 1 and a small conditioning plant was installed at the bottling stores in 1924-26 but Bass declined to put its name to the product and it was known as 'Circle Ale' until September 1930, when Bass 'Blue Triangle' and Worthington 'Green Shield' were openly marketed as such. The bays of the Old Ale Cellar were insulated and chilled by brine circulation to produce the low temperature for conditioning 'Blue Triangle' and 'Green Shield'. It was nearby at the Nile boilers that Les Day was driving when some wagons came off the rails and ran up the bank. The locomotive was about to leave the scene when it was pointed out that they could hardly remain there wedged on the bank. A rope was attached to the locomotive and the wagons were pulled off dropping straight back on to the rails!

The lines between Wellington Street Junction and Shobnall Junction, where the Dallow Lane Branch left, were very busy. All Bass' traffic from the loop lines joined on to the MR between these

boxes and road vehicles approaching the maltings passed over the lines just beyond Shobnall Junction. A small cabin called Shobnall Crossing Box was provided for the crossing keeper controlling road traffic but there were no gates and vehicles had to 'halt and await permission to proceed'. There was an old cross bar signal nearby and another was situated at the entrance to Klondyke Sidings. The latter was usually kept in the clear position but was placed at danger before a train entered the sidings, meaning that all shunting had to stop. This type of signal had generally disappeared elsewhere in the country with the coming of the conventional semaphore signals in the late 1870s. There were still one or two to be seen at Burton until the end of the railway branches and an example is preserved at the Bass Museum. When the locomotives were running alongside Shobnall Road, the drivers were warned not to sound their whistles until they were near to the home signals and they had to be careful not to whistle unnecessarily.

The railway company's locomotives were often to be seen marshalling trains at Shobnall. They took loads of empty casks to Klondyke, where the wagons were picked up by a Bass locomotive and worked round to the cask washing plant. Once there, they could be moved up by capstan. The general aim was to send out wagons with full casks which had originally come in with empty casks. On approaching Klondyke, the shunter checked whether empty casks were required immediately, and if so, the railway company's locomotive might sometimes take them directly to the cask washing bank, although usually the loop lines were shunted by Bass' locomotives. Klondyke was particularly busy in winter with the railway company bringing in many loads of barley and coal. All Bass' coal was worked to Klondyke where it was allocated to the boilers, stockyard and locomotive shed. On arrival, a man used to go along chalking on the wagons which malting kiln the coal was destined for. Anthracite came from South Wales and was never taken to the stockyard. About a hundred years ago, Bass had purchased anthracite from collieries at Bonvilles Court and Kilgetty near Saundersfoot, Cwmamman, Cross Hands and Pontyberem in the Gwendraeth Valley, Gwaun cae Gurwen, Garnant, Ystradgynlais in the Swansea Valley, Essery, and Rhos. The anthracite from the collieries around Saundersfoot was of especially good quality and held in high esteem for drying malt. Indeed, the colliery company claimed that it commanded prices 2% or 3% per ton above the next best qualities and that Bass always took as much as they could get, even though it cost Bass 5 shillings (25p) per ton more than Gwaun cae Gurwen and other good anthracites. In fact, the anthracite generated so much heat that it was difficult to use it for everyday purposes, such as steam raising, in the 1860s. Bass must have been impressed with its qualities because Mr Gretton seriously negotiated to purchase the Bonvilles Court Coal & Iron Company but the talks ended abruptly when his mineral surveyor died suddenly. Despite the quality of the anthracite, the seams round Saundersfoot were narrow and difficult to work, and this may have also influenced the decision. Anthracite mostly came in Great Western Railway wagons, although some private owner

Trains at Shobnall Junction on Thursday 11th August 1955

Locomotive	Time		No. of Wagons (where known)	Train	
41878	arr	6.35am		109T	
1	dep	6.42am		Bass R's	
41878	dep	7.15am		109T	
41878	arr	8.05am		109T	
41532	arr	8.34am		110T	
41532	dep	8.42am		110T	To Bond End Branch
44164	pass	9.01am	40	Derby–Wichnor	
58130	arr	9.15am		128T	Via main line
58130	dep	9.16am		128T	Via main line
41878	dep	9.19am		109T	
12	dep	9.27am		Bass R's (ex Worthington locomotive)	
41878	arr	9.30am		109T	
11	dep	9.57am		Bass R's	
44435	pass	10.07am	35	To Stoke Gifford	
41878	dep	10.15am		109T	
61733	pass	10.26am	30	Colwick–Wichnor	
41878	arr	11.13am		109T	
44185	arr	11.42am	40	121T	Bass tubs Via Dallow Lane Branch
41878	dep	12.08pm	35	109T	
43763	pass	12.16pm	33	Derby–Wichnor	
58130	arr	12.27pm		128T	Via main line
41878	arr	12.34pm		109T	From Klondyke
58130	dep	12.50pm		128T	To Locomotive Shed
44185	dep	12.53pm	38	121T	To New Dixie and New Wetmore
47257	arr	1.18pm		114T	From Allsopp's Sidings
47257	dep	1.24pm		114T	To Allsopp's Sidings
1	dep	1.40pm		Bass R's	
41878	dep	1.49pm		109T	To Loop
4		2.32pm	3	Marston, Thompson & Evershed	
41878	arr	2.35pm		109T	
44185	arr	3.20pm		121T	Via Dallow Lane Branch
7	arr	3.22pm	11	Bass	
41532	arr	3.40pm	2	110T	
41532	dep	3.47pm		110T	To Loop
41878	dep	3.55pm		109T	To Loop
1	dep	4.06pm		Bass R's	
44185	dep	4.12pm	7	121T	Via Dallow Lane Branch
1	arr	4.17pm	6	Bass	
7	arr	5.07pm	1	Bass	
41878	dep	5.12pm		109T	To Loop
41532	arr	5.24pm	2	110T	
41532	dep	5.27pm		110T	To Bond End Branch
41878	arr	5.49pm	9	109T	
47257	arr	5.53pm		114T	From Allsopp's Sidings
47257	dep	5.56pm	26	114T	To Allsopp's Sidings
41878	dep	5.59pm		109T	To Loop
41878	arr	6.30pm	17	109T	
48002	arr	6.37pm		Locomotive for the Leeds	
48002	dep	6.47pm		To Leeds via main line	
41878	dep	7.08pm	19	109T	To Sharp Bros & Knight's works
41878	arr	7.18pm		109T	From Sharp Bros & Knight's works
41878	dep	7.38pm		109T	To Locomotive Shed

Shobnall Junction Signal Box on 26th December 1965. It had opened on 17th December 1917, replacing an earlier structure on the same site, and closed on 24th April 1966 when the line to Wellington Street was singled. (C. Shepherd)

vehicles may also have been involved. Some wagons must have been regularly devoted to this traffic with Worthington because they carried small metal plates, charcoal grey in colour and with white lettering reading:-

'Empty to Cwmgwrach Colly
Glyn Neath GWR
For Worthington & Co
Burton on Trent'

Other plates referred to traffic from Glyncastle Colliery and Onllwyn Colliery. These three pits were situated within 10 miles of each other to the north east of Neath in the Dulais Valley and the Vale of Neath.

In later days, most railway company operations were concentrated at the Shobnall Exchange Sidings and Klondyke was run down in the 1950s, although a few wagons could be found stored there until 1967. Shobnall Exchange Sidings were generally the preserve of one of the old ex MR tank locomotives because only short trips were required; the most arduous task being the climb from under the Bridge Hole. Even in the mid 1950s, the Shobnall 'Jocko' could be a 1F 0-6-0 tank and 41878 was the favourite, with 41699 and 41839 occasionally standing in. The Jocko arrived from Burton shed about 6.30am and spent some of the morning bringing loads of about 35 wagons round from Leicester Junction Sidings. In the evening, it often ventured along Sharp Bros & Knight's timber yard siding before returning to the locomotive shed, usually at half past eight. Saturdays were similar but with less activity in the afternoon and work finished about 6pm.

The signalmen in Shobnall Junction Box in 1955 were G. King and P.D. Rowe, and they operated alternate 6am - 1.20pm and 1.20pm - 8.30pm shifts. There was some excitement on Tuesday 15th November when there was a derailment. The locomotive was soon rerailed by 5pm but Nos.8 and 10 points and Nos.2 and 3 sidings were out of use. Fred Dicken had to be called, but the points were not working again until ten o'clock, and the box shut late that night. No.10 points must have been fated because there was a locomotive derailment at them a week later and the breakdown train had to be summoned. The only goods train to start from Shobnall in 1955 was the 'Leeds'. Its locomotive arrived about 6.30pm and ran into an empty siding. The Jocko attached the wagons to the locomotive, and then pulled the complete train up to the main line with the train locomotive pushing, coupled on at the rear. After reversal, the train headed north, leaving the tank locomotive to return to the sidings. The 'Leeds' was regularly rostered for one of the few Burton 8Fs, such as 48002, 48401, or 48547. There were also trip workings from other yards including 121T and 128T often with elderly 2F 0-6-0s in charge, the constant coming and going of Bass' locomotives as they shunted the banks or set off for the New Brewery, the little Bond End four-wheeler, the 3F 0-6-0

119

Shobnall on 21st December 1963 with left to right – the curve to Bass' Shobnall Maltings; Shobnall Crossing Box; Bass's New Ale Stores and its cask washing plant complete with tall chimney; Shobnall Exchange Sidings with a BR 350hp diesel shunter; the single line leading to Marston, Thompson & Evershed's Brewery in the distance; the sidings to Shobnall Wharf; and the double track of the Dallow Lane Branch sweeping past the corner of Shobnall Junction Signal Box. (C. Shepherd)

tank on the Dallow Lane trip, Marston's green diesel, and the down through goods behind Burton 0-6-0s or a Colwick K2. What a fascinating mixture of mostly pre World War 1 locomotives!

No.8 Malting was used by the Ministry of Food during World War 2 and malting never recommenced afterwards although its railway connection with not removed until May 1964. With the decline in rail traffic, Shobnall Wharf closed on 6th July in the same year and the trade was transferred to the Derby Street coal depot. Bass' rail system enjoyed a brief period of increased activity when the Middle Yard cask washing plant was renewed because the plant at Shobnall was used in the interim but then closed about 1966. Traffic on the Tablet Road finished on 20th January 1968. Nos.3–6 Maltings were demolished in 1977-78 but Nos.1 and 2 continued, having been converted into box drum pneumatic/mechanical maltings in 1958. This justified the retention of a rail link to the main line for bulk grain vans after the remainder of the railway layout at Shobnall shut in 1967. The branch to Leicester Junction was, however, singled and reclassified as a siding on 17th March 1968. It was shunted by a BR 350hp diesel locomotive and the crossing over the now named Wellington Road was merely protected by two handworked semaphore signals. A new tower malting has since been erected at Shobnall which is serviced by road vehicles. BR could not guarantee the continuing availability of sidings at the barley collection centres and the line into Shobnall closed in 1979.

The Albion Brewery

London brewers, Mann Crossman & Paulin, came to Burton and erected the Albion Brewery in 1873-75 on 82 acres of land leased from the Marquis of Anglesey to the north west of the Trent & Mersey Canal. The brewery was designed by W. & S.T. Martin of Nottingham and comprised an impressive red brick brewhouse, together with a cooperage and stables. Workmen's houses, the Albion Hotel, and St. Aidan's Church were also built by the company. At first, the brewery did not have a railway system and four horses had the task of conveying the casks of beer from the brewery along the roads to the various goods depots in the town.

An agreement was made on the 29th December 1875 between Mann, Crossman & Paulin and the MR to construct a single railway line from the MR Shobnall Branch to the brewery. Each company was to be responsible for the cost of the work on its own property, the MR's territory ending just to the west of the bridge over the Trent & Mersey Canal. Mann, Crossman & Paulin had to pay the MR 'half the annual expenses of working and lighting the signals and the wages of the signalmen and pointsmen'. It had to meet the costs of labour for maintaining the track at a rate of 10s (50p) for every 22 yards and also provide gates to prevent trespass at the junction with the Shobnall Branch, although latterly there were none in existence. The line opened on 29th December 1876 and Mann, Crossman & Paulin's traffic could then be taken directly from the brewery to Shobnall Exchange Sidings. MR locomotives were also allowed to work over the line into the brewery.

By 1882, an additional siding had been laid so that the single line divided into two on entering the brewery. One passed by the brewhouse to the cooperage at the far end of the site, whilst the other ran by the racking room bank. The firm did not require its own locomotive and relied on the MR to visit the brewery every day. Incoming trains were usually made up into three sections. On arrival, the coal wagons were despatched to the bank in front of the boilers, the malt and hops were taken to the loading up cages, and the casks to the empty cask yard. After completing this shunting, the locomotive was ready to take any wagons laden with filled casks of beer back to Shobnall Junction. Workings were organised so that all orders received before 3pm on one day could be delivered to the most distant towns in the country on the following day.

Mann, Crossman & Paulin's annual output of beer at Burton never exceeded 50,000 barrels, and in 1896, it closed the brewery and withdrew back to London. The brewery and remainder of the lease, including the licensed houses, were purchased by the Albion Brewery (Burton on Trent) Ltd. This company had been formed in that year as a successor to Buckmaster's of Lincoln and Bell's of Boston who had traded as the 'Burton and Lincoln Breweries' about 1890. The latter had taken over E.P. Dawson's Brewery in Moor Street. Purchase of the Albion land was essentially a financial transaction because within two years, the licensed properties were leased to Salt in late 1897 and the brewery, hotel, and some houses were subleased to the newly amalgamated J. Marston, Thompson & Son Ltd in 1898. Bass took a sublease of the remaining open land and Shobnall Grange. The new company soon expanded becoming Marston, Thompson & Evershed Ltd in 1905 when Sydney Herbert Evershed joined and some of Evershed's brewing equipment was moved from his Bank Square Brewery to Shobnall.

Numerous extensions were added to the railway system until it generally assumed its ultimate

Shobnall Basin was one of the last remnants of the Bond End Canal. This 3rd May 1964 view shows 'The Mount Pleasant' public house on the left. It was leased by Marston, Thompson & Evershed from the MR. Beer used to be delivered by rail; a wagon was shunted the few hundred yards from the brewery and the casks were lowered down the embankment into the cellar. Later, supplies were brought by road to the Shobnall coal wharf, indicated here by the railway wagons, and then the casks were rolled to the public house. (C. Shepherd)

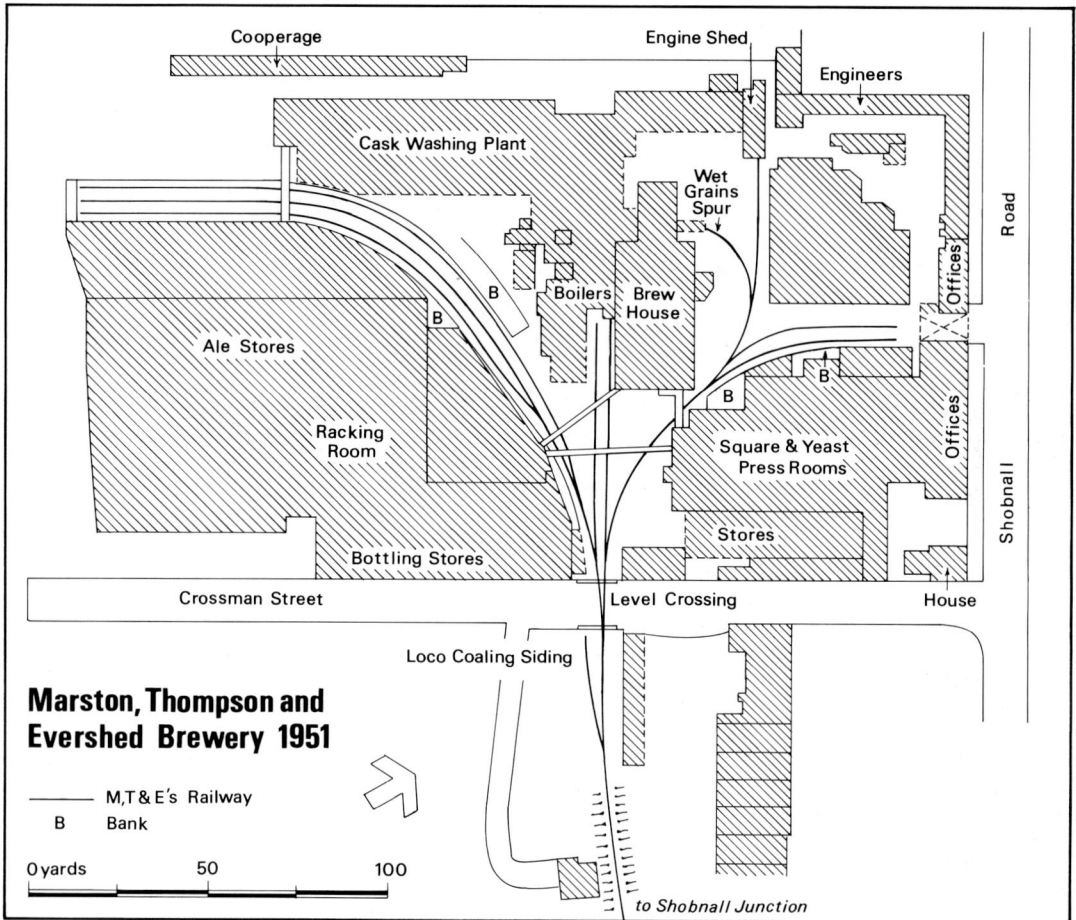

Marston, Thompson and
Evershed Brewery 1951

——— M,T & E's Railway
B   Bank

0 yards   50   100

form in the early years of the twentieth century. A siding continued to run to the brewhouse to serve the boilers under the main block and the maltrooms, but the extension to the cooperage was dispensed with. The other siding was enlarged to three lines, two of which served the ale stores and cask washing banks. A new siding was laid round to the north side of the brewhouse to permit the removal of wet grains and give access to the locomotive shed, which could accommodate two shunting locomotives. There was no signal box at the level crossing over Crossman Street and the operation of the gates was controlled by hand. A short spur was subsequently constructed near the crossing and the locomotives used to stand on this line to be coaled.

There were no maltings on the site but the company had its own maltings at Derby Road, Horninglow Street, and Park Street. Derby Road Malting, erected next to the Up Wetmore Sidings about 1900, was shunted by MR locomotives and was sometimes known as the Passburgh Siding. Possibly the name was derived from the first major victory by the British army in the Boer War at Madder River, near Paardeberg, on 27th February 1900. Some years later in 1925-26, a contractor attempted to demolish the chimney at the malting by setting fire to wooden shoring inserted in the base of the chimney,. with unfortunate results as the chimney fell through the malting doing considerable damage.

Marston, Thompson & Son's No.1 shunts the brewery yard near Crossman Street.
(F. Jones Collection)

In January 1901, Marston Thompson & Son Ltd ordered a new 4-coupled saddle tank locomotive from Hawthorn Leslie & Co Ltd. This proved to be the first of a number of similar purchases of standard 14in locomotives from this manufacturer. The locomotive arrived in the following June and had a 140lb/sq.in boiler, a tank carrying 600 gallons of water and bore long linear plates with the company's name. No.1 (maker's number 2502) began to take Marston's traffic to Shobnall Junction and thence either to the MR Shobnall Exchange Sidings or the LNWR Allsopp's Sidings on the Dallow Lane Branch on the 24th June 1901. Marston also purchased a 'brake' (van) for £66 from the MR and it was handed over in good condition on 21st September 1901. No.1 remained the sole locomotive for a long time until the company placed an advertisement in *Machinery Market* in January 1918 for a 4-coupled locomotive with 12in to 15in cylinders and weighing about 30 tons. The subsequent acquisition must have proved unsatisfactory because Marston soon returned it, and instead, purchased a second hand Hawthorn Leslie (maker's number 2837 of 1910) from A. Herbertson & Sons Ltd of Chollerford near Hexham in November 1918. This interpretation is based on an assessment of the company's accounts.

Marston, Thompson & Evershed quarterly financial transactions

March 1918	Loco	£2800 paid
September 1918	Loco	Cash part of deposit re loco retd £1000
March 1919	Loco	£2500 paid
March 1919	Loco	Contra ex Buck re loco £1100
September 1919	Loco	ex Buck re loco £987

From then on, it was the practice to have two locomotives and to work them alternately. Hawthorn Leslie 2837 and subsequent locomotives had the slightly longer cylinder stroke of 22in. The steam locomotives were painted in an attractive dark blue livery, relieved by a narrow straw and orange line, and with a broad vermillion line to the wheels. They were kept in an immaculate condition. The company was less dependent on rail transport compared with some of the other brewing companies in the town because many of its licensed properties were in country areas, where deliveries had to be made by road. It acquired a steam lorry as early as 1905, and the petrol engine fleet of lorries in 1921 included six reconditioned 5 ton Leyland vehicles, previously used by the Royal Flying Corps. By 1934, Marston, Thompson & Evershed had a fleet of 48 road delivery vehicles.

Marston ordered a new locomotive from Hawthorn Leslie (maker's number 3581) in March 1923 but it was not until over a year later in 1924 that it was delivered at a cost of £1,790. No.3 had a

No.3 taking on coal from one of Marston's wagons stabled on the short siding near Crossman Street on a pleasant Autumn evening, 9th October 1963. (P. Waterfield)

wheelbase of 5ft 6in, weighed 26 tons, and carried a boiler with a pressure of 160lb/sq.in; an increase of 10lbs on No.2 and 20lbs on the original locomotive. The water capacity of the saddle tank on these locomotives was 650 gallons, with the exception of No.1 which held 50 gallons less. No.1 was disposed of to Thos W. Ward Ltd which appears to have hired it out to the Clifton & Kersley Coal Company, before selling it by 1930 to the Ford Motor Company for use at its Dagenham Works. The entry in the *Hawthorn Leslie Engine Book* reads 'Collieries (Clifton & Kersley) Ltd. Ward. Ford Motor Co Ltd [by] 8/12/1930'.

It was not long before Marston purchased another new locomotive from Hawthorn Leslie of the same type as No.3. In this period of economic depression, No.4 (maker's number 3774) was sent out from the works in 1931, within two months of the order being placed by Marston and it cost £100 less than the previous locomotive. Both locomotives carried a brass plate with the owner's name and number. No.2 was sold in part exchange to Hawthorn Leslie, a figure of £250 being shown for it in Marston's accounts. Hawthorn Leslie subsequently sold it to the Priestman Collieries Ltd's Norwood coke ovens near Gateshead, where it was called VENTURE and worked until it was scrapped in 1965. Nos.3 and 4 shared the task of shunting the brewery for the next twenty years. When Eric Hannan visited the brewery in 1945 to see the two locomotives, he recorded of No.3 that it was 'the cleanest locomotive I have ever seen' which was indeed a complement in Burton.

The old driver had been Tommy Cheatle who was on the locomotives for 40 years. George Fowler was one of the cleaners and very good at his job, not missing much even in the gloom of the shed. When Tommy Cheatle retired, the new man co-opted to drive the locomotive soon got into trouble and was involved in a collision. Mr Stockton then sent for Jim Gaunt, who lived in South Uxbridge Street, saying that he had heard that Jim had once been on the footplate for the LNWR and asked him to take over the locomotive; that was in 1944. Jim Gaunt had joined Marston in 1926 when Charrington's Brewery closed and had then driven a lorry to Southampton. He stayed on the locomotives until the railway finished.

During World War 2, Marston's railway system was kept very busy, particularly as six of the company's lorries had been requisitioned by the Government. The locomotives had to be 'bagged up' to stop the glare from the firebox. There were two drivers and two shunters on the workforce, with one pair working the morning shift starting at 6am and the other pair on the afternoon shift. The locomotives were lit up by the cleaners; one of the cleaners was on 'days' and the other worked 'nights'.

The first job for the locomotive on a Monday morning about 7am was to take the wagons, which had been loaded with casks of ale for Winchester on the Sunday, down to the Shobnall Exchange Sidings. This beer would arrive at Winchester Bar End Goods Yard by Monday evening, although the return of the empty casks sometimes took weeks! Marston had absorbed the Winchester Brewery in 1923, and after brewing stopped there a few years later, ale was sent from Burton by rail and road. There were usually eight to ten wagons laden with assorted casks each week. The locomotive then brought back empty wagons which were placed by the ale stores bank. Next, the boilers would be set up with coal by taking wagons along the siding under the brewhouse. The driver and shunter had their breakfast while the cleaner coaled the locomotive and generally smartened it up. Marston obtained a lot of malt from Yeomans, Cherry & Curtis and so the locomotive ran down the bank to Shobnall Junction, where it would reverse along the Dallow Lane Branch to that company's maltings, and bring back malt vans for unloading in the brewery. They used to go to Dallow Lane three times a week on Mondays, Wednesdays, and Saturdays. This was followed by shunting the ale bank sidings, taking in wagons with empty casks for washing and storage, and then moving the empty wagons to the other bank so that they could be loaded with full casks from the ale stores. The middle line was used for spare wagons. After that, two loaded wagons had to be collected from the wet grains spur and these were stabled out of the way, sometimes on the 'coal road', whilst the locomotive coupled on to a string of wagons with full casks. It drew these carefully out over Crossman Street and attached the two wagons with wet grains at the rear of the train. This was to keep the dripping wagons out of the way of the locomotive because wet rails could cause the

Marston's No.4 was built by Hawthorn Leslie in 1931. It is seen here on 15th April 1952, not long before it was dismantled and minor parts were incorporated in the new diesel replacement.   (IRS K.J. Cooper Collection)

locomotive to slip; the driver did not want to use his sanding equipment as this would dirty the locomotive! There was a 1 in 82 gradient up to the canal bridge and the load was usually limited to 18 wagons, although more could be taken if there was a man on the level crossing. Jim Gaunt's locomotive once pulled 36 wagons in one load from the brewery. Charlie Gilman, the railway company's checker, used to come to examine the wagons before they went out, including putting the appropriate labels on them. If he found an unfit wagon, he would place a green label on it when it could still move, or a red one when it could not. Wagons which required repairs were sent to the Wagon Repairs Depot at Derby Road.

The routine of taking in empty casks and bringing out full casks went on throughout the day. Sometimes the locomotive went down the Bond End Branch to Park Street Maltings, when there was an urgent job and the railway company did not have a small shunter immediately available. It then took the wagons from the maltings to Leicester Junction Sidings via the curve from Dale Street, the driver obtaining permission from the signal box at the sidings before he could work round to the yard. Marston was not responsible for hauling the traffic between its maltings and the brewery.

Occasionally, the railway company's locomotive came into the brewery; indeed Jim Gaunt's father had done it on a LNWR locomotive. Once whilst Jim was waiting on his locomotive for the next job, he was very surprised to see smoke rising from what appeared to be another locomotive within the brewery. On investigation, it turned out to be a Bass' locomotive; the crew had on impulse decided to bring up six wagons destined for Marston and had already disappeared into the allowance house! Not surprisingly, different breweries' drivers were very partial to their own locomotives. Jim thought that the Hawthorn Leslie locomotives were better than Bass' because of their superior brakes, an important item on a shunting locomotive. He had watched a Bass locomotive stick on the bank at Shobnall when testing the brakes but had to acknowledge that they were well looked after and kept clean. All the repairs to Marston's locomotives were done in the shed, although Warren's of Newhall came to attend to the boiler repairs. Each locomotive had a boiler washout every other Sunday morning.

Baguley diesel No.4 stands on the siding near to Marston's offices at the brewery, 24th April 1964. *(R.K. Hateley)*

Loading No.3 on to the lorry which was to take it to the Foxfield Railway for preservation in April 1967. The diesel stands just beyond Crossman Street level crossing. *(C. More)*

In 1953, No.4 was dismantled and various parts are said to have been incorporated by Baguley in a new diesel locomotive (maker's number 3410), although this was probably restricted to such minor items as the buffers and number plates. The frame was almost certainly new because it did not show any holes, even plugged gaps, to correspond with the pattern of holes in the steam locomotive's frame for the ashpan and to permit attachment of the slide bars and cylinders. The new locomotive was a 0-4-0 with a Gardner 153hp 6L3 diesel engine and a Wilson epicycle gearbox, and was similar to the Ind Coope diesels. Livery was middle green, with unusual dark blue buffer beams, the same colours as the company's lorries. The order for the locomotive had been placed on 27th October 1952 but delivery was not until February 1955. It cost £8,918 and the remains of the steam locomotive went for scrap for £105.

The new No.4 worked for fifty weeks of the year leaving No.3 to fill in for the remaining two weeks when the diesel was having its annual overhaul. Rail traffic was declining and there was only a need to make the trip down to Shobnall Exchange Sidings once or twice a day. Loads of wagons were often in single figures. Although Marston relied on the railway company's wagons, it also owned a few of its own. Some had low sides for carrying refuse and others brought 'slack' (coal) from Derby Road. Jim Gaunt once inspected two reconditioned wagons with oil axle boxes at Wagon Repairs Ltd, Branston and these were subsequently purchased by Marston. The private wagons were finally kept within the brewery and included two railway vans for the storage of wines and spirits which stood on the siding near the offices.

Rail traffic eventually dwindled to such an extent that BR asked Marston to despatch the casks by road to Horninglow Yard where it would be prepared to accept them. Marston could not agree to this and turned all its traffic over to road transport. No more railway wagons were sent out after the beginning of June 1964, although No.4 moved some of the internal vans around the brewery in

127

the following November. No.3 had last been used on 11th October 1963. It was eventually purchased by Mr E. Trubshaw, with an undertaking that it would never be scrapped, and it is now at the Great Central Railway in Loughborough. No.4's last duty for the company was to pull the steam locomotive from the shed prior to it being loaded on to a lorry in April 1967. No.4 was sold to the Bristol Mechanised Coal Co Ltd's Filton Coal Concentration Depot for £2,925 and left about the middle of 1967. Seven internal wagons were disposed of at the same time. The diesel locomotive eventually returned to Marston by March 1990 for display.

A.B. Walker & Sons' Brewery about 1888 with the siding connecting it to the Shobnall Branch. *(R. Keene)*

Walker's Shobnall Brewery

On 30th November 1875, Andrew Barclay Walker leased 10 acres of land near Wellington Street Junction from the Marquis of Anglesey for £400 per annum with a stipulation that, within three years, he would build a substantial brewery in brick and slate at a cost of not less than £7,000. Walker's Brewery opened in 1877 and was served by a short railway line from the Shobnall Branch. The line was temporarily brought into use on 19th November 1878 and the LNWR's locomotive began to shunt its traffic on to the siding ten days later. An official opening took place on 1st January 1879. The railway crossed the lane (later Wellington Street Extension) in front of the brewery and entered the premises, where it divided into two sidings along the front and side of the brewhouse. A hand operated field gate protected the railway on the Shobnall Branch side of the lane. The brewery came under the control of Peter Walker & Son (Warrington & Burton) Ltd in 1890 until its closure about 1922. It was advertised for sale in 1923 as a 'pale ale and lager brewery', being purchased by Bass on 19th April 1923 probably to prevent other brewers securing a foothold in Burton, but was soon passed on to the English Grains Company in June 1924, which used it for processing spent grains. In view of the small size of the railway layout, Walker did not require a private locomotive, and the shunting was mostly carried out by one of the MR's small four-coupled locomotives. The sidings were busy almost to the end of their existence with wagons full of spent grains from the breweries. British Railway's 41532 was regularly seen in the yard about 4.30pm in the late 1950s and a BR 350hp diesel shunter then took over the duty until the rail connection was removed on 1st May 1964.

Baguley Cars Limited

The Ryknield Engine Co Ltd was formed in 1901 and registered as a company in the following year to manufacture cars using Ernest Baguley's design of steam car engine. Baguley had previously

128

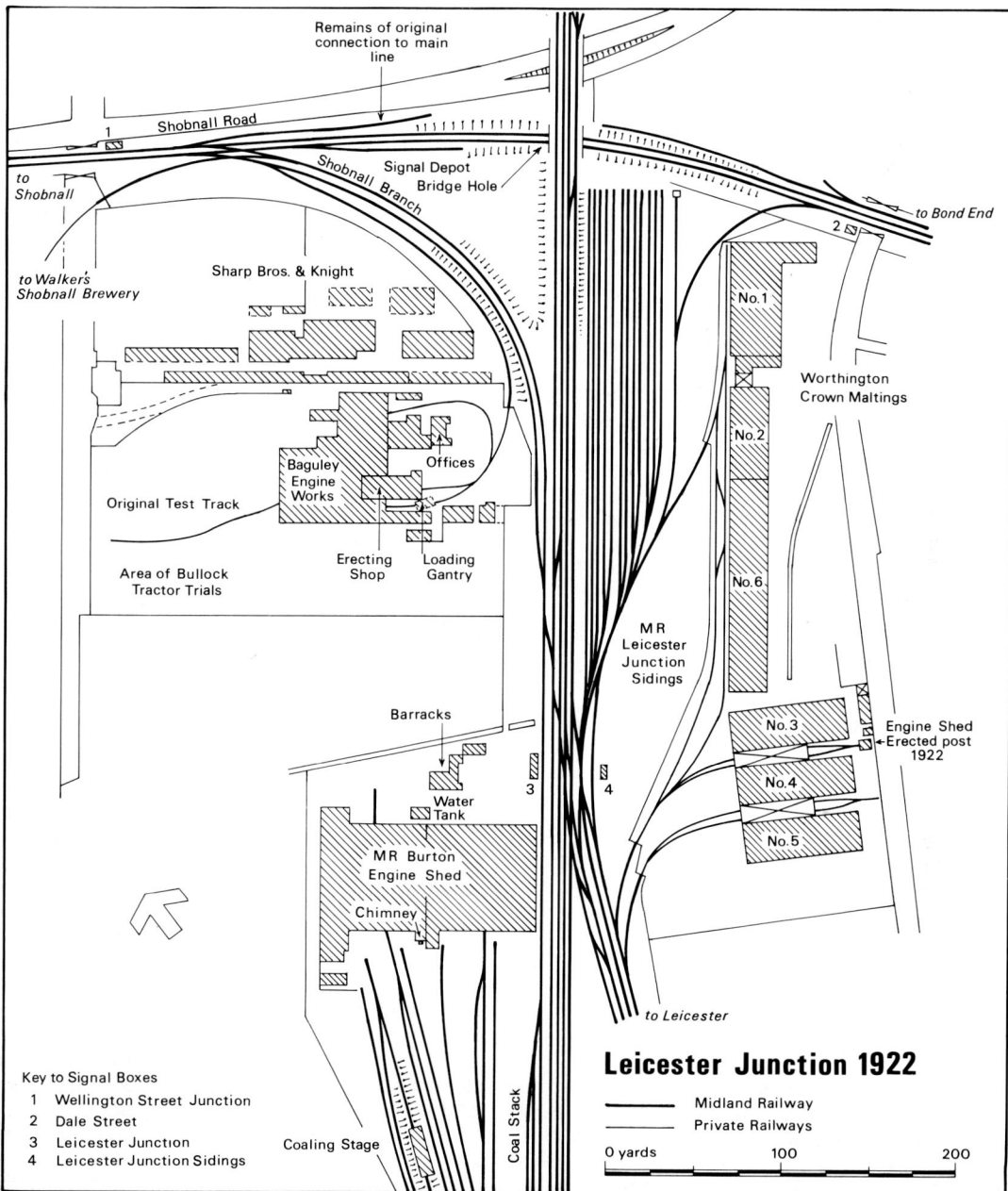

Remains of original
connection to main
line

Shobnall Road

1

to
Shobnall

Shobnall Branch

Signal Depot
Bridge Hole

to Walker's
Shobnall Brewery

Sharp Bros. & Knight

2

to Bond End

No.1

Worthington
Crown Maltings

No.2

Baguley
Engine
Works

Offices

Original Test Track

No.6

Erecting
Shop

Loading
Gantry

Area of Bullock
Tractor Trials

MR
Leicester
Junction
Sidings

Barracks

No.3

Engine Shed
Erected post
1922

3

4

No.4

Water
Tank

No.5

MR Burton
Engine Shed

Chimney

to Leicester

Leicester Junction 1922

Midland Railway
Private Railways

Key to Signal Boxes
1 Wellington Street Junction
2 Dale Street
3 Leicester Junction
4 Leicester Junction Sidings

Coaling Stage

Coal Stack

0 yards   100   200

been Chief Draughtsman at Bagnall's locomotive works in Stafford. A new factory was opened on
16th April 1903 on the open land between Walker's Shobnall Brewery and the MR main line.
Financial support came from the Clay family, Lord Burton, William Worthington, and Robert Ratcliff
but it proved an unfortunate venture for them all! William Worthington was a son of Albert Octavious
Worthington, and had been on Worthington's board of directors in the 1890s, but was not at the time

of the Ryknield flotation. The company eventually concentrated on petrol vehicles but soon ran into financial difficulties and the assets were purchased by the Ryknield Motor Company which was formed in 1906 by Wilfrid Clay, again with Ernest Baguley in charge. This concentrated on the production of commercial vehicle chassis, but it also experienced problems and a liquidator was appointed in April 1911. Undaunted, Baguley and Wilfrid Clay then formed Baguley Cars Limited which was registered on 3rd September 1911. The first of an eventual total of 94 motor vehicles appeared at the end of the same year with a few being supplied to the local brewers.

Baguley took over the manufacture of motorised railcars for a sales organisation called the Drewry Car Company, following the discontinuance of this work by BSA. In 1913, Baguley purchased the assets of McEwan, Pratt & Co Ltd, which had manufactured a standard range of early petrol locomotives with a good reputation, and a number of these were built by Baguley under the name of McEwan Pratt. The Shobnall Road Works went on to build 230 locomotives between 1914 and 1931. The majority were narrow gauge petrol locomotives but the total included 31 steam locomotives. Production reached a peak towards the end of World War 1 and almost a third of the total output was built in 1918. The most numerous type was the 60cm 10hp '677' class petrol locomotive, of which over 50 were built for the War Office. Baguley's early work on petrol locomotives was at the forefront of the development of internal combustion powered locomotives and they were built in a substantial manner in order to compete with contemporary steam locomotives. Details of them are given in Rodney Weaver's book *Baguley Locomotives 1914–1931,* published by the Industrial Railway Society. In 1915, Baguley was also involved in trials on American caterpillar tractors, which eventually led to the development of the tank. The Bullock 'Creeping Grip' tractor was tested at the Shobnall Road Works with Baguley providing the technical support. Although an alternative design was chosen, railways of various gauges were laid out on the resulting obstacle course giving a wide selection of gradients for testing locomotives.

Baguley's Works at Shobnall comprised an impressive office block, together with an extensive range of mostly single storey buildings. A siding ran round from near Wellington Street Junction to

The unusual 4-cylinder 2ft 6in gauge Baguley locomotive, maker's no.2020, built for the Rail Grip Syndicate and photographed on the Shobnall Road Works test track in 1923. Walker's Shobnall Brewery, then up for sale, dominates the background.

(Baguley (Engineers) Ltd, Staffordshire County Record Collection)

The chassis of Baguley Cars maker's number 533 in the Shobnall Road Works yard. This was probably the world's first successful application of hydraulic transmission to a rail vehicle. A locomotive was running past on the main line when the photograph was taken, obscuring the Leicester Junction Sidings. It is late 1913 and occupation of the Crown Maltings is already shared by R. Peach & Co (board on No.3 Malting) and Worthington (board on No.5 Malting).

the premises and had opened on 17th May 1902 to enable the construction of the Ryknield Engine Co's works to proceed. The LNWR was also allowed access from 19th June 1902. Inside the Works, the railway layout was very simple and there was a loading gantry near the erecting shop. The premises were originally surrounded by fields but Sharp Bros & Knight soon established a joinery works here next to the Shobnall Branch. Sharp Bros & Knight had been founded in 1887 when J.T. Sharp started a small business in Russell Street. He was subsequently joined by A.D. Knight and the company moved to Shobnall, extending the works in 1913.

The principal type of locomotive built by Baguley after World War 1 was the '774' design which was notable for the introduction of the 'Duplex' mechanical transmission; the largest example of this type being maker's number 800, a 0-4-0 locomotive with a 100hp 4-cylinder Baguley petrol engine. The latter remained at the Shobnall Works until it closed when the locomotive was taken over by E.E. Baguley Ltd and sold to Thos W. Ward Ltd for £180 in 1933. After resale to the London Brick Company, the locomotive was eventually preserved at the Museum of Staffordshire Life, Shugborough.

The fall in orders after World War 1 led Baguley to branch out into engineering work for the Burton brewers and the production of steam locomotives and rolling stock. To reflect this change, the name of the company became Baguley (Engineers) Ltd on 10th April 1923. It entered into a reciprocal agreement with the Yorkshire Engine Co Ltd of Sheffield and Baguley built a few narrow gauge locomotives for this company, but it was unable to direct any standard gauge orders to the Yorkshire Engine Company in return. During its existence, Baguley produced over 1000 railcars and trolleys, together with spares for other locomotive builders and machinery for local firms. This included vulcanising and pressing equipment for the India Rubber & Gutta Percha Company's new works at Burton. The output of rolling stock was particularly varied, with small 15cwt wooden bodied mine tubs, conventional 2ft gauge tip wagons, light railway passenger and freight stock, and heavier stock for overseas railways, such as a massive 85ft long 80tons 12-axle bolster wagon for carrying 10ft diameter pipes over the 3ft gauge lines of the Anglo Persian Oil Company. Baguley also built rolling stock, but not locomotives, for Honeywill Brothers. The production of railcars was based on

end of the MR's Horninglow Branch to preserve access to the canal. The line then descended from the Horninglow Road Bridge, before finally climbing at 1 in 132 to Stretton Junction, where catch points were provided to protect the branch from runaways.

More works were connected to the branch during the next 30 years. Immediately north of the Dallow Bridge, there had once been fields but a short siding was soon put in to Hallam & Sons Dallow Chemical Works and Grout & Co's Cooperage. The MR gained access to them on 7th December 1887 (Hallam) and 2nd March 1888 (Grout). Hallam supplied general chemicals to the brewing industry. The tall chimney at Grout's Cooperage carried the legend 'John Grout 1899'. J.B. Kind had been founded in 1875 and the company had a timber yard alongside the branch served by a line off the Dallow Lane wharf siding. There was also an internal hand worked two feet gauge system for moving wood from the yard to the various sawmills. There is a curious reference in the Goods Agent's notebook – 'Mr Kind's siding on the LNWR Dallow Lane Branch, this company can deal with traffic with their engine at this siding'. This was according to a letter dated 17th October 1885 but no trace of a locomotive has been found.

Dallow Lane ground frame controlled the sidings at the wharf because it was too far for point rodding to be provided from the signal box and the expense of another box could not be justified. In order to protect the connection with the branch, the points were locked. Trains stopped at Allsopp's Sidings and the signalman accompanied the locomotive to the wharf to operate the frame; the shunter performed the duty when the signalman was off. The Annett's key was originally kept at the frame but later was to be found in the signal box lever frame. A twisting action to remove the key operated the interlocking, thus holding the branch points and signal levers in position to prevent conflicting movements. The key could then be taken to the ground frame where it was placed in a similar lock to release the points to allow shunting of the wharf and Kind's siding to take place. Hallam's and Grout's siding was also protected by a lock and key. The mechanism had originally been invented by Mr J.E. Annett of the London, Brighton & South Coast Railway.

Two maltings were built in 1897 and 1898 respectively by Richards, Cherry & Yeomans on land behind Allsopp's Sidings Signal Box and these were also linked to the branch, with protection from the Annett's key. The maltings had passed into Yeomans, Cherry & Curtis's ownership by 1904. Alfred Henry Yeomans was one of the proprietors and he was followed in the company by his son Frank. W.M. Richards moved up to Marston's former premises at Horninglow in 1898 and specialised exclusively in coloured malts as Richards & Co (Malt Roasters) Ltd.

In 1909, Magee Marshall & Co purchased a piece of land from the LNWR at the foot of the Shobnall Road Bridge and put down a borehole to extract water. A siding was laid by the railway company to give access for a number of square tank wagons, which were used by Magee Marshall to transport the water to its Bolton Brewery. Although only small quantities were extracted up to the 1950s, the traffic was a remarkable testimony to the reputation of Burton water for brewing. It allowed Magee Marshall to advertise that it brewed pale ales with Burton water. The firm also appears to have used a borehole served by the Bond End Branch in 1904 before sinking its own borehole. On one occasion, Magee Marshall had problems with the yeast at its brewery. It transpired that somewhere between Burton and Bolton, some lads had opened the cock on the rail tank and run the water to waste. The railway yard foreman thought that it would be senseless to deliver an empty tank and had it filled up from a railway water crane with detrimental results for the yeast. Staton's premises on the opposite side of the branch had later become Frederick Jones & Company's Hercules Works (subsequently Jones & Broadbent Ltd) making fireproof partitions. Both sidings were locked by the Annett's key kept at Allsopp's Sidings Signal Box. The shunter on a locomotive wishing to enter either siding had to move a lever working an indicator in or near the box to show that the branch was occupied. The lever was kept in that position until the train was safely in the sidings, when it could be returned to the frame. It was necessary to operate the lever again before the points could be unlocked and the train could leave the siding.

The main function of the Dallow Lane Branch was to provide an alternative route between Shobnall and the town's railway system, and serve the various industrial premises, but it was also

138

The siding serving Magee Marshall's borehole near the Shobnall Road Bridge, with some of the tank wagons used to carry the water to Bolton. (A. Moss Collection)

used by some through goods workings which could avoid the congestion on the main line. Other locomotives came along the branch from Shobnall when it proved more convenient to hand over traffic to the LNWR at Allsopp's Sidings rather than at Horninglow Yard. Visitors included the MR and private locomotives from Bass, Marston, and Charrington. Bass' often propelled wagons to Allsopp's Sidings. With big loads, a shunter would stand in the first wagon to ensure that the line was clear, because it was difficult for the locomotive driver to see until the train was round the curve under the Shobnall Road Bridge. The person in Shobnall Junction Box used to tell the driver if the signal was in his favour.

The Dallow Lane Branch assumed a greater importance during World War 2 because it allowed diversions to take place from the main line, particularly for trains from Chaddesden and Toton. Allsopp's Sidings situation away from the main concentration of yards meant that it was comparatively safe from attack. The sidings were manned by head and under shunters and operated 24 hours a day, but the branch returned to a quieter existence after the war and activity lessened as the general level of rail traffic declined. In 1951, there were ten mostly coal trains booked to travel over the branch from Toton, Kirkby, Chaddesden and Colwick to Branston and Wichnor. Interestingly, they were all loaded trains and took on water at Allsopp's Sidings. Presumably the returning empties could travel faster and find a path on the main line. On some Sunday mornings, the branch was specially opened to allow three or four of the loaded goods trains to pass. By 1959, the number of regular through workings was reduced to three, the 6.20am Annesley–Pontypool Road, the 7.20am Colwick–Wichnor and the 4.18pm Toton–Wichnor. Trip workings 116, 114 and 121 all spent some time at Allsopp's Sidings each weekday during 1951. Also Trips 117 and 106 covered some of the duties between Horninglow Yard, Stretton Junction and North Stafford Junction.

Trip 114 10th September 1951

	am	am	pm	pm	pm	pm	pm	pm
Horninglow Goods	9.50				1.55	2.30		8.35
North Stafford Junction (South Cripple Sidings)				12.55	1.45			
Stretton Junction	10.00	10.15	12.35	12.45	1.50	2.37	7.40	8.20
Allsopp's Sidings		10.25	12.30			2.45	7.30	

The through goods trains ceased to run in 1961-62 and the down line between Allsopp's Sidings Box and Stretton Junction was given over to the mundane task of storing wagons. A number of sidings had also become disused, including Jones & Broadbent, Kind, and Hallam. Condemned wagons full of coal were stored in Allsopp's Sidings. The remaining premises were shunted by the Dallow Lane trip locomotive, usually a Burton 3F tank; ex MR 47233 and 47257 were particularly common.

It was a leisurely existence for the signalman at Allsopp's Sidings Box, a way of life not unique around some of the Burton signal boxes by October 1962. Although he signed on at either 6am or 7am, and a light engine might occasionally come from Shobnall to cross over, the first serious action of the day was not until the arrival of the principal trip working 9T80 at about 9.50am. This was the 9.25am from Horninglow Yard which came via Stretton Junction and was almost exclusively worked by 47643 during that month. We know this because the MR tradition was continued of recording the locomotive number in the train register book. Ahrons considered that this general practice had originated to ensure that signalmen kept a sharp lookout on trains. The trip continued on to Shobnall about an hour later. It collected some wagons and soon returned to Allsopp's Sidings taking coal wagons to Dallow Lane Wharf and coming back with empties. The locomotive 47643 stayed on the branch for most of the day doing what little shunting was required. Provision was made for it to go to Horninglow Yard at dinner time, departing back from Burton Goods at 2.35pm but there was rarely any need for it to undertake the journey. About midday, the 86T trip passed by the box en route from Old Wetmore to Shobnall, nearly always behind a Burton 4F. The shift ended at 1pm when the other signalman arrived to take over. After another hour, a light locomotive sometimes went by heading for Burton Shed. Then 47464 or 47313 on the 75T trip came from Shobnall to take water, and later 47643 made its last visit to the sidings at Yeomans, Cherry & Curtis; Allsopp's Maltings; Dallow Lane Wharf; and Grout's Cooperage about four o'clock assembling a mixture of bulk grain vans, empty coal wagons, and vans. A 4F on the 86T trip (4pm ex Shobnall) with between 10 and 17 wagons crossed over at the box before continuing on to Stretton Junction and Horninglow Yard. Finally,

Allsopp's Sidings after the signal box had ceased to be regularly manned. Yeomans, Cherry & Curtis's Maltings dominate the background with Kind's water tower further away. 8th June 1964. *(C. Shepherd)*

47643 took some wagons to Shobnall before picking up the remainder, usually 3 to 12 in number, and making for Horninglow Yard (6.55pm ex Allsopp's Sidings). The signalman's day of work was done and he signed off at 7pm.

Removing one of the running lines from the Dallow Lane Branch on 10th June 1964 near Staton & Newton's former siding.
(C. Shepherd)

The portion of the branch between Dallow Bridge and Stretton Junction closed on 7th October 1963, and the remainder became an extended siding from Shobnall Junction, with Allsopp's Sidings Box being opened by the shunter on the daily trip working. New coal hopper wagons, which had been stored on the branch, were removed by two BR 350hp diesel locomotives nose to nose on 17th June 1964 and work began immediately on cutting up the lines. The final traces of a connection with the branch at Stretton Junction were removed on 20th December 1964, not by the usual 350hp diesel on a permanent way train, but more appropriately by a borrowed 4F 44203. All Burton's allocation of 4Fs had gone for scrap, indeed, it was one of the last times that a 4F was seen in Burton, apart from occasional reports of one on the Lount–Drakelow coal trains. Dallow Lane Wharf had closed on 10th July 1964 and its business was transferred to the Midland Goods. The branch between the Dallow Bridge and Allsopp's Sidings Box shut about 1965 and the rest to Shobnall Junction in late 1967. Floor malting continued, albeit with much mechanisation, at Allied Breweries Shobnall Maltings until 1981 when they were demolished. At their closure, it was said that they had supplied one sixth of the malt for the company's Burton brewery.

CHAPTER EIGHT

BOND END AND THE 'COFFEE POTS'

Bond End, Duke Street and New Street Branches

Although these railways were sometimes described collectively as the Bond End Branch, each line had its own name and these will be used. A common feature was that they ran almost furtively behind the buildings in the centre of the town, every so often emerging to cross over one of the streets before disappearing away again behind the brick facades. Strictly speaking, the Bond End Branch was the railway opened in 1875 which went from Wellington Street Junction at Shobnall along the course of the filled in canal down to the river at Bond End. The name was derived from the fact that this area had once been occupied by serfs and bondmen who worked for the abbey but lived outside its walls. By the time that the Railway Bill had been deposited, much of the work of filling in the canal and levelling bridges had been completed so that the Act only provided for raising the land at Bond End by nine feet and removing the Branston Road canal bridge. This allowed the road to be lowered by four feet two inches, prior to construction of the railway. The mills at Bond End had long since ceased to be used for spinning but brewers such as Bell, Hill, Ind Coope, and Bowler had storage space in them.

Branston Road and Lichfield Street formed one of the main approaches to the town and it was natural that businesses should have developed where the road had crossed the canal. The Perks family had ties with the brewers and this encouraged the expansion of their timber business. The main premises and steam saw mill lay to the east of the Branston Road and the MR extended its Bond End Branch over the road to serve them on 2nd November 1875. Charles Hill's father had originally been in partnership with the Sherratts at the Abbey Street Brewery and he had built his own brewery on the west side of Branston Road about 1830. A few years after the arrival of the branch, a siding was provided to serve the brewery on 1st July 1879, with the LNWR also gaining access on that date. The siding was extended into the brewery yard on 14th June 1881.

From the end of the branch, another siding was constructed across to the timber store yard on the far side of Green Street allowing wagons to be reversed into these premises. Green Street was only a narrow lane and no gates were provided to protect the crossing. John Bell had leased and occupied a small malting next to the level crossing since 1873, storing ales in it, and the boiler chimney incorporated a block of stone inscribed with the symbol of a 'bell'. The siding was first used by John Bell and his successors at the malting, Roe & Pickering, adopted this agreement on 1st

Perk's offices were situated on the west side of Branston Road, with Charles Hill's Brewery behind them. The stone at the top of the building still read '1798 PS 1898' when this photograph was taken on 28th March 1965.   (C. Shepherd)

142

Bond End 1904

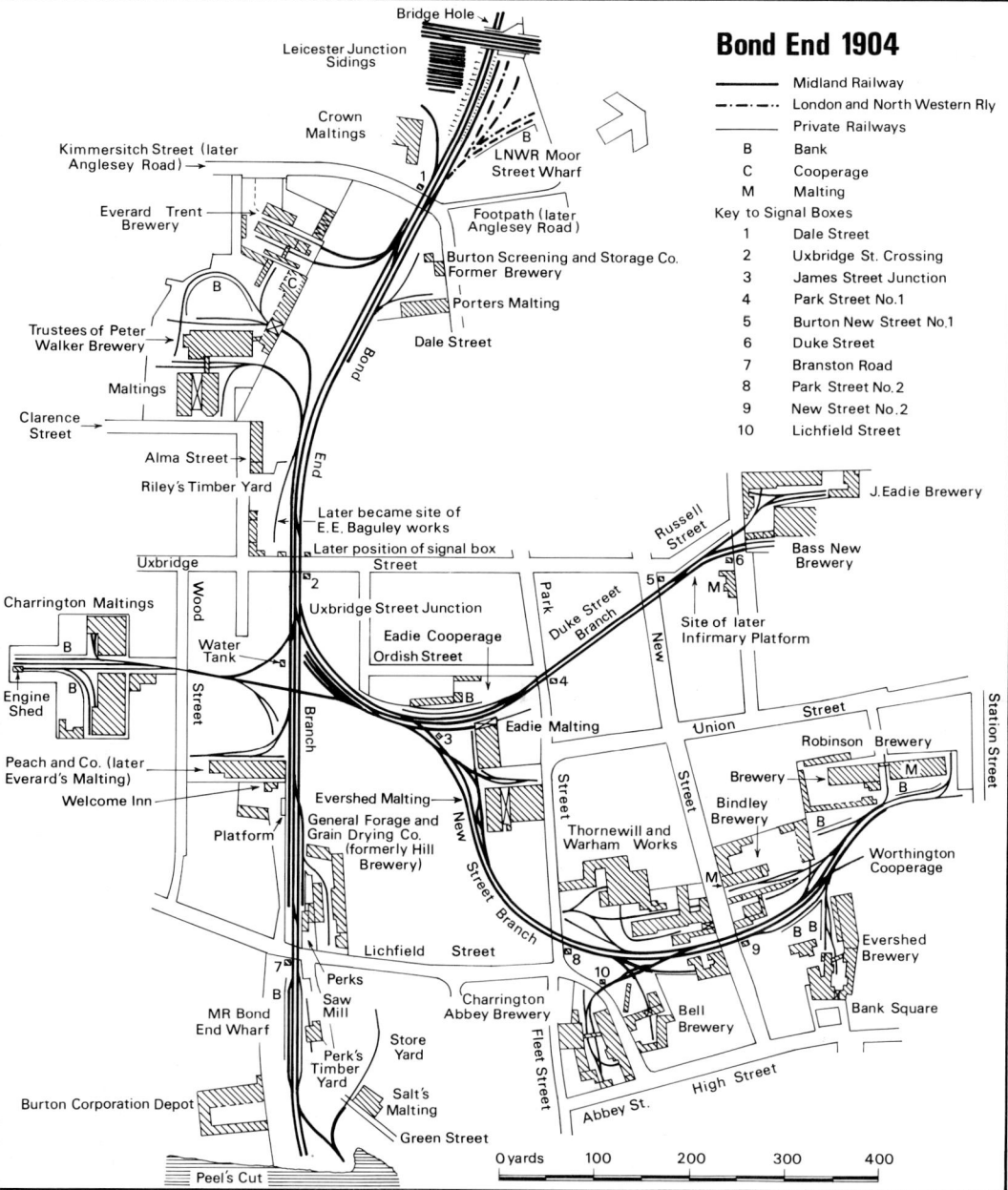

——————	Midland Railway
—·—·—·—	London and North Western Rly
—————	Private Railways
B	Bank
C	Cooperage
M	Malting

Key to Signal Boxes

1	Dale Street
2	Uxbridge St. Crossing
3	James Street Junction
4	Park Street No.1
5	Burton New Street No.1
6	Duke Street
7	Branston Road
8	Park Street No.2
9	New Street No.2
10	Lichfield Street

Bridge Hole

Leicester Junction Sidings

Crown Maltings

Kimmersitch Street (later Anglesey Road) →

LNWR Moor Street Wharf

Everard Trent Brewery

Footpath (later Anglesey Road)

Burton Screening and Storage Co. Former Brewery

Porters Malting

Trustees of Peter Walker Brewery

Dale Street

Maltings

Clarence Street

Alma Street →

Riley's Timber Yard

Later became site of E.E. Baguley works

Later position of signal box

J. Eadie Brewery

Russell Street

Bass New Brewery

Uxbridge Street

Uxbridge Street Junction

Charrington Maltings

Wood Street

Water Tank

Eadie Cooperage

Ordish Street

Park Street

Duke Street Branch

Site of later Infirmary Platform

Engine Shed

Station Street

Street

Union Street

Robinson Brewery

Peach and Co. (later Everard's Malting)

Welcome Inn

Evershed Malting

General Forage and Grain Drying Co. (formerly Hill Brewery)

Platform

Branch

New Street Branch

Eadie Malting

Thornewill and Warham Works

Brewery

Bindley Brewery

Worthington Cooperage

Evershed Brewery

Lichfield Street

Perks

Saw Mill

Charrington Abbey Brewery

Bell Brewery

Bank Square

MR Bond End Wharf

Store Yard

Perk's Timber Yard

Salt's Malting

Fleet Street

High Street

Abbey St.

Burton Corporation Depot

Green Street

Peel's Cut

0 yards	100	200	300	400

August 1882, with the LNWR also exercising its right to work on to the siding. Later, the malting was taken over by Salt and finally by Peach & Co in the 1930s and 1940s.

The land at Bond End on the opposite side of the branch belonged to the MR and it constructed a raised bank to allow wagons to be unloaded. Shortly before the Grouping, there was a large railway notice board standing on two posts close to the Branston Road Signal Box. It was painted black with white lettering and read 'Bond End Wharf. Midland Railway and LNWR' followed by reams of railway jargon. Coal was the principal traffic at the wharf. A short lived siding, opened on 30th September 1882, connected the wharf with the nearby Corporation Depot and Workshops. This was known as the Granite Siding; an indication that road stone, setts and kerbs were delivered and stored here. It is not always appreciated how the growth of the town required substantial amounts of road making materials. Shortly before the Bond End Branch was extended to Duke Street, the Town Commissioners had overruled a request by James Eadie to purchase land in the area of the Bond End Farm to build maltings and cask washing premises because they needed some of it to store granite setts, which could be bought for 6d (2½p) a ton cheaper during the winter months. Perhaps the opening of the siding at the Bond End Depot allowed Eadie to proceed with his cooperage at Ordish Street, now that alternative storage was available for the Corporation. Even so, the Corporation continued to require materials around the town. On 10th February 1887 Edward Clavey, the Borough Surveyor, put out to tender for the supply of about 8,000 tons of both broken and unbroken granite and granite setts and kerbs 'the same to be delivered in such quantities and at such times as may be directed, at the Midland Railway Station, Hay Wharf, Shobnall Wharf, Bond End Wharf or Horninglow Wharf.' *(Burton Chronicle)*.

After Hill's Brewery closed in 1900, the buildings were used by the General Forage & Grain Drying Company. By the end of World War 1, Perks was also in decline and the timber yard was taken over by the Midland Joinery in 1921. The latter developed an extensive network of 2 feet gauge hand worked railways for moving timber between the storeyard and the various mills.

Loaded wagons on the Midland Joinery's hand worked narrow gauge railway on 28th August 1967. (C. Shepherd)

The section of the Bond End Branch to the Wharf was never very busy compared with the Duke Street Branch, which diverged from the Bond End Branch at Uxbridge Street Junction, and formed an essential link to Bass' Breweries. It had been constructed by the MR across the long gardens at the rear of some of the houses in James Street and Ordish Street, on through the field behind Bond End Farm, and over Park Street. The signal box at Park Street No.1 opened on 2nd December 1875 and was replaced by a new structure on 13th December 1902. There was then a short straight stretch of track to New Street. This area was built up by 1875 and buildings on both sides of the road had to be demolished to make way for the railway. Russell Street represented another obstruction, and its alignment had to be altered so that it ran alongside the new railway, which followed the course of the old road. More property had to be removed at the corner with Duke Street. Salt had a malting on the opposite side of the railway and there was a small platform later placed near here for the Infirmary. The hospital had been reconstructed and enlarged in 1899. Bass had

Duke Street Signal Box was reckoned to have the best bell in Burton. 2nd August 1964.
(C. Shepherd)

a special relationship with the Infirmary, the equipment of which was serviced by the company's engineers. If more coal was required for the Infirmary boilers, a phone call would be put through to Bass' Engineers' Department which would contact the Railway Office. The foreman shunter at Shobnall then arranged for a wagon load of coal to be attached to the last train at night and this was left by the Infirmary platform for unloading.

The last signal box at Duke Street dated from 16th March 1907 and was reckoned to have the best bell in Burton. Charlie Harrison was in charge of it in 1958 and is remembered for his very deep voice. The crossing had one set of gates which not only protected the double track of the branch as it entered Bass' New Brewery, but also the single line into Eadie's Brewery (siding opened 17th May 1880), which had resulted in yet another minor diversion of Russell Street. James Eadie was a self made man who had begun brewing in a small way at the premises in Cross Street in 1854. Production in the first year was only 250 barrels and the stores were originally located on the site. The brewery was enlarged between 1883 and 1888 and further sidings added. These ran by the front of the racking room and twenty wagons could be loaded with casks of beer at any one time. Eadie also purchased land behind Bond End Farm and he had a handsome twin block of maltings erected by J. Maddock of Moor Street in 1877. A siding from James Street Junction extended under part of the malting permitting the despatch of malt. Barley was delivered to the top floor stores by way of railway lines at the end and south side of the building. These sidings opened on 28th November 1877 and the LNWR used its running powers over them from 10th June 1878. Ale stores in the basement could hold 2,500 barrels. A new cooperage and cask washing shed was also built at Ordish Street with a siding, opened on 3rd September 1884, off the Duke Street Branch. Eadie did not have its own locomotive and mostly relied on the MR to move its rail traffic between the various premises. The company became James Eadie Limited in 1893 and was reconstituted in 1896. Brewing stopped when it was taken over by Bass in 1933. Bass used the brewery as a wine and spirit store, replacing premises at Coventry, but its locomotive never went into the yard. The cooperage lay abandoned until the 1960s but the malting was taken over by the English Grains Company.

James Street Junction marked the start of the New Street Branch which ran across Park Street and New Street, before terminating at the back of the shops in the very centre of the town, one mile

145

from Wellington Street Junction. It was double track and constructed with some difficulty because of the built up nature of the area. The line squeezed between the houses leased by Sydney Evershed in New Street and passed the corner of his brewery, and a small malting and kiln occupied by Lewis Meakin.

Signal Boxes between Shobnall and Bass' New Brewery

Name of Signal Box	Distance between boxes (yards)
Shobnall Junction	-
Wellington Street Junction	247
Dale Street	435
Uxbridge St Crossing	437
James Street Junction	262
Park Street No.1	137
Burton New St No.1	150
Duke Street	80

The three branches together made a fascinating network of railways linking several small breweries and forming an outlet for some of the larger companies' traffic. It was in the years before World War 1 that the intricacy and colour of the branches reached its maximum extent. No one has left a description of them at the height of their popularity. Later amalgamations and closures reduced the quality of the spectacle, although some of the sidings continued to be visited by a few wagons, and there was the constant coming and going of Bass' locomotives up to 1967. Let us take an imaginary, but probably representative, trip along the railway in those earlier days – No.9, immaculate in the Turkey red livery of Bass, pulls away from the bank at the Shobnall Ale Stores with empty wagons returning to the New Brewery. It threads the railway lines past the exchange sidings where one of Marston's smart dark blue locomotives is busy collecting wagons to take up to the brewery. Gathering speed over the Wellington Street Junction level crossing, No.9 rushes down the gradient to the Bridge Hole under the MR main line before charging up the bank to Dale Street level crossing. A LNWR locomotive is busy sorting wagons in the Moor Street Wharf but its identity is hidden by the surrounding wall. Once on the level again, No.9 settles down to a steady pace as it puffs along the straight behind the properties in Dale Street, perhaps passing one of the little MR 0-4-0 tank locomotives just emerging from the archway of Walker's Clarence Street Brewery. After slowing for Uxbridge Street level crossing, No.9 swings its train away from the Bond End Branch. Steam issuing from Wood Street Maltings probably indicates Charrington's green locomotive getting the wagons of malt ready for the brewery. The driver of No.9 gives a cheerful wave to the signalman at James Street Junction where sometimes one of the graceful blue Worthington Hudswell Clarke locomotives is waiting with wagons for the Crown Maltings. After rattling over Park Street No.1, Burton New Street No.1 and Duke Street level crossings in quick succession, No.9 chuffs slowing through the cavernous gloom between the Delhi Maltings and the New Brewery ale bank, where men are busy loading similar empty wagons with casks of ale for despatch to the ale stores, prior to their being sent to some distant part of the country.

The Bridge Hole

The busiest part of the Bond End Branch was from Shobnall under the main line through the Bridge Hole to Dale Street and the Shobnall Jocko came this way, stopping beyond the crossing before reversing back round the rising curve (opened 25th February 1884) past the Crown Maltings to Leicester Junction Sidings. Old Harry Hawkes recalled one memorable journey along the line during the Zeppelin raid on 31st January 1916. This is recounted in Denis Stuart's book *History of Burton upon Trent* "I went on duty at 8.12 at Leicester Junction. On a little engine No.1602, a little 0-6-0 shunter. And my mate says 'Shut that ejector, Harry. There's such a blinking noise above us.' And he no sooner said this than the bomb dropped in the sidings, fifty yards away. I was in a bit of a ditch there and I saw this great black object in the sky. Our lights were on at Leicester Junction, so I put out as many as I could. Then the incendiary bomb dropped on the Ind Coope bottling stores. They immediately went up into flames. That would be about 8.45, 8.50pm. As we went round to Dale

James Eadie's premises. The upper illustration shows a MR 0-4-0 saddle tank locomotive leaving the brewery about 1888. In the lower photograph, the Duke Street Branch curves past the former Eadie's malting, then occupied by English Grains, and approaches Park Street No.1 Signal Box. 26th December 1965.

(A. Barnard, C. Shepherd)

Bass' No.2 rushes down to the Bridge Hole picking up speed for the climb to Dale Street on 8th June 1964. The grey Worthington medium sided wagon number 68 is carrying ash. *(C. Shepherd)*

Street up to Wellington Street crossing, an old signalman called Tony Mycock shouted 'What's going off?' he said, 'Come here' and I went up into the signal box and he'd got a great incendiary bomb on his lamp-cleaning bracket. Seemed twice as big as a hurricane lamp. He says 'This here's hit the signal box and its bounced in front of here', and he went and picked it up and brought it into the signal box. So I says 'That's an incendiary bomb, Tony', I says 'you want to get shot of that bugger'."

Sometimes signalmen who were nearing retirement or had become less fit were moved to signal boxes on the town's branches, on the theory that the work was more suitable for them. One man transferred from Wetmore Sidings Box to Wellington Street Junction Signal Box after an illness, but the move hardly entailed less effort, because he unfortunately now had to handle the large wheel for the heavy gates across Wellington Street Extension. The MR had a wharf along the Bond End Branch near the Bridge Hole which was served by a single siding. This was the Burton Signal and Telegraph Engineers' Depot, complete with a forge and a small signal box used as an office. On the opposite side of the branch was the short remnant of the original link to the main line, which was retained in case spare capacity was needed to store traffic waiting for accommodation on Sharp Bros & Knight's Siding.

The LNWR had attempted to run its own locomotives over the Shobnall and Bond End Branches on 6th June 1878 but had been stopped by the MR. Further negotiations took place and the terms of the agreement were set down in Mr Harrison's letter dated 10th June 1878. The LNWR was allowed to work its own traffic to and from the Shobnall Basin Sidings, Bass's Shobnall Maltings, Evershed's Malting, Eadie's Malting and Bass's New Brewery but it was not permitted to run its own trains to the 'Shobnall Station' (presumably the MR's coal wharf), 'Mann & Crossman's' Branch (later amended on 20th June 1881 from which date the LNWR worked its own traffic), the Bond End Wharf

148

and Perks' Siding at Bond End. Any goods for these places had to be handed over to the MR at Wetmore as previously. The LNWR subsequently gained approval that it could haul its traffic using its own locomotives to the Shobnall and Bond End Wharves from 1st May 1879. MR employees still dealt with the traffic at the wharves and kept the accounts.

The LNWR's locomotives also shunted its own coal depot at the Kottingham and Moor Street Wharf. This had opened on 6th July 1880 and the MR was able to work its goods into the wharf, although it was the LNWR employees who unloaded the wagons and kept a record of the produce handled. The term 'Kottingham' came from the nearby cooperage, which had been founded by Alfred Newton who had originated from Cottingham near Hull. He later used the cooperage to dry and process waste barm from the breweries for resale. The wharf had two road entrances. Once a funeral cortege wanted to take a short cut across but the old employee, who looked after the wharf, refused and was later complimented by the railway company, which said that he could finish his days there. Apparently there was an old belief that the action of carrying a corpse across the land created a public right of way. In later years, a little ex MR 0-4-0 locomotive could often be found waiting at the wharf for its next duty. It was renamed Moor Street Wharf in the years after World War 1.

Whistle code approaching Dale Street Signal Box from Leicester Junction Sidings

Whistles

2	Eadie's Brewery, Duke Street
3	Bass' New Brewery
4	Robinson's Brewery
5	Branston Road

When the Bond End Branch was built, the land to the south west was largely undeveloped and the crossing took its name by virtue of being located at the end of Dale Street. Anglesey Road was

41536 on Trip 110 pulls out of Moor Street Wharf on 7th May 1955 to rejoin the Bond End Branch. The signal box behind the solitary wagon is Burton Station South on the main line. Closure of the wharf took place on 6th July 1964.

(B.J. Miller Collection)

Dale Street was one of the older surviving signal boxes in Burton when this photograph was taken on 10th April 1964. *(C. Shepherd)*

originally only a farm track and the level crossing was probably little used by road vehicles in the beginning. The farm track was previously known as Kimmersitch Street and there was a complaint in a Burton Town Council meeting in 1905 when the attention of Members was drawn to the 'dangerous state' of the railway crossing in Kimmersitch Street. Only a few weeks before, a horse had trapped one of its hooves in the metals and been killed by a locomotive. In some MR deeds, the level crossing was referred to as 'Meakin's Crossing'. Dale Street Signal Box was probably erected in 1882 when the crossing was widened. It eventually became a late surviving example of a MR Type 1 box. The MR had begun to use its familiar standard design of signal box in about 1869-70 and what is now known as the Type 1 was built up to about 1883. It could be most easily distinguished from later types by the shallow depth and high waist line of the 3ft 6in deep front windows. Each window comprised four panes with weatherboard timbering underneath. Like most MR boxes, it was of all wood construction and built up from substantial horizontal timbers set in the ground. This was the undoing of some of these boxes as the timber rotted. The MR had an accelerated programme of signal box replacements from 1890 which meant that Type 1 boxes, such as Dale Street, became fewer in number. Dale Street Box was extensively repaired in 1911 when the walkways and front locking room windows were probably added, and officially closed on 20th January 1968.

If the locomotives had a heavy load, both the brewery and railway companies' drivers used to wait at Dale Street home signal for the distant signal to be pulled off. When clear, they took a good run down the bank and up to Shobnall in the knowledge that Wellington Street gates would be open. The positioning of a distant signal so near to a signal box was unusual and Wellington Street Junction home signal was on a tall post so that it could be easily seen. Sometimes, when the locomotive boiler was full of water, working through the Bridge Hole had a tendency to cause priming and this resulted in a few complaints from the public. Loading gauges were provided to warn drivers approaching the Bridge Hole of the restricted height and they had to look back and check the passage of the last wagon to see that the gauge was not shaking. It did happen on rare occasions, such as when a van had been fitted with new wheels and springs. Some of the vans had rails on the roof and Joe Slater recalled these hitting the gauge once. Flooding could also take place at the

41536 runs along the down goods line by Leicester Junction Sidings on 30th May 1960. In the background are part of the Crown Maltings and the Leicester Junction Sidings Signal Box. This latter structure had opened on 20th June 1909 replacing an earlier box.   (R.C. Riley)

Bridge Hole and sometimes a railway company locomotive would be deputed to take the wagons through the water, with Bass' locomotives delivering them to Dale Street and collecting them between Wellington Street and Shobnall Junction. In the Great Flood on 21st October 1875, the water reached a depth of 12 feet under the bridge and a plaque was subsequently placed in the wall recording the level.

The Crown Maltings

The curve round to the Leicester Junction Sidings also gave access to the Crown Maltings which formed an impressive sight, particularly when viewed from passing trains on the main line. Meakins were long established maltsters who had started by using various small maltings scattered about the town. Probably with the proceeds from the sale of the old Abbey Brewery, they initially built two maltings at Crown in 1875 (later Nos.1, 2) on land leased from the Marquis of Anglesey. Henry James Meakin signed the lease but he soon died, because in 1877, the land was leased by the trustees of H.J. Meakin and Lewis Meakin. The maltings were then controlled by Lewis and George Meakin and were connected to the Leicester Junction Sidings by a single line, possibly put down for the Machine Cooperage Company's building (Neave Prescott Steam Cooperage in 1869) that had previously occupied part of the site. Meakins began to send out traffic over the line on 9th October 1878, the MR's locomotives collecting the wagons. The LNWR gained powers on 22nd June 1881 for its locomotives to also work to the maltings. In 1882, the Meakins started the construction of three more maltings (Nos.3, 4 and 5) to an advanced design and incorporating considerable mechanisation. The railway layout was expanded to serve the new maltings by taking additional lines off the Leicester Junction Sidings shunting spur. These lines were opened on 12th September 1883 for the receipt of rail traffic, although Worthington occupied one of the maltings by this date. Later No.6 Malting, containing a kiln for drying barley, was added to No.2 malting. In 1887, the Meakins employed 3 managers, 6 foremen and 70 maltsters, and L. & G. Meakin made 7,292 qtrs of malt for Bass in 1890-91.

The Burton Foundry Company also had a siding off this spur following the establishment of its works in 1916. It became part of Allied Ironfounders in 1929 and was still receiving rail traffic on 6th July 1965 when an ex LMS designed 350hp diesel shunter 12077 was noted in the siding. The railway company always shunted this siding.

It is thought that the Meakins had no sons to follow them in the business at the Crown Maltings, although a daughter of George married Ernest Manners, who was to become managing director of Worthington. By 1898, Worthington seems to have taken over the lease of some of the maltings. According to a 1903-04 LNWR plan, Meakin still occupied Nos.1 and 2 with Worthington in Nos.3-6. Meakin's name had disappeared from the list of sidings by 1912. A photograph of the maltings in late 1913 has R. Peach & Co's name on No.3 and Worthington on Nos.4 and 5. There are memories of 'Peach & Co' on a board over the passage between Nos.1 and 2. In 1914, the 6th North Staffordshire Regiment was billeted at Peach's Maltings and there is a photograph of the Regiment being mobilized at the beginning of August with the men standing on the sidings outside No.3 Malting. On a LMS rating plan, Peach was shown to occupy Nos.3-5 Maltings. Eventually Worthington controlled all of the maltings.

The Crown Maltings shunt was one of the jobs which persuaded Worthington of the need for Planet locomotives. A small corrugated iron shed was specially built abutting on to Anglesey Road capable of accommodating one of the early Planet locomotives. Its dimensions were based on the low cab profile of these locomotive with unfortunate results, because the later tall cab variety could not get into the shed! The Crown Maltings job therefore had to be reserved for one of the low cab locomotives, which was permanently stabled at Crown and was only brought to High Street when repairs were needed. A spare Planet was kept at High Street in good condition in case of breakdowns, and this would replace it until the repairs had been carried out, when the original Planet would return to Crown. The driver booked on at Anglesey Road at 6am and usually worked up to about 4pm. His main task was to manoeuvre wagons between the different hoists. One of Worthington's steam locomotives dealt with traffic to and from the maltings. Bass' locomotives never worked round to Leicester Junction Sidings until after the amalgamation with Worthington. In more recent years, Bass' 'Barley Engine' used to go to Crown about 10.30am and collect malt vans for the Hay Sidings, where they were handed over to a Worthington locomotive. Traffic for exchange with the railway company was mostly hauled round to Shobnall or up to Dixie. Once, when flooding blocked the normal route, Bill Bennett worked a Bass locomotive along the main line through the station to Dixie. The change to the mechanised handling of malt created difficulties for the little Planet locomotives. They could manage four or five bulk grain vans on the straight but on the tight curves into the maltings, they would often ride up and come off the rails with as little as one bulk grain van. Floor malting ceased at Crown about 1965-66 and the buildings were eventually sold to the Clarke organisation which converted them to other uses.

The 'Coffee Pots'

Some of the breweries were small concerns which did not require their own locomotive and relied on the railway company to carry out most of the shunting. The tight curves, with lines penetrating into virtually every corner of the premises, forced the MR to develop its own range of short wheelbase locomotives. Although these could once be seen in various parts of the town, they were particularly associated with the Bond End branches; earlier this century, it could be truly said that the Bond End trip was 'a proper ale carrying job'.

Typical of these properties were the three breweries located between Dale Street and Uxbridge Street level crossings. Walker's Clarence Street Brewery was designed by Scamell & Collyer of London and built by Lowe & Sons in 1883. Two railway lines ran across the open ground from the Bond End Branch, one of which entered the yard through a covered archway. Once inside, this line split into two sidings with a railway lying alongside the ale stores bank. Stores occupied the whole basement area of the brewery and casks were delivered to the loading point by a steam lift. A semi-circular ale bank, which could accommodate up to 10,000 casks between October and May, was served by the other sidings. The second line from the branch passed between the brewery and the maltings, one block of which had an unusual octagonal shaped kiln, with a weather vane in the form of a goat on the cupola. The kiln was circular inside and its shape was dictated by the use of steam driven prongs and brushes for turning the malt. Barley was brought in by the railway but the malt could be delivered directly to the maltrooms in the brewery by a conveyor belt running along a covered bridge above the railway.

The sidings to Walker's Brewery came into use on 12th April 1883. They connected with the up line of the Bond End Branch, but by 1900, the sidings joined to form an additional line which went over the Uxbridge Street crossing adjacent to the branch and continued almost up to Branston Road. The signal box at the crossing was located on the south side of the branch in 1882 but had to be moved to the opposite side to make way for the new line. On 20th June 1910 the position of the box

Part of Crown Maltings and offices as seen from Anglesey Road on 29th March 1966. The small corrugated iron building was the locomotive shed specially built to accommodate one of Worthington's first Planet locomotives.   (C. Shepherd)

One of the little MR 0-4-0 saddle tank locomotives at Walker's Clarence Street Brewery about 1888.   (A. Barnard)

was changed yet again and a new signal cabin was erected on the west side of Uxbridge Street! The *Sectional Appendix to the Working Timetable* referred to 'Uxbridge Street Junction, Canal Branch as late as 1937'.

Walker's Clarence Street Brewery closed about 1925, but Yeomans, Cherry & Curtis took over the maltings and continued to receive grain vans until 1967, when the maltings were converted to grain stores. Baguley used the cellars underneath the brewery to store wooden patterns up to 1965.

The final position of the Uxbridge St Crossing Signal Box. 21st March 1967. (C. Shepherd)

The land between Walker's Brewery and the Dale Street crossing was occupied by Thomas Sykes' Trent Brewery in the late 1870s, with an annual production of only 3,000 to 5,000 barrels. Thomas Sykes had come from Seaforth near Liverpool. In 1885, he signed a new lease with the Marquis of Anglesey for the land with the brewery, storerooms, stabling and cottages. In the same year, his son Benjamin Corliss Sykes leased a piece of land adjacent to the brewery from Phillip Robinson and more land was leased in 1885. On 31st March 1890, the leases were assigned from the trustees of Thomas Sykes (deceased) and Benjamin Sykes to the Sykes Brewery Co Ltd. Meanwhile, the brother-in-law of Thomas Sykes was James Porter and he, with his son John H. Porter, had the little brewery and malting across the branch in Dale Street. They had taken over these premises from Bryan Brothers in 1878. Previously the site had been Joseph Outram's timber yard when the Bond End Canal still flowed past its boundary. The Porters lived in a nearby house called The Maynes which they had named after the family home in Poulton-le-Fylde. John H. Porter married a daughter of R.W. Abbots who was Bass's head maltster. They had a son called James Porter who followed his father into the business and ultimately became Vice Chairman of Scottish & Newcastle Breweries Ltd.

Initially neither brewery made use of the branch but sidings were opened into the Dale Street Brewery on 20th October 1882 and to the Sykes Brewery Company on 28th July 1890. The latter was served by two lines which ran across open ground into the brewery, but these premises were soon to change hands. On 29th March 1893 Harold Elkington, the liquidator of the Sykes Brewery Company, conveyed them to the newly registered Trent Brewery Co Ltd. The property was leased to Everard & Welldon on 17th February 1898; the Trent Brewery Co Ltd having gone into voluntary liquidation in June 1896. Everard had started brewing in 1849 and the firm came to Burton as Everard, Son & Welldon, acquiring the Bridge Brewery off the Burton Bridge. T.W. Everard completed the purchase of the former Sykes premises from the Trent Brewery Co Ltd on 18th January 1901. The business was called W. Everard & Co until October 1925 when it became a

BR 204hp diesel shunter D2384 eases round the curve leading to Everard's Brewery on 25th March 1966. The remaining sidings on the Bond End Branch could be dealt with by a 0-6-0 locomotive by this date.   *(C. Shepherd)*

private limited liability company. It was registered as a public company, Everard's Brewery Ltd, in October 1936. Most of the public houses were in Leicestershire and beer was regularly sent by rail to Leicester. Movement by road began in 1926 using two Super Sentinel articulated 6-wheel steam lorries. These continued to run from Burton to Leicester until June 1946 when diesel lorries took over. Everard brewed at the former Sykes brewery until 1985, although the railway sidings had of course gone before then, and it later functioned as a working museum.

The brewery in Dale Street subsequently became Sykes & Porter and was later included in the Robinson property. Beer was then brewed at Robinson's Union Street premises and only the malting was used at Dale Street. The brewery was rented to a grain drying company, called the Burton Screening & Storage Company, with the malting eventually passing into Ind Coope's ownership, together with the other Robinson possessions.

Everard also had a malting alongside the Bond End Branch at Wood Street. It had been built by Charrington but was in Peach & Co's ownership when it caught fire on 7th July 1908. Water from a huge tank on top of the engine house at Charrington's Maltings was used to stop the fire spreading to Perk's timber yard. The siding to Peach's Wood Street Malting had opened on 10th September 1896 but the tight curve meant that only small locomotives, such as the MR 0-4-0 shunters, could enter. This malting came into Everard's possession after World War 1 and railway wagons continued to be delivered to the malting until the Bond End Branch closed. A siding passed under the external loading hoists at the side of the building and connected with the railway which ran next to the branch. In the early 1960s, Conder Engineering Co (Midlands) Ltd had a gantry crane over the Branston Road end of this railway and steel was brought in by BR on bogie bolster wagons. Malting finished at Wood Street when it was found more economical to buy malt from outside suppliers.

The New Street Branch also had its share of small breweries worked by the MR's 'Coffee Pots'. Two of the brewers had some previous involvement with Worthington whose cooperage was also connected to the branch. Thomas Robinson had the brewery in Union Street and may have been

In the 1870s, the MR had a varied collection of short wheelbase locomotives which it had taken over from a number of industrial concerns. These were becoming due for replacement and Samuel Johnson brought out a new design, having similarities with the Sharp Stewart locomotives acquired from the Staveley Coal & Iron Company. The locomotives had inside cylinders which, combined with four-coupled wheels, gave them a rather quaint appearance. Most industrial locomotives with this wheel arrangement had outside cylinders because speed was not essential and the overhang at the front end could be tolerated. This also left the rear axle free from inside cranks and the firebox could be placed close to it. The MR was a great believer in inside cylinders, even if it meant that the locomotives had to have a considerable overhang at the back end so that the firebox could clear the crank axle and connecting rod big ends. Eighteen locomotives (1500-17) were built between 1883 and 1897 with 13in x 20in cylinders and a type J boiler with a raised round topped firebox. A slightly larger version was then brought out using a J1 boiler and a flush topped firebox, together with 15in x 20in cylinders. Ten (1518-27) of these locomotives were built. At Burton, the *MR 1911 Working Timetable Appendix* laid down the following limits:-

'Shobnall & Bond End, Burton
Loads for small tank engines of 1500 class will be 25 loaded and 37 empties and for shunting engines of 1601 class, 35 loaded and 50 empties.'

Locomotives at Burton

Locomotive number	Years when at Burton					
	1929	1937	1944	1948	1958	1962
1510	✓					
1516	✓	✓	✓	✓		
1523			✓	✓		
1530		✓		✓		
1532	✓				✓	
1533				✓ 1947		
1535	✓	✓	✓			
1536	✓	✓	✓	✓	✓	
1540 (7000)				✓		
1543 (7003)		✓ 1935				
1544 (7004)		✓ 1935		✓		
11205	✓ 1932					
11217		✓		✓		
11230	✓					
11235	✓		✓	✓		
16020		✓	✓	✓		
D2859						✓

( ) Later numbers of locomotives.

There were still twenty six of the small locomotives distributed between nine MR sheds in 1920. Burton had 1500, 1504, 1516, and 1519. The LMS soon scrapped most of them during the next decade but three of the four survivors in regular service soldiered on at Burton. In addition, 1506 had been withdrawn in 1924 but was retained by Derby Works as the 'Bottom Yard Jinty' and it operated until 1949. When 1506 (renumbered 1509 in 1930) was under repair, 1516 was sent from Burton to deputise. Sometimes 1509 came to Burton to help out. The early locomotives were only given a spectacle plate but they eventually sported a piece of metal bent over to form a rudimentary cab. On 1506, this extended to the back of the locomotive but 1516 did not have the rear section.

Of the Burton locomotives, 1510 was withdrawn in 1936 but 1516 and later 1523 continued to shunt round the Bond End Branch. The Grammar School boys often climbed on to the wall surrounding the school field at Peel Croft to jeer at these old antiquated MR locomotives. Mocking enquiries such as "What time are you mashing?" and "Getting the copper ready for washday?" invariably elicted a shower of small coal from the fireman who was often a youth not much older than the schoolboys themselves. Occasionally the ball would go over the wall and there would be a shout from the direction of James Street Junction signal box as a boy was seen creeping over the line to retrieve it. When Frank Holmes worked on the Bond End trip, he usually had 1523.

"I was on that job one week and one of the crank pins started to run hot on it. We worked it. The next day, they told us to take it and they would send us a fresh one later in the day. Anyway, they sent us 1516. Well she was absolutely useless. The tubes were blocked up on it. We managed with it like. It was down for the job the next day. I said to my mate 'We'll do something about this', I says 'Put a great fire on it, I'm going to have a scrounge round'. I found two or three old sacks and two or three old overcoats. I went into the Oil Stores and I soaked 'em with paraffin, brought 'em on a barrow and chucked them up on that there and said 'Shove 'em in the firebox and when you have done', I says 'Shut it up and keep it shut, keep the independent steam jet on. We went to the Belling Out Box. Running out from the Belling Out Box down towards the relief cabin at Leicester Junction (by the side of the engine shed), they caught fire. There was fire everywhere, round the engine, underneath but it burnt all the muck out and she steamed like an old tin kettle afterwards. You should have seen them run out the blinking relief cabin. It was a laugh that was."

Locomotive 1516 was loaned out during World War 2, and even before then, it had spent short periods at Wingfield Main Colliery and Chilwell Ordnance Depot. On at least three occasions it stood in for a Sentinel at Ley's Malleable Castings Ltd's works at Derby. The last general overhaul of 1516 was in 1948 and it was withdrawn on 1st October 1955 after covering 636,694 miles. It was the last example of the smaller class with the J type boiler; 41523 had also gone a few months earlier.

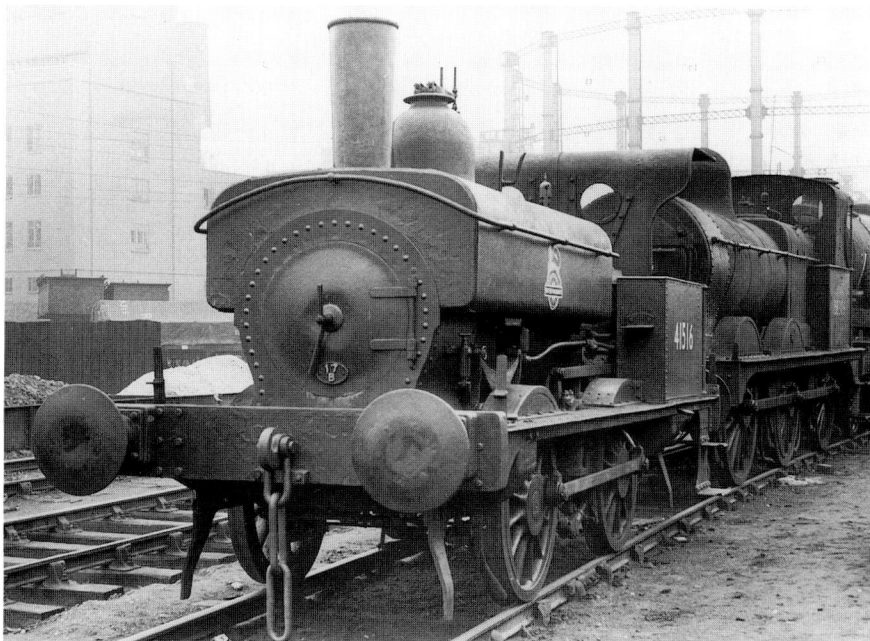

41516, the last example with the J boiler, at Derby for scrapping about 1955. One side was cleaned and new transfers applied for the official pre-scrapping photographs. *(Frank Ashley)*

In 1907, a new design of shunter was introduced by Richard Deeley of the MR. These locomotives had a radically different appearance with side tanks extending to the front of the smokebox, outside cylinders, and Walschaerts valve gear. The latter was certainly a departure from standard MR practice. Five locomotives were built (1528-32) and some of these went to shunt the Staveley Ironworks. Another five were erected in 1921-22 (1533-37) and the type was seen on the New Street Branch shortly after. The later locomotives carried 'rebuilt' plates when new and were supposedly conversions from the inside cylinder 0-4-0 saddle tanks but they were virtually new locomotives. It was a sign of the inflation during the latter half of World War 1, and for some time after, that the cost of building the later series of Deeley locomotives had risen to £3,889 each, compared with £1,361 for each 1907 locomotive. In 1927, Burton had 1532, 1535, and 1536. Number 1532 went to Staveley in 1930 but 1530 arrived six years later; 1536 was allocated to Burton for most of its existence and was given a new boiler in 1928, the old boiler having a recorded mileage of 109,847. Later, it received reconditioned boilers which had been on other members of

Use of Deeley 0-4-0 tank locomotive 1536 at Burton 1927-1961

	Mileage (includes amount on loan)		Heavy/ light repairs	Weekdays out of service Running repairs/ examinations	Not required	Comments
1927	14,165		3	50	23	
1928	12,787		27	44	31	Heavy general overhaul. New boiler fitted
1929	13,909		0	28	65	
1930	9,040		0	44	90	Stored part of year
1931	13,398		8	19	75	Stored part of year
1932	8,500		0	46	85	
1933	11,182		25	53	15	Major repairs. Fitted with boiler ex 1534
1934	13,337		37	6	20	Heavy general repair. Boiler ex 1528 fitted
1935	18,443		0	7	23	
1936	16,593		0	35	17	
1937	18,389		16	11	10	Major repairs
1938	18,365		11	5	9	Light repairs
1939	13,465		80	10	1	Major repairs. Boiler ex 1531 fitted
1940	17,845		0	14	5	
1941	15,407		48	12	5	Light repairs
1942	16,175		0	21	9	
1943	14,663	(8,839)	7	29	10	Light repairs
1944	15,707	(1,800)	23	20	9	Heavy general repair. Boiler ex 1529 fitted
1945	13,184	(6,193)	0	46	16	
1946	9,843	(6,751)	32	21	11	Light repairs
1947	12,054	(6,342)	0	3	1	
1948	12,531	(9,749)	22	24	25	Major repairs. Boiler ex 1535 fitted
1949	14,244		0	28	25	
1950	11,686	(a)	0	21	15	
1951	12,228	(a)	27	8	32	Heavy intermediate repair
1952	10,868		0	31	73	Stored serviceable 66 days
1953	9,801		0	39	18	
1954	11,841	(b)	16	42	18	Heavy general repair 1954-55. Boiler ex ? fitted
1955	9,190		9	15	37	
1956	8,697		0	34	32	At Rowsley 5.5.1956 to 15.9.1956
1957	12,323		0	12	22	
1958	8,118		0	9	97	
1959	10,363					
1960						
1961	800					Withdrawn week ending 4.3.1961

a   Includes loan to other regions
b   Includes loan to private companies

the class. The dramatic effect of the Depression is revealed by the number of days, totalling 90 in 1930, when it was not required. Annual coal consumption was down to 133 tons in 1932 compared with the more usual figure of about 250 tons. It saw greater use later in the decade and was loaned to the 'USA authorities, Burton' on a daily hire basis from 26th December 1942. This continued until 1948. Both 1530 and 1535 were also lent to the United States army until 17th June 1944, when the former departed for Gloucester and the other went to Derby. They were replaced by Kitson 1540 (7000) and Lancashire & Yorkshire Railway pug 11217. Despite the number of four-wheel shunters at Burton, 1533 also had to be temporarily borrowed from Staveley in 1947. It was a different story in the 1950s as traffic declined. Although serviceable, 41536 was placed in store for the first quarter of 1952. It was also loaned out to other regions and private firms. At the beginning of 1955, 41536 had a major overhaul emerging from Derby Works repainted but unlined and was joined at Burton by 41532 in April. In the same year, the ex North London Railway tank on the Cromford & High Peak Railway had also gone into the Works for repairs and 41536 went up to the little Sheep Pasture Engine Shed to deputise while it was away.

Usually only one 0-4-0 shunter was now required at Burton, and with 41536 absent, 41532 was the main performer on the 110T Bond End trip. It began its day at Shobnall Exchange Sidings about 8.10am before setting off down to Bond End. Frank Holmes describes what it was like "Picking up and putting off at breweries down Bond End. Started from Shobnall, then down into Dale Street, across the road from the Forest Grape, mess about in there, do a bit of shunting with your train and then into Everards. Put them some wagons in there and perhaps two or three loads of grain. Go in the allowance room and have a glass of beer. Down then to the Welcome – that's at Uxbridge Street. A bit of messing about there. Then down to Bond End. 'Little Hitler' as used to work the crossing gates there. He would come and we'd do a bit of shunting there. Into the market. Do a bit of shunting round there and perhaps come back again and fetch some more stuff. You was messing about, perhaps never had no more than fifteen or sixteen wagons to you all day. You was dodging about at work all the while." Whilst 41532 might make a brief return to Shobnall at 11.30am, it mostly brought wagons back about 3pm, before often visiting Ind Coope & Allsopp's Bottling Stores. It put in a final appearance at Shobnall during the evening and then travelled back to the shed. If 41532 was not available, another locomotive was pressed into service. On 8th August 1955, 41516 was working on the trip, and although 41532 was back the next day, 41516 was also out on an 'oil train' going along the Dallow Lane Branch. An ex Lancashire & Yorkshire Railway pug was sent from Derby to replace 41516 and it saw some use on 110T for a few days in mid September. A week later on 24th September both 41532, and 51235 on a 'coal train', were working. The arrival of the new diesel made 41532 and 41536 redundant and both were sent to Derby for scrap in March 1961; 41536 reputedly with a cracked frame. It had covered 958,105 miles during its career.

For more modern power, the LMS had turned to a private manufacturer, Kitson, and it supplied five of a traditional industrial type in 1932. It had originally been intended to base the new locomotives on a development of the Deeley class but presumably the depressed economy meant that buying 'off the peg' was cheaper. Each new locomotive cost only £1,525. This batch had the saddle tank extending almost the whole length of the boiler. They were numbered 1540-44 but this was later changed to 7000-04 under the 1934 renumbering scheme. Another five were built at Horwich Works in 1953-54 but this time the cost was £7,479 each. The BR version (47005-09) had the saddle tank cut short before the dome to permit larger coal bunkers holding two tons to be installed. Burton received two of the new LMS locomotives, including 1544 which was initially fitted with a patent smoke eliminator. They did not stay long and Burton generally had to make do with the older locomotives. Perhaps the new locomotives were more suited to the heavier work at iron and steel works. Burton men considered the Kitson locomotives 'a bit tight on some of the curves' despite their having the same wheelbase as the Deeley locomotives. 47000 was at Burton for eight years until 1952 and both it and 47006 stood in on the few occasions when the diesel shunter was out of action.

Ex Lancashire & Yorkshire Railway pugs more typically seen around the Liverpool docks, such as numbers 11205, 11217, 11230 and 11235, became quite a common sight in Burton, though little

Kitson saddle tank 47000 deputises for D2859 on 25th June 1964 and runs across New Street. *(C. Shepherd)*

use was made of 11230. It was in the town for 3½ years before it returned to its native haunts and during that time, it was in store for 592 weekdays. Number 11217 did more work at Burton but even it had several periods out of use. Ind Coope borrowed it in 1937, and a week later, it was sent to the Bromford Tube Company at Birmingham, being transferred to Saltley Shed at the end of the loan. It came back to Burton in 1944 and did quite a lot of miles on hire, presumably for the United States army. It was not long before 11217 was on its travels again, this time to Maltby Main Colliery and then further afield to the North Sunderland Railway again on loan. The locomotive left Burton

51217 and 56020 stored at the back of Burton Shed yard in 1951. *(P. Rickard, Courtesy Pendon Museum Trust)*

162

for the last time in 1952. The last steam locomotive type was the Caley pug 16020 (later 56020) which stayed for a long time until condemned at Derby in mid 1955. Despite this, it had suffered from the censure that "you couldn't get round the curves". In 1941 the Royal Ordnance Factory No.10 Rearsby was built near Queniborough on the Syston and Peterborough line. During the construction, Burton's 1536 and 16020 and Derby's 11235 were all stationed at Leicester for varying periods to work on the site. The railway company's shunters at Burton were a remarkably well travelled set of locomotives.

The four-coupled locomotives were not without their problems. The steep pull up from the Bridge Hole meant that with anything like a load, they were usually struggling by the end of the journey. There was very little space for carrying coal and the quite deep firebox had to be filled up with lumps at the start if adequate steam pressure was to be maintained. More coal could be picked up during the day from small wooden stages located around the railway system but it required a fair amount of skill to work these locomotives economically. Otherwise, there were frequent stops to take on water and attend to the fire. The early Johnson locomotives, such as 1516, only had a water capacity of 400 gallons and a sharp blast would soon deplete the fire. The injector water regulator on the Deeley locomotives often jammed because it ran along the top of the tank where extra coal was stowed. It could be bleak for the crew on 1516 with its austere 'cab', although visits to the allowance rooms provided some relief. In comparison, the Deeley locomotives were very hot to work on in the summer because of the confined space within the cab.

The requirement for small specialist locomotives did not quite disappear with the diesel era. Twenty 179hp diesel shunters were constructed by the Yorkshire Engine Company for BR. Only one of these was required at Burton and D2859 arrived in December 1960. Its reign was short and it moved on to Derby in the autumn of 1964. The few remaining sidings on the Bond End and New Street Branches could be dealt with by one of the BR 204hp 0-6-0 diesel shunters, D2377 or D2384.

E.E. Baguley Limited

After the closure of Baguley (Engineers) Limited's works at Shobnall in October 1931, Baguley and the Souster brothers set up a small repair business for their products in premises believed to have been situated near the corner of Clarence Street and Alma Street. Some old machinery, part finished components, and three unsold locomotives (800, 1721, 1797) were acquired. The new company of E.E. Baguley Limited was registered on 20th April 1932. Orders began to come in for new locomotives and it was evident that more space was required. The adjacent plot of land had previously been used by W. Riley & Sons as a timber yard and a siding had been opened into the premises on 10th December 1883. According to the MR, this siding was stated to belong to Berry & Co in 1919. Baguley purchased this land and erected a new but modest factory facing on to Uxbridge Street. The single siding from the Bond End Branch was retained and later developed into a multi gauge test track.

During the 1930s, the company built small numbers of petrol and diesel locomotives rated from 10 to 55hp, together with a number of Drewry railcars based on older designs. Some of the locomotives were fitted with Baguley transmissions until the early 1940s. There was also some general engineering work and a reasonable trade in spares for the railcars already in service. During World War 2, the works was involved in munitions work but afterwards it concentrated more on locomotive construction. Many of the orders came via Drewry, and Baguley produced all of this agent's narrow gauge and one off standard gauge locomotives, including such classic designs as the 107hp and 153hp Gardner engined locomotives; whilst the Vulcan Foundry and Robert Stephenson & Hawthorns continued to build Drewry's larger standard orders, including the 204hp locomotives. Baguley also began constructing battery locomotives, making many 13 tons mining locomotives under contract to suppliers English Electric and Metropolitan Vickers. In response to the contraction of the British locomotive manufacturing industry, Drewry acquired a controlling interest in E.E. Baguley Ltd in September 1962 and all Drewry's work was then carried out at the Uxbridge Street Works.

163

Two recently constructed 2ft gauge 25hp diesel locomotives stand in Baguley's Uxbridge Street Works yard. Maker's numbers 2104-05, they are destined for Cornwall County Council's Lostwithiel By-pass road contract. Behind, ex MR 0-4-4 tank 1240 pauses next to the Uxbridge Street Crossing signal box on the Bond End Branch. Although the date is July 1937, one of the wagons is still lettered prominently 'LNWR'.

(E.E. Baguley Ltd, courtesy Staffordshire County Record Office)

The company changed its name to Baguley-Drewry Ltd on 1st June 1967 and the Drewry Car Company Ltd went into voluntary liquidation in September 1970. A number of modernised designs appeared from the works based almost universally on hydraulic transmission. The orders included a series of four and six-coupled locomotives for Indonesia, 140hp 0-6-0 diesel locomotives for the Sena Sugar Company of Mozambique, and new narrow gauge locomotives for military establishments in Britain. Railcar production appeared to have ceased in the early 1960s, but more recently a number of modern diesel hydraulic railcars were built for the Ministry of Defence. Railway Mine & Plantation Equipment Ltd secured an initial order for ten locomotives, with a further two added later for sugar estates in Mozambique. The order was for equal numbers of 600mm and 2ft gauge locomotives to be built by Baguley-Drewry Ltd. Tate & Lyle Ltd placed the order as agents for the Mozambique State Sugar Corporation, financed by a loan from a large United Kingdom bank. Two of the locomotives were shipped about April 1983 and a further six were completed by June when a total stop of shipments was made by the bank because of Mozambique's failure to make repayments on the first instalment of the loan. Efforts were then made to dispose of the remaining locomotives and kits of parts, with some going to preserved railways in this country. This unfortunate episode marked the finish of Baguley-Drewry Ltd which ceased operations at the end of 1984.

Thornewill & Warham

In the eighteenth century, Burton achieved some significance as a distribution point for imported bar iron, because of its position at the head of the Trent Navigation and the proximity of the South Staffordshire area. The trade encouraged some ironworking in the town and Thomas and Francis Thornewill had established a small works on the south side of New Street by 1740, and a forge at

Clay Mills in 1755 using the water power of the River Dove. The New Street Works was gradually expanded with the freehold being secured for £140 in 1760. Thomas Thornewill ran the New Street Works with 15 employees producing spades, axes, scythes, hoops, and nails for mainly local use. William Bass also frequently carried goods from Thornewill including dresser weights for the looms at Hinckley and over 4000 spades each year during the 1760s to London. Thornewill supplied bundles of plate hoops to John Walker Wilson in 1778 and iron bars to Benjamin Wilson between 1791 and 1796.

Thornewill overcame the decline in the local hardware industry by concentrating on the manufacture of iron castings. In 1846, the business was described as 'iron and brass founders, and steam engine makers'. It may have produced engine components since the beginning of the century but the company was unlikely to have manufactured complete stationary engines prior to 1840. The growth of the local breweries and collieries no doubt encouraged Thornewill to expand his business beyond the simple manufacture of castings. Midland pits were early users of pumping engines, and steam engines were becoming more widely adopted for a variety of purposes by the mid nineteenth century.

Thornewill & Company added more land around its New Street Works between 1839 and 1847 in order to lay out the large engine shops. After his uncle's death in 1843, Robert Thornewill was in sole charge of the works until he entered into partnership with John Robson Warham, an engineer from South Shields on 2nd July 1849. John Warham had been senior draughtsman at the well known locomotive firm of R. & W. Hawthorn, Newcastle, and would be able to offer much practical advice on the new business of engine building. The works prospered with the growing markets of the brewing and coal industry. In 1851, Thornewill & Warham employed 75 men and 25 boys and were producing twelve pumping and winding engines a year, and by 1861, its workforce had increased to 178, a number only exceeded by the three leading brewers in the town.

High pressure steam engines advertised by Thornewill & Warham

5	Horsepower for a fixture,		Boiler included	£75
5	" "	travelling,	"	£100
10	" "	fixture,	"	£140
10	" "	travelling,	"	£180

Advertisement *Derby Mercury* 26th October 1842

Colin Owen was able to inspect Thornewill & Warham's *Engine Order Book* when researching the development of industry in Burton. Unfortunately, subsequent to his visit, the Order Book was destroyed in a fire and so the chance to resolve some of the queries about the early Burton brewery locomotives was lost. The Order Book started at number 115 about 1855 and so number 1 probably dated back to around 1842. It is not known when its first locomotive was built but the Babbington Coal Company in Nottinghamshire is reputed to have had a 2-4-0 well tank called NAPOLEON which came from Thornewill & Warham about 1850. The first record of a locomotive in the Order Book was for the sale of a 'tank locomotive' about 1858 to Ibstock Colliery in Leicestershire (maker's number 148). Owen noted that Thornewill & Warham supplied sixteen locomotives to the Burton brewers up to 1902 when the Order Book finished.

By 1870 Thornewill & Warham had acquired a national reputation for steam engine manufacture, supplying firms as far afield as Glasgow, London, and South Wales, and had begun to develop an export trade. According to Colin Owen 'Of the 329 engines and locomotives traceable in their Engine Order Book, 202 were supplied to collieries, 66 to breweries, 12 to waterworks, 10 each to ironworks and potteries, 6 to engineering works, 5 to sewage works, 4 to railways, 3 each to gas works and quarries, 2 to lead mines, and one each to a building works, brickworks, canal company, flour mill, dock company, and woodworks'. The company was involved in constructional engineering and was responsible for much of the iron work in the new Burton breweries. Substantial extensions had to be made to the works, notably in 1876 and 1880, and it stretched from New Street to Park Street. The arrival of the New Street Branch in 1880 provided the site with rail access. One siding ran by

D2859 on the New Street Branch passes Brigg's Works (ex Thornewill & Warham) and approaches Park Street level crossing in March 1964.   (P. Waterfield)

the side of the fitting shop, another entered the iron stores, whilst a third ran by the side of the boiler house and beam engine house.

Robert Thornewill died in 1858, and ten years later, a new partnership was formed in which his widow (6/12ths), J.R. Warham (5/12ths), and Thornewill's son Robert (1/12th) held the total capital of £44,000. J.R. Warham died in 1886 and the business was in the sole charge of Robert Thornewill by 1893. Mr G. Sheffield began his working life at Thornewill & Warham and in Denis Stuart's book *History of Burton upon Trent* describes what it was like. 'I started work with Thornewill & Warham when I was thirteen – that would be in 1910. I got four shillings a week, with a shilling rise every year. We worked from six in the morning until five at night. The gaffer, old Mr Robert Thornewill, used to drive up to the New Street Works every morning at eight with a coachman who had a billycock on the side of his top hat. Mr Thornewill died in 1914. I remember Mr Davis, the engineer manager, and Mr Schofield, the chief draughtsman, Mr Beaton, the foreman moulder. The moulders all came to work in a hard hat and swallow tail coat, some of them green with age.'

Thornewill & Warham had built the Ferry Bridge across the River Trent in 1889 at the expense of Lord Burton, but towards the end of the nineteenth century the fortunes of the Company waned. Indeed, Bass' Engineer Couchman was moved to comment in 1904 that 'It is of course only in accordance with Messrs Thornewill & Warham's usual dilatoriness.' Approaches to purchase Thornewill & Warham were made by Mountain & Gibson Limited from Bury who manufactured tramcar trucks, tramway works cars and spares. The *Sheffield Daily Telegraph* on 22nd May 1909 reported that the Bury works was too circumscribed and that they had decided to acquire Thornewill & Warham's New Street Works and to transfer their operations to that site. The New Street Works was said to be well laid out, having good transport facilities with railway sidings, and sufficient land to enable extensions to be made to the workshops. Mountain & Gibson & Thornewill Limited was formed to take over Mountain & Gibson on 6th June 1908 as a going concern and the New Street

Previous page. A Thornewill & Warham brochure dated about 1883, although the locomotive designs belong to the 1860s and 1870s. It is not known whether locomotives were also built at the Company's Severn Works in Derby.
(C. Shepherd Collection)

Works after the completion of the purchase. The prospectus for the newly incorporated company appeared in *The Times* on 24th May 1909. For some reason, the deal fell through and Thornewill & Warham remained in control of the New Street Works until it went into voluntary liquidation in 1919.

A new company known as Thornewill & Warham Ltd was formed which lasted until it was taken over by S. Briggs & Co Ltd in 1929. The latter was a firm of brewery engineers which had occupied Dawson's old brewery in Moor Street. New Street Works was run by Thornewill & Warham Successors until 1950 when Briggs concentrated all its operations at the works. There was a reminder of the old days when Briggs rebuilt an elderly Hunslet locomotive (maker's number 498 of 1890) named GOOD LUCK from Griff Colliery in 1952-53. The sidings at the works changed little in the first half of the twentieth century although their use declined. A simple spur was all that was required in 1959 and this probably saw little if any traffic. The name did not disappear entirely because John Thornewill, an offshoot of the family business (and owned by Lobbs after 1929), had an iron and steel stockholders warehouse located off Wood Street which was served by the remains of the direct line from Wood Street Maltings to James Street Junction.

Charrington & Company

For more than fifty years, and long before the days of the giant Bass Charrington combine, Charrington had its own brewery at Burton located in the triangle formed by Lichfield Street, Abbey Street, and Fleet Street. The Abbey Brewery was designed by Martin and Hardy, architects of Nottingham, for Charrington Head & Company and brewing began on 7th November 1872. Output in the first year was 10,000 barrels and it had increased to 80,000 barrels by 1887. This mainly comprised pale ales and a large amount was sent by rail to London, with the remainder going to towns in the Midlands and the North. Head had died in 1880 and the title once more became Charrington & Company. The brewery was connected to the New Street Branch by a line, which crossed Lichfield Street, and was opened on 8th June 1880. There were sidings serving the buildings

Charrington's Brewery at Burton about 1888.
(A. Barnard)

Bass' No.12 en route from Shobnall, approaches James Street Junction Signal Box on 30th December 1966. Charrington's locomotive used to travel along the New Street Branch past Evershed's and Eadie's Maltings and over the metals on the right to reach its Wood Street premises. *(C. Shepherd)*

on either side of the brewery yard. The block on the Lichfield Street frontage contained the New Union Room, racking room, and the lofty brewhouse which according to Barnard 'by reason of the various roofs being broken up into different heights, surmounted by tall chimney stacks, presents a striking picturesque appearance.' On the opposite side of the yard was the Old Union Room. The repair cooperage was across Fleet Street and was not linked to the railway, the casks probably being taken across the road by horse and dray.

To reach its Wood Street Maltings, Charrington's locomotives had to back out of the brewery yard over Lichfield Street and across Bell's sidings to make contact with the New Street Branch. The junction was controlled by Lichfield Street Crossing Signal Box (replaced by a new structure on 11th March 1905). Then the locomotive headed off along the branch past Thornewill & Warham's Works, Park Street No.2 Signal Box and crossing, and Evershed's and Eadie's Maltings before reaching James Street Junction. There were a few sidings here and a separate single line off one of them gave direct access to the Wood Street Maltings, crossing the Bond End Branch at right angles in the process. The original signal box at James Street Junction began operations on 26th April 1880 but was replaced by a new box on 13th January 1929.

Initially, there was only one malting at Wood Street and this was linked to the Bond End Branch by a line opened on 18th October 1878 which curved round to a point near Hill's Brewery. The other

Locomotive whistle code at James Street and Uxbridge Street Junctions 1921

Whistles

1	To Charrington's Wood Street premises
2	To Eadie's Brewery, Duke Street
3	To Bass' Brewery, Duke Street
4	To Robinson's Brewery
5	To Branston Road

malting was completed on the Uxbridge Street side of the site probably shortly after 1882. Part of the stores in both maltings were built over the railway sidings so that bags of malt could be dropped directly into the wagons. The 1879 Act gave approval for the original railway connection to be replaced by a new curve which joined the Bond End Branch at Uxbridge Street Junction. Wood Street Stores had begun loading ales on 17th March 1880. The direct line from James Street Junction to Wood Street was brought into use on 4th October 1886.

MR locomotives initially worked the traffic between Charrington's premises, but on 1st May 1885, Charrington began using a new four-coupled 12in saddle tank locomotive, which it had purchased from Hudswell Clarke (maker's number 276). The locomotive carried an oval owner's plate with the words 'CHARRINGTON & CO BURTON ON TRENT' around the perimeter and the date '1885' in the centre. It shunted the sidings at the brewery and the maltings, and also took a couple of loads of ale destined for London and the other agencies up to Allsopp's Sidings on the Dallow Lane Branch. The MR levied an annual charge of £40 for the Charrington locomotive's use of the Bond End Branch in 1905. MR locomotives continued to deliver wagons from the main line and Barnard recalled how he narrowly escaped being run over in the brewery yard as some coal wagons moved in one direction and a train with malt came the other way. He also noted on his visit in 1887-88 that 'the firm had one powerful locomotive which is kept in the shed at the maltings.' The private sidings at Wood Street ran between the two maltings to terminate at the end of the yard, next to the locomotive shed, whilst other lines served ale banks used for stacking casks. Charrington, like all brewers, also kept store ales on the ground level working floors of the maltings. They were piled up, cask lying on cask, during the summer. The accommodation was cool, well ventilated, and had the advantage that it could be locked up! With the change to running ales, Bass no longer followed this practice because it had adequate space in its ale stores.

Charrington's last locomotive arrived early in 1921 and was a powerful 15in Hudswell Clarke 0-4-0 saddle tank locomotive of the Abertawe type (maker's number 1437). It was supplied in a middle green livery, carried the maker's plate (unusually) on the smokebox, and oval owner's plates

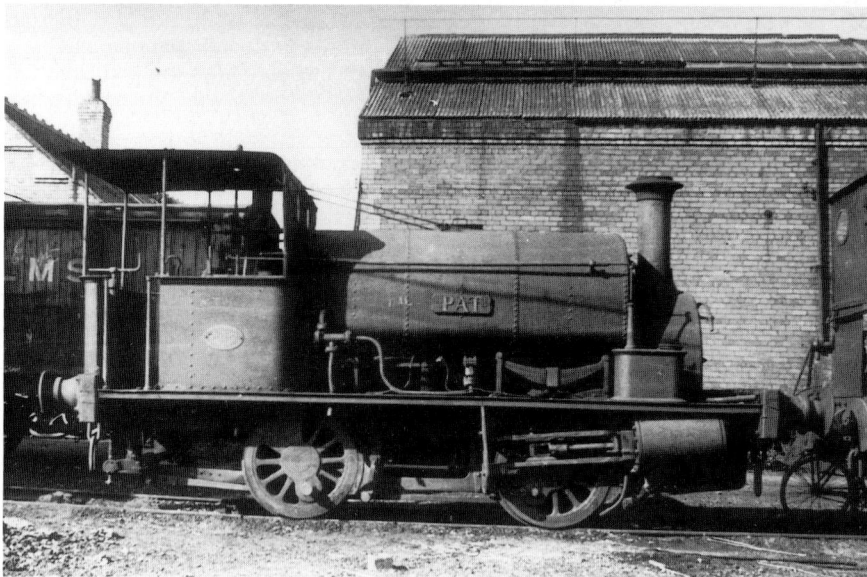

Hudswell Clarke 276 of 1885, once owned by Charrington at Burton, but seen here at Gresford Colliery, near Wrexham, on 3rd October 1936. (F. Jones Collection)

Charrington's former locomotive shed at the Wood Street Maltings on 25th March 1966. (C. Shepherd)

on the bunkers reading 'CHARRINGTON & CO LTD, BREWERS, BURTON ON TRENT'. No running number was displayed. Fitted with both steam and hand brakes, the locomotive weighed just over 24 tons and cost £4,090. It is likely that the old locomotive was traded into the manufacturer in March 1921, once the new acquisition had settled in. Hudswell Clarke rebuilt 276 and then resold it to the Taf Fechan Water Authority on 14th June 1922 for £1,625, plus £16.75 extra for tyre washing gear. These are the only two locomotives for which we have precise details, although Jim Gaunt worked at Charrington until it closed, and he reckoned that the company had two locomotives before 1437 arrived, all from the same manufacturer.

In 1925 Charrington decided to finish with its Burton operations and concentrate production in London, disposing of its scattered public houses in the Midlands and North of England, and the Abbey Brewery closed in the following year. There was an interesting advertisement in *The Contract Journal* on 4th May 1927 which stated that a standard gauge four-coupled Hudswell Clarke saddle tank locomotive with 10in x 22in *(sic)* cylinders was for sale. It could be seen at Burton on Trent and was being sold by Honeywill Bros Ltd of London. A similar advertisement appeared in the *Machinery Market* on 23rd April 1926 (no reference to Burton) and 6th May 1927. It is strange that Honeywill Brothers should have branched out into dealing in secondhand steam locomotives, although they were involved with the Worthington petrol locomotives at this time. The cylinder dimension is a mistake. Hudswell Clarke never provided small cylinders with such a long stroke and it is likely to be 15in x 22in. The manufacturer only built eight of these locomotives before 1927. By coincidence, two of them were at Burton and were disposed of at this time. Allsopp's locomotive was reputedly scrapped in 1926. Charrington's would have been for sale after the brewery closed, and it went to J. Crosfield & Sons Ltd's soap works at Warrington.

There was a consequent loss of traffic on the New Street Branch and it was singled; the Up line from James Street Junction to New Street No.2 Box, including the link to Charrington's Brewery, being removed on 2nd July 1935. It had operated on a 'one locomotive in steam' basis since 7th May 1928 but still using both lines in the correct direction. Most of the direct line from James Street Junction to Wood Street was removed about World War 2 but the maltings continued in use operated by the Atkinson Brewery Limited. This company relied on the LMS to bring wagons in round the curve from the Bond End Branch. Atkinson became part of the Mitchells & Butlers group, so that when the latter amalgamated with Bass in 1961, it was logical for Bass to take over operation of the maltings. From then on, they were shunted by a Bass locomotive.

Bass' No.2 shunting some internal grain vans at the Wood Street Maltings on 6th June 1963.
(C. Shepherd)

The Last Years at Bond End

The branch from Uxbridge Street Junction to Bond End Wharf closed on 2nd March 1964, with the withdrawal of facilities at the wharf. On 23rd May, contractors comprising five men and a lorry were busy cutting up the rails into short sections. The separate line serving Wood Street, Everard's Malting, and Conder Engineering remained in use. There was then only one daily trip along the New Street Branch, which was said to have remained open at Bass-Worthington's insistence, because it formed an alternative exit from Worthington's Brewery. On a typical day in June 1964 when 47000 was standing in for D2859, the locomotive ran light round the curve from Leicester Junction Sidings, down the Bond End Branch and through the vegetation which was rapidly taking over the New Street Branch. This 'return to nature' so confused one motorist that she had parked her car on the New Street crossing under the impression that it was not used because 'the dandelions and grass were at least 6in high.' Unfortunately, the episode resulted in a forty minute delay for the locomotive and some wagons, and a £2 fine for the motorist. Reverting to our typical day, 47000 removed a mineral wagon

Unloading railway vans at Bindley's former brewery on 25th March 1966; G.L. White, potato merchant was then in occupation. (C. Shepherd)

Bond End Wharf closed on 2nd March 1964. The photograph shows D2859, reputedly on the last working, pulling out past the Branston Road Signal Box (erected 6th July 1902).

(P. Waterfield)

Almost the end; Burton New Street No.1 Signal Box on 26th March 1967. The background has been transformed by the construction of Bass' new central boiler plant on the site of Eadie's Brewery. This box had opened on 15th November 1901. (C. Shepherd)

out of G.L. White's premises at the former Bindley Brewery and also collected two vans by the old Robinson Wharf. It gingerly made its return, the shunter operating the crossing gates at New Street where Fred Morse had once been the regular signalman.* It was only a short distance to the Park Street crossing where the box (erected 15th May 1909) had been replaced by a ground frame on 2nd July 1935. There was another 16 ton mineral wagon to be picked up from English Grains premises near James Street Junction. After crossing and recrossing Uxbridge Street, 47000 left its wagons by the water tower on the third line near Wood Street, and ran up to Yeomans, Cherry & Curtis's Clarence Street Maltings to fetch a bulk grain van. It then coupled on to the other vehicles and still propelling the bulk grain van headed back to Leicester Junction Sidings. The New Street Branch closed on 28th April 1966 and the land behind New Street and Station Street was cleared and laid out as a car park in time for the Christmas shopping. The remaining lines finished about the same time as Bass' railway although the official closure date was 20th January 1968. Signals and boxes were left intact and it was not until four years later, that the Midland Railway Trust dismantled numerous items of historical interest for its site at Butterley. These included Burton New St No.1 Signal Box, with spares from Duke Street Box, together with three sets of signals.

* New Street No.2 signal box was the second structure on the site and it opened on 1st July 1905. It was downgraded to a ground frame when the branch was singled but remained in place, albeit with increasingly faded paint work.

CHAPTER NINE

INDUSTRIAL RAILWAYS OFF THE MAIN LINE

A Derby bound express had an easy run over the generally favourable gradients from Birmingham but there was a need to begin braking as the train swept through the remains of Branston station. There would probably be an escape of steam from the locomotive's safety valves and that distinctive aroma announcing the approach of Burton would enter the open carriage window. The overriding impression was of the train slowing past railway yards full of trucks, with the occasional shunting or goods locomotive tucked away amongst the wagons. Branston Sidings was the first yard to be met when coming from the south, with its three signal boxes Branston Junction, Branston Sidings No.2 and Branston Sidings No.1. The line to the Branston Factory diverged at the Junction box.

The Branston Factory

Thomas Lowe & Sons began to construct the National Machine Gun Factory at Branston to the designs of the Enfield Company during World War 1 but work was not completed by the end of hostilities, and the factory's only contribution to the war effort was the re-conditioning of 1000 machine guns. The long wall marking the boundary of the premises was built by German prisoners of war housed in Peach's maltings in Anglesey Road. At least one locomotive, a 0-4-0 well tank built by Hawthorn & Co of Leith (maker's number 366) is known to have worked at Branston. Rail traffic entering the factory siding (opened 24th March 1918) had to reverse before it could reach the 'gun works' After the War, the premises were no longer required by the Government and, about May 1920, they were purchased by Crosse & Blackwell Ltd whose existing works in London was too small and threatened by redevelopment.

All of Crosse & Blackwell's food preserves were made at Branston. A locomotive was required to shunt the works and a small 10in Hudswell Clarke & Rodgers product was acquired. Maker's number 139 had been built in 1874, was carried on four 2ft 9in diameter coupled wheels, and weighed 11 tons. It was renovated by the manufacturer in 1914, prior to the contractor Hugh Symington & Co Ltd using it to help lay out the extensive railway system at the new Gretna Munitions Factory, near Carlisle. The locomotive was called DORA then and was subsequently taken over by the Ministry of Munitions as part of its operations at the factory. Peacetime meant that it was surplus to requirements and Crosse & Blackwell bought it. It was renamed DAISY and, according to Jim Gaunt, had a dark brown livery. There is an alternative possibility that the locomotive may have come to Branston under the ownership of the Ministry of Munitions and had been acquired with the factory.

Production at Branston soon proved to be uneconomic because most of the raw materials and exports still passed through London. Crosse & Blackwell returned to the capital in 1924 and the Branston Factory closed in the following year. Only the name 'Branston Pickle' remains as a reminder of the company's brief stay in Burton. The *Machinery Market* magazine on 20th February 1925 carried the announcement that J. Sulley was to auction Crosse & Blackwell's plant, including a Hudswell Clarke *(sic)* standard gauge locomotive, on 4-5th March 1925. DAISY was sold to the Trent Concrete Co Ltd at Colwick, near Nottingham.

The unfortunate history of the Branston Factory continued when Martin Harman Coles formed the Branston Artificial Silk Co Ltd in 1927. He began to produce artificial fibres at the factory on the 7th June 1928 initially using imported viscose but later making his own. Eight tons of viscose were being produced each day by March 1929. A 0-4-0 locomotive was ordered from Baguley (maker's number 1654) on 8th October 1927 at a cost of £750 and it was delivered on 9th January 1928. The locomotive had a Baguley 4-cylinder 45hp petrol engine and Baguley combined mechanical transmission. It was a centre cab '1648' design and locomotives of this type gave long and reliable service. Unfortunately, Coles was involved in various dubious financial transactions and the result

175

The 45hp diesel mechanical locomotive supplied by Baguley (maker's no.1654) in 1928 to the Branston Artificial Silk Company.
(Baguley (Engineers) Ltd, courtesy Staffordshire Record Office)

was that the Branston Artificial Silk Company ceased trading at the end of 1930. The factory then lay empty in the hands of the official receiver, although the Commercial Lead Company leased some of the premises for a short time.

The MR had an agreement dated 20th November 1922 to carry out temporary shunting over Crosse & Blackwell's railway lines, which were near to the Branston Sidings, as long as it did not interfere with the company's traffic. This agreement was transferred to the Branston Artificial Silk Company on 7th April 1927. Subsequently, it was noted that the traffic to and from the factory had reduced and that only one line was required for it. The railway company used the remainder for marshalling and storage.

Hillier Parker held an auction of 'plant including a 60hp *(sic)* standard gauge petrol locomotive' on 6th April 1937, but with war looming again, the War Department took over the factory, together with the Baguley locomotive, in July 1937. It became the Central Ordnance Depot, Branston supplying clothing and equipment. This role continued after the War and it was later known as an 'OSDD' or an Ordnance Storage and Disposal Depot, a title which covered a multitude of activities, excluding explosives. The Ministry of Defence ran the depot down in the 1960s and eventually closed it in February 1975, although it was used by the Government for storage after that date.

There was naturally a great increase in rail traffic as World War 2 developed. The War Office ordered a batch of five new Hunslet standard diesel mechanical locomotives, with Gardner 6-cylinder 6L3 153hp engines, on 20th May 1939 to work in the various ordnance factories. There was some delay and the War Department had to borrow locomotives from the LMS, such as 11235 and 1516, to help shunt the Branston Depot during January and February 1940. Two months later, the pair of new Hunslet locomotives (maker's numbers 2065 and 2066) arrived at Branston. They were initially numbered 2 and 3, later becoming 71681 and 71682 and subsequently 847 and 848. The Baguley

After taking over the Branston Depot, the War Department sent Baguley 1654 to the maker's Uxbridge Street Works. It was photographed there in the yard in March 1938 after overhaul.
(E.E. Baguley Ltd, courtesy Staffordshire Record Office)

locomotive remained until about 1944 when it was transferred to the Royal Ordnance Factory at Rotherwas, Hereford.

For more than twenty years, the two Hunslets formed the main motive power at Branston, the only exception being when overhauls became due. In 1955 number 2066 was sent to the Central Workshops at Bicester for overhaul and, on its return, 2065 went away also to be refurbished, coming back in September 1957. During some of this period, the Branston Depot received one of the War Department standard 153hp diesel mechanical shunters, Andrew Barclay 357 of 1941. With the completion of the Hunslet overhauls, the Barclay was sent away to the Cairnryan Military Railway near Stranraer. When major repairs were again due in the mid 1960s, another locomotive from the WD's batch of Hunslet machines (maker's number 2068) helped out. It went to Bicester when no longer required.

Wagons for the depot were brought by the railway company from its Branston Sidings and left just inside the gate. The War Department locomotive then collected them and placed them in the works' own fan of sidings for the checker to examine. Most of the day was spent in moving these wagons to the different buildings and taking other wagons to the sidings for eventual handing over to the railway company. Because the depot was used for storage, loaded wagons would be worked both in and out. The two locomotives at the depot were used on alternate weeks with Ron Lightfoot as a driver and Morris Low a shunter. When Bass' railway closed, George Ashmole went to the Branston depot as its only platelayer. He not only maintained all of the internal track but had to travel to other depots within a radius of 40 miles to look after their railways as well.

The Ministry of Defence introduced a classification scheme for its locomotives from 1964 and the two Hunslets were allocated type B5. By this time, the Ministry possessed an over abundance of elderly diesel shunters and two more locomotives were sent to Branston to give whatever assistance was needed with the declining rail traffic. War Department 212 (Drewry number 2169) arrived in 1968 and 247 (Andrew Barclay maker's number 342) came in the following year. The Drewry Car Company was only the supplier of 212 to the War Department; it was in fact built by the Vulcan Foundry, maker's number 4861. Hunslet 2066 paid another visit to the Sinfin Lane Depot at Derby, returning in 1971 before going to Bicester in the following year. It was stored there for four years and then sold to Bird's scrapyard at Long Marston.

177

Two Andrew Barclay 0-4-0 diesel mechanical shunters arrived to cover the final work at Branston. It was interesting to note the reappearance of Barclay maker's number 357, now identified as 202, and last seen in this area heading through Stretton and Clay Mills station in 1964. It replaced Drewry 2169 in May 1972. The other Barclay was maker's number 344 which took over from Barclay 342 on 4th January 1973. These Barclay locomotives were originally fitted with Gardner 153hp 6L3 engines. Barclay 344 had been built with an exhaust quenching system for use at the Bishopton Ordnance Factory at Glasgow and it was also one of the locomotives involved in a programme of fitting new engines, receiving a Paxman 193hp V6 unit. Its classification changed from B10EQ to B11SA as a result.

MoD number 859 (Andrew Barclay 357) and brakevan pass Stretton and Claymills Station in the course of transfer from Featherstone, near Bescot, to Ruddington on 6th April 1964.   *(C. Shepherd)*

The other original Hunslet locomotive (2065) was scrapped in 1974 after the purchaser had removed the engine. With the departure of Barclays 357 and 344 in March 1975, locomotive working at the Branston Factory came to an end.

Wagon Repairs Limited

From among the maze of railways at the Branston Sidings emerged the double track of the Birmingham Curve which swept round to join the Leicester line at Birmingham Curve Junction Signal Box, thus completing a triangle of railways. The first box at Birmingham Curve Junction had opened in March 1873 and it was succeeded by two replacements, the last dating from 23rd September 1906.

The Branston Wagon Works was built early in the twentieth century by the Birmingham Railway Carriage & Wagon Co Ltd but about 1920, it changed ownership becoming part of Wagon Repairs Limited. There were two main buildings both served by transporters for moving wagons from one line to another, together with a fan of storage sidings adjacent to the Birmingham Curve. Presumably horses were originally responsible for any shunting, but in July 1931, the company ordered a locomotive from Baguley (Engineers) Ltd (maker's number 2071). This was a four-wheel chain driven design very similar to the Simplex and Planet types and it proved to be the last locomotive to come from the Shobnall Road Works. It was fitted with a transverse 4-cylinder Ford petrol engine producing 25hp and a Baguley assembled Planet gearbox as found on the narrow gauge locomotives. The new locomotive was cheap and simple, using as many components as possible from a 10 ton open wagon. Indeed, it was said that someone went down to the Branston Wagon Works to select suitable components from their stock of spares! The locomotive remained at Branston until about 1948 when it was transferred to Wagon Repairs' Gloucester Works.

No information appears to have survived about whether there was a locomotive at the Branston Wagon Works during the next seven years, but on 25th October 1955, Wagon Repairs Limited placed an order with Ruston & Hornsby for a new locomotive to be delivered by road to the Branston Works. This was a standard 4-wheel 48DS diesel shunter (maker's number 393303). It had a Ruston 4VRH engine, 2ft 6in diameter wheels, weighed 7½ tons, was equipped with a Type G25 gearbox and was driven by roller chains to the axles. Warm weather was obviously expected as a cab heater was not provided! The locomotive cost £2,598 and arrived at Branston on 21st January 1956. These 48hp locomotives were comparatively tiny but proved ideal for those operators with a limited number of sidings and modest haulage requirements. Wagon Repairs' locomotive stayed until 1968 when it moved away to the Wellingborough Works; shortly after the Burton Works closed in October 1968.

Lloyds' Wellington Works

Continuing our journey along the main line into Burton, the substantial buildings of Burton locomotive shed appeared on the left. Behind the depot was a foundry established by F.H. Lloyd & Co Ltd in 1932 and was served by a siding off the shunting spur for the shed. The FNF Machinery Manufacturing Company also had a works making textile machinery with a siding off the same spur. During World War 2, the foundry was taken over by the Ministry of Supply, reputedly as a supply depot. It was during this tenure that a locomotive was purchased to transport goods between the warehouse and the exchange sidings. This locomotive was ordered on 22nd June 1942 by H.A. Brassert & Co Ltd of Granite House, Cannon Street, London, which was an agent acting on behalf of the Ministry of Supply. The new machine was built by Ruston & Hornsby (maker's number 218045) and was one of its 48DS locomotives, although the manufacturer's files still made use of

One of Lloyd's Ruston locomotives shunting at its Wellington Works. (J.A. Peden)

the older '44/48HP' designation. It had a Ruston 4VRO 4-cylinder engine, a three speed gearbox and was also fitted with an electric starter, lights, and sanding. In October, Brassert wrote requesting that a metal oval plate bearing the inscription 'M OF S BURTON', in letters approximately 1½in high, should be fixed to each side of the cab. The agent also asked that the locomotive be painted black, lined out in white, although it was prepared to accept a standard finish if the manufacturer was limited to one. Ruston & Hornsby charged £1,340 for the locomotive and it was delivered just before Christmas.

Although Ruston's spares records suggest that the foundry was still connected with the Ministry of Supply until 1947, Lloyd's name had appeared on orders two years before and the company stated that it took over the locomotive in 1945. Duties included transporting scrap and coke to the foundry and the despatch of iron and steel castings. The locomotive usually worked every weekday but when not required, it was left wherever it was convenient for the driver; there was no locomotive shed. The name of the company changed to Lloyds (Burton) Limited in 1947.

The first locomotive worked at the foundry for over a decade but in 1955, Lloyds decided to order a replacement. It was obviously satisfied with the service given by the previous shunter and a new 48DS locomotive was obtained from Ruston & Hornsby (maker's number 386873) at a cost of £2,460. This had the more modern 4VRH engine. The older locomotive was sold for £100 to C.J. Driver Ltd of Great Barr in 1957; the latter was a Ruston & Hornsby stock holder and engine specialist. Ruston 386873 continued to shunt the declining amounts of traffic until use of the railway ceased and the locomotive was scrapped about 1970.

It was usually only possible to catch a glimpse of Lloyds' locomotive because most of the works was hidden from the railway company's main line by Burton Shed and its coal stage. The latter was a traditional MR structure with a railway on a ramp leading up to the covered coal stage. Small hand

On 4th June 1963, 92080 pulls condemned locomotives 47417, 43734, 43645 and 43593 past Burton Station South Signal Box. This box opened on 20th December 1914 and closed on 15th June 1969; an earlier box at this location was named Moor Street. (C. Shepherd)

propelled carts were used for transferring coal from the wagons to the locomotives. The shed yard was usually occupied by lines of steam locomotives being serviced or waiting their next duties. In earlier days, there was a long coal stack between the main line and the yard but later supplies were stored in coal wagons. This part of the main line was always very busy because of locomotive movements to and from the shed. In addition, the branch from Leicester came in from the right, beyond lay the Leicester Junction Sidings and the Shobnall Branch dropped down to the left. After passing over the Bond End Branch and the Moor Street level crossing, the main running lines swung either side of the island platform of Burton station, with the Birmingham end of the station protected by the Burton Station South Signal Box. After stopping at Burton – most passenger trains used to call here – the express would head off towards Derby past Burton Station North Signal Box and between the imposing facades of Allsopp's and Truman's breweries.

Truman, Hanbury Buxton & Company

The Black Eagle Brewery dominated the northern side of the main line with the tallest part of the building surmounted by a turret. Originally based on Phillips Brothers' Brewery, the premises had been substantially enlarged to the design of George Scammell in 1874-76. In addition to the main block, there was a cask washing shed, joiner's shops, sawmill and offices. The cooperage comprised a long range of buildings next to Derby Street and in the late 1880s, the casks were manufactured by hand from the finest quality Russian oak. Timber was stored in the open and protected by hop sacking, whilst nearby were four large stacks each made up of as many as 10,000 empty casks. The brewery's convenient location meant that a private railway could be laid from the MR up main goods line at the Iron Bridge to the far end of the premises, before returning round the back of the brewhouse to a spur by Derby Street East. Another reversal gave access to the line at the front of the brewery. Over the years, there were numerous derailments when the railway company's shunting locomotive attempted to pull out a rake of wagons from the front of the brewery, neglecting to check that the points at the rear of the train were not set for the cask washing plant. More sidings were later added to serve the No.1 and No.2 Maltings. Both buildings were four storeys high; No.1 was

The impressive frontage to Truman's Brewery, with the connection to the MR, and the sturdy fence separating the brewery from the lines to the NSR shed. Later these sidings were used for Truman's exchange traffic.   (J.A. Peden Collection)

181

Truman, Hanbury, Buxton Brewery 1951

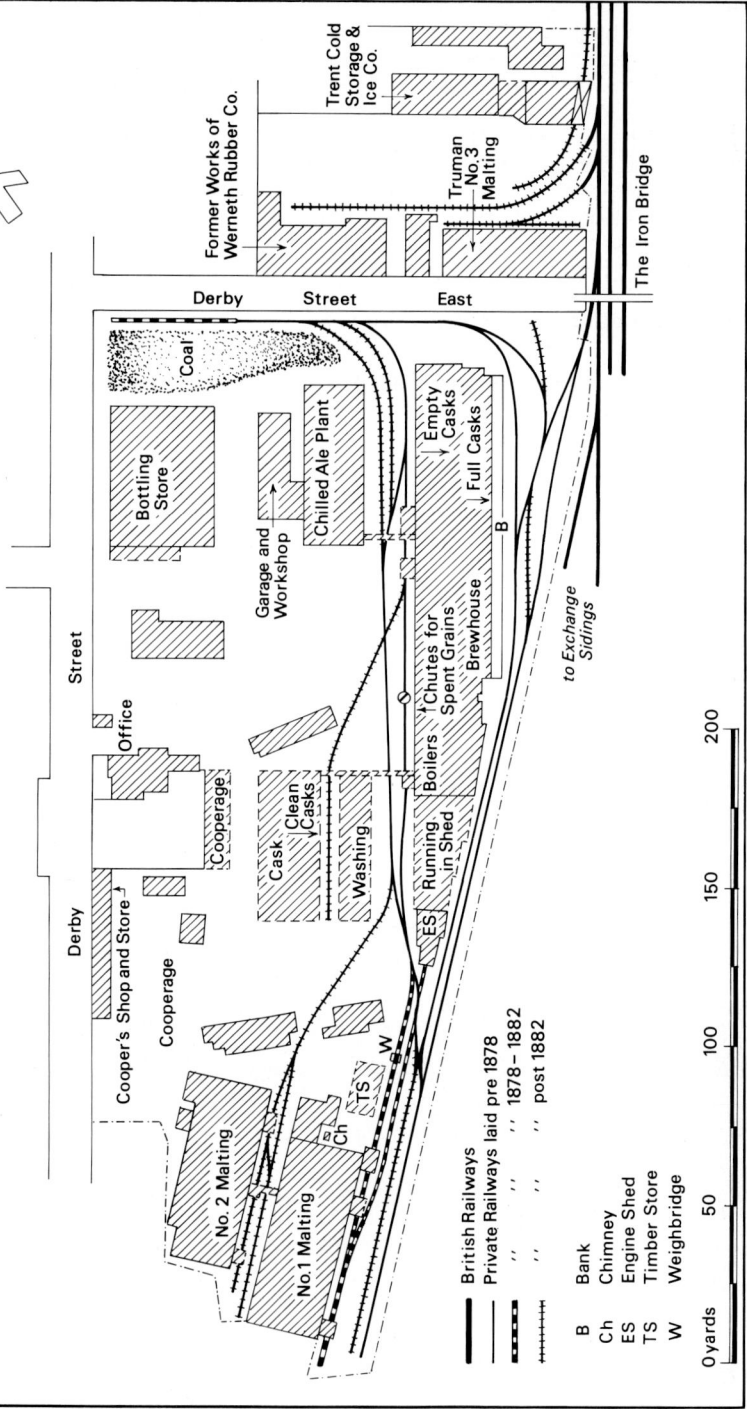

Trent Cold Storage & Ice Co.

Former Works of Werneth Rubber Co.

Truman No.3 Malting

The Iron Bridge

Derby Street East

Coal

Bottling Store

Garage and Workshop

Chilled Ale Plant

Empty Casks

Full Casks

B

Brewhouse

Chutes for Spent Grains

Boilers

to Exchange Sidings

Derby Street

Office

Cooperage

Cask Cleaning

Clean Casks

Washing

Running in Shed

ES

Cooper's Shop and Store

Cooperage

No. 2 Malting

No. 1 Malting

Ch

TS

W

British Railways
Private Railways laid pre 1878
  ,,   ,,   ,, 1878 – 1882
  ,,   ,,   ,, post 1882

B   Bank
Ch   Chimney
ES   Engine Shed
TS   Timber Store
W   Weighbridge

0 yards   50   100   150   200

182

Bass No.9, now preserved at the Bass Museum, stands by Delhi Maltings in the New Brewery. Note the Bass wooden grain van behind. (B. Mettam)

Ind Coope and Allsopp's Sentinel locomotives, Nos.7 and 8, outside Allsopp's shed, with the ex LNWR Horninglow Street Goods Depot to the left. (R.C. Riley)

Truman, Hanbury, Buxton's last Peckett, maker's no.2136, stands in the brewery yard. The background is formed by Ind Coope & Allsopp's Brewery. (B. Mettam)

No.5, a Worthington's Bagnall locomotive, brings a load of vans under the Mount Pleasant Bridge and past Hawkins Lane Signal Box on 26th May 1959. (R.C. Riley)

Marston, Thompson & Evershed's No.3, Hawthorn Leslie 3581 of 1924, poses on the branch to the brewery near Crossman Street. (B. Mettam)

Bass' Repair Shed at Guild Street with No.3 (Thornewill & Warham 609 of 1891) outside on 30th May 1960. The central part of the shed was built in 1864.
(R.C. Riley)

Another fine owner's plate is visible on Worthington's Planet locomotive No.10 at Shobnall on 12th April 1958. The Bass internal wagon 112 attached was built in 1901 and purchased in 1949. (R.C. Riley)

Rundown of the brewery railways; Worthington's High Street crossing has been converted to manual operation. Bass' No.1 (Bagnall 3568) passes Worthington's signal box on 22nd March 1967. (C. Shepherd)

built by Joseph Chamberlain of Burton in 1879-80 and No.2 by George Hodges in 1897-98. They were sometimes known as the Old and New Maltings. Increases in traffic soon meant that there was a need for a private locomotive to shunt the brewery railways. The spur alongside Derby Street East was extended to allow for the longer trains and a locomotive shed was built at the end of the main block. It had an inspection pit and Truman carried out repairs to the locomotives in the shed, although Warren's men came to do the boilers and fireboxes. The locomotive crew had a cabin at the side of the shed and this usually had a big roaring fire in it, which not only kept them warm but was also used for lighting up the locomotive. There was a tray on top for drying the sand to go in the locomotive sandboxes. The railway's basic layout was thus completed and the brewery was to remain substantially in this form until the 1960s, the main additions being the erection of the chilled ale plant in the mid 1930s and the bottling stores.

From the 1st July 1880, Truman began to use its own locomotive to take wagons to the MR 'cheese line' at the nearby MR Goods Yard. The brewery was separated from the railway company's sidings by a fence of old sleepers, with a gate adjacent to the Iron Bridge. In later years, when the NSR locomotive shed had been removed, the four lines outside were used exclusively by Truman as its exchange sidings and Truman's locomotive made numerous visits to these sidings throughout the day. Permission had to be obtained from the nearest signal box before the locomotive could venture out. Traffic was then picked up or delivered by the railway company, usually by the trip which took it to Wetmore or Horninglow Bridge Yards. If it was urgent, a passing light engine might stop and deliver it to the appropriate sidings.

The identity of the first locomotive and its eventual fate are unknown but it was soon supplemented by a new 0-4-0 locomotive with 12in cylinders purchased from the Yorkshire Engine Company (maker's number 406) in 1886. It carried an ogee shaped saddle tank, which was a typical feature of this manufacturer's designs at that time, and a rudimentary weatherboard giving it an antiquated appearance. Not surprisingly, it was known as 'Old Coffee Pot'.

In 1901, it was joined by a standard 0-4-0 saddle tank from Hawthorn Leslie (maker's number 2507). This was a more powerful locomotive with 14in x 20in cylinders and a boiler pressed to 140 lbs/sq in; driving wheel diameter was 3ft 6in. Hawthorn's must have done good business in Burton because Marston had obtained a similar locomotive just three months before. Truman recognised the new locomotive's origins by giving it the name NEWCASTLE, an unusual action amongst the Burton brewers and one not to be repeated. The company was to rely on the Yorkshire and Hawthorn Leslie locomotives for the next twenty years. NEWCASTLE was originally only fitted with hand brakes and it was later sent back to Hawthorn Leslie accompanied by a fitter for steam brakes to be added. Unfortunately, small hand lubricated tank locomotives are not designed to travel long distances and the bearings consequently ran hot en route so that it finished its journey loaded on a wagon. Truman's locomotives were painted dark green, but during World War 1, the Yorkshire temporarily received an austere grey livery. Ben Ward remembered seeing it in 1917, a small grey locomotive with a metal eagle on each side of its unusual shaped tanks. It shrieked and clanked as it worked a few trucks round the curves in the brewery.

In the twentieth century, a man named Blant drove the locomotive for a long time and he was followed by a driver called Bell. The next and final driver came from the railway company and was only at Truman's for a short time before use of the locomotive ceased. An engine cleaner worked a 4am to 12 noon shift and his first duty was to raise steam on the locomotive. He also relieved the driver at meal times. The driver and shunter clocked on at 6am to check over the locomotive and to do any necessary oiling. One of their first tasks was to fetch wagons of empty casks from the exchange sidings. With the old grease lubricated wagons, there was always the danger that they would freeze up in cold weather, and then the crew had to spray them with hot water in order to get them moving. Dirty casks were unloaded by the sheds, which housed two Goliath cask washing machines, and then clean casks were put into the wagons for the short journey to the bank at the rear of the brewhouse. Full casks from the stores underneath the brewhouse were rolled into wagons via the bank on the main line side of the building. Ale for London was given priority so that it could as it traversed no less than four level crossings. What is less known is that there were two separate railways.

The first was a simple private affair constructed in 1855-56 linking Tooth's London & Colonial Brewery on the south side of Victoria Crescent with the canal. Wagons were pulled by horses and Mr Tooth paid the sum of £1 a year wayleave to the Town Commissioners for crossing Victoria Crescent. The precedent was later quoted in the argument over the town centre level crossings, although Samuel Allsopp said that the Commissioners 'have a pound a year for it but have no power to grant the permission.' The railway ran along King Street to Tooth's malting and stores which stood next to a canal basin, the only one in Burton to be owned by a brewery. Although Tooth had established his business not long before the railway was built, he developed a wide ranging trade and several embossed beer bottles have been excavated from an early settled area at Balwyn in Victoria, Australia. These bore the Company's trademark of a rampant horse and the word INVICTA, similar to the coat of arms of Kent where the family originated. There was another small brewery tucked away on the corner of King Street and William Street, behind the Dingo Hotel. This was owned by Cooper but did not have any physical connection with Tooth's railway. The Dingo Hotel could have been indicative of another Australian association. Michael Thomas Bass had agents for his high gravity beers in Australia and urged young people to go out there to take up land for sheep farming, he even subsidised some of them and would not accept repayment.

In 1867, the MR obtained powers for its Horninglow Branch and this replaced the original line. The new railway was laid some yards to the east and parallel to the horse worked line, which was mostly removed, apart from a short section forming the Crescent Brewery's first siding. Despite objections from the proprietors of Cooper's Dingo Brewery in November 1866, the MR was able to acquire enough land from both breweries and small portions of Arthur and William Street in order to construct the branch. King Street disappeared and part of it was used to form the MR's Horninglow coal wharf. The London & Colonial Brewery Company had gone out of business and so T. Cooper & Company, then owned by Herbert Keeling and Edward Wright, transferred its operations to the Crescent Brewery. Clayton later took over the Dingo Brewery but produced only small

On the Horninglow Branch, 47643 shunts some vans for the Cyclops Works over Victoria Crescent, next to the former Cooper's Crescent Brewery on 31st July 1963. Tooth's private railway once crossed the road immediately behind the train.

(C. Shepherd)

Tooth & Co's Horse Worked Railway 1865

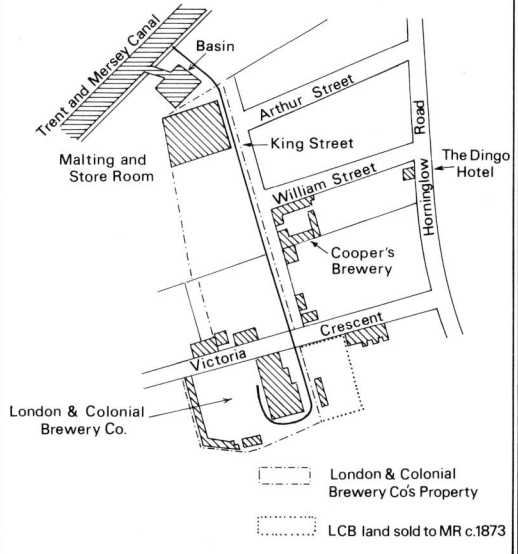

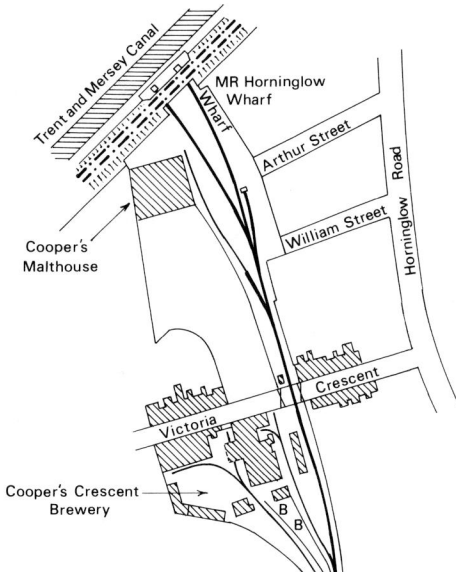

- Trent and Mersey Canal
- Basin
- Malting and Store Room
- Arthur Street
- King Street
- William Street
- Horninglow Road
- The Dingo Hotel
- Cooper's Brewery
- Victoria
- Crescent
- London & Colonial Brewery Co.

London & Colonial Brewery Co's Property

LCB land sold to MR c.1873

Trent and Mersey Canal

MR Horninglow Wharf

Cooper's Malthouse

Arthur Street

William Street

Horninglow Road

Crescent

Victoria

Cooper's Crescent Brewery

B

Stocal Enamelled Tile and Iron Works. Note: Established 1913, works shown as 1920

Horninglow Branch 1900

	Midland Railway
	London & North Western Rly.
	Private Railways
B	Bank
C	Cooperage
SB	Signal Box

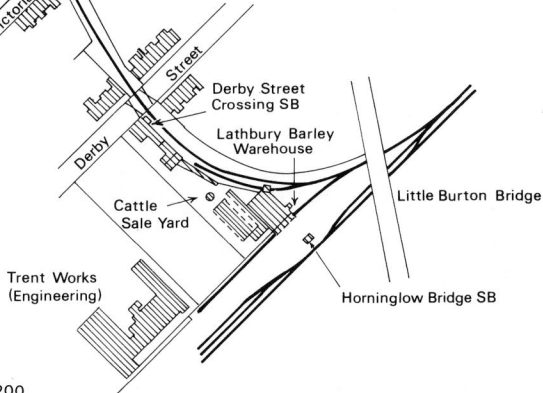

Midland Brewery (disused)

Dallow Street

Victoria Street

C

Later became Burton Pure Ice and Storage Co.

Street

Derby Street Crossing SB

Lathbury Barley Warehouse

Little Burton Bridge

Derby

Cattle Sale Yard

Trent Works (Engineering)

Horninglow Bridge SB

0 yards 100 200

quantities of ale, an annual production of about 500 barrels compared with Cooper's 40,000 to 50,000 barrels at the Crescent Brewery. Nevertheless from 1st May 1880, Clayton was making use of a nearby siding. Back in 1872-73, the MR had been trying to dispose of the Dingo Hotel.

The MR branch, opened on 27th February 1873, left the main line immediately passing underneath the Little Burton Bridge before sweeping round in a tight curve to Derby Street. The signal box near the Little Burton Bridge was called Horninglow Bridge; opened in 1864, the box structure was replaced three times before being closed on 26th November 1933. There was a cattle sale yard at the Smithfield abutting on to the curve and a siding was provided for it. The bridge carried Horninglow Street over the main line and was erected before 1850. Although the alignment of the road was slightly altered to cross the bridge, its original route could still be easily seen at both ends of the bridge. Some of the cattle destined for the Smithfield were unloaded on the east side of the main line and driven over the Little Burton Bridge. This so upset pedestrians that a cantilevered footway, protected by railings, was attached to the bridge in order to keep the cattle off the pavement. The Smithfield Hotel was situated next to the signal box controlling the Derby Street Crossing, although in later years (probably between 1937 and 1945) the box had disappeared and manual operation of the gates was the rule. At least two houses previously occupied by John Gibbons and John Hanson, and leased by Frederick Gretton from the Marquis of Anglesey, had to be demolished to make way for the construction of the branch.

The line then continued over two more level crossings in quick succession. Between them, a short siding was provided for the few wagons stopping at Ball's Midland Brewery, which had been established in the early 1870s. Green & Clarkson (W. & G.R. Clarkson 1875-95) later occupied the premises, expanding the brewery and putting in an extended siding. Annual production in the 1880s was between 6,000 and 10,000 barrels of beer. The business is thought to have closed about 1895, although Peter Walker & Sons was said to have acquired 'the old established brewery known as the Midland in Burton in January 1891!'. Shortly after 1900 the Burton Pure Ice & Cold Storage Co Ltd took over the western half of the site and supplied blocks of ice for preserving perishable produce. When the larger Burton brewers turned to carbonated beers in the mid 1920s, cold rooms were urgently required in which to store chilled beers, until they were ready for bottling. In the interim before the brewers developed their own cold space, they rented it from both the Trent Cold Storage & Ice Company and the Burton Pure Ice & Cold Storage Company, which made use of suitable empty brewery premises in the town. The tall narrow former brewery building on the eastern part of the site was first occupied by Renwick & Hunt, bakers and corn merchants, followed by Oldham's Cooperage Company. In the 1950s, Magee Marshall purchased water from a well controlled by the Burton Pure Ice & Cold Storage Company. The water was carried in 13 rail tank wagons to Bolton and on arrival there, the wagons were connected to a pipe and the water was pumped into a large storage tank in the brewery. These tank wagons were cleaned and the interiors repainted by Magee Marshall at Bolton, empty wagons being consigned back to the 'Victoria Street sidings' at Burton. This traffic probably ceased at the end of the decade.

The branch ran across an open area of land, known as the Blakeholme and leased by Frederick Gretton, before reaching Cooper's Brewery. A second siding was opened into Cooper's premises on 26th October 1874. Later, the MR built a 'wharf and ale dock near the Crescent Brewery' in 1882 but it is not clear to what this refers. Brewing ceased after Salt took over the company in 1919. A number of firms then made use of the accommodation, including The Derby Fertiliser Ltd (1921) and David Hill Ltd (1925), whilst the paving contractor J. Hoult & Son had some of the outbuildings. During World War 2, H. Wesley & Sons Ltd's factories in London and Manchester were bombed and the company moved out to various parts of the country, including Burton where it occupied Cooper's former brewery. It made cardboard cases for shells and mortars during the War, and later produced a wide range of paper products. A siding agreement with the LMS was dated 14th August 1946. The Crescent Brewery buildings were eventually demolished in 1981.

Beyond Victoria Crescent level crossing was Horninglow wharf, which in 1882 possessed a 5 ton travelling crane but this had gone by 1888. An extension to the wharf was brought into use on

4th December 1890. Contemporary maps show a signal box at Victoria Crescent but the gates were opened by hand for many years, and it is doubted whether there was ever a signal box at this location. The structure was subsequently described as a 'checker's cabin' before it disappeared. At the wharf, the MR had put in a siding to service Cooper's Malting and, although this building was subsequently demolished, in 1916 the site became the Cyclops Engineering Works, which continued to use the siding. The works was established by F. Peeters, a Belgian refugee, who was one of many who stayed in the town during World War 1. Jackson's bottling and mineral water company had occupied the malting briefly before Peeters came on the scene.

The Stocal Enamelled Tile and Iron Works was built by Stocal Enamels Ltd on part of the Blakeholme in 1913 to make all sorts of vitreous enamelled products, including railway signal arms and a platform was put up alongside the branch for loading wagons. According to Stuart, the company was still in existence in 1952, but subsequently Renold Chains Limited opened a new factory on the site on 7th May 1959. This had its own short siding next to the branch.

The final premises on the branch to receive our attention is the grain store erected on a corner of the Smithfield which belonged to Lathbury, according to the 1895 Railway Clearing House list, and there was a hoist over the cattle sale yard siding. Another railway line was later added on the side of the building parallel to the main line. The grain store subsequently belonged to the Burton upon Trent Screening & Storage Company, until Yeomans, Cherry & Curtis gained possession of it in 1921; a siding agreement with the LMS was dated 20th September 1921. Use by Yeomans, Cherry & Curtis ceased at the end of the 1960s. Sandars, the maltsters from the Eastern Counties, briefly took it over but then Bass acquired the premises so that it could eradicate the right of way through the former market, which was already in its possession, and it formed Bass' road transport depot in the 1960s. The grain store was demolished in 1976.

The single line branch was worked on a one engine in steam basis, the round black staff being kept in Horninglow Bridge Signal Box. Usually forming part of the 74 trip duties, the branch was mostly in the capable hands of a 3F 0-6-0 tank locomotive by the 1960s, although on very rare occasions, one of the tender version might turn up. The curves were not sharp enough to require a short wheelbase 'coffee pot'; although they are reputed to have been on the branch in the past.

The final train on the Horninglow Branch pulls over Derby Street level crossing on 1st January 1970.
(A. Moss Collection)

A regular performer latterly was 47643 and it often propelled wagons up the branch on its daily visit, puffing past Wesley's factory in the mid morning as the author struggled to move his trolley laden with Woolworth's Christmas wrapping paper about a building designed as a brewery. In 1966, half of Wesley's paper products still went out by rail and some were stored in the ex GNR Sugar Shed at Hawkins Lane until the festive season arrived. After shunting the coal wharf and collecting a few vans filled with steel drums from Cyclops, 47643 returned to sort Wesley's two banks. It would then retrace its way back along the branch to Renold Chains, where it left its train to pick up a couple of wagons from the swarf recovery plant. There were vans to propel into the Burton Pure Ice & Cold Storage Company's siding and sometimes a few grain vans at Yeoman's Cherry & Curtis' curious many angled building. After its last booked visit on 19th June 1965, 47643 was replaced by a 350hp diesel shunter, but it continued to act as a stand in until 25th July 1966. By the next week, D3572 was working on the branch. Horninglow Wharf had closed on 6th July 1964 and there was a gradual decline in other traffic. The line between Victoria Street and Cyclops was taken out of use on 28th February 1969 and the branch was cut at the level crossing. Closure of the branch took place on 1st January 1970 and the track was removed in the following May. So ended the story of a short branch which was typical of many similar lines in our towns and cities. They were for the most part rarely noted but together they provided a lot of business for the railway companies. Today, such lines are a rarity in Britain.

The Rubber Industry

The main line continued on towards Derby under the Little Burton Bridge. On this next stretch, it was difficult to see more than railway lines and wagons, so extensive were the yards. There was the Old Dixie/Horninglow Bridge Sidings on the right, and New Dixie on the left with the No.4 Grain Warehouse, Hydraulic Pumping Station and Wagon Repairs Depot beyond. At North Stafford Junction, the branches to Tutbury and the Hay diverged. The main line then passed between Old Wetmore and New Wetmore Sidings, entry to which was controlled by Wetmore Sidings Signal Box near the ex NSR overbridge. With our train now beginning to get into its stride, BTR's Oxford Works would be noted on the left.

The coming of the rubber industry provided much needed diversification of Burton's industrial structure and a number of factories were built in the town. First was the small Oxford Works in Derby Street East, immediately behind Truman's No.3 Malting. It was founded by the Werneth Rubber Company in 1911 and the gable wall bore this inscription for a long time. The same company also erected the much larger Oxford Works, making rubber soles and heels, just beyond Wetmore and next to the main line, with a siding extending the whole length of the site, and another line entering the building at right angles via a wagon turntable. In 1929, B.F. Goodrich took over and it became part of the British Tyre & Rubber Co Ltd.

There were also two factories with sidings off the ex NSR line near Stretton Junction. The India Rubber & Gutta Percha Company erected its Silvertown Works in 1916 on a 50 acres site off Horninglow Road to make complete car and cycle wheels. A railway line was laid parallel to the Trent & Mersey Canal from Stretton Junction to the works. In 1930 the factory closed but in the following year, it was taken over by B.F. Goodrich to manufacture V belts for the automobile industry; the business eventually traded as the British Tyre & Rubber Co Ltd from 1933. The Silvertown Branch was certainly used for taking coal to the boiler house but had become disused by 1950. Pirelli also opened a large works on the other side of Stretton Junction in 1929 and a lengthy siding involving a reversal was provided. Rail traffic did not last long apparently finishing in 1935 due to a dispute over demurrage charges, although the track remained in situ until after World War 2.

Burton Constructional Engineering Company Ltd

These premises were located on the opposite side of the main line to BTR's Oxford Works. Production began in 1914 and concentrated on rolled steel joists, angle iron, and steel plating. The railway company reached the works by a line from Wetmore Down Yard which ran parallel with the main line. A private siding trailed off this line into the works and stockyard under various gantry

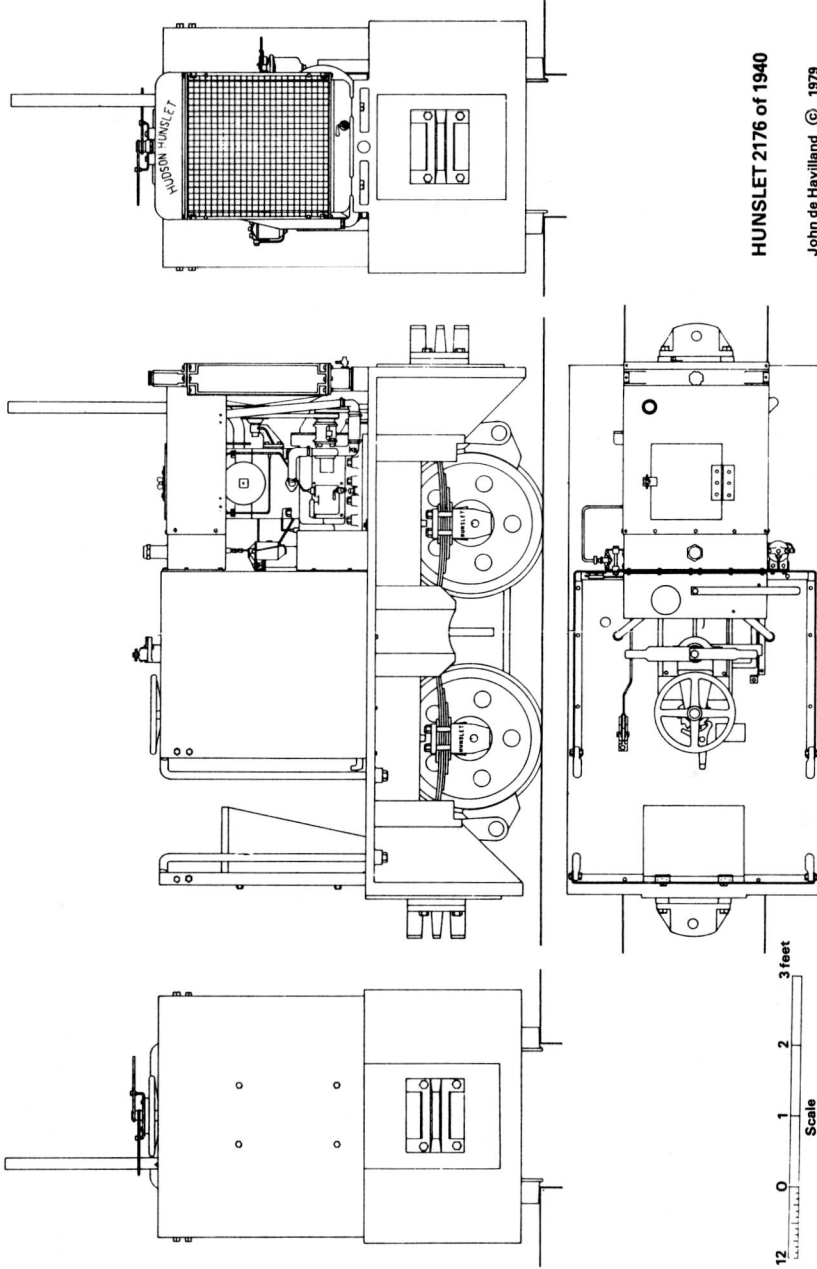

HUNSLET 2176 of 1940

John de Havilland © 1979

This drawing by John de Havilland shows Hunslet 2176 as it appeared in early 1979 at the Great Bush Railway without the engine covers carried at Burton on Trent, these having been lost in the intervening years. The illustration first appeared in The Narrow Gauge No.91.

0   1   2   3 feet
Scale

12

193

cranes. During the factory's later existence, a Class 08 350hp diesel shunter delivered the bogie bolster wagons, laden with steel bars, to the siding. The latter was subsequently extended to the British Ropeway Engineering Co Ltd's factory (Agreement dated 15th April 1946).

The stockyard at Burton Constructional had a 2ft 0in gauge railway system, which allowed steel to be manoeuvred about on bogies, connected by lengths of metal tubing, and taken into the main building. A 4-wheel petrol locomotive built by Hibberd or Motor Rail provided the first motive power but little seems to be known about it. The next locomotive was second hand, having been purchased from the First National Housing Trust Ltd's Perry Beeches Estate contract at Birmingham. It was a 4-wheel diesel mechanical machine built by Hibberd, maker's no.1869 of 1934, and it worked at Burton Constructional until 1960 when it was replaced by a locomotive from Cohen's scrapyard at Kingsbury. This was Hunslet diesel mechanical shunter (maker's number 2176) which had been constructed for the War Department in 1940. It was one of a batch of 25 Hudson-Hunslets, all incorporating a McLaren LMR2 diesel engine rated at 25hp at 1500rpm. The engine drove through a two speed forward and reverse gearbox and a Hunslet patent friction clutch and heavy roller chains to both axles giving track speeds of 3½mph and 7mph. Its brakes were operated by a pillar hand wheel in the centre of the open cab. Weighing approximately 4½ tons in working order, the locomotive had unusually large 2ft diameter wheels for a narrow gauge locomotive and a consequently high running plate and substantial buffer beam. Many of this batch of locomotives delivered to the War Department were stored at Donnington and it is possible that some were never used by the WD at all, being disposed of at 'war surplus' sales, still in their original packing. At Burton, the locomotive shunted around the works narrow gauge system until, by 1971, it was no longer required. It was sold to Mr John Thomas in 1972 and he loaned it to the Leighton Buzzard Narrow Gauge Railway Society.

English Grains Company

Beyond the next farm bridge, the main line passed by one of English Grains' premises. This company had been incorporated on 29th February 1892 and initially it occupied various old maltings around Burton, taking wet spent grains from the brewers, drying and turning them with additives into

MR 0-6-0 number 343 shunting wagons at English Grains Derby Road Works.
(A. Moss Collection)

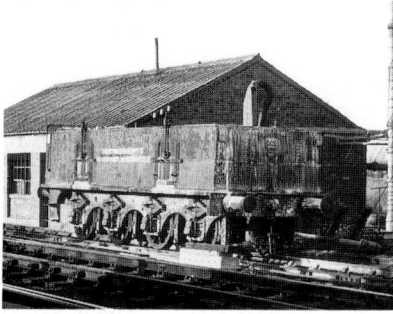

Taking coal to Burton Corporation's Clay Mills sewage works involved a lengthy trip along the Up Goods line. The wagons could be propelled but a maximum number of ten was specified. On 6th April 1964, D3568 pushes wagons past the English Grains factory on Derby Road, with its sidings occupied by dripping wagons full of spent grains. Sewage disposal was always a problem at Burton, because of the slight gradients and large quantities of water discharged from the breweries. At Clay Mills, there was a short siding (opened on 12th July 1875) off the Down Goods line to serve the boilers, which supplied steam to the four engines pumping treated sewage to Etwall. The railway company had a water treatment plant on the up side at Clay Mills and there was usually an ancient locomotive tender positioned next to it for the resultant sludge; the tender in the 1st February 1964 photograph carried a plate 'L & Y No.909 3600 galls'. Clay Mills Junction Signal Box illustrated the MR's liberal use of the 'Junction' suffix, even when it only controlled the division into passenger and goods lines. A box was opened here in 1874, the replacement being brought into use on 17th September 1899. It closed in 1987.   (C. Shepherd)

cattle food. Spent hops were also processed and added to cattle tonic foods, whilst another interest was yeast foodstuffs for humans and cattle. It is not known when the Derby Road Works was built but the MR line to it opened on 4th February 1894. The 550 yards single line from Wetmore was worked by the MR on the one engine in steam basis and the round black staff was kept at Wetmore Sidings Signal Box. Wagons could be propelled and no brake van was required. Heaped grains in a wet condition are prone to spontaneous combustion because of the rapid oxidisation and the company suffered numerous fires. There was one in some premises at Derby Street in 1893 and a very bad fire at the Derby Road Works in 1924. The Burton deputy fire officer was killed and Bass' old Merryweather fire engine is said to have pumped continuously for eight hours. Lines of wooden wagons full of spent grains were to be seen in the Derby Road Works sidings until the brewery railways finished.

CHAPTER TEN

IND COOPE AND ALLSOPP

Samuel Allsopp & Sons

For much of the nineteenth century, Allsopp was the second major national brewer in Burton and, although the company ran into problems at the end of the century, it remained a substantial undertaking with premises throughout the town. Henry Allsopp had taken over the running of Samuel Allsopp & Sons on the death of his father, Samuel, in 1838. Until the 1850s Allsopp relied on its brewery in High Street, together with three maltings and a cooperage near Henry Allsopp's family residence in Horninglow Street. The brewery had been considerably enlarged over the years and the first brick of the two large chimneys was laid on 23rd May 1843.

Henry Allsopp also owned land alongside the main line near the station. Production was rising and the need for malt led to the erection of three new maltings on this land. By 1855 barley could be brought in by the MR along a short railway line laid past the ends of the maltings, the first private siding in Burton. Two years later on 19th June 1857, the *Burton Weekly News* reported that 'Messrs Allsopp & Co [sic] have found it necessary to construct new malthouses' and the resulting complex was made up of seven maltings. Some of the blocks were joined together by a barley floor which spanned over the roadways between the buildings and powerful hydraulic hoist could lift barley up from the railway. Allsopp still relied on horses and carts to carry the malt to the brewery in High Street. The scene in Brook Street, the main approach to the maltings, was chaotic with an average of 350 carts a day passing along it.

Above. *Allsopp's Old Brewery seen from the High Street level crossing, with Burton Corporation tram No.17 passing.* *(Bass Museum Collection)*

Allsopp was already embarking on a much grander enterprise, the erection of its New Brewery next to the maltings and adjoining the main line. Additional land in the form of Lowes Close had been acquired from the Marquis of Anglesey in 1858, together with other small parcels from Hugh Brookes and Ind Coope. Hunt and Stephenson of Westminster were responsible for the design, and with the adjoining maltings, the new premises occupied a large self-contained 20 acres site. The 1907 *Commercial Handbook* described it as 'the largest single brewery in the world'; the brewhouse containing eight mash tuns of about 4,000 quarters a week capacity and attached to another block including a union room with 1,376 casks, a racking room, and the No.2 ale stores. It was possible to cross over the railway lines outside by an iron latticed bridge to reach the Great Union Room which was built in 1860. The impressive facade of this building can still be seen from the main line; it originally contained 1,624 casks, with a racking room underneath and below that substantial ale stores. The company's offices were at the Station Street end of the building. In the middle of the yard stood an Italianate clock tower, which in reality was a hydraulic engine house with a water tank at the top.

All this construction coincided with the opening of the first branch railways in Burton. A new connection was quickly provided by May 1860 to link the brewery to the MR, although initial amounts of traffic were small, because the New Brewery had barely begun production. A complex network of lines was laid around the site, and in the best Victorian traditions, considerable reliance was placed on the railway to transport materials both within the brewery and to the other premises. That original simple siding to the maltings had already been extended to reach the newer premises and it now ran by the long bank which served the ale stores below the Great Union Room. Four powerful hydraulic lifts could raise the casks to the bank at the rate of eight a minute. Another access to the railway company's system was established by a line which curved round the corner of the MR Grain Warehouse No.1. There were also links in either direction with the Guild Street Branch at the Brook Street Ground Frame. One of these led directly into the New Cooperage, which occupied the whole of the south eastern end of the site from Station Street to Brook Street. Two hundred people were employed here at the washing and unheading sheds, the running in, and the repairing sheds. On

The New Cooperage at Allsopp's New Brewery and the company's No.5 locomotive in attendance. (Bass Museum Collection)

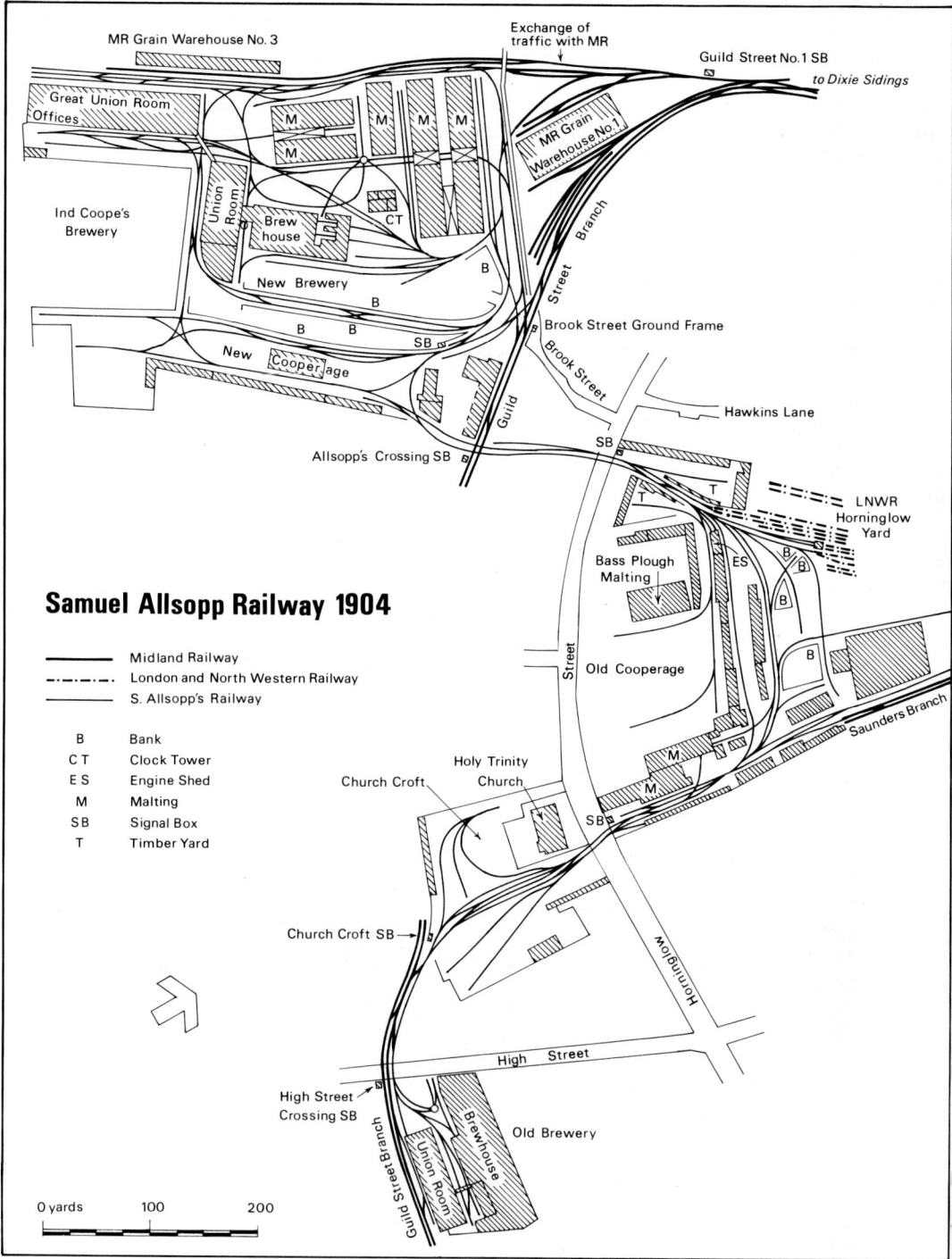

Samuel Allsopp Railway 1904

MR Grain Warehouse No. 3

Great Union Room
Offices

Ind Coope's
Brewery

Union Room

Brew house

New Brewery

New Cooperage

M M M M

CT

B

B

B B

SB

Exchange of
traffic with MR

Guild Street No.1 SB

to Dixie Sidings

MR Grain
Warehouse No.1

Guild Street Branch

Brook Street Ground Frame

Brook Street

Guild

Hawkins Lane

Allsopp's Crossing SB

SB

SB

LNWR
Horninglow
Yard

T T

Bass Plough
Malting

ES

B B

B

B

Old Cooperage

Street

Saunders Branch

Church Croft

Holy Trinity
Church

M

M

SB

Church Croft SB

Horninglow

High Street
Crossing SB

High   Street

Guild Street Branch

Union Room

Brewhouse

Old Brewery

	Midland Railway
	London and North Western Railway
	S. Allsopp's Railway

B	Bank
C T	Clock Tower
E S	Engine Shed
M	Malting
SB	Signal Box
T	Timber Yard

0 yards   100   200

198

Barnard's visit, he recorded that 14,000 casks were received at the washing plant each week for cleaning. After treatment, the casks were taken in railway wagons round to the two racking rooms, or else moved down to the Old Brewery. A private signal box was located at the end of the New Cooperage to control the traffic. Dominating the busy scene were the ever present pyramids of casks. In April 1864, Allsopp had laid out between 4 and 5 miles of private railway and the layout was virtually complete three years later with little subsequent alteration until the retrenchment of the business. The MR always fetched and delivered its traffic with Allsopp, the exchange being made between the Iron Bridge and the Little Burton Bridge, and Allsopp's locomotives did not work into the Old Dixie Sidings.

It was necessary to connect the New Brewery to Allsopp's earlier property and the double track private railway ran from the New Cooperage yard, over the Guild Street Branch at right angles, and across Horninglow Street to the Old Cooperage (later known as Allsopp's Middle Yard). According to the Act, the crossing of the Guild Street Branch on the level was to be protected by gates which would be supervised by the MR and normally closed against the private line, although no-one remembers there being any gates. P.F. Halbard's Britannia Foundry blocked the way in Horninglow Street and had to be demolished. Much of the fine cast iron work to be found round Burton had come from his foundry. Moor Mill Dam stream was put in a culvert and the railway was constructed along its course between the site of the Foundry and the properties facing on to Hawkins Lane. Allsopp's signal box, latterly painted green, controlled the Horninglow Street level crossing and there was a stone set into the wall of the box with a horizontal line to show the level reached by the water in the floods of October 1875.

After the New Cooperage opened, the Old Cooperage mostly concentrated on the manufacture of casks by hand. Many tradesmen were to be found here, including the wheelwrights, painters, blacksmiths and bricklayers. The site had been partly occupied by William Saunders' brewhouse from

An ancient crossbar signal controlled the movement of traffic where Allsopp's private railway passed over the Guild Street Branch. The MR Allsopp's Crossing signal box seen here dated from 6th February 1893 and closed on 16th July 1967. On 21st July 1967, No.2 made the last journey over this section of Allsopp's railway. (P. Waterfield)

No.6 in front of Allsopp's maltings and New Brewery with the glass lined tanks from the Pfaudler Vacuum Fermentation Company. *(R. Farman Collection)*

There was very little money for the revitalisation of the locomotive fleet, what with the debacle of over capitalisation and the unsuccessful lager venture. Most reliance was still placed on the Hudswell Clarke & Rodgers locomotives despite them beginning to show their age. They were noisy locomotives and made a distinctive sound as they shuffled round the brewery. Livery was green, something akin to malachite, and each locomotive had an oval owner's plate on the side of the cab with the legend 'Allsopp & Sons Ltd' and the trade mark of the open hand in the centre.

There is uncertainty about what happened to some of the early locomotives. It is known that the Manning Wardle was sold to the Carlton Ironworks in County Durham. The manufacturer's spares records suggest that this was in the period 1870-77, if the Ironworks owner's name is correctly recorded; however, when Barnard visited the brewery in 1887, he noted that Allsopp had six locomotives. Another contemporary report in 1901 spoke of Allsopp owning six locomotives.

The fate of No.6, the 1876 Hudswell Clarke & Rodgers' locomotive, is uncertain. This was once thought to have been rebuilt by Thornewill & Warham in July 1901 but various features of the new design discount this. The Hudswell Clarke & Rodgers' product was more likely traded into Thornewill & Warham for another substantially rebuilt locomotive. The rivetted front plate between the main frames on the replacement locomotive, also called No.6, suggests that this had originally been a well tank. In addition, the large dome had presumably once covered spring balance safety valves, as on the Bass' Faery locomotives, although the associated levers and springs were missing. It is mere conjecture but was it coincidence that Bass' old No.9 was replaced in 1901. Another unusual aspect of the design was the use of Walschaerts valve gear. This was very rare on a British industrial locomotive and again may have indicated the presence of a well tank. Whatever its origins, the 'new' No.6 was of sufficient modern appearance to be featured in a 1930s Thornewill & Warham (Successors) catalogue, where it was described as a 14in locomotive built for Samuel Allsopp.

Allsopp purchased a brand new locomotive from Hudswell Clarke in 1903. Ordered in the previous December, No.7 (maker's number 647) was marginally more powerful than the traditional Burton brewery shunter and had 15in x 22in cylinders, 3ft 7in diameter wheels, weighed 24 tons 14cwts and cost £1,295.

The fate of locomotive No.2 (Hudswell Clarke & Rodgers maker's no.75) is not known but in 1912, numbers 3 and 5 were sent to Hawthorn Leslie & Company for rebuilding. During World War 1, Allsopp was still having problems with its motive power and it bought Bass' No.6 from Isaac Hill & Son's scrap yard at Burton. The locomotive was repainted green in the wooden paint shop in the Old Cooperage yard, near the Holy Trinity level crossing, early in 1917. Apart from the livery, it retained the appearance of a typical Bass locomotive. Its arrival allowed the worst Hudswell Clarke & Rodgers locomotive to be scrapped in 1920 and the ex Bass locomotive took its number 4.

A closer view of the unusual No.6 which was probably a rebuild by Thornewill & Warham of an older well tank locomotive. (F. Jones Collection)

Allsopp's No.7 at the Old Brewery after the latter had been refurbished to produce lager. (F. Jones Collection)

World War 1 witnessed the continued decline in the fortunes of the Old Brewery. Much of the cold storage was given over to keeping food during the hostilities. A disastrous fire in July 1916 gutted most of the cold storage cellars and it was decided not to rebuild the plant at Burton, lager production being transferred to Alloa, where it was initially sold as Arrol's lager and Calder's lager. The small amounts exported still went under Allsopp's name. Archibald Arrol & Son Limited of Alloa had become a subsidiary through the connection of J.J. Calder, managing director of Allsopp. Eventually, Graham's Golden Lager Company came under Allsopp's control and all the lager was then sold under that label. There was an obvious requirement to move beer and lager in bulk quantities between the production centres in the country and the various bottling stores. Allsopp was an early user of tank wagons, the first batch entering traffic in 1929, and these were later often seen standing in a row under the Belfast Roof next to the Great Union Room. One of the functions of the tanks was to travel to St Pancras station where they were lifted down to the bottling stores underneath. When repairs were required, the wagons were sent to Wagon Repairs at Branston, often for attention to hot boxes. The tanks had either one, two, or three compartments; the first design built by Charles Roberts & Co Ltd of Wakefield had three and could carry a load of ten tons. Subsequent versions between the wars followed the same pattern, although some were of an increased capacity holding 12 tons. The wheelbase and springing was altered to accommodate the additional load. There was a metal plate on the wagons advising that they belonged to 'S. Allsopp & Sons Ltd., Burton on Trent'. Even a Graham's Golden Lager tank wagon built in 1939 carried a similar plate, but by this time, it was lettered 'A. Arrol & Sons Ltd., Alloa'.

About 1923-24, Bass had inadequate chilling space for its new carbonated beers. The move of lager production meant that Allsopp's Old Brewery had spare capacity and Bass temporarily rented space at the cold stores. Bass' locomotives took wagons loaded with hogsheads of beer from its Old Dock up to Church Croft Signal Box, then crossed over on to Allsopp's private line and ran back down to the Hay, before gingerly working round the tight curve into the Old Brewery. On the very rare occasions when the floods under the Burton Bridge became impassable, Bass' locomotives also pulled wagons along Allsopp's railway over Horninglow Street to the Saunders Branch. The union and racking room block at Allsopp's Old Brewery was taken over by Eatoughs in the early 1920s to manufacture footwear and this company prospered despite a fire in 1926. Allsopp's locomotives continued to work into the brewery yard until quite late but about 1934, the remainder of the Old Brewery closed down and was subsequently demolished. The two tall chimneys were felled in 1937 and the *Burton Observer* recounted that the contractor had to burrow three feet into the base of the second chimney and was then only through the outer cover. A sheet of glass was found in the base engraved with the statement that 'At 50 minutes past 7 o'clock in the morning of the 23rd day of June, 1843, the first brick of this chimney was laid. . . by Samuel Charles Allsopp, Esquire aged 15 months. The adjoining bottle of ale was brewed at the time of his birth, March 24th 1842.'

The closures reduced the amount of the railway system which had to be worked by the company's locomotives. Holy Trinity level crossing over Horninglow Street became disused in the 1930s and the Midland Cooperage's siding was shunted by the LMS from the Guild Street Branch. Allsopp's locomotives were confined to shunting around the lines of the New Brewery, with trips over Horninglow Street to the Old Cooperage and Horninglow yard. Some of the stock had been dispensed with and the old Hudswell Clarke & Rodgers locomotive number 5 was scrapped in 1922, to be followed by the ex Bass locomotive No.4 in 1926. It is reputed that No.7 was scrapped in 1926, but this seems to be a remarkably short life for a relatively modern Hudswell Clarke product and it has been already mentioned that Honeywill Brothers were advertising a Hudswell Clarke locomotive for sale at this time. These disposals by Allsopp were also made possible by the purchase of a new locomotive in 1925. It departed from the normal pattern of acquisitions by coming from Andrew Barclay Sons & Co Ltd of Kilmarnock (maker's number 1858) and was one of the manufacturer's standard 14in 0-4-0 saddle tank locomotives. Dimensions were 3ft 5in diameter wheels, 5ft 6in long wheelbase, a 618 square feet total heating surface, a grate area of 9.5 square feet, and a weight in working order of 27.75 tons. It could carry 700 gallons of water and 11cwts of coal. Allsopp appears to have relied on just three locomotives – 3, 6 and the Barclay 8 – in the

Allsopp's No.8 after completion at Andrew Barclay's works, Kilmarnock in 1925.
(University of Glasgow Archives)

years leading up to the amalgamation with Ind Coope in 1934. The date when No.3 was sold to the Redbourn Hill Iron & Coal Company at Scunthorpe is unknown and the Thornewill & Warham rebuilt locomotive was also not included in the amalgamated fleet, being scrapped about 1934.

Ind Coope

Ind Coope began brewing on the north side of Station Street in 1858. The land between Station Street and Mosley Street, formerly in use as a hop yard, was also acquired and by 1863 ale stores and a cooperage had been erected on it. A year later, the MR laid its third of a mile long Mosley Street Branch to connect these premises with the main line.

Ale loading on to the railway started on 13th March 1865 when the branch opened and the LNWR began to work into the premises in August 1867. The branch left the main line near Moor Street and swept round to Mosley Street, where it crossed the road, and then ran between the cooperage and the ale banks. Ind Coope also had some of its own sidings here and one of the lines served Wilson's bank. Mushrooms used to grow on some parts of the ale banks where beer spillage was a frequent occurrence. Some railway wagons had to be loaded from ground level because of the inadequate length of the banks on the east side. This was more difficult and could be particularly hazardous in icy and snowy conditions. The Mosley Street Branch terminated on the far side of Station Street, where an end-on connection was made with Ind Coope's private sidings to the brewhouse and union/racking rooms; the 'malt line' running round the north side of the brewhouse. Apart from the casks being taken to the ale stores, there were wagons full of spent hops to be removed. In later years, these were sent to Barons of Borrowash who were horticulturalists growing roses. Other wagons stood around waiting for farmers to come with their carts to collect the spent grains. The brewery yard was very congested with little siding space and workings continued well into the night to clear the casks of beer.

For much of its existence, the branch was worked by Ind Coope's horses and locomotives, and traffic was exchanged with the MR near the main line. Incoming wagons were left by the railway company on sidings at the cattle dock, or alongside the branch west of the Mosley Street crossing. In the space between, Bass purchased a sizeable area of land and constructed its Mosley Street

Pumping Station about 1864, with the water being stored at the top of the 118 feet tower. The remainder of the site was used as a timber yard. Two long sidings off the Mosley Street Branch allowed timber to be brought in, together with coal for the boilers. An early Bass trip comprising four trains to Crystal Palace started from the yard. By 1882, Bass had sold much of the land to the MR and the timber was then sent to the stave yard at Shobnall. Ownership of the land immediately around the well was retained by Bass, which was now served by a much shorter line from the branch shunted by the MR until the boilers and steam engine was superseded by electric motors about 1925. The MR laid three sidings on the former timber yard and both Ind Coope's arrival and departure traffic were stabled on them. There must have been a slight gradient up to the main line because the railway company's locomotives had to work hard pulling wagons out. Occasionally on damp misty mornings a long plume of smoke marked the efforts of a driver to regain the main line. The exceptions to these arrangements were the wagons of yeast for Newton Husband which were taken to the cattle dock to await attachment to a passenger train.

Ind Coope's premises were continually enlarged to meet the growing demand for beer. The ale stores could hold 45,000 casks in 1888 and the company's supply of malt had been improved by the construction of four maltings on the opposite side of the main line between 1872 and 1882.

A lovely photograph taken about 1888 of Ind Coope's Thornewill & Warham locomotive standing next to the ale stores, with Station Street and the brewery behind. *(R. Keene)*

One of Ind Coope's Hawthorn Leslie locomotives on the Mosley Street Branch surrounded by the company's casks.
(A. Moss Collection)

Acquisition of this site had been originally to secure adequate supplies of water. A borehole was sunk and the surrounding area was initially used as a sports ground until Ind Coope began work on the maltings. Ind Coope's railway to the maltings was opened on 12th January 1870 via a sharp curve behind Burton Station South Signal Box. The sidings on the open ground next to Shobnall Road were used for loading casks which had been stored in the maltings. This area was of course separated from the brewery by the main line and any shunting carried out by Ind Coope had to rely on its horses. The railway company's four-coupled 'Coffee Pot' used to squeal its way round the curve to fetch and deliver wagons. So far, most development had taken place at one end of this site but, by 1900, a portion near Borough Road was taken over by Lowe as a builders yard. One of the brewery company's lines was extended into Lowe's yard and was known as the Curzon Street siding; a gantry crane being later installed to facilitate the handling of builder's materials. The remainder of the site between the maltings and Lowe's yard was used by Ind Coope to erect new bottling stores and the sidings were extended from the maltings on 1st August 1901. The two railway companies agreed that the LNWR would place 'Ind Coope's traffic on the avenue of their Shobnall maltings sidings and it is pushed down to their bottling stores by our [MR] engine,' a rather pedantic arrangement! Ind Coope agreed to pay the MR £100 a year for the haulage of its traffic with MR locomotives between the brewery and the new bottling stores from 1st January 1904, although it could vary the agreement if it acquired a locomotive for the Shobnall Road premises. The latter could be seen from the platform of the new passenger station, although stock standing on the MR's two up Garden Carriage Sidings partly obscured the view. There was a short extension of one of these sidings to the small MR Engineer's works depot.

Regular shunting competitions were held on Ind Coope's sidings at Shobnall Road every Good Friday. Both the railway companies' and the brewers' shunters competed for the splendid trophy, a sterling silver bowl going to the person who could couple and uncouple 20 wagons in the shortest time. Lord Burton presented the bowl which was hallmarked 1896-97, and engraved with 'Burton on Trent Railway and Brewery Shunters Coupling Championship.' Around its neck were the trade marks of breweries coloured with enamel:

Worthington	White shield with red dagger
Bass	Red triangle
Allsopp	Red hand
Salt	Red Maltese Cross

211

There was also the town's coat of arms and at each of two sides was the buffer end of a railway wagon having a coupling hook protruding from the drawbar. Harry Toplis was one of the winners before he became a driver on a Worthington Planet locomotive. A few competitions took place after 1919 and Harry Briggs of Bass won one but the event petered out after the Grouping. A NSR shunter called Holmes was the last winner and he kept the trophy, until he gave it to the LMS in 1931 to be competed for in ambulance tests. Since then, the trophy has returned to Burton where it can be seen at the Bass Museum.

Horses shunting wagons at Ind Coope's brewery.   *(Bass Museum Collection)*

Ind Coope began to use its own locomotive on 17th October 1867 but unfortunately its precise identity has not been established. A locomotive shed was built with a short spur off the Mosley Street Branch near the junction with the main line. The first locomotive for which records survive was ordered on 8th December 1884 from R. & W. Hawthorn Ltd (maker's number 2022), immediately before that company amalgamated with Andrew Leslie & Co Ltd, and it arrived in the following year. A traditional 0-4-0 saddle tank with 12in x 18in cylinders and 3ft 0in diameter wheels, it was the precursor of numerous purchases from Hawthorn Leslie. The locomotive was made No.1 and given the unusual name ESCA. When Barnard visited the brewery in 1888, Ind Coope also had a Thornewill & Warham locomotive. This was very similar in design to Bass's first locomotive. It was a well tank, carried no saddle tank or cab, and had an ornamental dome. Thornewill & Warham had subsequently updated its locomotive design to include a saddle tank and so it is quite likely that this locomotive was built in the 1860s and may have been the 1867 acquisition.

The Thornewill & Warham locomotive was almost certainly replaced when Ind Coope bought new locomotives in 1895 (No.2 maker's number 2295) and 1896 (No.3 maker's number 2345). These were more powerful 14in locomotives of a Hawthorn Leslie standard design, with 3ft 6in diameter wheels and a boiler pressure of 140 lbs/sq in. The saddle tank stopped short of the chimney and could hold 600 gallons of water. No.2, probably laid down for stock by the manufacturer because the

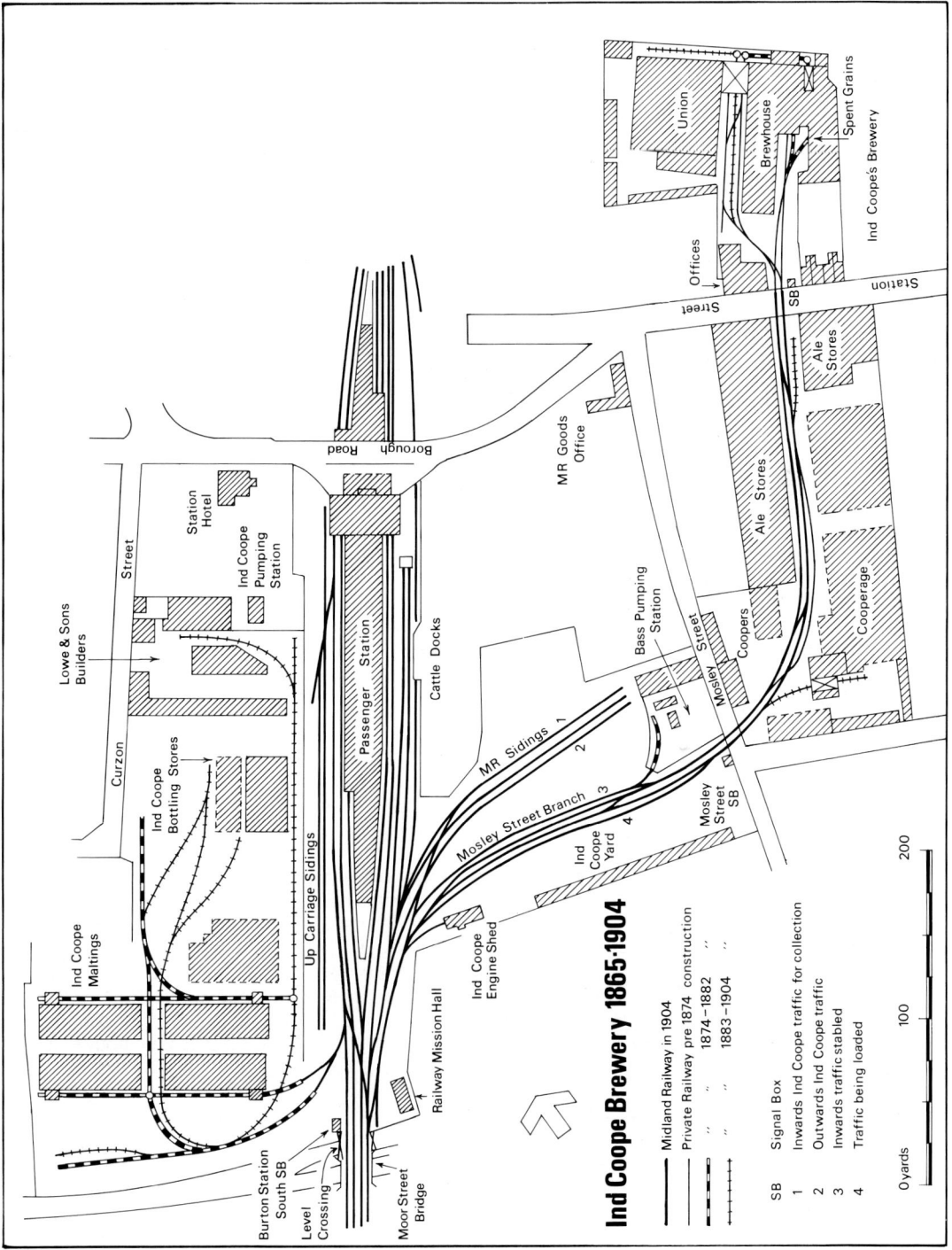

Ind Coope Brewery 1865·1904

Legend:
- ———— Midland Railway in 1904
- ———— Private Railway pre 1874 construction
- " " 1874–1882 "
- " " 1883–1904 "

- SB Signal Box
- 1 Inwards Ind Coope traffic for collection
- 2 Outwards Ind Coope traffic
- 3 Inwards traffic stabled
- 4 Traffic being loaded

Scale: 0 yards — 100 — 200

Map labels:
- Union
- Brewhouse
- Spent Grains
- Ind Coope's Brewery
- Offices
- SB
- Station Street
- Ale Stores
- Ale Stores
- Cooperage
- Coopers
- Mosley Street
- Mosley Street SB
- Bass Pumping Station
- MR Goods Office
- Ind Coope Yard
- Mosley Street Branch
- MR Sidings
- 1 2 3 4
- Ind Coope Engine Shed
- Railway Mission Hall
- Moor Street Bridge
- Level Crossing
- Burton Station South SB
- Ind Coope Maltings
- Ind Coope Bottling Stores
- Curzon Street
- Lowe & Sons Builders
- Station Hotel
- Ind Coope Pumping Station
- Borough Road
- Passenger Station
- Cattle Docks
- Up Carriage Sidings

LMS number 11205 passing by Garden Carriage Sidings and Ind Coope's Shobnall Road Maltings on 19th April 1932. (Dr Hollick)

next locomotive had the same order number, was lettered 'Ind Coope & Co Ltd'. It is likely that No.1 had gone by 1901 because Wade recorded in the August 1901 *Railway Magazine* that Ind Coope had two locomotives at Burton. There was generally only a need for one operating locomotive, with the other spare in the shed. Signal boxes controlled the level crossings and that at Station Street was of a Romanesque design to match the offices. It was erected in the 1860s, presumably when the railway opened, and was probably constructed by Ind Coope. The box originally had three arched

A Thornewill & Warham locomotive pauses during shunting at Ind Coope's cask washing siding, whilst a horse brings wagons along the branch about 1888. (R. Farman Collection)

214

Ind Coope's signal box at Station Street was an attractive Romanesque design; the original arched windows at the front having been replaced by a bay window, presumably to give better visibility of the faster moving road traffic. 12th April 1958.

(R.C. Riley)

openings on each of its four sides. Later a bay window extension was provided to give a view down Station Street. Before 1900, those windows facing into the brewery yard had been replaced by one large rectangular panel, divided into numerous panes by glazing bars. There was always a distinct possibility of being held up at the Ind Coope level crossing in Station Street, usually when hard pressed to catch a train at Burton Station. Then a dark green Hawthorn Leslie locomotive would shuffle across the highway. It could well be one of those with the short saddle tank and there are still recollections of 'the dumpy steam dome and flared chimney'.

Despite its difficulties soon after the start of the twentieth century, Ind Coope continued to trade. Arthur Whinney of the London chartered accountants Messrs Whinney, Smith & Whinney was appointed Receiver and Manager of the whole of the company's business on 15th January 1909. He carried out a reorganisation, making economies and giving up unprofitable houses and trade. The resultant reconstruction of the company's finances meant that a profit was shown during the years in receivership. Ind Coope & Company (1912) Limited was set up on 21st October 1912 to acquire the undertakings and business of the old company, as from 8th October 1910 for £1,392,257.

With both locomotives approaching thirty years of age, Ind Coope decided to obtain two new replacements from Hawthorn Leslie. No.1 (maker's number 3539) arrived in 1923 and No.3 (maker's number 3632) came in 1925. They had a 2in longer cylinder stroke compared with the earlier locomotives and an increased boiler pressure of 160 lbs/per sq in. Both bore owner plates typical of the Burton brewers with the company's title and the locomotive's number above it. The older locomotives were disposed of in 1925. No.2 was sold to the Synthetic Ammonia & Nitrates Co Ltd (later ICI Ltd) but No.3 (maker's number 2345) was considered worthy of retention and was given a major overhaul by Thornewill & Warham before being sent to the Romford Brewery.

Ind Coope & Allsopp

In 1934, these two well known companies amalgamated. There had been an agreement between them since about 1927, but in effect, it amounted to a takeover of Allsopp by Ind Coope.

215

Ind Coope & Allsopp's locomotives at the entrance to the Old Cooperage yard with No.4 (Hawthorn Leslie 3540) in the upper photograph. Below is No.7 (Sentinel 9376) seen on 6th September 1948; it was later fitted with electric lights. (IRS K.J. Cooper Collection)

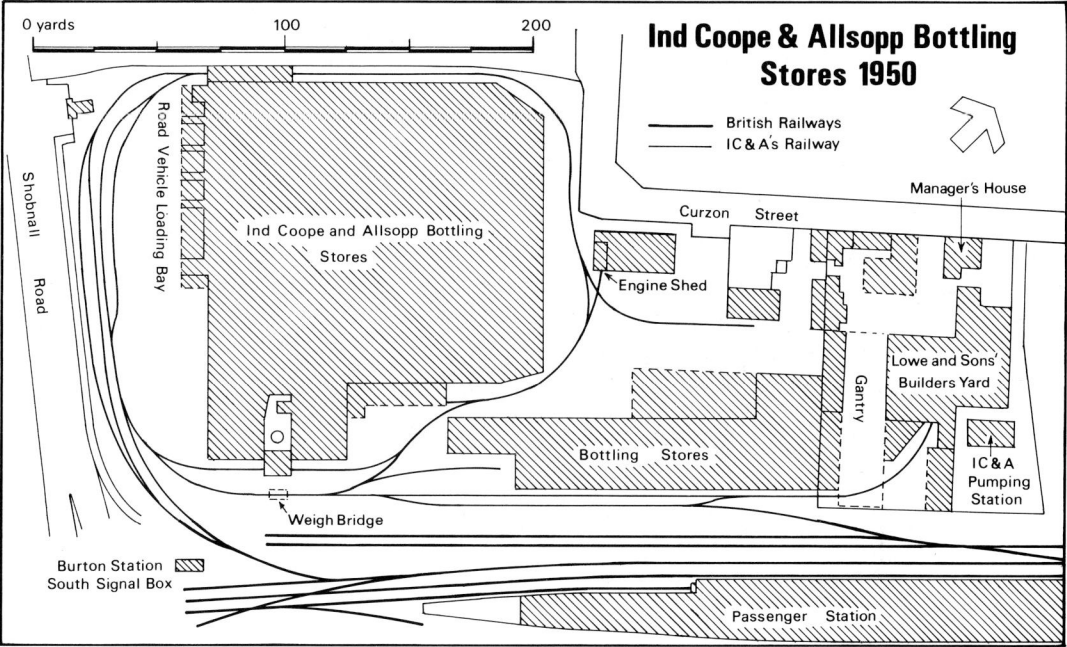

Ind Coope & Allsopp Bottling Stores 1950

| British Railways |
| IC & A's Railway |

Shobnall Road

Road Vehicle Loading Bay

Ind Coope and Allsopp Bottling Stores

Curzon Street

Manager's House

Engine Shed

Gantry

Lowe and Sons' Builders Yard

IC & A Pumping Station

Bottling Stores

Weigh Bridge

Burton Station South Signal Box

Passenger Station

0 yards 100 200

were put in wooden crates with masses of straw to try to reduce the number of breakages. A new high speed bottling plant was officially opened at Curzon Street by the deputy Chairman on Thursday 30th September 1948. This had been very economically accommodated by converting the four maltings and old stores to take the new equipment. Very little outside labour was used and much of the work had been done by German and Italian prisoners of war. The railway layout was extensively modified and it formed a large circle around the new bottling stores. Beer was initially brought from the brewery in rail tanks but these were soon replaced by road transport. Rail traffic at Curzon Street also declined because of the need to avoid the breakages caused by shunting. Caustic soda and coal still came in by rail, whilst wagons of cullet (broken glass) were sent to the Garston Glass Company at Liverpool. There were also a few Ferry wagons, which handled exports to Belgium, but these soon ceased when the beer began to be bottled in Belgium. Meanwhile, there could still be as many as twenty wagons standing at the New Brewery waiting for composite loads of casks and bottles to be made up. A lorry was sent over from the bottling stores with the crates to be added. If the contents of the load mainly comprised bottles, then the railway wagon was taken to Curzon Street. The amount of shunting at the bottling stores was not particularly arduous and the acquisition of a second hand battery powered electric locomotive from the War Department at Bramley Depot in 1946 suited Ind Coope & Allsopp's requirements. By coincidence, the locomotive had visited the town in the previous year, when it was at Baguley's works for some repairs. Then it had been lettered 'WD No.1 OC Reme Long Marston'.

The battery locomotive had a number of advantages, including instant availability for use and low maintenance costs, but its greatest asset was the complete lack of any emission of smoke, fumes, or dust when shunting around the bottling plant. Admittedly there was the need for charging the batteries, but the makers claimed that the locomotive could deal with intermittent shunting totalling 2 to 3 hours during each day and this would be adequate. A shed was provided for it so that a locomotive could be kept on this side of the main line for the first time. Although built as long ago as 1922 (maker's number 533), the English Electric design of battery locomotive had undergone little change over the succeeding years. There were variations in the type's detailed outline, differences

219

No.9, the battery locomotive, at Ind Coope & Allsopp's New Brewery on 12th April 1958.   *(R.C. Riley)*

in the rating of the traction motors and batteries, and the weight could vary from 9 to 20 tons. Nevertheless, it was basically a very simple machine with a central cab and battery compartments at both ends, all carried on two substantial longitudinal steel channels with laminated springs above each of the axle boxes. There was considerable standardisation of the power and electrical equipment. Ind Coope & Allsopp's locomotive was classified as a Type 3B weighing 15 tons and delivering 38hp at a one hour rating. The controls were based on tramway practice with a standard hand operated controller, starting resistance, and circuit breakers.

By the 1950s, most of Ind Coope & Allsopp's railway operations were concentrated on the brewery, maltings, ale stores and cooperage at the New Brewery site. These were still linked by private railway to the former Old Cooperage yard, although workings were mainly restricted to light engine movements from the shed, coal from the stockyard to the boilers at the brewery, and exchange traffic with BR at Horninglow Yard. Coal came by road from Leicestershire and was stockpiled until required. In 1952 Ind Coope & Allsopp bought some new hopper wagons from Charles Roberts & Co Ltd for transporting the coal from the stockyard by railway to the New Brewery. Some of the maltings near the main line were destroyed by fire and were replaced by the new Saladin Maltings in 1958. Ind Coope & Allsopp continued to operate the four maltings up at Shobnall, latterly with the barley kept in compartments under controlled conditions.

The Sentinel locomotives do not seem to have impressed because, just one year later in 1949, a diesel locomotive was ordered from Baguley. Some minor parts of No.3, the Hawthorn Leslie steam locomotive, were used in the construction. The new diesel mechanical shunter (maker's number 3227) was delivered in 1951. It was similar to Marston's locomotive with a four speed gearbox and the drive via a jackshaft to the side rods but it had a Paxman 6RW 150hp engine. Like Marston's locomotive, it could also be classed as an 'accountant's rebuild'. This was a fairly common practice amongst the railway companies when a new locomotive could not be justified as capital expenditure, either because of shortage of money or when it was to replace a locomotive which had not been written down to a nominal value and had therefore to be paid for out of revenue. They were officially regarded as rebuilds of existing locomotives, this being a legitimate use of the revenue account. Another reason for the practice was that completely new plant was taxed as capital. If a reasonable proportion of the older plant was incorporated in its replacement, the job could be classed as a repair and set against profits. In brewing, for example, it was permissible to put back the existing wood of a wort copper upon an absolutely new copper vessel (the essential part) and call the job 'repair'. Such practices were entirely lawful under the tax system. Only a few parts would probably be reused to make certain that the resultant locomotive was not technically a new one. It

Baguley number 3227 shortly after delivery to Ind Coope & Allsopp on 14th March 1951.
        (E.E. Baguley Ltd, courtesy Staffordshire County Record Office)

was of course generally cheaper and easier to build from scratch rather than to modify well-worn, second hand machinery.

Ind Coope & Allsopp's diesel was made No.2 and was soon sent down to Romford in order to replace its steam locomotive. Another diesel was immediately ordered from Baguley on 30th March 1951 for the Burton brewery and this was made No.1 (maker's number 3357). The old steam No.1 locomotive returned but was sold to Thos W. Ward Ltd on 3rd November 1951 for £1,350. It cost Ward £68 to transport the locomotive by Pickford's low loader to its Templeborough Depot in Sheffield. Here it was put to good use by being hired to the National Coal Board, which ultimately purchased it on 25th March 1953. The price had risen to £3,500, less half the hire charges of £163. Its sister locomotive, No.4, was also sold to Ward on 1st April 1953 for £1,350. This figure included a lot of spares which were obviously no longer needed. Ward used its own transport to move the locomotive to Templeborough at a cost of £55. No.4 was also in good enough condition for Ward to sell it for £2,000 on 10th February 1954 to its subsidiary, the Low Moor Best Yorkshire Iron Ltd at Low Moor, Bradford. The last orthodox Ind Coope & Allsopp steam locomotive at Burton was the Barclay and it was scrapped in 1954. With the arrival back of the original Baguley diesel in 1955 to complete the 'new look', the stock formed a curious mixture in contrast to that with which the amalgamated company had begun.

Ind Coope & Allsopp locomotives in 1955

Number	Maker	Works number	Built	Type
1	Baguley	3357	1952	diesel
2	Baguley	3227	1951	diesel
7	Sentinel	9376	1947	steam
8	Sentinel	9384	1948	steam
9	English Electric	533	1922	electric

Rapidly declining traffic meant that there was no need for the two Sentinels and they disappeared from the scene. No.7 was sold to Sentinel agents Thomas Hill (Rotherham) Ltd at

On 21st July 1967, Allied Breweries' No.2 has the privilege of being the last locomotive to leave the former Allsopp's shed. *(P. Waterfield)*

222

Crossing Horninglow Street for the final time.   *(P. Waterfield)*

Kilnhurst in 1960 which was converting a number of Sentinel locomotives to diesel shunters at this time. It spent several years in obscurity passing through the hands of various owners, before being acquired, still in its original form, by the Railway Preservation Society at Quainton Road. No.8 also disappeared from view of the general public until its presence was once again revealed to local enthusiasts in the mid 1960s by the demolition of some buildings near the former Holy Trinity level crossing.

The remains of the Mosley Street Branch were lifted in 1966-67 and the railway between the New Brewery and the Old Cooperage yard, together with the locomotive shed, closed on the 21st July 1967. On that date, the Horninglow Street level crossing was opened to allow through No.2 driven by Eric Rose. The latter had been a locomotive driver at the brewery for 32 years and he was accompanied by retired former drivers Tommy Moss, with 50 years service, and Mr R. Hackett with 47 years service. The final trip brought to an end more than one hundred years of working over Horninglow Street. As the locomotive approached the gates from the shed, foreman shunter Bill Elliot who had been with the company for 38 years gave a defiant ring on the signal box bell, before the gates opened to stop the traffic for the last time. The line was soon dismantled and the signal box was demolished on 2nd September 1967. A small amount of shunting left at the brewery could be handled by a single Baguley diesel and the other locomotives were stored next to the Saladin Maltings. Bulk grain vans from Alloa and Mistley were brought in via the connection from Horninglow Bridge and this proved to be the last rail traffic to be received by Allied Breweries. Within about a year, a tractor took over the remaining shunting. No.9 disappeared, presumably for scrap, and the two Baguley diesels were sold to Derbyshire Stone Ltd in March 1970 for further work in its quarries. There were thoughts of preserving No.8 but it was in such poor condition that it was eventually scrapped in January 1971. A few rail wagons continued to come into Allied Breweries for another decade.

CHAPTER ELEVEN

LOCOMOTIVES OF WORTHINGTON AND BASS

Worthington and Company

When rail traffic began to be loaded at Worthington's High Street Brewery on 30th September 1863, following its connection to the MR, it was worked by horses. Worthington's horses pulled the wagons along the Hay and up the Guild Street Branch, where they were handed over to the MR. In August 1864, the MR's horses took over and Worthington's horses were restricted to shunting within the brewery. The MR began to use locomotives to work traffic to and from the brewery in February 1865 but Worthington continued to rely on horses for internal shunting until 1872 when its first locomotive was purchased.

With output growing and the onset of another brewing season, Worthington decided to obtain a second hand locomotive from the LNWR. Number 1205 was a 0-4-0 saddle tank with 14in x 20in inside cylinders, 4ft diameter wheels on an 8ft wheelbase, a working weight of 23 tons and was finished off with a typically tall LNWR chimney. Inside cylinders were unique for a brewery locomotive, although the railway companies had some of the type. It is probable that the LNWR used examples of the 1201 class at Burton and Worthington would have had the opportunity to examine them at work. There was also the advantage of early delivery at this, the busiest time of the year. The locomotive was virtually new having been built at Crewe (maker's number 1473) in April 1872. Worthington set it to work on the 19th November 1872 and the account for £1,475 was settled in the following month. During this period, the LNWR built some locomotives for sale in competition with the recognised builders, and contrary to what its Act of Parliament allowed it to do. Selling 1473 as a second hand locomotive just a few months later was a way of getting round this technicality! Later

Hudswell Clarke 262 was recorded in workshop grey livery before delivery to Worthington. It carries an oval owner's plate reading 'WORTHINGTON & CO, 1883, BURTON ON TRENT' together with the company's white shield trade mark. This plate was soon replaced by the rectangular owner's plate, which all of Worthington's locomotives carried for much of their existence. *(F. Jones Collection)*

Worthington locomotives No.1 (Hudswell Clarke 262), No.2 (Thornewill & Warham 434) and No.3 (Hudswell Clarke 452) in the brewery yard about 1896 with the old engine shed behind. By this date, the Thornewill & Warham locomotive had been fitted with a similar design of rudimentary cab.

(J. Challen Collection)

the LNWR had to stop such sales to private customers when the major locomotive manufacturers took out a court injunction against it. Worthington's next locomotive was a Thornewill & Warham product (maker's number 434) acquired in 1876 and very similar in external appearance to the Bass Faery locomotives, even carrying a number plate on the footplate backsheet.

When Worthington's brewery and railway were enlarged, a new locomotive was purchased from Hudswell Clarke (maker's number 262) in 1883; it was made No.1 and the Thornewill & Warham locomotive became No.2. A traditional saddle tank design which set the pattern for future purchases, 262 had 4-coupled wheels of 3ft 6½in diameter and 14in x 20in outside cylinders. Like the Thornewill & Warham locomotive, it did not have a cab. Worthington then disposed of the ex LNWR locomotive, advertising it for sale on 12th October 1883. When Barnard toured the premises in 1887-88, he remarked that the company owned "two powerful locomotives constructed to run round sharp curves" which they did with perfect smoothness and safety. Perhaps the story had been different for the LNWR locomotive; certainly its comparatively long 8 feet wheelbase must have been something of a handicap.

The rapid expansion of the brewery's trade in the late nineteenth century called for more locomotives. Tenders were invited from three manufacturers. John Fowler quoted £1,340, Thornewill & Warham indicated that it did not wish to tender because it could not meet the required delivery date of mid January 1896 and the third, Hudswell Clarke, was actually given the order on 22nd October 1895. A duplicate of 262 was completed on time and forwarded to Worthington, becoming No.3 (maker's number 452). It cost £1,310 and this was to be paid £655 in cash on delivery, with

mistake caused by the sight of a photograph in an old album showing a locomotive with a square top tank. In fact, the locomotive was a more modern Faery machine and the alteration was simply a sketch to see what it would look like.

More new locomotives came from Thornewill & Warham (maker's numbers 249 and 259) in 1864 and these were given running numbers 1 and 2. They were well tanks and generally similar to the initial acquisition. Early in the same year, an engine shed with two lines was constructed alongside the Guild Street Branch with space for four locomotives. This was to the north west of Guild Street because locomotives were, of course, still restricted from going over the level crossing until August 1865. Two years later, Bass still had the single engine shed and it was valued at £413.

Further purchases again from Thornewill & Warham took place in 1869 (No.3 maker's number 303) and 1872 (No.4 maker's number 353). These two locomotives were more powerful than their predecessors; the diameter of the cylinders was increased to 13in, and in the case of No.4 to 13½in, whilst their unladen weight was greater at 16½ tons. According to the 1925 Notes 'they were also the first of a series which carried overhead tanks as well as underneath tanks.' They were very similar in appearance to the following Faery class locomotives.

The tremendous growth in the company's business and the expanding scale of the premises, particularly with the developments at Shobnall, called for even more locomotives. In fact, Bass was so hard pressed that it was forced to advertise on 28th November 1873 for a locomotive which it could hire for 3 or 4 months; the specification was for a 4-wheel tank locomotive with 13in or 14in diameter cylinders, and locomotive owners were asked to contact Mr Canning. Between 1873 and 1877, Bass purchased five new locomotives built by Thornewill & Warham, numbered 5 to 9 and always referred to as the Faery class. This was presumably derived from the French word faerie meaning sprightly. They had 14in x 20in outside cylinders, 3ft 11¾in diameter wheels (No.5 had 3ft 9¾in) and weighed 18½ tons when unloaded. The Salter safety valves were located on the centre of the boiler, together with a large brass dome. No.8 cost £1,650. There was no cab or weather board for the protection of the crew and the locomotives carried both a saddle tank and a well tank. This is confirmed by the *Locomotive Repairs Log Book* which recorded on 3rd September 1892 that No.5 had its top tank taken off and its bottom tank taken down. No.1 was also rebuilt in 1876-77 to the Faery form, although this was probably an accountancy exercise with little of the old locomotive used, it being valued as a new Faery locomotive. No.2 had been modified prior to 1876 giving Bass a fleet of nine similar locomotives.

Bass' locomotives 1876-1883 and 1892-1893.

Locomotive		Valuations in £ at 1st July									
		1876	1877	1878	1879	1880	1881	1882	1883	1892	1893
No.1		500	1450	1375	1300	1275	1225	1175	1125	650	700a
No.2		700	600	525	475	475	475	460	430	170	170
No.3		750	700	600	525	550	550	530	500	240	b
No.4		850	750	700	575	825	800	775	740	c	-
No.5	Faery	1300	1200	1150	975	1000	975	950	910	500	500
No.6	Faery	1550	1400	1350	1280	1225	1200	1150	1100	560	500
No.7	Faery	1550	1400	1300	1300	1250	1200	1150	1100	655	650
No.8	Faery	1600	1400	1350	1260	1250	1200	1150	1100	650	625
No.9	Faery	-	-	1375	1300	1275	1225	1175	1125	650	625
No.2	Triangle	-	-	-	-	-	1350	1300	1250	740	750a
No.3	Triangle	-	-	-	-	-	-	-	-	1200	1110

Notes

a   Being repaired
b   At Thornewill & Warham
c   Being repaired at Thornewill & Warham

There does not appear to have been a standard rate of depreciation applied to the valuation of

The Thornewill & Warham locomotive fleet of Bass in 1878-79. Top – what are thought to be Nos.2, 8, 1 and 7 stand in front of the Running Shed. The man leaning against a buffer might be William Walters and the other gentleman in the broad rimmed hat could be the lamented John Pheasant. Bottom – Assumed to be Nos.9, 5, 4, 3 and 6 on the curve from the Guild Street Branch by the engine sheds to the Middle Brewery. The small building behind No.9 was used by the chargehand shunter; Charlie Mansfield was its occupant in later years.

(G. Renwick, courtesy G. Thursfield)

TRANSVERSE SECTION

Extension to Bass's Original Engine Shed 1871

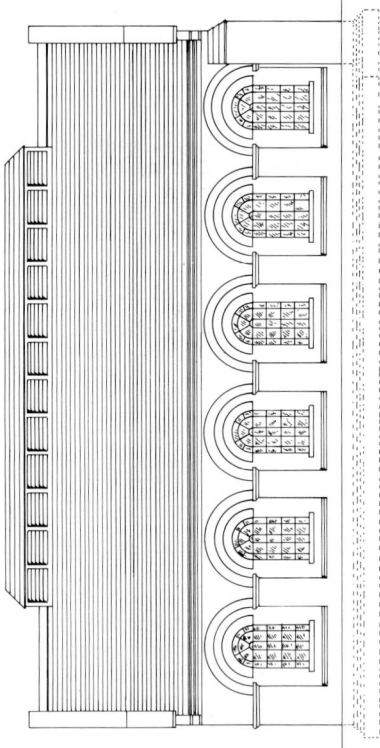

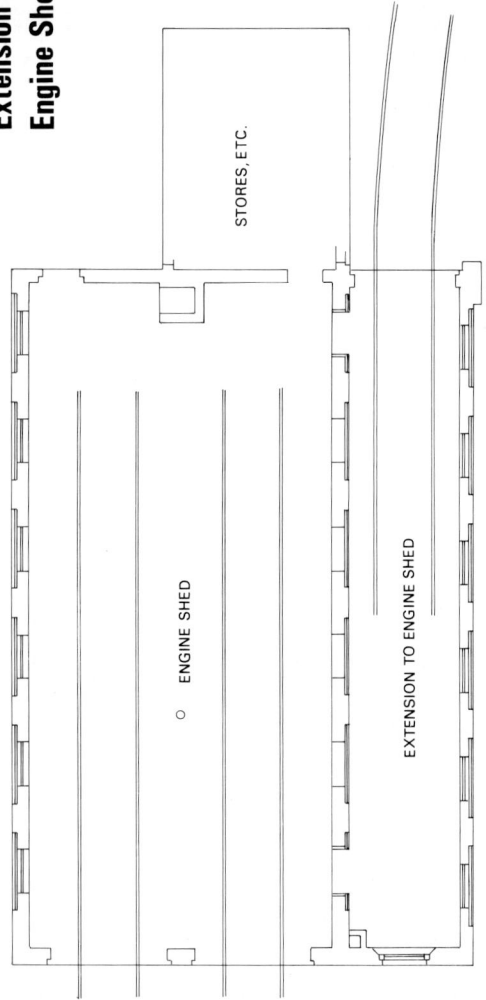

NORTH ELEVATION

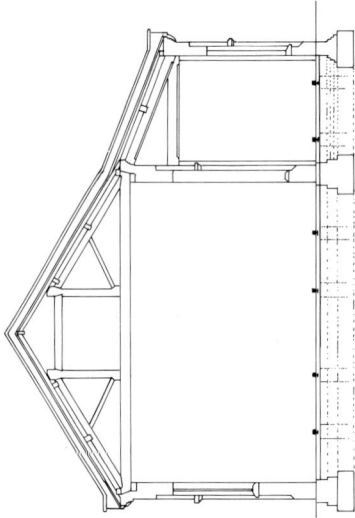

STORES, ETC.

ENGINE SHED

EXTENSION TO ENGINE SHED

GROUND PLAN

0 feet   10   20   30   40

238

the locomotives, either straight line or on a reducing balance. It is likely that the change in values was decided on the basis of locomotive condition and yearly profits as suggested by the auditors, John Bewley & Son of Liverpool.

The imminent arrival of the Faery locomotives led to a demand for more space and Bass extended its engine shed by adding an extra bay on the side next to the Guild Street Branch, with the roof being carried over at a reduced pitch to give sufficient headroom. It was originally intended to serve this bay by a siding which entered from the back of the shed, and this was shown on the plan of the building approved by the Town Surveyor on 12th June 1871, but there was also a need for better repair facilities and so it was decided to omit the railway line and make the bay into the locomotive fitting shop. To compensate for this loss, another bay was constructed on the opposite side of the shed, capable to accommodating one locomotive, and entered by a siding from the front. The building was subsequently known as the Repair Shed (or No.1 Shed). At its maximum, it could hold five locomotives including one dismantled for overhaul. The Bass Directors' Saloon was eventually kept on the line in the bay. Raising the locomotives to remove the wheels had to be done by jacks and the boilers were lifted by block and tackle suspended from the wooden beams above. There were often two or three men from Warrens of Newhall at the shed repairing a boiler. The 7½ tons pulley crane and gantry was not installed at the Repair Shed until March 1946. Overhaul of a locomotive took about nine months with the choice being decided on the basis of the one in worst condition, rather than in strict rotation.

Bass still did not have adequate cover for all of its motive power and the Running Shed (or No.2 Shed) accommodating five locomotives was erected next to the original shed. Although the *1925 Notes* assert that this event took place in 1876, it was probably already a firm proposal by 1871 and built to house the Faery locomotives. The 1871 plan mentioned above referred to the original shed as the 'Old Engine Shed.' Bass' double track from the Guild Street Branch to the Scutari Maltings had to be singled to make way for the new shed.

*Overhauling a Bass loco-
motive at the Guild Street
sheds.
(Bass Museum Collection)*

239

Bass' No.6 (Thornewill & Warham 393) before rebuilding. It is standing on the curve leading to Shobnall Maltings, with the Exchange Sidings behind. *(F. Jones Collection)*

At the back of the Repair Shed was an upstairs room over the office. This had pews and was originally used as both a messroom, where the men could leave their clothing, and for the morning service with which they began their day. During this century, stores such as lamps were kept in the room and it was only a messroom once more when the regular facilities at the locomotive shed near Scutari Maltings were being redecorated. The main locomotive stores were located in the extension at the rear of the Repair Shed. Brickwork at the back of the Running Shed showed signs of having been extensively renewed. This was the result of an over-confident cleaner who reckoned in about 1920 that he could drive; unfortunately the locomotive was in reverse and he knocked down the wall of the shed. Alongside the approach lines to the sheds were the 'sandhole', where dry sand was kept for the locomotives' sandboxes, and a store of coal. In July 1876, there were 14 tons of Staveley coal in stock for the locomotives, but by 1892, the coal came from the Moira Colliery Company. The engine sheds were situated in a triangle of railway lines which proved useful in turning locomotives and an ashpit was provided between the two buildings.

Maintenance of the locomotives was the responsibility of the Engineers' Department, whilst the Railway Department controlled the working of them. The first engine shed supervisor for which records survive was John Pheasant, who was accidentally killed on 15th August 1882, and a framed memorial to him used to hang in the upstairs messroom. In addition to the fitters, the Engineers' Department employed two chargemen dressed in short white coats who worked alternate day and night shifts. They also supervised the men and boy cleaners, who belonged to the Railway Department, and were in theory upgraded fitters so that they could attend to mechanical matters. In the early 1920s, Joe Sharp and Bob Lines were the chargehands, but strangely they had been locomotive drivers, and so any major repairs required during the night shift had to wait until the morning. At that time, the fitting staff comprised an apprentice, a fitter and a senior fitter. When Barnard Nisbet started, Arthur Blincow was the senior fitter. 'Bright young men' had to serve some time in different parts of the brewery and this included the railway fitting shop where they learnt about the various types of engineering. John Gretton as a young man was no exception and he spent some time at the engine shed, his first job being to make a pair of callipers. There was a copper ladle used for heating their allowance beer in the shed and, on cold days, the men added ginger to the beer. William Warden, John Parr, and the young Bernard Nisbet were working as fitters in the engine shed in the mid 1920s. It was heavy work and the minor injuries which they suffered says much about the nature of the job.

Accidents at Bass' Engine Shed 1st April 1924 to 31st March 1927

William Warden. 9th April 1924. Lost skin off left thumb due to hitting it with a hammer whilst cutting angle ring out of No.3 locomotive smokebox during its rebuild.

William Warden. 10th February 1925. 1½ months off work due to bruised ribs caused by leaning heavily on the footplate of No.3 locomotive when fitting feed valve.

John Parr. 2nd October 1925. Bruised arm working under locomotive.

Bernard Nisbet. 19th November 1925. Cut finger whilst fixing new spring hanger on No.9 locomotive and the chisel bar slipped.

Bernard Nisbet. 24th March 1926. Cut and bruised leg when fixing new chimney on No.11 and slipped off footplate. The locomotive was having a major overhaul.

John Parr. 19th April 1926. Fitting rods on No.11 when in striking the spanner, a piece of grit flew out bruising his eye.

William Warden. 11th October 1926. Cut a finger whilst working on the sand pipes for No.10 locomotive. The hammer slipped off the chisel.

John Parr. 15th March 1927. Strained groin lifting brake block into position on No.1 locomotive.

It took about fifteen years to become a driver at Bass. A boy started as a 'general dogsbody' at the shed. All learned some fitting before eventually opting to become a driver or a fitter and as a result the drivers had some mechanical knowledge. From cleaning boy, the next step was to spend some time on the footplate firing and learning the job. They worked one week on days from 6am to 4pm followed by one week on nights from 4pm to 2am. The last part of the night shift was devoted to helping clean the locomotive. They then graduated to relief driver, during periods of holidays and sickness, and became a full time driver when a replacement was required. In 1915, the drivers worked 54 hours per week, excluding meal times (½ hour for breakfast and one hour for dinner), for 37 shillings per week. The general agreement left it to the individual brewers to decide whether firemen should be employed and later there was only one man on the footplate of each Bass locomotive. This wage compared with the standard rate of 25 shillings per week for an able bodied brewery labourer at that time.

On 16th April 1880, Bass' Board agreed to purchase a new locomotive at a cost of £1,600, less £600 for trading in an old locomotive. The company turned again to Thornewill & Warham, which supplied a new design (maker's number 455) to replace No.2, which was by then the poorest of the locomotives. This new acquisition had no well tank or dome and the safety valves were placed over the firebox. Removal of the 'underneath side tanks' was an important improvement because they had been most inconvenient and had made access to the valve gear very difficult. The locomotive became No.2 and the type was known as the Triangle class; a value of £1,350 being entered in the Stock Book. Old No.2 was retained for some years, no doubt as a spare to cope with any unexpected exigencies. In 1891, it was No.3's turn to be replaced and a new No.3, again of the Triangle class, was bought from Thornewill & Warham (maker's number 609) for £1,195. This was a low price and suggests that a locomotive may have been traded in although no evidence has been found to prove this.

Old No.2 could now be safely disposed of and Bass' Engineer advertised it for sale in the 1st November 1893 issue of the *Machinery Market* magazine. It was described as a standard gauge four-coupled locomotive with saddle and under tanks, 12½in x 20in cylinders, 3ft 4in diameter wheels, a wheelbase of 6ft 2½in, and a boiler with 72 tubes. The Coton Park & Linton Colliery Company soon agreed to buy the locomotive. Payment was conveniently arranged by deducting the purchase price of £270 from Bass' account for coal delivered from the colliery for the month ending

An engraving of Bass' Triangle class locomotive No.2 at the Middle Brewery in 1887-88.
(A. Barnard)

31st December 1893. A cheque for the outstanding balance of £9 17s 3d was forwarded by Bass three weeks later. It was no coincidence that William Canning was one of the directors of the Coton Park & Linton Colliery Co.*

The original No.3 was despatched to Thornewill & Warham's works in 1892-93 and kept there until at least 1895 and possibly later. It may be that Bass was considering sending the locomotive to Sleaford to help in the construction of the maltings. Work did not start on the erection of these buildings until 1901, at which time old No.3 was reported to be having minor repairs. No.2 of the Triangle class had been rebuilt in 1896 and was last used at Burton in December 1900 before being sent to Sleaford on 2nd October 1901. When the maltings were completed, No.2 was disposed of by Bass and went directly to Sheffield in 1906. According to Alan McCrea, whose father was an apprenticed joiner at Sleaford during the construction, there were two Bass locomotives involved on the contract, together with the mobile No.60 portable steam boiler and its 10hp engine. The latter came back to Burton in 1907 and was stabled at Mosley Street for emergencies. The identity of the second locomotive at Sleaford is not known but it was likely to have been old No.3.

This period at the turn of the century was one of considerable change with the arrival of several new locomotives. Another engine shed was required and this was erected next to the Scutari Maltings at the end of the 1890s. It was an example of Couchman's work and the single line building could accommodate four locomotives. Trade increased until after 1902 when demand declined with a national depression. It did not pick up again until after World War 1 when it was still about a fifth of a million barrels below the 1902 production, thus the trade never warranted the replacement of the three Faery locomotives disposed of in 1916-17.

The Faery locomotives were of a similar vintage and the time was approaching when all would need major renewal. Bass' active stock in 1895 comprised:

Faery type locomotives	1, 4, 5, 6, 7, 8, 9
Triangle class locomotives	2, 3

*   Coton Park Colliery was situated two miles north of Church Gresley and was difficult to work because of the badly distorted and faulted seams. It also suffered from serious drainage problems; hence its local description of 'the strip and at it.' Large quantities of coal and bricks were supplied by it to Bass.

Bass New Engine Shed, Scutari Maltings

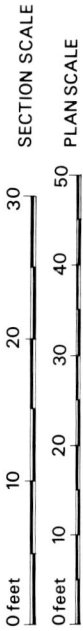

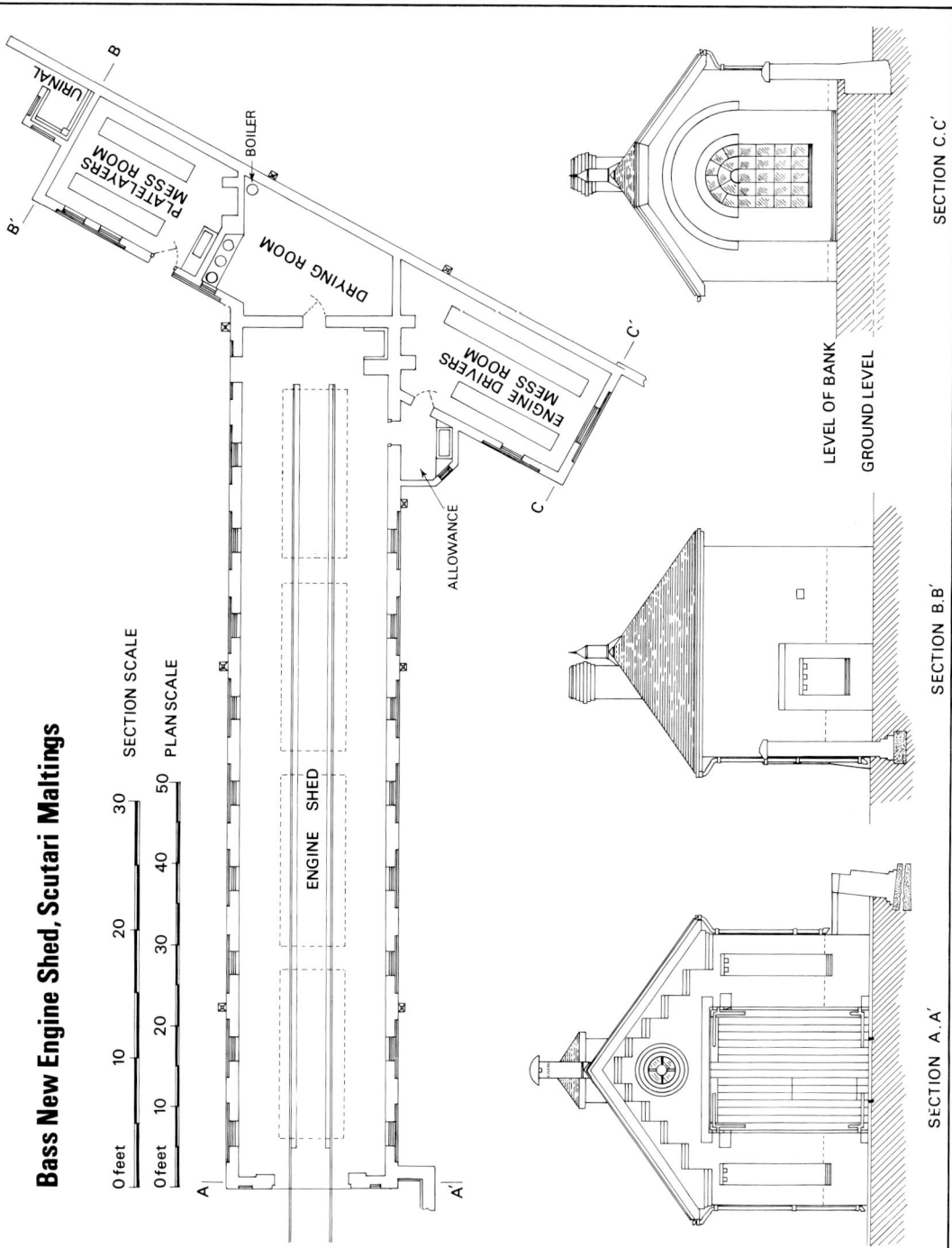

SECTION SCALE

0 feet 10 20 30

PLAN SCALE

0 feet 10 20 30 40 50

URINAL

PLATELAYERS MESS ROOM

BOILER

DRYING ROOM

ENGINE DRIVERS MESS ROOM

ALLOWANCE

ENGINE SHED

A A'

B B'

C C'

SECTION A.A'

SECTION B.B'

SECTION C.C'

LEVEL OF BANK

GROUND LEVEL

When No.3 of the Triangle class was built, it was specially painted in a grey livery so that it could have its official photograph taken in Bass' Middle Yard.　　　　　*(C. Shepherd Collection)*

No.4 had been repaired at Thornewill & Warham in 1892-93, and therefore work began in May 1896 on No.5, the poorest of the remaining locomotives. The opportunity was taken to bring the locomotive up to a modern standard and the well tank was removed. Rebuilding took place in the shed at Guild Street and was very extensive. Parts received from the Hunslet Engine Company included one boiler, one cab, one ashpan, one chimney, one saddle tank, and boiler, firebox, and cab fittings. Couchman was very much involved in the rebuilding and his dealings with Hunslet again demonstrate what a perfectionist he was. His specification for the cab included a very large cut out portion at the back to aid visibility and rounded corners. The locomotive was put to work on 24th May 1897 and must have been regarded as an asset to the Railway Department. It formed the basis for subsequent rebuilds and was to be a significant factor in the design of the new locomotives. Two new brass owner's plates were fitted on 23rd June 1897.

The locomotives had originally carried two or three different plates. Owner's plates with the name of Bass, Ratcliff and Gretton, together with the date of construction, were usually located on the cab side sheets, although the Triangle class carried them on the saddle tank. Thornewill & Warham's maker's plate was positioned on the side of the sand boxes. In the 1870s, the locomotive also had a number plate on the rear of the cab back sheet. Couchman would not have manufacturer's name plates displayed and they were removed from the locomotives as well as much of the machinery; even moulded maker's plates on pumps and engines were chiselled off! From then on, only oval brass owner's plates were carried by the locomotives. These were engraved by Barratt who owned a gun shop on the site of the present Blue Posts public house. Later plates also displayed a red enamelled triangle which was a trade mark of Bass and was incidentally the first registered trade mark in the world following the approval of the Trade Marks Act in 1875.

Couchman had already decided to rebuild the other Faery locomotives and he wrote to Hunslet asking for its price for the work on four of the locomotives.

'Messrs The Hunslet Engine Company   10th May 1897
Dear Sirs,
        I shall be glad to receive your quotation for the manufacture and supply of 4 complete sets of Boilers, Tanks, Cabs, also for cylinder drain cock gear, sparging gear, steam and exhaust pipes and connections, also sanding apparatus etc, same as previously supplied, all for our Locomotives Nos.6, 7, 8, & 9. The work to be carried out as per the drawings and specification in your possession. Your quotation must state the shortest time in which you would be able to execute the whole of the order. I should propose to send you one engine at a time for repairs to machinery which would be settled upon after the engine was dismantled for which I should expect you to give an approximate price. I shall be glad to receive your quotation this week.
                                                              Yours truly,
                                                              H.A. Couchman'

Other companies were also asked to quote, including Thornewill & Warham and Ruston & Proctor. The latter's figure for the 'boiler, tank, cab etc' complete was £760 per locomotive and Couchman invited Ruston & Proctor's Engineer to come and look 'at the engine I have just completed as I want him to be quite aware of the class of workmanship required.' Ruston & Proctor supplied steam pumps for the Middle Brewery and No.14 Engine House.

No.5 was the first of Bass' locomotives to be fitted with steam sanding apparatus when it was rebuilt. The system was described as the 'Holt and Gresham Steam Sanding Apparatus in *Bass' Engine Log and Repair Book.* Francis Holt had been the MR Works Manager at Derby when he

No.5 shortly after being rebuilt, together with the Directors' Saloon, between the Ale and Hop Stores and the Railway Office in Bass' Middle Brewery. The gentleman at the front of the locomotive is thought to be T. Williamson.   (Bass Museum Collection)

applied compressed air sanding gear to a number of locomotives in 1886. Following objections from the Westinghouse Brake Co about the possible effect on the braking system, Holt modified the device and used steam. It was ultimately commercially marketed by Gresham & Craven. In 1897, the latter supplied a further six sets of steam sanding apparatus for fitting to some of the Thornewill & Warham locomotives. Nos. 3 and 8 retained the old arrangement of sandboxes on the running board with a vertical pipe on each side of the locomotive which allowed the sand to fall by gravity between the wheels. Couchman obtained parts for the forthcoming rebuilding from a variety of suppliers. He wanted to be sure that everything going into the revitalised locomotives was to his standards. They included the following ordered on 30th June 1897:-

Storey & Co	6 steam whistles, as previously supplied in April 1896.
John Smith & Co	Clack valves, globe wheel valves, and steam feed junction valves all to be polished of the very best gun metal and to be capable of working to a steam pressure of 140lbs/sq in.
Dewrance & Co	Gauge glass fittings, valves, and cocks as previously supplied. To be of the very best gun metal polished.
Körking Bros	6 compound injectors right hand and 6 left hand.
Salter & Co	6 steam pressure gauges with 6in diameter dials, brass cases, and indicating up to 200lbs/sq in.

It is clear that following the success of the work on No.5, Bass was intending to rebuild six more of its locomotives, but not all of this work was carried out, and soon some new locomotives were being ordered. In the meantime, No.4 received a new boiler, motion and other parts in 1897-98 apparently at Guild Street. Ruston & Proctor supplied the slide bars and brake gear in July 1897.

The first two of the new locomotives were ordered from Neilson Reid's Hyde Park Works in Glasgow in August 1898 and delivery was to be 'in 6 months (8th February 1899) under heavy penalty.' In fact Bass was not able to put the locomotives, Nos.10 and 11 (maker's numbers 5567 and 5568) to work until August 1899. They cost £1,700 each and were known as the Class A or more affectionately as the 'Scottish engines'. The design was based on a development of the rebuilt Faery locomotives. Bass not only provided the drawings to Neilson Reid, insisting on adherence to them, but also ordered the materials and had them tested before they were handed over to Neilson Reid. Bolton's of Widnes supplied copper sheets for the fireboxes and were rebuffed when tests showed minute quantities of lead in the copper. When a query arose about plates, Couchman wrote on 23rd September 1898 that 'I should prefer these plates to come from Messrs Taylor Bros of Leeds as I think they will be found more reliable for flanging if made of Yorkshire Iron as specified.' Even the smallest detail was not overlooked, for example, on the rebuilds he wrote to Hunslet on 15th December 1898:

'. . . We simply use Cotton Trimmings for our axle box lubricator as per the sample sent herewith. The cotton is folded as per sample and pushed through the brass holder and tamped up sufficiently tight until the whole width is filled and then the tops and bottoms are cut off and the wick opened out thus.'

Couchman travelled up to Glasgow to check on progress and to examine the quality of work. In April, an inspection of the boilers revealed that they were not quite true. The centre portion of the width was satisfactory but they were high at the corners. Couchman maintained that if the plates had been set up properly, this could not have happened. He was quite prepared to ask Neilson Reid to make two new boilers, but on this occasion would accept the boilers, because it had happened through the neglect of the manufacturer's foreman. He acknowledged that the company would suffer to an unreasonable degree but every other detail of the locomotives had to be made strictly in accordance with the drawings. To its cost, Neilson Reid found what H.A. Couchman meant by specification. In the next month, he sent a coloured drawing showing the painting and lining for the locomotives. This was followed by a wooden panel giving the precise colours and the full size lettering for the numbers. At that time, Couchman was personally conducting the rebuilding and furnishing of the London offices, the revitalisation of the old locomotives and the erection of new ones, building Plough Maltings, putting mechanical screens, conveyors, and elevators into the existing Burton maltings, making preliminary arrangements for Sleaford, designing and

Neilson Reid's photograph of No.10 carrying a maker's plate which will soon be removed in favour of a Bass owner's plate.   *(C. Shepherd Collection)*

superintending the building of new public houses and advising the Bass directors on church work. He was a very remarkable man.

The new locomotives were heavier and more powerful than the rebuilt Faery locomotives. They had 14in x 21in outside cylinders, 3ft 6in diameter coupled wheels, and weighed 23 tons 10cwt when unloaded and 28 tons 14cwt when loaded. The difference was partly made up of coal in the firebox (3cwt) and bunker (7cwt), water in the boiler (1 ton 2cwt) and tank (3 tons), and sand (2cwt). In practice, about 5cwt of coal was kept in the bunker on one side only. Boiler pressure was 140 lbs/sq in, although 135 lbs was sometimes later quoted. The locomotives were fitted with a copper firebox and 103 brass 2in diameter boiler tubes which gave a total heating surface of 612.5 sq ft. Dixon steam brakes and steam sanding were fitted. Overall height of the locomotive from the rail was 11ft 6in and the length over the buffers was 24ft 1½in.

The decision to continue with the rebuilding programme before the arrival of the new Scottish locomotives placed a difficult burden on the Railway Department. Early in 1897, Couchman began to look around for some temporary assistance. When he failed to locate a suitable cheap secondhand locomotive, he turned to the MR who no doubt were pleased to assist such a valued customer and it meant that No.8 could be sent to Hunslet's works at Leeds for rebuilding in 1898. Unfortunately, the small shunter borrowed from the MR came to grief.

'Samuel Johnson Esq, MR Derby   3rd December 1898
Dear Sir,
re 4 wheel coupled locomotive
I am sorry to have to inform you that the above locomotive which we have on hire from you, has given way in the boiler.
The smokebox tube plate has burst along the belly of the barrel of boiler in consequence of corrosion which has gone nearly through the plate.
We had to send for your people earlier in the week to put in one new tube and new ferrules as the latter were worn quite out and the tube was so thin that it burst.
I am writing to inform you of this matter as the engine will have to be returned to Derby. Of course you will not hold us responsible for the damage done, as the defect

was not due to our neglect but existed in the engine when she was sent to us. Mr. Hodges is aware of the damage and kindly promised to let us have another locomotive.

Yours truly,
H.A. Couchman'

The replacement was 1428A (later numbered 1505) which was one of the MR inside cylinder four-coupled locomotives, so familiar a sight around the town. The 'A' signified that the locomotive had been put on the duplicate list in 1892 but it was still in active service.

There was obviously much pressure on the available locomotive stock around the turn of the century. Couchman wrote to Hunslet on 6th September 1898 saying 'I should like some definite idea as to when we are likely to have No.8 Engine back. I should propose to send you another loco in say 5 weeks time if you can put it in hand at once. . .' Four days later, Couchman was writing to Ruston & Proctor 'I am at present taking my holidays and shall not be able to do anything in the matter of the 13 x 18 engine until next month.' It is not known to what this refers. No.8 did not return to Burton until 2nd February 1899, No.7 having taken its place at Leeds. By May 1899, the MR was enquiring when it might have its locomotive back! Bass responded that it could not be spared until the new locomotives turned up.

No.8 was thoroughly tested the day after its arrival and performed satisfactorily. In fact, Couchman was sufficiently pleased with the way that Hunslet's man had brought the locomotive to Burton and got her ready for steaming that he sent a £1 postal order for Hunslet to hand to him. This was then almost equivalent to one week's wages. The altered locomotive met Bass' requirements and had cost much less than the price for a new purchase. Couchman even contemplated pressing ahead with completing the rebuilding of the six locomotives. There was one minor problem when, two weeks later, several pieces of ¼in round iron broken into small bits were taken out of the cylinders through the drain cocks. It was presumed that they had been pounded up between the piston and the cylinder cover. Fortunately, there had been no damage to the cylinders and Hunslet was let off with a warning to take more care with No.7.

'Samuel Johnson Esq   19th January 1899

Dear Sir,

I shall be obliged if you will kindly send over a man tomorrow to take charge of our loco No.7 which we are sending to Leeds by an afternoon train. The engine will be in our running sheds and your man can take her over there and we will haul her out to any point he may direct to pick up the goods train. The engine was passed on Monday last as fit for running on your main line.

Yours truly,
H.A. Couchman'

No.7 was sent to Leeds on 20th January 1899. After it had been dismantled, Couchman carried out his usual inspection and drew Hunslet's attention to the new wheels and axles, that its cylinders had been rebored four years ago, and that the pistons, rods, crossheads, and slide bars were also new. All parts from the outside suppliers were sent with the locomotive. Hunslet was also asked to ensure that the wheels and axles were interchangeable with the other rebuilt locomotives by making the eccentric sheaves alike and all having the same angle of advance. No.7 was returned on 14th November 1899.

During the year, problems had arisen with Nos.4 and 5 when it was found that the wheels were loose on the axles. Oil was coming through between the axle and the eye of the wheel and the paint was cracked all round the axle. The wheels and axles had been fitted together by Vickers of Sheffield and it was suspected that there had been some deficiency in either boring out the eyes of the wheels or in turning the axles too small. Vickers sent an employee to Burton to inspect them and it was agreed that the axles and wheels would be returned to Vickers, although the company continued to dispute its liability for carrying out the work free of charge, but Couchman was having none of that! He commented "nothing will test the grip of the axle better than outside cylinders with constant curve work all day long. I cannot agree to paying anything towards the new axle." A set of

Top. *No.7 in its rebuilt form stands outside Bass' Repair Shed at Guild Street.* Bottom. *No.1 and the Directors' Saloon alongside the Middle Brewery and Hop Stores on 12th April 1958.*
(IRS K.J. Cooper Collection, R.C. Riley)

wheels from No.5 was sent to Vickers on 20th February so that a new axle could be put in without delay. Loss of a locomotive for even a short duration at this time was obviously a serious matter. The material in the axle was to be hammered steel of the best quality and capable of withstanding an estimated tensile strength of 38 tons per square inch. In addition, Couchman asked for the burr on the tyre edges to be skimmed off, and added as an afterthought, that the tyres also seemed to be showing signs of movement. They were to be replaced by new tyres if necessary. A month later, Vickers was still complaining about the cost of the work but Couchman pointed out that no railway company would have accepted such workmanship and Bass was as particular as any railway company. He went on to suggest that the fault had arisen because Vickers had turned the axles perfectly parallel and that the locomotive builders used grease rather than oil when the wheels were being pushed on to the axle.

Despite the delay in work on the two new locomotives and the success of the rebuilds, Bass still had it in mind to order another three new locomotives from Neilson Reid. A tender was received quoting a price of £1,875 each. Couchman was disappointed because he had hoped to replace more of the old Thornewill & Warham locomotives if the price had been right. Nevertheless, two more locomotives were ordered from Neilson Reid in October 1899. The builder was given eight months to complete the work under heavy penalty but it was over a year before the new locomotives, Nos.1 and 2 (maker's numbers 5759 and 5760) began their duties at Burton in November 1900, having cost £2,100 each. Bass must have been satisfied because it continued to order locomotives from Neilson Reid, later stating that the locomotives were 'very efficient for their size, economical to run and light on the road; the firm is justly proud of its little engines.' Neilson Reid had been left in no doubt as to the arrangements for the new locomotives. Couchman had made sure of that writing 'You must please understand that the work is to be carried out under exactly the same conditions as the previous order, and the price of course includes the small extra details which you have just supplied.'

The new No.9 (maker's number 5907) was outshopped by Neilson Reid on 2nd November 1901, arrived at Burton a week later and began operating on the 20th. The cost was £2,150. Shortly afterwards, King Edward VII visited Bass' breweries. He left Euston on Friday 21st February 1902 aboard the royal train, only stopping at Lichfield to change locomotives, and the entourage reached Barton & Walton Station at 6.30pm where they disembarked for Lord Burton's home at Rangemore Hall. The next day the King toured round the breweries and popular legend has it that he travelled in the Directors' Saloon pulled by No.9, the company's newest locomotive. The truth was less glamorous because all of the moving was done in an open horse-drawn carriage and the locomotives were deployed at several vantage points for effect! The King returned from Burton on Monday 24th February at 1pm accompanied by various officials of the LNWR and MR. The LNWR Jubilee class compound 4-4-0 POWERFUL arrived with the train at Euston; the rough weather through which it had travelled reputedly shown by the appearance of the locomotive which was said to be brown with dirt. It was more likely to have been unburnt coal!

Three new Scottish locomotives meant that further withdrawals could take place. Old No.1 was disposed of despite the fact that it had received a thorough overhaul with the addition of many new parts in 1893. Faery No.9 was not rebuilt and it was also let go. Their fate is not known but various possibilities exist, including sale to Thornewill & Warham for rebuilding or possibly going to Sleaford as an alternative to No.3. What we do know is that an ex Bass Thornewill & Warham locomotive worked at Hemingways Ltd, an iron and steel engineering company at Haverton Hill in County Durham, shortly after the turn of the century. The last of the Faery rebuilds had taken place when No.6 had gone to Hunslet's works in 1900.

Between 1902 and 1904, No.3 was 'completely rebuilt in the shed at Burton.' It was fitted with a new boiler supplied by Hunslet but kept the rear safety valves over the firebox which were a distinctive feature of the Triangle class. A cab made by Hunslet to the design of H.A. Couchman was fitted and this had a hole in the roof to allow the steam to escape from the safety valves. The locomotive was given a false dome to match the appearance of the other stock. In 1909, No.3 was

*The rebuilt Bass' No.6.
(Bass Museum
Collection)*

fitted with a new boiler and firebox, thus enabling it to revert to the same arrangement of safety valves as the other Bass locomotives. Its Bass owner's plate recorded the date of construction as 1891 but only mentioned in the 1909 rebuild. The photograph of some of the locomotives outside the Guild Street sheds in 1906-07 reveals one locomotive with a taller cab and rectangular spectacle. It was originally thought to be No.3 because of its different safety valves but examination of a photograph by Frank Jones indicates that it was old No.4. Contemporary records for old No.4 do not exist before 1895 but the valuations indicate that it was at Thornewill & Warham in 1892-93. It seems likely that old No.4 was the first Bass locomotive to receive a saddle tank and cab, probably as part of the rebuild by Thornewill & Warham. The latter was rapidly falling out of favour and hence Couchman's resolve to carry out his own rebuilding starting with No.5, and it was this locomotive which set the standard for future work.

Repairs and renewals to the other locomotives continued. No.5 was fitted with four new wheels supplied by the North British Locomotive Company, successors to Neilson Reid, in 1903 and No.8 received new wheels from Hunslet two years later. No.8 was also sent to Hunslet's works in the first half of 1911 for boiler repairs and to be fitted with a new copper firebox, smokebox, and tube plate. It re-entered traffic on 2nd September 1911. The firebox of No.4 was in poor condition by this time and it required repairs or patching six times between 1905 and 1911. In the following year, a new No.4 was ordered from the North British Locomotive Company (maker's number 19848) which was to be the 'same in all respects to those previously supplied.' Although the North British list and the Bass owner's plate quoted 1912, it did not reach Burton until 14th May 1913 having cost £2,148. It was given a trial run to Shobnall five days later. Old No.4 was sent to Sheffield on 30th June 1913 presumably for scrap.

This left Bass with a fleet of eleven locomotives:-

Scottish   Nos.1, 2, 4, 9, 10, 11
Rebuilt Faery   Nos.5, 6, 7, 8
Rebuilt Triangle No.3

In 1916, it was discovered that No.6 had a cracked firebox. Bass could not obtain a new copper firebox because of the war and so the locomotive was sold to Isaac Hill & Son on 2nd August 1916. Hill had two scrapyards, one at the Hay Wharf and the other at Derby. Additional locomotives were difficult to obtain at this time and so 'Scrappy' Hill fitted it with a steel firebox and sold it to Allsopp early in 1917. All Bass' scrap was sent to Hill until about 1934. Items from the locomotives, such as worn tubes, were dumped in a wagon which stood by the rear of the locomotive shed.

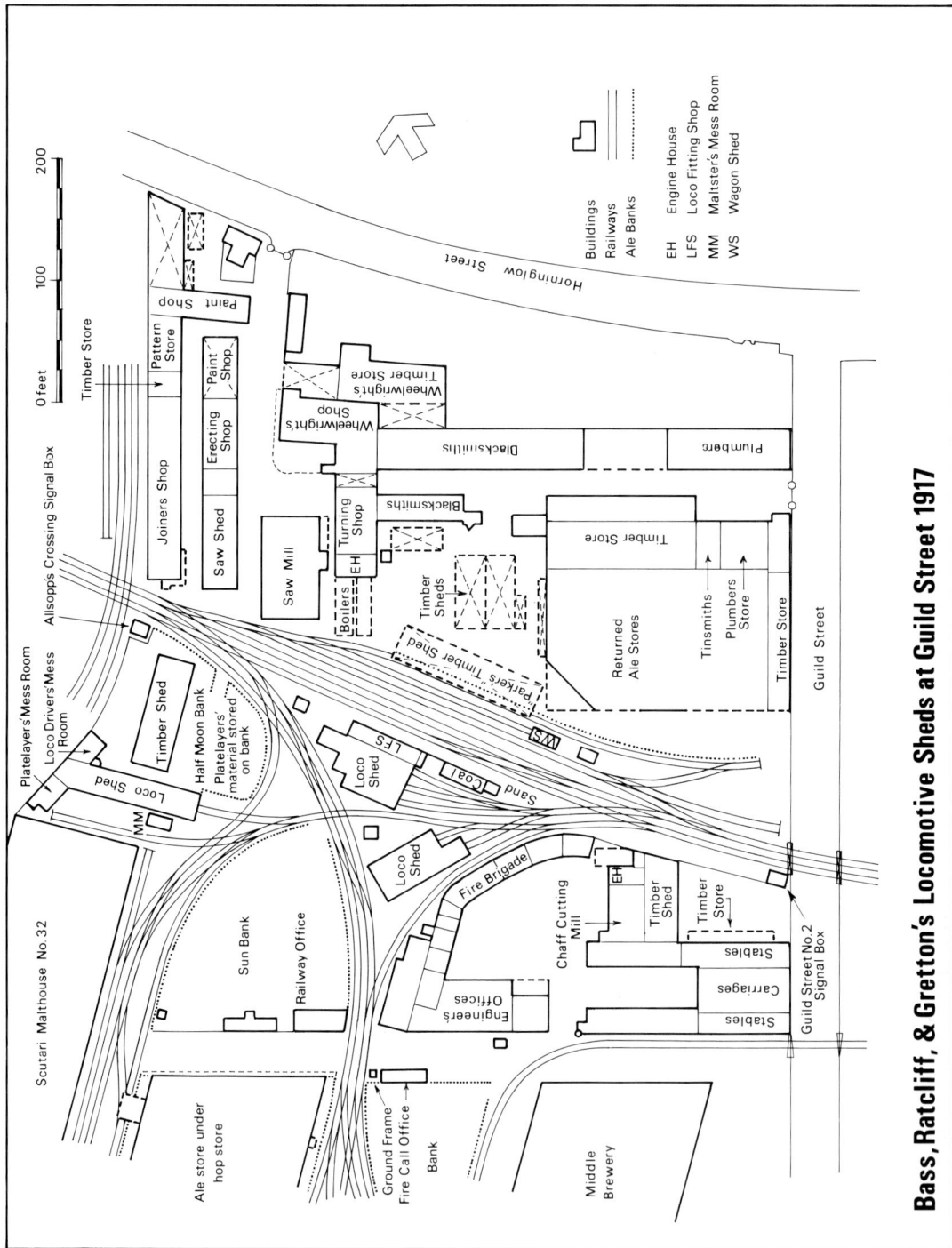

Bass, Ratcliff, & Gretton's Locomotive Sheds at Guild Street 1917

Legend:
- Buildings
- Railways
- Ale Banks
- EH — Engine House
- LFS — Loco Fitting Shop
- MM — Maltster's Mess Room
- WS — Wagon Shed

Labels on map:
- Horninglow Street
- Timber Store
- Paint Shop
- Pattern Store
- Joiners Shop
- Erecting Shop
- Saw Shed
- Saw Mill
- Turning Shop
- Boilers
- EH
- Wheelwright's Timber Store
- Wheelwright's Shop
- Blacksmiths
- Blacksmiths
- Plumbers
- Timber Sheds
- Parker's Timber Shed
- Timber Store
- Returned Ale Stores
- Tinsmiths
- Plumbers Store
- Timber Store
- Guild Street
- Allsopp's Crossing Signal Box
- Platelayers' Mess Room
- Loco Drivers' Mess Room
- Timber Shed
- Half Moon Bank
- Platelayers' material stored on bank
- MM
- Loco Shed
- Loco Shed
- LFS
- Sand
- Coal
- WS
- Loco Shed
- Fire Brigade
- Scutari Malthouse No. 32
- Sun Bank
- Railway Office
- Chaff Cutting Mill
- EH
- Timber Shed
- Timber Store
- Guild Street No 2 Signal Box
- Stables
- Carriages
- Stables
- Engineer's Offices
- Ale store under hop store
- Ground Frame
- Fire Call Office
- Bank
- Middle Brewery

Scale: 0 feet — 100 — 200

252

A group of Bass' locomotives outside the Guild Street sheds in 1906-07. The locomotive with the contrasting cab is thought to be old No.4. (Burton Mail Collection)

As World War 1 developed, there was an increasing demand by the Government for locomotives which could directly assist with the war effort. On 15th August 1916, an advertisement appeared in the *Locomotive Magazine* and the Ministry of Munitions subsequently conducted a census of all industrial locomotives in the country.

'To Makers and Users of Locomotives. THE MINISTRY OF MUNITIONS are prepared to receive offers for Good Second-Hand Shunting Locomotives of various sizes. The following information must accompany each offer, which must be addressed to Mr Hubert Baines, Deputy Chief Engineer, H.M. Office of Works, King Charles Street, Whitehall, London S.W:- Type, size and weight; maker's name; when built; when and by whom last overhauled, condition, price.
H.M. OFFICE OF WORKS, &c 11th July 1916.'

As a result A.H. Roberts, plant draughtsman in Bass' drawing office under Couchman, compiled a report in February 1917 giving details of all the company's locomotives including information on the major repairs for the older locomotives. A statement was made that they 'are all employed in Brewery work generally, and at present time one engine is employed at our Maltings [Anderstaff Lane] taken over by the Ministry of Munitions as Shell Stores.' As a result of the report, Nos.5 and 8 were sold to the Ministry of Munitions on 20th April 1917 and were sent to the Purfleet Deep Wharf & Storage Co Ltd's premises on the north bank of the Thames. The wharf was operated by the Royal Engineers on behalf of the War Department. Shortly after the end of hostilities, the wharf was handed back to the former owners and the War Department locomotives were sold. No.5 went to the Mapperley Colliery Company in Derbyshire, where it was named WILLIAM HENRY and worked at Stanley and Mapperley Collieries until it was scrapped on site by William Bush & Co of Alfreton in 1957. No.8 was purchased by the Purfleet Deep Wharf & Storage Co Ltd, becoming No.1 PURFLEET. In 1952 its boiler and saddle tank were put on a 0-6-0 Hudswell Clarke locomotive (maker's number 823 of 1908) which had begun its existence on the Weston, Clevedon & Portishead Railway. The redundant frame, which was cut up in 1957, was stamped with the number 400 and there must have been an exchange with that of No.7 at some time before it left Burton.

253

Bass' last Scottish locomotive No.4 approaches Guild Street level crossing about 1955.   *(M. Taylor, courtesy J. Peden)*

For many years Bass used untreated water from the South Staffordshire Water Board at Lichfield for the locomotives. This was hard water and must have meant that the boilers required frequent descaling. In 1909 Bass received one cask of Algor Boiler Syrup from the Liverpool Borax Company and began to add this to the water. In the first half of 1912 a water treatment plant was installed, a ton of Calcium Hydrate being received from the Sofnal Water Softening Co Ltd on the 5 March. The next day, a ton of pure Alkali arrived from Brunner Mond followed by a load of wood fibre from the City of London Woodwool Company. Part of the Running Shed at Guild Street had been extended forward and in the roof over the entrance was a large rivetted iron tank which held treated water taken from the softening plant on the opposite side of the railway branch. The tank acted as a header for the standpipe serving the locomotives outside the Repair Shed. This plant continued to function until the end of the railway using materials purchased from the original suppliers, although a refinement was added about 1954 when a final treatment with Alfloc was introduced to give neutralisation of the feed water. Sometimes the water became too soft, and this led to the locomotives priming and ejecting dirty water which resulted in complaints from nearby people.

The reduction in the locomotive stock meant that there was little need for the newest engine shed adjacent to the Scutari Maltings. Bass' locomotives had once been painted in this shed, but by 1924, it was occupied by a horizontal aluminium tank mounted inside a railway van. This had briefly transported bulk Red Triangle beer to Southampton for bottling. The tank was subsequently put on a Carrimore road chassis for moving high gravity beers from the Old Brewery to Shobnall Bottling Stores and was towed by a large Latil petrol tractor. In October 1926 Bass purchased its first Scammell lorry which ran to Coventry and this was kept in the shed with the rail tank pushed to the back. The shed was later used for garaging tractors and was not demolished until 1964 at the same time as the Scutari Maltings.

In 1914-15 No.7 spent a year at Hunslet's works undergoing an extensive overhaul, which included repairs to the boiler and the fitting of a new copper firebox, tubeplate, and smokebox. It was retyred and the cylinders were bored out. No.7 returned on its own wheels and was painted at Burton. Some modifications must have also been made to the design during the overhaul because the *1925 Notes* recorded that it was not until 1915 that No.7 was brought into line with the other locomotives. In 1924 the hole in the cab roof of No.3 was filled in and the Bass coppersmiths made a new dome cover which could always be subsequently recognised by its slightly taller top. The boilers of these two locomotives both had 84 tubes.

Bass now had six Scottish locomotives, categorised as Class A, and two (Nos.3 and 7) Class B. The latter were lighter and less powerful, with an unladen weight of 22¼ tons, boilers operating at 120 lbs/sq in, 14in x 20in cylinders and retaining their larger 4ft diameter wheels. According to the Engineers Department, a Class A locomotive should pull 40 loaded and a Class B 30 loaded 10 ton wagons. The following maximum loads were specified.

Haulage power of Bass' locomotives

	Class A	Class B
Adhesive power in ordinary weather	5 tons	4.6 tons
Draw bar pull	4.8 tons	3.4 tons
Tractive effort	11,240 lbs	8,330 lbs
Maximum load	30 to 35 wagons	20 to 25 wagons

The railway van built by Metropolitan Cammell with an aluminium tank mounted inside for transporting Bass' beer to Southampton.
(Historical Model Railway Society Collection)

No.3 settled down to a fairly uneventful existence following its rebuilds. Apart from a new firebox, no major replacements took place until 1954 when it was fitted with a new boiler and firebox received from Hunslet. These weighed 5 tons 3cwts and the boiler was lagged with the old magnesia slabs. Fractures in the frame at the front end were welded and strengthened by fitting plates. Although No.7 had two major repairs, it did not receive a new boiler and firebox until 1953. A crack in the frame was welded in 1956 and strengtheners fitted.

The Class B locomotives generally worked on the lighter duties particularly in the Middle Yard and at the Middle Brewery. Harold Cox had originally started as a cleaner and he eventually drove No.3, whilst Bob Jowett from Brook Street was on No.7. Bob's eyesight was none too good although it must have been acceptable because the MR tested the drivers' eyesight regularly. About 1924, he was instructed to take 'Master John' (later Lord Gretton) round the brewery on the locomotive and teach him to drive, so he bathed his eyes in boracic powder evening and morning to ensure that they were in good condition! John Gretton must have profited by the experience because he later fired the railway company's locomotives on the local lines during the 1926 General Strike. Old Bob Hartshorne was subsequently on one or the other Class B locomotives with Harry Birkin as his relief man. Whilst the Class A locomotives had steam brakes, Nos.3 and 7 had to depend on handbrakes.

The elm brake blocks supplied by the wheelwrights only operated on two wheels and, with a heavy load, there was a tendency for the wooden blocks to be very noisy when the brakes were applied. About 1927 Bass' Engineer tried to get rid of the noise by calling in Ferodo who recommended fitting its linings to the brake blocks. The experiment was not a success and the wooden brake blocks remained to the end.

The first two Class A locomotives had an eventful start. No.11 was involved in an accident at the end of 1902, it required extensive repairs and was out of action for 2½ years. In 1909 the boiler began to give trouble and 70 tubes had to be replaced, but it was not successful and had to be sent to the North British Locomotive Company. A year later, Bass gave the locomotive an extensive overhaul including the fitting of a new boiler and firebox. The problems were finally overcome and, apart from retubing in 1926, it did not receive its next new boiler and firebox until 1951. This boiler was steam tested at 150lbs and hydraulically at 260lbs, the pressure gauge being set at 140lbs/sq in.

In November 1908, No.10 was sent to Glasgow for a new boiler and firebox. Parts of the valve gear were also renewed. On its return, a further three months were spent in the shed being fitted with various other new parts, including a front buffer beam, so it too appears to have been damaged. The boiler and firebox were repaired in 1922 and replaced in 1936, when the smokebox was also rebuilt at the blacksmiths' shop. It was out of action for a year in 1952-53 when the boiler was reconstructed by Warrens in Bass' engine shed and a new firebox was fitted. No.10 was Joe Slater's regular locomotive. It once broke a tyre up at Dixie because of a cracked pin, but fortunately the tyre did not come off the wheel; it was due for retyring anyway.

Apart from an accident to the firebox top and the replacement of 103 tubes in 1921-22, No.1's original boiler and firebox lasted until 1948, when the replacements cost £1,640. It is noticeable that all of the locomotives received less attention during World War 2 because of the shortages of materials and the preoccupation of manufacturers with other priority work. After the War, an attempt was made to improve the condition of the locomotives.

No.2 had been fitted with a new boiler and firebox in 1938-39. This was repaired in 1947 and the steel rivets were taken out of the firebox seams and replaced by copper studs. It received a new copper firebox in 1955. Little of note happened to No.9 until 1929 when it failed a hydraulic test and Warrens rebuilt the boiler fitting 101 new micro copper tubes and a new firebox. The water tank was also scaled and cleaned out. No.9 was out of action for 1½ years at the end of World War 2 for an extensive overhaul. It had a new boiler and firebox in 1956. No.4 had some repairs after a derailment in 1929 but did not require a new boiler and firebox until 1949.

There were four principal duties for the Class A locomotives and the drivers spent a week in turn on each of these duties. They comprised the 'Old Brewery Engine' which serviced the Old Brewery and took ale up to the Dixie Ale Stores; the 'New Brewery Engine' which performed the same role for the New Brewery, but this time moved ale up to the Shobnall Ale Stores; the 'Shobnall Engine' which worked at Shobnall and delivered filled casks to the railway companies' sidings; and last but not least the 'Barley Engine'. The latter was responsible for moving barley and malt about the premises. Prompt delivery was essential and the drivers on the other locomotives often used to say "Out of the way, the Barley Engine's coming." The head shunter on the Barley Engine had a great sheet of paper with the details of the malt to be moved and the kilns to be set up. In winter, the Barley Engine's traffic was so heavy that the work was shared between two locomotives.

With one locomotive dismantled for overhaul and another having a boiler washout, there was only one spare locomotive. If traffic was heavy and a locomotive had broken down, it was necessary to get the fire out of one of the locomotives on arrival at the shed, wash the boiler out during the night, so that it could be ready for work the following day. This happened a lot in later years. The pressure on the locomotives was also evident in that the Class B locomotives saw greater use on the Class A rosters; for example, No.7 was often up at Shobnall in 1955.

William Dennis was in charge of the engine shed by the turn of the century and last signed the *Locomotive Logbook* on 2nd May 1920. He was not a fitter by trade but had previously been a driver on the MR. George Maurice Wright succeeded him and stayed until he retired on 31st March 1931, when he must have been at least 70 years old. Known as 'Gun Metal' or 'Loco' Wright to distinguish him from another George Wright, who was the Outside General Fitters foreman, he also acquired the name 'Ticker' Wright because he always used to have his watch out. He was a modest retiring man who had been born in the Whitby area and had served his apprenticeship in a Teesside shipbuilder's yard on marine steam engines. His method of testing locomotives after overhaul was to take them out through the brewery to Shobnall where they would be examined to check that all was satisfactory. If this was so, he would thrash the locomotive down the bank under the Bridge Hole on the return and reckoned that he reached a speed of 40mph on one trip!

The painting of a Bass locomotive after overhaul was a work of art. It required a total of 658 hours and cost £36 (labour) and £5 8s (£5.40) (materials) in 1916-18.

Work carried out on a Bass locomotive by the Painters' Department

	Hours
Thoroughly cleaning off oil and grease	140½
Rubbing down, stopping, filling, painting	329½
Setting out and lining	72
Flatting and varnishing	105
Writing, shading and gilding numbers	11
Total	658

Locomotives were painted in the Repair Shed after World War 1. On varnish days, nine feet long sheets were hung to separate the bay from the remainder of the shed. After varnishing, the locomotive was left completely undisturbed for 48 hours. Great was the joy when George Maurice Wright opened the sheets to reveal a resplendent locomotive, 'a Bass job.' When Wright retired, the jobs of the Locomotive Fitters' foreman and the foreman of the Middle Yard machine shop were combined. Bill Potts had come from Baguley and he was made joint foreman, to whom the senior fitter in the engine shed was responsible. The foreman spent most of his time in the main machine shop but visited the engine shed early in the day, usually combining his visit with a trip to the office to see the Engineer. Bill Potts remained in control until 1955 when Dick Stubbs took over until his retirement in 1965.

Livery of Bass' Locomotives

Black (grapholine)	Inside work before engine is put together - firebox, boiler (and underneath tank for early Thornewill & Warham locomotives).
Turkey red (light)	Boiler, tank, cab, edge plates, outside of frame and wheels
Brown	Inside cab.
Black	Top of cab (outside), smokebox, chimney, buffer stocks, steps, brake, tackle.
Vermillion or Goodlass Empire fast red	Buffer planks, inside of frame, eccentric rods, and injectors
Yellow	Number on saddletank.
Black lining picked out with a pale yellow or straw colour fine line	Boiler tank, cab, edge plates, outside of frame, wheels, buffer planks.
Bright work	Burnished copper chimney cap, burnished brass dome, burnished steel handrail running round locomotive. The steel buffers and copper sandpipes were also polished metal.

Over the years, minor improvements were made to the locomotives. At the beginning of the 1930s, they were equipped with Dunbar & Slater mechanical cylinder lubricators. Then spark arrestors made by the blacksmiths were fitted; these had a wide mesh and it is doubtful if they had much effect. Some locomotives were also given Neil's patent rocker firebars, although those on No.7

257

were replaced in 1952 by straight firebars. A wheel tyring plant was introduced into Bass' Fitting Shop and the locomotive wheels were retyred there after September 1930, No.7 being the first to receive attention. At the same time, there were frequent renewals of the crank pins on the front wheels and occasionally on the rear wheels. Retyring had previously been contracted out to Thornewill & Warham, Hunslet, Baguley Cars Ltd and Hawthorn Leslie. For example, No.9's wheels were retyred with Vicker's 'Australia' brand steel tyres by Hunslet in 1911-12.

In 1931 the well known firm of Armstrong Whitworth & Co Ltd of Scotswood on Tyne opened a diesel traction department and laid down an early stock order for six diesel electric shunting locomotives. They were built in 1933 for demonstration purposes in the hope that sales would quickly follow. One of these locomotives (D24) was lent to Bass Worthington for a month's trial. It worked around the railway system but appears to have had problems coping with the constant heavy shunting which caused the electricity supply to keep cutting out. The locomotive weighed 15 tons in working order and had a six-cylinder 85hp Armstrong Saurer diesel engine with jackshaft drive. Bass did not purchase the locomotive although the type generally enjoyed quite long careers. D24 was eventually bought by Thames Board Mills at Warrington and was not scrapped until 1957.

Bass changed to the bulk handling of barley in 1939-40 and this reduced the cost of labour considerably by the use of bulk grain vans, mechanical elevators and conveyors. On 19th May 1939 Bass ordered its first diesel shunting locomotive from E.E. Baguley Ltd at a cost of £1,941 2s 5d (£1,941 12p) and it arrived in the following December. The diesel was required to shunt the pumping machinery around the maltings because this was too heavy for the horses. It was designed jointly by Baguley and Bass; special consideration being given to the problems of exhaust fumes, the small radius curves, and the many short hauls over the working area. The locomotive had four-coupled wheels with a 4-cylinder 85hp Gardner 4L3 diesel engine and mechanical transmission. A two speed

No.5 in the Middle Yard, near High Street, on its first outing with Alan Shipley and Ralph Hoe, the shunter. December 1939.

(E.E. Baguley Ltd, Courtesy Staffordshire County Record Office)

Bass' Ruston & Hornsby diesel No.8 passes Shobnall Crossing Box on 29th March 1966.
(C. Shepherd)

gearbox was fitted and the weight of the locomotive was 17 tons. It became the responsibility of Alan Shipley, the Grain Department millwright (maintenance foreman) instead of the Chief Engineer. Alan was a clever inventive man who had served his apprenticeship with Wolseley Motors. His main responsibility was the repair and overhaul of the screening at the maltings. Both 'Grain Department' and 'Malting Department' were used as styles for the one department. Payments were made in the accounts to the 'Malting Department' but the men handed in checks in the form of 'GD211'! Grain department has been adopted here because it covers both barley and malt.

The new diesel was kept in the small shed by the side of the Middle Yard Storeroom which had originally been provided for the Directors' saloon carriage. It became No.5 and gave good service, although it was too small to do all of the jobs. Bass tried it out on a full load of ale from the New Brewery to Shobnall; that was fifteen wagons. Theoretical calculations said that it would not be powerful enough to get up the bank from the Bridge Hole. Joe Slater was driving and, making sure that the back peg was off, the train rushed down under the Bridge Hole. Joe put the locomotive out of gear and let the load push it up the bank. As soon as the train began to hang back, he turned on full power, opened the sanders, and just managed to get up to Shobnall. The theory had been disproved but the reserve was obviously too fine for No.5 to perform on the heaviest duties. It was either on this or another occasion, that a telephone message was sent to Baguley on 21st November 1940 that No.5 had climbed up the 1 in 50 from under the Moor Street bridge pulling a load of 172 tons including itself. No.5 had a complete overhaul at Baguley's works in 1957.

Although the locomotive stock of Bass and Worthington was merged in 1960, it is appropriate to consider the combined fleet from 1957. By this date, most of the steam locomotives were approaching sixty years of age and the decision was taken to replace them with new diesel locomotives. The next ten years were to be a period of quite radical change not only with the introduction of the diesels but also with the rundown of the railway as a whole and the subsequent disposal of the recently acquired diesels. A group of men had to be sent on a course at Rolls Royce's works at Derby for a fortnight to learn about the new form of motive power. They included Bernard Nisbet the chargehand, Eric Caps the fitter, and a driver Sid Smith. The mornings were taken up with a series of lectures and the afternoons were spent in the workshop. On the Thursday, they went to Rolls Royce's locomotive works at Shrewsbury, and then had examinations on the Friday to see what they had learnt. On his return, No.5 was transferred to Bernard Nisbet's care, although it was generally kept on its former duties. It was often temporarily stabled by the west side of Shobnall Maltings coupled to the pumping vans. It returned to the Guild Street Engine Sheds for servicing and refuelling, and was also kept at the sheds if it had been working at Brook Street. Bass eventually decided that it was too expensive to have No.5 standing around doing nothing for lengthy periods. No.3 was in for repairs and they were intending to replace it with a Scottish locomotive, but the suggestion was made that No.5 should be tried on the Middle Brewery job. It performed well and was subsequently used on this and other suitable duties.

Bernard Nisbet took over the responsibility for the locomotive repairs at Worthington's shed and he would go over to do the running repairs; more major items were dealt with at Bass' shed. The two locomotive liveries were retained but they were also used to distinguish between the power of the diesel locomotives. Those over 200hp were painted Turkey red with similar lining as previously, and those under 200hp were blue with red lining. The blue was a slightly lighter shade than the Worthington steam locomotives which kept their dark blue livery. A visit to Worthington's New Engine Shed on Sunday 8th March 1964 revealed Nos.11, 21, and 22 present, with No.5 in the process of being repainted blue to accord with the scheme.

At the end of 1957, a new diesel locomotive was obtained from Ruston & Hornsby Ltd of Lincoln at a cost of £5,835. It was obviously part of a lot built for stock because delivery took place less than two weeks after the order. No.8 (maker's number 416566) was an 88DS locomotive, a type which proved to be very popular throughout the country. Ruston & Hornsby produced 254 of them and they replaced many four-coupled steam shunters. No.8 was fitted with a Ruston & Hornsby four-cylinder 4VPH 88hp diesel engine and the drive was transmitted from the engine to the two axles by roller chains. The locomotive weighed 17 tons and was painted blue. It and later acquisitions were no longer fitted with brass owner's plates, 'No.8' being painted on each side of the cab with the 'RH' monogram plates underneath. Couchman would have turned in his grave! Joe Slater was on the footplate of No.8 for the first few weeks and he took it over to Worthington to try it on their workings for a fortnight. It caused much consternation because of its ready availability. There was no need to stop for coal and water and so the men on the ale banks and shunters were given no opportunity for a rest. Joe Slater's grandfather was reputed to have been the first shunter killed at Burton. He died at the station in the same week that the *Burton Chronicle* (first published 18th October 1860) came out.

There was evidently a need for a more powerful diesel shunter to take over the main steam jobs and so Bass placed an order with Baguley on 30th May 1957. No.6 (maker's number 3509) was a 0-4-0 diesel weighing 31 tons and was delivered in September 1958 at a cost of £13,176. Although Baguley's output of locomotives was small, the new machine was based on the popular well tried combination of the Gardner diesel engine and mechanical transmission used by several manufacturers, the 8-cylinder 8L3 engine producing 204hp. Another similar locomotive, No.1 (maker's number 3568), was ordered from Baguley in May 1960 and arrived a year later, having cost £13,530. The wheelbase was 3in shorter at 6ft 0in and it subsequently had its sand boxes modified to allow it to operate in two feet of floodwater under the Burton Bridge.

Bass tested a more powerful Ruston & Hornsby locomotive when the 200DE Class demonstration diesel number 412716 arrived for trials in April 1959 but no sale resulted. Earlier that year, Rolls Royce had produced its first Sentinel diesel hydraulic locomotive which was to have a major impact on the market. This was powered by a Rolls Royce supercharged diesel engine, with a Rolls Royce CF 11,500 torque converter. From this, a short drive shaft transmitted the power to a centrally mounted forward–reverse gearbox. A change of direction could be pre-selected while the locomotive was moving and the two axles were driven by duplex roller chains from each end of the gearbox. The chassis was very similar to the 200hp Sentinel steam locomotives but slightly longer at 24ft 4¾in with a 6ft 6in wheelbase. This range of diesels included 4-wheel, 0-4-0 and 0-6-0 types with a range of engine horsepowers and locomotive weights. The third locomotive to be built by

Bass' Baguley diesel No.6 and a solitary grain van travel along the Guild Street Branch on 6th November 1965. Allsopp's former railway once curved round from here behind the grain van to the Holy Trinity level crossing. (C. Shepherd)

Sentinel was 10003 in 1959 and it was initially used by the manufacturer for demonstration purposes. In 1960 Bass purchased this locomotive from Thomas Hill (Rotherham) Ltd, the marketing company for Sentinel locomotives, at a cost of £12,000 and made it No.12. A similar locomotive (maker's number 10085) was also acquired from Thomas Hill, was allocated No.7, and arrived by rail under its own power from Shrewsbury on 28th September 1961. Both locomotives were fitted with a Rolls Royce 6-cylinder 207hp C6SFL diesel engine and S.C.G. Type RF11 gear box. They were 4-wheel machines and weighed 34 tons. The order for 10085 had been placed by Bass on 29th August 1961 and it was built to a standard specification but with the customer's painting requirements – 'Cab,

Bass' No.12 drifts down towards the Bridge Hole and Shobnall on a snowy 10th March 1964. (C. Shepherd)

Sentinel diesels, Bass Nos.12 (left) and 7 (right) shunting Shobnall cask washing plant on 29th March 1966. *(C. Shepherd)*

Casings and Skirts to be painted Turkey Red, lined Black (7/8" wide) and Pale Cream (1/8" wide). Buffer beams to be painted Signal Red, outlined with a 7/8" Black and a 1/8" Pale Cream line. Frame and Running Gear to be painted Black as standard and standard painting for Cab and Casings interior.' Mr G.H. Ridsdill from Thomas Hill accompanied the locomotive and give it a final examination at Bass. One of the Sentinel diesels was soon in trouble when it fractured an axle at Shobnall in February 1963. The axle and wheels were sent to Sentinel's works at Shrewsbury and a new axle was subsequently fitted at Bass' Engine Shed.

The Rolls Royce engines were considered to be not quite as powerful in practice as the Gardner engines of Nos.1 and 6. On one occasion, a Baguley diesel was pushing a fairly long train into Dixie No.8 Road. It was necessary to clear the points, and so it continued pushing, until the shunter gave a shout that it was propelling the wagons out of the Wetmore end of the siding and was fouling those points. They counted 68 wagons which the Baguley had moved. Bass' Rule Book advised care in pushing wagons into the No.8 Road because there might be shunting operations taking place on the BR Nos.8 and 9 Roads at the Old Dixie end. Rolls Royce was always sending letters about updating details on its locomotives in contrast to Baguley, the products of which were nevertheless considered very reliable and powerful.

The arrival of the new diesels meant that three of Worthington's Hudswell Clarke steam locomotives could be scrapped; also Nos.1, 7 and 15 were stored in Worthington's Old Engine Shed. No.15 had a new boiler and firebox in 1952 and was still in reasonable condition so it was taken to the Old Shed in October 1961 where it was cleaned and stored ready for service if required, although this did not materialise. It is reputed to have sunk into the floor after standing in store for some time. There was an intention to preserve No.1 for display alongside the new 'Locomotive' public house which was then under construction in Station Street near Worthington's former level crossing. This proposal did not come to anything and a wall sign showing Bass' first steam locomotive was used instead. On 28th February 1963 the three locomotives were removed from the Old Shed and taken to the Hay Sidings. Next day they were pulled away by one of the Baguley diesels to be later placed in a goods train bound for Sheffield and scrapping. As they rolled slowly by the Old Brewery ale bank, the men there gave the solemn notes of the funeral march.

The final two diesel locomotives came from Baguley at the end of 1962 following an order placed on 23rd August 1961. No.4 (maker's number 3589) and No.11 (maker's number 3590) had

Nos.15, 7 and 1 wait in the Hay Sidings on 28th February 1963 to be taken away for scrap. *(C. Shepherd)*

a 0-4-0 wheel arrangement and were fitted with a Gardner 4L3 107hp diesel engine. Baguley's records incorrectly state that they had 6LW 112hp engines. The new locomotives weighed 20 tons and cost £8,939 each. All Baguley locomotives with the Gardner 4L3, 6LW, 8LW and 8L3 engines were fitted with Vulcan Sinclair hydraulic couplings and four speed Wilson Drewry epicycle gearboxes made by Self Changing Gears of Coventry. Final drive was by a Wiseman reverse/reduction bevel drive mounted on the jackshaft. The combination of the Gardner engine and Wilson epicycle gearbox was arguably the best of all the diesel mechanical power plants and remained a standard Drewry specification from 1934 until 1969, with Baguley building a number of these locomotives from 1949 onwards. No.11 was officially handed over on the 11th December 1962 at a reception at Shobnall. The heavy rain was defied by those present and Mr W.E.C. Souster, managing director of Baguley, remarked on the good relations which had existed for a long time between the two companies. He recalled the several occasions when Bass had placed its sidings at his company's disposal for testing new locomotives. Nos.5 and 6 of Baguley manufacture were also made available for inspection.

The new diesels took the numbers of the steam locomotives they replaced, so No.4 was stored in Worthington's Old Engine Shed where it was later joined by No.11, which had previously been dumped by the side of Bass' Running Shed. When No.11 was moved into Worthington's shed, it caught its chimney on the smoke vent and knocked a hole in the roof which had to be patched up. Both locomotives were removed in July 1964 and sent to Thos W. Ward's yard at Derby for scrap. Ward had established a temporary yard next to Baker's premises at Derby Friargate mainly to deal with railway scrap.

The efficiency of operating the railway locomotives was kept under review, particularly as the level of traffic was declining. Locomotive drivers were given books in which to record every movement and their times, and these were scrutinised each morning to see whether it was possible to reduce the number of locomotives in commission. This proved difficult although a locomotive was occasionally taken off when amounts of traffic were low. With the reduced production at Worthington's Brewery from February 1963, it was possible to replace the Baguley working there with a small Planet, and this in turn enabled Bass to take another steam locomotive out of regular service. In addition the night shift was reduced from two men to one man. The latter could not be dispensed with because he was needed for steam raising. Bass tried out a German Mercedes Benz 'Unimog' road/rail shunter as another possible option. It is reputed to have dealt competently with a long line of wagons totalling more than 160 tons but no order resulted from the trial.

In April 1963, all of the diesels and five of the Planets were generally in use apart from when servicing or repairs were required. Two steam locomotives were also regularly operated. The other four steam and remaining Planet were spare, although an attempt was made to rotate the steam locomotives. In that month, Nos.3, 9, 10 and 16 had all been working, No.9 having just passed a boiler inspection. There had been thoughts of withdrawing No.2 earlier in the year but it was eventually overhauled using the wheels and parts of the motion from the condemned No.1. No.13 was dumped by the side of the Running Shed with one of its cylinder heads requiring attention. At the end of the month, terms were agreed with Thos W. Ward Ltd for the sale of Nos.3, 10 and 13 and they were withdrawn on 6th May 1963 and sent to Bolton on Dearne for scrap two weeks later. They stood in Wetmore Yard and were picked up by a passing goods train.

Bass' locomotive workings mid 1963

Type	Number	Builder	Power	Duty
Steam	No.2	Neilson Reid		Barley
	No.9	Neilson Reid		Spare
	No.16	Bagnall		Boiler washout
Diesel	No.1	Baguley	204hp	Old Brewery
	No.4	Baguley	107hp	Extra spare
	No.5	Baguley	85hp	Shobnall Maltings
	No.6	Baguley	204hp	New Brewery
	No.7	Sentinel	207hp	Shobnall
	No.8	Ruston & Hornsby	88hp	'Middle Brewery'
	No.11	Baguley	107hp	Worthington 'Outside Engine'
	No.12	Sentinel	207hp	Maintenance
Planet	No.17	Kent Construction	40hp	Worthington 'Inside Engine'
	No.18	Kent Construction	40hp	Dixie Ale Stores
	No.19	Kent Construction	40hp	Middle Yard
	No.20	Kent Construction	40hp	No.2 Ale Stores
	No.21	Hibberd	40hp	Crown Maltings
	No.22	Hibberd	40hp	Spare

Locomotives continued to work from Worthington's New Engine Shed, particularly on longstanding Worthington rosters, but there was a greater sharing of locomotives between it and the Bass sheds. The remaining steam shunters operated for another year until 6th August 1964 when they were withdrawn from service. Although still in reasonable condition, rail traffic had declined rapidly. No.16's last recorded repair was the fitting of five new copper stays in the firebox and replacement of the brake blocks in May 1964. Nos.2 and 16 stood in the Midland Goods yard before being picked up and transported to Ward's yard at Derby in August 1964.

No.9 had been earmarked for preservation in 1961. It was being overhauled when withdrawal came and the repairs were stopped. It was reassembled, including some parts from No.2 which were in better condition, had its tyres turned, and a new chimney fitted. According to Bass' records, it was repainted in Worthington's shed but John Giles, foreman painter at Bass, worked on the locomotive himself in the Bass shed and confirmed that it was repainted before moving to Worthington's shed. Ernest Chapman spent a whole week cleaning the brass work. In February 1967, it was sent to the Staffordshire County Museum at Shugborough for preservation and subsequently returned to Burton on 4th April 1977 for display at the newly opened Bass Museum.

Bernard Nisbet was in final control of the locomotives until the railway system closed, having been the chargeman at the shed for many years. He had served his apprenticeship in No.8 Shop at the MR's Derby Works starting at the age of fourteen. He was out of work after completing his

Baguley diesel No.4 at Guild Street with (top row) Moor, S. Smith, L. Hawksworth, B. Brunt and (bottom row) ? , Castledine, J. Slater, F. Shilton, S. House, L. Haywood, D. Bacon, S. Riley, ? , ? . (Bass Museum)

Nos.10, 13 and 3 make their final journey to Ward's scrap yard in a goods train heading towards Derby on 22nd May 1963. (P. Waterfield)

apprenticeship until he met the Honourable Evan Baillie, grandson of Lord Burton, who arranged for him to join the Engineers' department at Bass' shed in 1920.

Work began on pulling down some of the buildings at Guild Street in early 1966 and the Repair Shed was the last to go, demolished in November of that year. Locomotives were then stabled in the open on the opposite side of the Guild Street Branch near to the former Wagon Repair Shop. Any final repairs were carried out on a spare line in Worthington's New Engine Shed with some working over the High Street level crossing as a result.

The Planet locomotives had been withdrawn in 1965 and Nos.17, 20, 21 and 22 were stored in Worthington's Old Shed, whilst Nos.18 and 19 remained on a siding at Guild Street. On 30th March 1967, the Worthington site was cleared of locomotives because demolition of the brewery was fast advancing. No.6 hauled the four Planet locomotives, with their driving chains removed, from the Old Shed to Guild Street. They were followed by No.7 which had just been repaired and was the last locomotive to pass over Worthington's High Street crossing. Nos.17, 18, 19 and 22 went to Alfred Loom's scrapyard at Spondon near Derby in August 1967, although No.22 survived a little longer to shunt around the yard. Nos.20 and 21 were saved by the Railway Preservation Society at Chasewater and No.20 returned to the Bass Museum about June 1980 on loan from the Society.

With the closure of Bass' railway department on 31st March 1967, the locomotives were stored awaiting disposal. There was still the stock to be collected together and there were occasional journeys after this date. Indeed on 17th April, three locomotives were busy moving wagons out to Dixie. In September, No.4 went to work at George Cohen's scrapyard in Canning Town; No.11 moved to Wagon Repairs Ltd, Port Tennant, West Glamorgan in March 1968 and No.5 was sold to the Honourable John Gretton for preservation in July 1967 going to the Great Western Society depot at Didcot at the end of August 1968. The dealers L. Sanderson of Birtley, County Durham obtained No.8 in March 1968. The four largest diesels were amongst the last to go. No.1 had some alterations made to its cab reducing the profile before it was sold to P.D. Fuels Limited at Dibles Wharf, Northam in Hampshire where it replaced an ex London & South Western Railway locomotive. Thomas Hill bought Nos.6, 7 and 12 in November 1968, No.12 moving by road to Kilnhurst on the 20th of that month and No.7 following on the next day, thus ending approximately 105 years of Bass locomotives.

CHAPTER TWELVE

OPERATION OF THE BASS RAILWAY

Management of the Railway

The range of Bass' railway operations was pre-eminent amongst the brewery companies in the town and it became even more extensive after the merger with Worthington. Allsopp's was the only other railway to approach it in size but much of its track was concentrated at its New Brewery, particularly after the closure of its premises in High Street. As late as the 1960s, Bass-Worthington locomotives could be seen working between the company's breweries and Middle Yard in the centre of the town, over the Bond End Branch to Shobnall and the Wood Street Maltings, to the ale stores and exchange sidings at Dixie via the Guild Street Branch, and also over the Hay Branch to Anderstaff Lane, Walsitch Maltings and Dixie. On an average day in 1925, Bass' locomotives handled some 1,000 wagons, of which 350 to 400 were empties received directly from the LMS and LNER or wagons liberated from other traffic. A similar number of loaded wagons were sent out each day and about 300 to 350 of these contained casks of ale equivalent to approximately 6,000 barrels. The balance of wagons was involved in internal traffic between the various premises. With exchange sidings at each end of the railway system and cask washing plants and ale stores located at widely dispersed points, there was no simple flow of inward traffic and the amount of internal working merely added to the complication. In addition, there were a number of single line sections and some form of efficient train control was essential.

While there was a centralised Railway Department after the 1926 merger manned by the Traffic Manager and his staff, and both this and the Forwarding Office staff were located in Bass' General Office in High Street, the workings of Bass and Worthington's railway systems continued to operate separately. The cessation of cut throat competition in the market place had obvious advantages but the two companies' outside Railway and Forwarding Departments were retained until after the merger with Mitchells & Butlers in 1961.

Some of the Traffic Managers were autocratic figures who were not averse to giving orders (in both senses) to the railway companies' goods agents in Burton who were anxious to secure their share of the brewery traffic. John Cosgrove was Bass' traffic manager from at least 1865. He was evidently well thought of because £500 was paid to him in 1880 for savings which he had made in the Railway Department. Unfortunately, he was not a fit man, and on 21st March 1881, the Board voted to give him £100 to enable him to seek a warmer climate in the hope of restoring his health. He died two years later and the Board gave £800 to provide investment income for his son. The money was to revert to the company if the son died before reaching the age of 21. William Walters and John Lambrick were the trustees.

William Walters became the next Traffic Manager and held this position until his retirement on 31st December 1915. He had been born at Worcester in 1842. When he was about 20, he went to Derby Trinity School as a teacher but almost immediately moved to the MR at Derby. After about a year, he transferred to the LNWR at Euston under Mr Turnbull. About 1867 Michael Thomas Bass enquired about the availability of a bright young man to join the company and, on the recommendation of Mr Turnbull, William Walters was appointed deputy to the Traffic Manager at the age of 25. An insight into the character of William Walters has already been gained through his organisation of the Bass trips. He died on the 23rd March 1923 at the age of 80.

Frank Haynes took over on the first day of 1916 having moved to Bass in the previous April from his position as the MR's resident Assistant District Goods Manager at Liverpool. He was known as 'Puffer' Haynes, to distinguish him from W.A. Haynes who was head of the Grain Office, or less kindly as 'Itchycoo' from a mannerism of twitching. It is thought that latterly he was away ill and he died on 23rd March 1943. His successor, Cecil or Captain Welch, had previously come from J.S. Fry

Bass' No.5 on grain vans at the Middle Yard Grain Store.

(Bass Museum Collection)

Engine often worked until late at night. If there was a steady input of barley, it was possible to screen it before storage; a rush of incoming barley and some would have to go into temporary storage until it could be dealt with. A wet season meant that much of the barley would have to go on the kiln floors to reduce the moisture to 4%. When barley arrived before floor malting commenced, the malt kilns could also be used for drying. Otherwise the barley had to go into store until the drying kilns could deal with it. Even after the concentration of screening at Brook Street it was still necessary for the barley to go to Klondyke initially for sampling.

Most of the malt came from the garners on the premises and was taken to the breweries in ½ quarter (168lbs) sacks. Consistent punctuality was maintained by means of trip trains which had a scheduled timetable and only stopped to set down wagons at the three breweries.

		am	am	pm	pm
Shobnall Maltings or Exchange Sidings	depart	9.00	11.00	12.45	2.00
New Brewery	arrive	9.10	11.10	12.55	2.10
Middle Brewery	depart	9.25	11.25	1.10	2.25
Old Brewery	arrive	9.35	11.35	1.20	2.35

The trains carrying casks from the washing plants to the breweries for refilling ran three or more times daily. Some examples of regular trips are shown below:-

Middle Yard to Middle Brewery	*Shobnall Cooperage to Middle Brewery*	*Shobnall Cooperage to New Brewery*
8am	7.40am	7.40am
10am	9.30am	8.15am
12pm	11.15am	10.15am
	2.15pm	11.30am
		12.30pm
		2.45pm

The Old and New Breweries lacked adequate stores of their own and the filled casks had to be worked to the ale stores.

270

Old Brewery to Dixie Ale Stores	New Brewery to Shobnall Ale Stores
7.30am	8.40am
10.30am	10.40am
1.00pm	11.50am
2.30pm	1.10pm
5.00pm	3.05pm

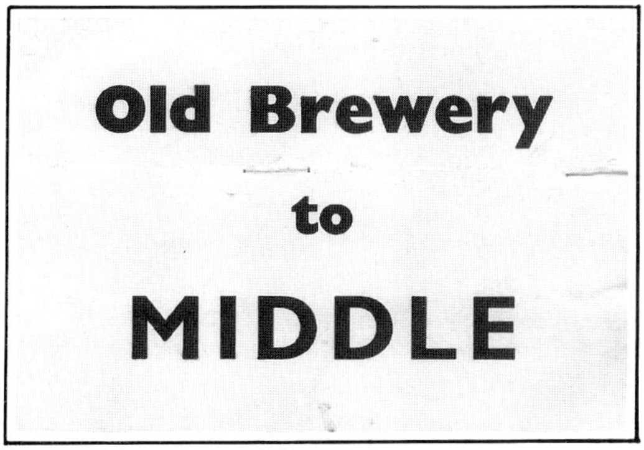

Old Brewery

to

MIDDLE

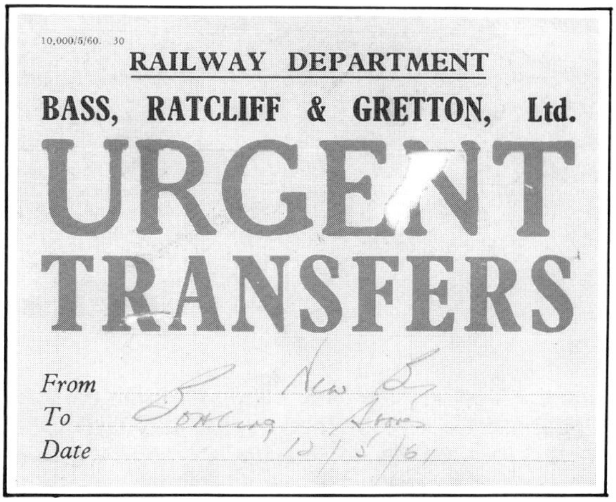

10,000/5/60. 30

RAILWAY DEPARTMENT

BASS, RATCLIFF & GRETTON, Ltd.

URGENT

TRANSFERS

From

To

Date

DEPARTURE TRAFFIC

Trains were despatched at specified times each day from the ale stores to the railway companies' exchange sidings. The arrival of empty wagons at the five loading stations was timed to permit the departure of outgoing trains because the wagons of beer had to connect with the specified service, otherwise they would not go out that night. Wagons were marshalled in junction order according to the information on the ale loaders' slips to encourage the prompt departure of the railway companies booked outward services. Once the loaded wagons taken by the Bass locomotive were sometimes identified by their ultimate destination and the accompanying photograph shows the 'Scotch Special' about to be propelled round to Dixie Sidings. Later, no external identification was used on the trains for many years, although at least one board seems to have been discovered at the very end of the railway's operations.

Train loads of spent grains and hops despatched to the manufacturers of cattle and pig foods required immediate handling. Other wagons sent out contained ash for tipping on colliery spoil heaps by special arrangement, and there were also a few empty wagons.

In 1925 three complete trains were sent by Bass to London every weekday except Fridays when it was only two. The wagons for the London beer trains were loaded at the Middle Brewery ale stores and a Bass locomotive pushed them down to Dixie No.8 Road, where the guards van and LMS locomotive were coupled on, and the train was away to London. These trains left at 5pm, 7.30pm, and 11pm.

Rules and Regulations

A return was completed each morning giving particulars of every wagon standing on the brewery premises or exchange sidings and this control resulted in the practical elimination of demurrage charges. There was also another return covering wagons standing under load, including a specification of the amounts of coke, coal and dust. An empty wagon requisition form was used to advise the railway companies as to the number of wagons which should be made available. These

271

No.11 displays an old 'Newcastle Special 12.30pm' board as it slowly makes its way past the works associated with the construction of Bass' new No.1 Brewery on 21st March 1967. Such boards had not been used for many years.
(C. Shepherd)

and the loading slips used by the foremen ale loaders were prepared in advance by the Forwarding Department and distributed by the Railway Department. Bass had a set of labels for placing on each wagon to show its destination. Wagon labels with blue or black lettering covered transfers and emergency labels were red. The latter included urgent traffic and those wagons which required repairs.

The brewery companies' employees were expected to be familiar with and comply with the railway companies' rule books. The MR, LNWR, and NSR also jointly produced a smaller booklet which comprised 'Extracts from the Rules and Regulations for the guidance of Engine-drivers and others in charge of Brewery Companies' engines when working on the MR, LNWR, and NSR at Burton on Trent.' British Railways issued a subsequent edition of the publication. As if these instructions were not enough, both Bass and Worthington's Railway Departments had their own Rule Books. Information on signals was based on the railway companies' practice so that there was constant observation of the rules on the jointly worked lines. The Bass version had to allow for the existence of the crossbar signals and drivers were informed that when the bar was in a position across the line, it denoted 'Danger–Stop'. The introduction to the text was quite specific:-

BASS - WORTHINGTON

NOT to be **LOADED**

FOR REPAIRS

DESTINATION ....

WAGON No. ....

DATE ....

REPAIRS ....

INSPECTED ....

> 'All servants employed by Bass, Ratcliff, and Gretton Ltd, on their
> Railways, must strictly observe all signals used by British Railways, and
> be guided entirely by their officials when working on and in connection
> with their Branch Railways.'

Bass' General Regulations made it abundantly clear that obedience and careful attention to the employees' duties were very much the order of the day.

> 'Every servant of Bass & Company will be liable to immediate dismissal
> for disobedience of orders, negligence, misconduct, or incompetency.
> Any instance of intoxication whilst on duty will be punished by instant
> dismissal.
> Smoking on duty is strictly prohibited.'

This continued until after 1948 although Worthington omitted the warning about smoking.

Trains on Bass and Worthington's railways were subject to signals controlled by the private boxes in a similar manner to the MR's branches. Attempts were made to minimise delay to the public caused by trains crossing the streets. The signalman or gateman had to satisfy himself that no road vehicle was so near the gates that it would be delayed by the gates opening and he had to give the public preference as far as possible. (The rules did not recognise that there might be signalwomen although, of course, there were!). In working wagons over the crossings, 'the person in charge of the horses, tractor, or engine' had to approach the gates cautiously, because it was not always possible to open the gates immediately. A book was kept by each signalman in charge of the gates and the movement of trains over the public thoroughfare was recorded. The time allowed was one minute but if the delay exceeded two minutes, the causes were investigated by the Railway Office. In the few cases where this was found to be necessary, the delay was due to the locomotive slipping in frosty weather or the presence of fog. Bass would not allow more than fifteen wagons to be taken across the streets in one journey unless special authority had been given. A driver often indicated to a signalman by a whistle code which track he wished to take or that he was going over the crossing in order to shunt back over another line. The head shunter with the train had to inform the railway companies' signalmen when Bass had finished work so that they could then close the box and leave.

Although perhaps seen as a rather menial job, the shunters' duties required a good deal of care and several of Bass' railway regulations dealt with their activities. Indeed it was the Head Shunter who was responsible for the train; the driver only looked after the locomotive. The shunter had to make sure that the wagons were secured and properly coupled, and that any stabled were in a safe position which did not conflict with other movements. When wagons were propelled, the shunter had to stand in the first wagon or walk alongside it to see that there were no obstructions. The shunter also had to look after his own welfare, only coupling poles could be used to join wagons. A 'prop or pole' was not to be generally employed as a lever to move wagons, but if one was, it had to be 'supplied by Bass & Company'!

Bass relied on horses for localised shunting for a long time. The Shires with the largest muscles were preferred for moving railway wagons but even they sometimes slipped as they strained to start the wagons, despite the ridges cut in the Mountsorrel granite setts. Later eight electric capstans were introduced at the busiest points where there was a continuous need for shunting. Whilst the horses were limited to pulling one loaded or two empty wagons, the capstans were capable of moving eight loaded or twelve empty wagons.

Employees in the Railway Department included sidings foremen, locomotive drivers and firemen-cleaners, head and undershunters, number takers, signalmen, capstanmen, pointsmen, and crossing men, together with clerical and other staff. The operating employees worked on a double shift system.

273

Agreement between the Burton Brewers and the Workers' Union made on 14th June 1915

Concerning the standard rate of wages, working hours, payment for overtime and other conditions of the work of brewery workmen.

Locomotive drivers

Rate of wages	37 shillings (£1.35) per week
Hours	54 per week excluding meal times
Overtime	To be paid at the same rate as brewery labourers
Firemen	It is agreed that this is a matter for the employer to decide whether firemen are employed or not
Holidays	Christmas Day, Good Friday, and Trip day, and three additional days; or where no Trip day, four additional days not necessarily consecutive - six days in all

Firemen, including cleaners

Rate of wages	Firemen 26 shillings (£1.30) per week of 54 hours excluding meal times Cleaners 25 shillings (£1.25) Youths age 13 - 7 shillings (35p), age 14 - 8 shillings (40p), age 15 - 10 shillings (50p), age 16 - 12 shillings (60p), age 17 - 15 shillings (75p), age 18 - 17 shillings (85p), age 19 - 19 shillings (95p), age 20 - 21 shillings (£1.05)
Overtime	To be paid at the same rate as brewery labourers
Holidays	Same as drivers
Youths over 18	As agreed above

Spare drivers called upon to take charge of locomotives

Rate of wages	When driving – 1st year 33 shillings (£1.65) 2nd year 34 shillings (£1.70) 3rd year 35 shillings (£1.75) and then 36 shillings (£1.80) and 27 shillings (£1.35) when in shed

Youths as cleaners. When youths are doing this work, to receive youths' rates.

Head shunters

Rate of wages	34 shillings (£1.70) per week. No overtime to be paid
Holidays	One week clear in addition to Christmas Day and Good Friday

Under shunters

Rate of wages	26 shillings (£1.30) per week
Hours	54 per week, exclusive of meal times
Overtime	Same as brewery labourers

General hand in engine shed

Rate of wages	To be paid at the rate for the work he does

The new rates to be calculated so that the men will receive a full week's wage at such new rates on the first pay day after the 1st May 1915. This agreement shall remain in force for a period of at least two years from the 1st August 1915 and six months prior notice shall be given by either party, if they should desire to amend or terminate the agreement.

Burton brewers who are parties to this agreement

Samuel Allsopp & Sons Ltd	Marston, Thompson & Evershed Ltd
Bass, Ratcliff & Gretton Ltd	Peter Walker & Co Ltd
The Burton Brewery Co Ltd	Peter Walker & Son, Warrington & Burton Ltd
T. Cooper & Co	Robinson's Brewery Ltd
W. Everard & Co	Thomas Salt & Co Ltd
Ind Coope & Co (1912) Ltd	Yeomans, Cherry & Curtis Ltd
James Eadie Ltd	

Bass & Worthington's Railway Department in 1960-61

Moving forward to 1960-61, there had obviously been many changes including the recent amalgamation of Bass' and Worthington's Railway and Engineers' departments. Malting and brewing still retained their separate identities. Annual sales of beer were equivalent to 1,473,168 barrels. Not only was most of this delivered in casks (79%) but more went by rail than road (61.5% of all casks, 57% of all casked barrelage by rail). At that time, the Railway department employed 71 people, together with 21 locomotives to help move this output.

Occupation	Number
Drivers and Shedmen	26
Shunting Foremen	3
Head Shunters	11
Under Shunters	14
Relief Shunters	9
Signalmen, Gatemen	7
Cabin man	1
Total	71

This figure excludes the ale loaders. Ninety two of the Bass ale loaders were controlled by the Traffic department and shown on the Railway department's wages list. In 1961 Worthington's beers were sent from High Street to the ale stores at Dixie and No.2 (Newton) Stores; Old Brewery beers were taken to Shobnall Ale Stores, and the Middle Ale Stores received New Brewery beers. The stores at No.3 (Wetmore Road) were used only for beer which had been returned. The ale loaders were scattered around the company's premises at strategic locations.

Cask handling personnel

Racking room or ale store	Labour engaged solely on cask handling		Labour engaged mainly on cask handling	
Old Brewery	Brewery	6		
	Traffic dept.	16	-	
New Brewery	Brewery	16		
	Traffic dept.	18	-	
Worthington Brewery	Brewery	16	Forwarding dept.	19
Middle Brewery	Brewery	6		
	Traffic dept.	34	-	
Shobnall	Brewery	4		
	Traffic dept.	24	-	
Dixie	-		Forwarding dept.	49
No.2 (Newton)	-		Forwarding dept.	21
Nos.5 and 10	-		Included under Worthington Brewery	
Totals		140		89

The number of wagons involved in the brewery trade was still substantial particularly around Bass-Worthington's system. In fact, internal movements exceeded the combined incoming and outgoing traffic. In an average week, at least 2,220 wagons were moved between the premises. About 900 wagons containing empty casks arrived in Burton for Bass-Worthington each week. Other incoming traffic was more variable depending on the season. It might only be 50 wagons or could be as many as 220 wagons. Apart from the despatch of full casks, there was not much other traffic to send out. The 25 wagons each week probably contained spent grains.

Internal movement of railway wagons

Movement		Wagons per week
Tunhouse (cleaned) casks		
Shobnall Yard to New, Old, and Worthington Breweries		360 - 510
Middle Yard to Old and Worthington Breweries		200 - 250
	Total	560 - 760
Other empty casks		
Shobnall Yard to Middle Yard and Cooperage		150
Middle Yard to all Cooperages and branding shed		100
Brought in by road and loaded into wagons for		
cask siding (as temporary storage)		65
	Total	315
Full casks		
Old Brewery to Dixie, Middle, Shobnall and No.2		
Ale Stores (plus ex racking to agency stores)		500 - 600
New Brewery to Middle, Shobnall, Dixie, No.2 Ale Stores		
and bottling stores (plus ex racking to agency stores)		400 - 500
	Total	900 - 1100*
Less 10% (to exclude ex-racking ale)		90 - 110
	Revised total	810 - 990
Grain		
Barley from Dixie Sidings to drying kilns at Middle Yard,		
Shobnall, Anderstaff Lane, New Brewery, and Station		
Street. All Bass barley is transferred to Brook Street for		
screening and then moved to the maltings for stowing or		
malting		145
Malt from maltings to breweries		30
Haulage from Crown Maltings for Worthington		35
	Total	210
Coal		
Coal for maltings		15
Shobnall to New Brewery		50
Coal to Engine Shed		3
	Total	68
Miscellaneous		
Ashes from maltings to Shobnall ash screen		8
Hops from Dixie to stores (during season)		24
Spent hops		3
Wet grain		17
Bottled beer from bottling stores at Shobnall to		
Middle Ale Store		15
Other		1
	Total	68
	Overall total	2220*

* Unfortunately the surviving records appear to omit the traffic in full casks from Worthington's Brewery.

Platelayers

There were originally about two dozen platelayers in the Engineers' department at Bass. Their messroom was located at the engine shed next to Scutari Maltings with some of their materials kept on the Half Moon and Allen's bank. The main store was near the blacksmiths' shop and there was some stock at Klondyke. After the merger, Bass' platelayers looked after Worthington's railway as well and the latter just had one man who walked around their track knocking in keys. Charles Solloway was Bass' foreman platelayer in 1927. There were eventually fourteen men in the gang because it took this number to lift a rail with two on each hook. At weekends when they were relaying, the gang was strengthened to twenty two men by using some of the ale loaders. Rails were 85 to 95lbs of the bullhead type. Tight curves round some of the banks often meant that there was limited space to carry out renewals. A 'Jim Crow' was used for bending rails; this was hand operated and had a heavy buttress screw thread. All derailments were dealt with by the platelayers and they were once up to 2am trying to free seven bulk grain vans which had all locked their buffers on the curve round to Anderstaff Lane Maltings. Injuries sometimes occurred. About 1930, a platelayer was knocked down and killed by a wagon near Worthington's High Street Signal Box whilst oiling and cleaning the points. Other less serious incidents could happen, such as that in November 1928 to Frederick Alesbrook who lived in Canal Street. This man with the appropriate name received a cut over his eye when a spike flew out during setting keys in rail chairs. Fortunately, it was not too bad and he continued at work. Percy Ford was a foreman in charge of the platelayers and he had come from one of the railway companies. The story was often recounted about the day when Percy Ford was supervising a job. He told Wilf Birkin, who later went into Station Street Box, to "hit the bugger here" indicating the place with his foot whereupon Wilf promptly did just that, unfortunately for Percy who broke a toe as the hammer hit his foot. Tommy Haynes was his deputy and he was followed by George Ashmole. George had worked at Fauld between 1946 and 1957. He stayed at Bass until 1965 when he left to go to the Branston Depot. Rail traffic was decreasing rapidly and the platelayers were disbanded, contractors being used for the last couple of years.

Bass Private Wagons

It is perhaps surprising that Bass did not own a large fleet of railway wagons in view of the enormous volume of traffic which it sent out. Instead, it preferred to rely on the railway companies for a regular supply of wagons, an arrangement which was certainly very much cheaper as careful control meant that there were few demurrage payments. Examination of the *Assets Register* suggests that this dependence on the railway companies was a longstanding feature. No large scale sales of wagons took place to the MR in the 1882-95 period when that company was trying to reduce by acquisition the number of poorly maintained private owner wagons running along its tracks. It

Tank wagon B38. (Bass Museum Collection)

Wagon Works at Derby and Eveson's at Birmingham were often visited. The Wheelwrights repaired the railway wagons with English timber obtained from Mason's and Kind's yards. It was bought in the round and then cut up according to requirements. Replacement of the wagon floor planks was frequently required. The Wheelwrights only had two men responsible for wagon repairs and there was a limit to how much work they could handle, so any excess was contracted out to Wagon Repairs Limited at Branston.

Twenty three replacement internal wagons were purchased on the 3rd December 1945 at a total cost of £898 18s 3d (£898.91), although they were hardly more modern, having been constructed in 1898. They were numbered in a separate series known as the 'A' type and were not disposed of until the 1960s. Additional lots of wagons were added to the A series as the older wagons disappeared. The A47-56 lot was for fuel only but A47, A48, A52, A53, A55 and A56 were converted to medium sided wagons in February 1964.

Bass A Series open wagons purchased for internal use 1945-1954

Numbers	Description	Load carried	Built	Acquired	Cost each	Disposal
A1-23	Low & medium sides	8 tons	1898	1945	£39	1959-66
A24-29	Low sides	8 tons	1907-08	1948	£45.47	1964-66
A30-34	Low sides	8 tons	1907-08	1949	£51.54	1962-67
A35, 36	Medium sides	10 tons	1906, 1901	1949	£58	1965, 1966
A37-42	Medium sides	10 tons	1907	1953	£91	1962-66
A43-46	Medium sides	10 tons	1907	1953	£89	1962-64
A47-56	High sides	12 tons	1910	1954	£101	1966-67

In 1949, Bass also purchased nine open low sided wagons for £21 each, which could carry 10 tons but were not included in the A series, presumably because they had a lower life expectancy. Originally built in 1901, they were allocated numbers in the old series (112, 113, 116-121, 124) and

Number 119, a Bass low sided internal wagon with rounded ends, at Shobnall No.8 Malting on 21st August 1964. The wagon still has grease axle boxes.
(C. Shepherd)

were disposed of between 1957 and 1966. Many of the three plank low sided wagons had been modified with slightly higher rounded ends supported by vertical outside stanchions to carry ash. Some still had grease axleboxes. The only other open wagon purchased in this period was number 148 which was also not included in the A series. It was a high sided wagon with a capacity of 12 tons, was purchased for £135, and lasted until 1st March 1967.

Bass' internal open wagons had originally mostly been built by the MR and had wooded bodies and frames. Whilst the main variation was in the height of the wagon, there were occasional differences in the arrangement of the doors and the type of axleboxes with which they were fitted.

High sided wagons generally had metal plates at each corner and a tare weight of about 6 tons 2cwt. The body and solebar of Bass' internal open wagons were painted a pinky red and carried a bright red triangle on the black doors. Wheels, brakegear and the metal strengthening plates were painted black. At the bottom of the side planks in the left hand corner the number of the wagon was displayed in white. The right hand corner showed the information that the wagon was 'For internal use only' and the tare weight. In their latter days, the wagons did little work and were to be seen standing in sidings by the Brook Street Warehouse or up at Shobnall.

The Bass railway vans used for the internal movement of barley and malt were called 'malt vans', but grain vans was a more accurate description because they carried both commodities. Some barley and malt was also transported in railway company vans, and by road in horse drawn carts or later by tractor and trailer. Plough Malting always relied on road transport. Bass' wooden grain vans were mostly purchased secondhand in the 1930s; the first eight (1-8) sack vans coming from the LNER in November 1932 at a cost of £26 each. They were followed by some vans purchased from the LMS, which had mostly begun life with the MR around the turn of the century. Numbers 9-38 were acquired between September 1935 and February 1936 at a total cost of £2,022; 39-42 arrived in 1937 and 43-48 in May 1939. The ex LNER vans were broken up in 1950-53, having been replaced by more ex MR vans (49-64) purchased from BR in 1949. These were similar to the other vans and varied in building date from 1903 to 1914.

The grain vans initially carried sacks but with the change to the bulk handling of barley at some of the maltings in 1939-40, Bass' wheelwrights and blacksmiths converted them to handle bulk grain by lining them with zinc and inserting covered apertures in the roof for filling. They were arranged for side discharge, but as the maltings were suitably adapted, this was changed to sloping false bottoms with discharge chutes beneath, which reduced the capacity of the vans. The roofs were subjected to a lot of hard wear and frequently needed attention. Livery comprised a grey body and solebars with a prominent red triangle on each side; the number appeared in white at the left hand corner of the sides, and the wheels and brakegear were black. Some of the vans were sold in 1961-63 but others lasted to the end of the railway although often out of use. Number 59 was dismantled for spares in August 1961.

Three grain vans (65-67) dated from 1912-20 were obtained from the dealers, Eveson, in 1949 and were sent to Sleaford. They were sold on 24th November 1960 with the closure of the maltings. Bass also bought some steel vans from Eveson in 1951-52 with a capacity of ten tons. Two series of numbers are shown in the Register, 11-25 and 101-115, and the latter were those finally borne. Eight of these vans were sold in 1959 and the remainder on 19th April 1966.

The procedure for the mechanised handling of barley consisted of the grain van dropping its load through a grid into an elevator boot. The head of the elevator then discharged on to a band

A Redler unit for pumping out malt at Sleaford, September 1958. (C. Shepherd Collection)

When built by Charles Roberts & Co Ltd, bulk grain van No.3 only carried the name 'Worthington' in small lettering.
(Charles Roberts Collection, National Railway Museum. (ROB 4712)

conveyor and the barley was dispersed as required by a moveable 'throw-off' carriage. To remove barley out of the store, 6in diameter piping was used with one end connected to a vacuum pump and the other to a flexible pick-up nozzle dropped into the barley. Power for the pumps was provided by three of the vans being converted into 'Bass Railway Grain Veyors' by the company. These Redler units only required one van for the pump because the power came from an external electricity supply. They were less powerful than the Boby units and were only employed removing malt from the garners. Number 58 went to Worthington whilst 61 and 62 became Grain Veyor No.1 and No.2 respectively. In addition, No.1 Mobile Pneumatic Pumping Unit was put on the books on 31st March 1940. It consisted of a Boby vacuum pump fitted in a 12 tons steel railway van with dust arrestors, constructed by Charles Roberts & Company in 1939 (No.1048). Power was provided by a Gardner diesel engine (4LZ/47255) fixed in another 12 tons steel van, again built by Roberts (No.1047). The Boby was more powerful but delivered the grain with less force which minimised the risk of damage to the germ. It was No.5's job to shunt these vans around the premises and set them where they were required. No.2 unit was based at Sleaford and later worked at the Crown Maltings after 1958.

Bass went over to the mechanised handling of malt starting in 1955. To begin with, the malt was transported from the garners at the maltings to the breweries in the Eveson steel vans. Then new all-steel bulk grain hopper vans were purchased based on an older LMS design. They were built by Hurst Nelson and numbers 1-6 were acquired in 1956 at a cost of £1,221 each, to be followed by numbers 7-11 in 1959 at the increased cost per van of £1,478. Each van carried twenty tons but the first group had double compartment hoppers and the second group single compartments. Worthington also obtained two single compartment vans from Hurst Nelson in 1958. Another eleven vans were purchased by Bass (12-18) and Worthington (3-6) from Charles Roberts & Co Ltd in 1959-60. These were basically similar but adopted the later BR design of bulk grain van. The Bass vans were painted grey with a central panel inscribed with 'Bass' and the red triangle. On either side of the panel were the words 'MALT VAN'. The Worthington vans were also grey but had the name 'Worthington' across each side. Ironically after the closure of the railway, they were used on the main line to bring barley from East Anglia to Shobnall. This was after the amalgamation and they then carried the name of 'Bass Charrington' on the side.

No.11 with empty Bass grain vans runs past the former Burton Brewery Company's cooperage at Anderstaff Lane on 30th December 1966. The Gas Works and Anderstaff Lane Signal Box can be seen in the distance. (C. Shepherd)

Worthington Private Wagons

In 1948 Worthington had fourteen open wagons with medium sides, each with a capacity of eight tons, in use on the main line (29, 31-41, 44, 47) presumably on the coal and ash traffic. The majority were built in 1894 and had been acquired in 1919 for £84 each. Worthington's name was displayed across the side. The wagons were taken over by the British Transport Commission on 1st January 1948 and £16 10s 0d (£16.50) compensation was paid for each wagon. In the mid 1920s, Worthington was sending ash back to the colliery at Rawdon. One day, a wagon load of ale was mistakenly included in the train, but the error was not discovered until the next day and a clerk was sent out post haste to locate the missing wagon. He managed to find the casks but by then they had been well and truly emptied. A similar incident once happened when a wagon of full casks was wrongly sent to Worthington's Station Street Cooperage among a load of returned empty casks. Again the opportunity was not lost by those present at the cooperage. The Head Cooper was given the task of finding who had consumed the ale but all his enquiries were met with blank expressions. It was not for nothing that Worthington's Rule Book stated:

'IMPORTANT
Wagons delivered to British Railways
must carry current Forwarding Labels
or be certified empty by Inspection.'

Worthington had twenty two open wagons for internal use which had been purchased in February 1934 for £12 10s 0d (£12.50) each. They were 'little old things' in their grey livery with white lettering. It is not known when they were built because the register only shows them as being 'converted' between 1903 and 1914. These wagons were mostly used for spent grains and were to be often found stabled near Worthington's New Engine Shed so that farmers could bring their wagons to collect the grains. Often, the drivers had to move them before they could get their locomotives into the shed. One of the wagons stood here at the stop block to receive ash from the boiler fires. By 1948, these wagons were in need of replacement and they were disposed of in the early 1950s for £5 each.

Worthington's No.4 in the brewery yard in the 1930s. Two of the company's main line coal wagons can just be seen in the distance. *(IRS H.W. Robinson Collection)*

Worthington wooden internal wagon number 25 has a tare weight of 4 tons 14cwts. The body is 3 planks in height but with raised rounded ends. Built by the MR in 1907, it was used by the Malting Department.
(C. Shepherd)

Worthington grain vans at the company's brewery in January 1964. Number 202 is 14ft 11in in length and has the short brake handle. The other van 232 represents the 16ft 6in version. *(C. Shepherd)*

Forty six open wagons were obtained between 1949 and 1956 and numbered in Worthington's own series. Of the last lot, all except number 86 were subsequently converted to medium sides. Most of the wagons had originally been built by the MR and, apart from the colour, were similar to Bass' open wagons even to the higher rounded ends added to the low sided wagons. They were painted grey with inscriptions 'For internal use only' and the 'TARE' weight in white on the right hand side and the number in the bottom left hand corner. Sometimes the word 'Worthington' was painted in white on the middle of the side and at other times on the left hand side. The function of the wagon was occasionally shown and some of the 72-83 series were for the wet grains traffic.

Worthington open wagons purchased for internal use 1948-56

Numbers	Description	Load carried	Built	Acquired	Cost each	Disposal
20-29	Low sides	8 tons	1899-1901	1949	£61-£75	1962-67
54-56	Medium sides	8 tons	1901	1949	£54-£65	1961-62
57-71	Medium sides	10 tons	1898-1908	1949	£59	1961-67
72-83	Medium sides	10 tons	1907	1953	£90-£91	1961-66
84-89	High sides	12 tons	1910	1955	£124	1st March 1967

Worthington also owned 45 grain vans for internal use which were mostly built by the MR between 1902 and 1914. Bass sold them on 1st March 1967. MR goods van construction was divided into three basic sizes according to length. Most of the vans built before the end of the nineteenth century measured 14ft 11in over the headstocks on a 9ft 0in wheelbase, with the last of this type comprising some 2,967 vans being built to diagram D357 immediately after the turn of the century. Numbers 201-10 could carry 8 tons and probably came from this lot. Their shorter length was evident in the design of the bracing timbers on the side. The MR had already begun to build vans 16ft 6in in length on a 10ft 0in wheelbase, and construction concentrated on this design after the completion of the D357 work. They were built up to 1916 with a more uniform pattern of bracing timbers. Worthington vans 211-42 could carry 10 tons and were representative of the longer vehicles. Additional supports were added by the LMS to the end stanchions both at the top and bottom. There were examples of both sliding and folding doors and the vans were painted grey. Worthington also had two ex sugar vans which came from the LNER. They were latterly painted slate grey and used to carry spares for the Planet locomotives after these had been removed from Worthington's Engine Shed. The word 'Worthington' was written across the side of the vans in white.

Worthington grain vans for internal use

Numbers	Description	Source	Load carried	Built	Acquired	Cost each
100, 200	Sugar	ex LNER	8 tons	1901	1934	£28
201-210	Bulk grain	-	8 tons	1902	1937	£54
211-214	Bulk grain	ex LMR	10 tons	1909-14	1949	£50-£136
215-217	Bulk grain	ex Eveson	10 tons	1910-12	1949	£59
218-222	Bulk grain	ex Rly Executive	10 tons	1909-14	1949-50	£50-£113
223-232	Bulk grain	-	10 tons	1909-10	1953	£250-£288
233-242	Bulk grain	-	10 tons	1907-09	1956	£272-£274

The ex LNER sugar vans used for storing Planet locomotive spares stabled on the Returned Ale Stores siding at Guild Street on 3rd January 1967. (C. Shepherd)

Bass' No.1 on some of the B series wagons in the Hay Sidings on 29th March 1966.
(C. Shepherd)

The B Series Wagons

By the beginning of the 1960s, Bass-Worthington's internal rolling stock stood at a total of 186 vehicles. This was quite a sizeable fleet considering that the bulk of internal movements took place in British Railways' wagons.

Bass-Worthington rolling stock in 1961

Type	Total
Wagons	87
Roll top s.v. vans	7
Bulk vans	59
20 tons vans	24
Grain veyors	3
Sugar vans	2
Saloon and units	4

In April 1964, BR approached Bass concerning the payment it was making for the use of the BR wagons for its internal traffic. The charge was £2,720 per annum and had stood at this level since January 1943. BR justifiably considered that this payment was inadequate compared with the daily internal wagon user charge of 75p per wagon per day. Bass was of course aware of this; it was using over 200 wagons a day to transport clean casks to the breweries and racked ale to the storerooms and it would cost approximately £55,000 per year if Bass hired them from BR at the new charges.

Bass decided to purchase cheap second hand railway wagons to avoid this extra payment. Unfortunately, the BR Scrap Sales Controller could only offer wagons at the following rates and there was nothing cheaper in sufficient quality to meet Bass's needs – built up to 1944 at £100 each and built after 1944 at £120 each. Len Haywood then contacted Wm Rigley & Sons Ltd of Bulwell Forest and purchased 150 previously condemned wooden wagons and vans at a cost of £78 per vehicle in August-September 1964. This outlay of £7,200 was meant to cover the last year or two of internal railway working. Rigley also undertook to take the wagons back off Bass at their current value when Bass wanted to dispose of them.

289

p   New. To work 8.12.1900
q   New. To work 20.11.1901
r   New. To work 19.5.1913
s   On trial from AW c1933
t   New. Acquired 30.12.1939. Ov Bg 1957
u   From Worthington & Co Ltd 4.1954
v   New. Acquired 1.11.1957. RH records say 6.11.1957
w   New. Acquired 12.9.1958
x   From RH 4.1959 on trial
y   From Worthington & Co Ltd 27.5.1960
z   Sold to Bass 5.1960. From TH 6.1960 (ex demonstration locomotive)
aa   New. Acquired 23.5.1961
bb   New. Acquired 28.9.1961
cc   New. Acquired 9.11.1962
dd   New. Acquired 11.12.1962.

14   Allocated No.14 but not carried. To G.E. Baker (Metals) Ltd, Derby for scrap 20.6.1961
15   Returned to RH after trial 1959
16   Stored Worthington Old Engine Shed 25.5.1961. To Thos. W. Ward Ltd, Sheffield for scrap 1.3.1963
17   Stored Worthington Old Engine Shed 14.8.1961. To Thos. W. Ward Ltd, Sheffield for scrap 1.3.1963
18   Stored Worthington Old Engine Shed 14.10.1961. To Thos. W. Ward Ltd, Sheffield for scrap 1.3.1963
19   Withdrawn 14.11.1962. Stored Worthington Old Engine Shed 1963. To Thos. W. Ward Ltd, Derby for scrap 14.7.1964
20   Stored Worthington Old Engine Shed 1963. To Thos. W. Ward Ltd, Derby for scrap 14.7.1964
21   Withdrawn 6.5.1963. To Thos. W. Ward Ltd, Bolton on Dearne for scrap 22.5.1963
22   Withdrawn 6.7.1964. To Thos. W. Ward Ltd, Derby for scrap 20.8.1964
23   Withdrawn 6.7.1964. Stored Worthington Engine Shed 21.8.1964. To store for Staffordshire County Museum, Shugborough for preservation 17.2.1967. Returned for display at Bass Museum 4.4.1977
24   Stored Worthington Old Engine Shed 6.1965. To Railway Preservation Society, Chasewater, Staffs 7.1967. No.20 returned on loan for display at the Bass Museum c6.1980
25   Stored Worthington Old Engine Shed 27.5.1965. To Albert Looms Ltd, Spondon for scrap 8.1967
26   Withdrawn 9.1965 and stored at Guild Street. To Albert Looms Ltd, Spondon for scrap 8.1967
27   Withdrawn 11.1965 and stored at Guild Street. To Albert Looms Ltd, Spondon for scrap 8.1967
28   To Geo. Cohen, Sons & Co Ltd, Canning Town, Essex 9.1967
29   To P.D. Fuels Ltd, Dibles Wharf, Northam, Hants 2.1968
30   To L. Sanderson Ltd, Birtley, County Durham (dealer) 26.3.1968. Then to South Staffs Wagon Co Ltd, Princes End, Tipton 1969
31   To Wagon Repairs Ltd, Port Tennant, West Glamorgan 28.3.1968
32   Sold to John Gretton for preservation 24.7.1967. To J. Gretton, Melton Mowbray, Leics 8.1967. Transferred to Great Western Preservation Society, Didcot 31.8.1968
33   To TH 11.1968. Then to Boulton & Paul Ltd, Lowestoft, Suffolk 14.4.1969
34   To TH 20.11.1968. Then to CEGB North Tees power station, Haverton Hill 10.1969
35   To TH 21.11.1968. Then to Marchon Products Ltd, Marchon Works, Whitehaven 8.1969

APPENDIX 5

REFERENCES

Published Sources

Ackworth W.M. 1900 The Railways of England
Ahrons E.L. Locomotive and Train Working in the Latter Part of the Nineteenth Century Volumes 1-2
Anderson P. Howard 1973 Forgotten Railways: The East Midlands
Anderson V.R. & Fox G.K. 1981 A Pictorial Record of LMS Architecture
-      Baguley 621. Industrial Railway Record August 1975
Bagwell P.S. 1963 The Railwaymen, The History of the National Union of Railwaymen
Baker A. & Civil T.D.A. 1973 Bagnalls of Stafford
Barnard A. 1889-91 The Noted Breweries of Great Britain and Ireland Volumes 1-2
Barnes E.G. 1966 The Rise of the Midland Railway 1844-74
Barnes E.G. 1969 The Midland Mainline 1875-1922
Baxter D. 1977-84 British Locomotive Catalogue 1825-1923 Volumes 1-4
Biddle G. 1973 Victorian Stations
Blakemore M. Didn't we have a lovely time, the day we went to Scarborough. Railway World November 1988
Booth A. 1977 A Pictorial Survey of Standard Gauge Industrial Diesels
Brooks P. 1978 Seventy Five Years, the Story of Public Transport in Burton upon Trent
Brown M. Mining and Industry in South Derbyshire and North West Leicestershire
-      Burton LMS Warehouse. Railway Magazine June 1974
Burton upon Trent CBC 1928 Jubilee Celebrations of the Borough
Campbell Highet 1976 All Steamed Up
Camwell W.A. The Stafford & Uttoxeter Railway. Railay World May 1957
Carter E.F. 1959 A Historical Geography of the Railways of the British Isles
Casserley H.C. The Staffy. Trains Illustrated March 1951
Charlewood R.E. The Last Decade of the Midland. Railway Magazine 1947-48
Charlewood R.E. The MR's West of England service. Railway Magazine August 1907
Christiansen R. 1985 Forgotten Railways: The West Midlands
Christiansen R. 1973 A Regional History of the Railways of Great Britain: West Midlands
Christiansen R. & Miller R. 1971 North Staffordshire Railway
Clinker C.R. The Birmingham & Derby Junction Railway. Dugdale Society Occasional Paper No.11 1956
Clinker C.R. The Birmingham & Derby Junction Railway. Railway World July 1954
Clinker C.R. The Leicester & Swannington Railway. Transactions of Leicestershire Archaeological & Historical
      Society Volume 30 1954
Clinker C.R. The Leicester & Swannington Railway. Railway World April 1953
Clinker C.R. London & North Western Railway Chronology 1900-60
Clinker C.R. New Light on the Leicester - Swannington Railway. Railway Magazine March 1953
Clinker C.R. 1978 Register of Closed Passenger Stations and Goods Depots in England, Scotland and Wales
      1830-1977
Clinker C.R. & Hadfield C. 1978 The Ashby de la Zouch Canal and its Railway
Cole D. 1963-70 Contractors Locomotives Parts 1-4
Cook A.F. 1990 LMS Locomotive Design and Construction
Cooksey J. 1984 Brewery Buildings in Burton on Trent. (Victorian Society)
Cramp A.G. West of Basford. Railway Magazine January 1987
-      1908 Directory of Warrington
Dix C. Running Powers & Working Arrangements: NSR. Railway Magazine April 1909
Dorman C. 1967 LMS Album
Dorman C. & Casserley H.C. 1967 Midland Album
Dorman C. & Casserley H.C. 1969 Railway History in Pictures: The Midlands
Dow G. 1978 Great Central Recalled
Dow G. 1975 Midland Style
Dow G. 1970 North Staffordshire Album
Dunn J.M. 1966 Reflections on a Railway Career LNWR to BR
Dyos H.J. & Aldcroft D.H. 1969 British Transport
Egerton E. 1766 History of Inland Navigation
Essery R.J. 1980 Midland Wagons Volumes 1-2
Essery R.J. & Jenkinson D. 1984-89 An Illustrated Review of Midland Locomotives from 1883 Volumes 1-4
Essery R. & Morgan K. 1977 The LMS Wagon

Essery T. Firing Days at Saltley
Essery T. More Firing Days at Saltley
Evans G.E. 1970, Where Beards Wag All
- 1884 Fortunes Made in Business Volume 2
Franks D.L. 1975 The Ashby & Nuneaton Joint Railway
Gairns J. West to North by the Midland Railway. Railway Magazine July 1910
Gent B. Hunslet 2176 - The Biography of a War Surplus Diesel. Narrow Gauge 91
Glendenning S. Burton & Ashby Light Railway. Railway Magazine July 1906
Godfrey A. 100 Years Ago, Men of the Midland. Railway World December 1976
Goodman R.E. Burton Jubilees. Railway World December 1973
Gotheridge I. The Leicester - Burton on Trent Line. Railway World April 1986
Gough J.V. 1989 The Midland Railway: A Chronology 2nd edition
Gourvish T.R. 1972 Mark Huish and the LNWR, a Study of Management
Greenslade & Stuart 1965 History of Staffordshire
Gringling C.H. 1903 The History of the Great Northern Railway 1845-1902
Hadfield C. 1966 The Canals of the East Midlands
Hadfield C. 1966 The Canals of the West Midlands
Hall W.T. The Ashby & Nuneaton Branch of the LMSR. Railway Magazine 1932
Hamilton Ellis C. 1953 The Midland Railway
Harman F.W. Manning Wardle 60 The 1862 Exhibition Engine. Industrial Railway Record May 1984
Harris M. 1976 Preserved Railway Carriages
Hawkins C. & Reeve G. 1981-84 LMS Engine Sheds Volumes 1-4
Hawkins K. & Pass C. 1979 The Brewing Industry
Hawkins K.H. 1978 A History of Bass Charrington
Higginson M. 1989 The Friargate Line
Higson M.F. 1972 London Midland Fireman
Industrial Railway Society 1992 Industrial Locomotives of North Wales
Industrial Railway Society 1993 Industrial Locomotives of South Staffordshire
Industrial Railway Society 1992 Industrial Locomotives of the West Midlands
Industrial Railway Society 1992 Locomotives of the Ministry of Defence
Jones P. 1981 The Stafford & Uttoxeter Railway
Jux F. 1985 John Fowler & Co Locomotives Works List
Kalla-Bishop P.M. Locomotives at War
Klapper C. 1962 The Golden Age of Tramways
Lambert A.J. 1978 East Midlands Branch Line Album
Leleux R. 1976 Regional History of Railways of Great Britain: The East Midlands
Lindsay J. 1979 The Trent & Mersey Canal
Lowe J.W. 1975 British Steam Locomotive Builders
Manifold 1952 The North Staffordshire Railway
- 1909 Manual of British & Foreign Brewery Companies
Marshall J. 1978 A Biographical Dictionary of Railway Engineers
Marshall J. Midlands Coal on the Great Northern. Railway Magazine September, November 1975
Mathias P. 1959 The Brewing Industry in England 1700-1830
Matthews P. 1976 Private Owner Wagons
Molyneux W. 1869 Burton on Trent, its history, its Waters, and its Breweries
Moss A. 1984 A Burtonian's Diary
Nelson J. 1975 LNWR Portrayed
Newman R. & Budd A. Midland Railway Signal boxes. The Wyvern Nos.66-73
Nock O.S. 1958 Great Northern Railway
- A Notable Brewery Railway System. Railway Magazine February 1926
- NSR Workings over Foreign Railways. Railway Magazine October 1907
NUR 1971 The Railway Servants, a Century of Railway Trade Unionism 1871-1971
Owen C.C. The Early History of the Upper Trent Navigation. Transport History Volume 1 No.3 1968
Owen C.C. 1978 The Industrial Development of Burton on Trent
Owen C.C. 1984 The Leicestershire and South Derbyshire Coalfield 1200-1900
Owen C.C. 1992 The Greatest Brewery in the World. A History of Bass, Ratcliff & Gretton
Paar H.W. The Romford Brewery Railway. Industrial Railway Record December 1982
Parr R.B. 1970 An English Country Tramway
Pearson R. 1993 The Bass Railway Trips

Peaty I.P. 1985 Brewery Railways
Peaty I.P. 1988 English Breweries in Old Photographs
Perseus Locomotive Sheds, London & North Western Railway. Railway Observer May 1958
Peters Ivo 1976 Somewhere Along the Line
Pitt W. 1808 General View of the Agriculture of the County of Stafford
Plot R. 1686 Natural History of Staffordshire
Price M.R.C. 1982 Industrial Saundersfoot
Radford J.B. 1971 Derby Works and Midland Locomotives
Radford J.B. 1986 Rail Centres: Derby
Railway Clearing House 1883-1962 Handbooks of Railway Stations, Sidings etc
-       The Railways of Nottingham. Railway Magazine February, March 1932
-       1935 Railway Wonders of the World
Rannie J.A. The Midland of 35 Years Ago. Railway Magazine May-June 1946
RCTS 1963-90 Locomotives of the LNER Parts 1-10B
RCTS Locomotive Stockbooks
RCHS 1989 The Midland Counties Railway
Read R.E.G. Locomotive Activity on the NSR. Railway World September-December 1951
Read R.E.G. The NSR and its Neighbours. Railway World March-April 1954
Redman R.N. 1972 The Railway Foundry, Leeds
Riley R.C. 1962 A Night on the Beer. Trains Illustrated Annual
Robinson E.E. The South Staffordshire Railway & its Locomotives. Railway Magazine September 1935
Rose R.E. The Midland 0-6-4Ts: Sinners or sinned against. Railway World September 1987
Rowledge P. 1975 The Locomotives of the LMS Built 1923-1951
Shaw S. 1798-1801 History and Antiquities of Staffordshire
Sherlock R. 1976 The Industrial Archaeology of Staffordshire
Stanier D, West K., Stanier L. 1991 Trams and Buses in Burton 1903-1985
Steel W.L. 1914 History of the LNWR
Stevenson P. 1963 Transport in Burton on Trent RCHS Tour Notes No.13
Sowerby G. & Farman R. 1983 Burton upon Trent and District on Old Postcards
Sowerby G. & Farman R. 1984 More Old Postcards of Burton upon Trent and District
Stephenson Locomotive Society 1954 Railways of the West Midlands 1808-1954
Stretton C.G. 1901 History of the Midland Railway
Strong L.A.G. 1957 A Brewer's Progress 1757-1957: A Survey of Charrington's Brewery on the Occasion of its
        Bicentenary
Storer J.W. Burton and Ashby Light Railways Tramcar No.14. The Wyvern No.49
Stuart D. 1975-77 History of Burton upon Trent Volumes 1-2
-       41516 Technical Notes. Railway World April 1956
Tee D.F. The 0-4-0T's of the Midland Railway. Railway Observer May-June 1950
Thomas A.R. & J.L. 1987 The Sentinel 1930-1980
Thornley W.G. 1975 Breath of Steam Volume 1

Tonks E.S. 1974 Ruston & Hornsby Locomotives
Tonks E.S. Whitacre - Hampton in Arden. Railway Magazine March 1950
Townsley D. A Small Brewery Locomotive. Railway Modeller April 1972
-       1966 Trumans the Brewers 1666-1966
Tuplin W.A. 1973 Midland Steam
Twells H.N. 1985 Leicester and Burton Branch Railway
Twells H.N. 1982 LMS Miscellany
Twells H.N. 1984 Railways in Burton and the Trent Valley through 145 years
Underhill C.H. 1941 History of Burton upon Trent
Vaizey J. 1960 The Brewing Industry 1886-1951
Victoria County History 1967 Staffordshire Volume 2
Wade G.A. A Town of Railways and Beer. Railway Magazine August 1901
Walsall Local History Society 1981 Walsall Stations
Wain H.J. 1966 The Story of Drakelow
Webb B. 1973 The British Internal Combustion Locomotive 1894-1940
Webb B. Kent Construction Engineering Ltd. Industrail Railway Record June 1967
Webb B. The Origin of the Species. Industrial Railway Record December 1974
Weaver R. Baguley 800. Industrial Railway Record September 1967
Weaver R. 1975 Baguley Locomotives 1914-1931

Weaver R. Drewry Car Co. 1906-70. Industrial Railway Record December 1971
Weir H. The Midland North to West Dining Expresses. Railway Magazine September 1897
Wesley W. 1857 History and Description of the Town and Borough of Burton upon Trent
White P.M. & Storer J.W. 1984 Around the Wooden Box
White P.M. & Storer J.W. 1983 Sixpenny Switchback
Williams F.S. 1875 The Midland Railway
Willan T.S. 1936 River Navigation in England
Wilson H.S. 1971 A History of the Travelling Post Offices of Great Britain Part 1
Wingate H. & Gillham C. 1962 Great British Tramway Networks
Wishaw F. 1842 Railways of Great Britain and Northern Ireland
Wood A. History of Trade and Transport on the River Trent. Transactions of the Thornton Society of Nottinghamshire 1950
Worsencroft K. 1978 Bygone Sleaford
Wrottesley J. 1979 The Great Northern Railway Volumes 1-3

Original Records
Act for more effectively repairing and widening roads 8th May 1818
Samuel Allsopp Customers Ledger 1822-26
Allsopps Sidings Signal Box Train Register 1962
M.T. Bass Letterbooks 1842-55
William Bass Daybook 1760-70
Bass & Cos premises description 1876
Bass & Worthington Assets Register 1948
Bass, Ratcliff & Gretton Engine Log & Repair Books 1892-1964
Bass, Ratcliff & Gretton Locomotive Department Stock Book 1876-83, 1892-98, 1947-67
Bass, Ratcliff & Gretton Revised Rules and Regulations for Railway Department
British Railways Industructions for the Guidance of Drivers and Others in charge of Brewery Companies' Engines when working on the lines of BR (LM Region) at Burton on Trent 1960
British Railways Rule Book 1950
H.A. Couchman letters
English Electric Co Ltd, Battery Locomotives for Use in Power Station Sidings
Extracts from a Goods Agent's Notebook at Burton on Trent
General statement of turnpike income and expenditure 1822-71
Hawthorn Leslie Engine Book
Thomas Hill (Rotherham) Ltd, Specification of 'Sentinel' 100hp 25 tons BE/DG industrial locomotives
History of Bass & Co's Railway Department submitted to Railway Magazine May 1925
Hudswell Clarke Engine Book (Courtesy K. Plant)
Industrial Locomotive Society, Extracts from the Contract Journal 1881-1959, Machinery Market 1879-1970 and The Engineer 1917-24
LMS Appendix to Working Timetable March 1937
LNWR Sidings Agreement Diagrams (Courtesy Peter Lee)
Manning Wardle Engine Book and History Sheets
Musgrave & Bass Daybook 1794-96
MR, LNWR, NSR, Rules & Regulations for Brewery Companies' Servants, Burton on Trent 1921
Neilson Reid Order Book
NSR Locomotive Shed, Agreement with MR 11th August 1914
Ruston & Hornsby files - extracts 1931-49 (Courtesy Andrew Smith)
Shobnall Junction Signal Box Train Register 1955
Staffordshire Register of Canal Boats 1795-97
Title deeds to Bass & Worthington Burton properties
Benjamin Wilson Letterbook 1791-92, Miscellaneous ledger 1794-96, Customers ledger 1791-96 and Letterbooks 1801-10
John Walker Wilson, Daybook and stock valuations 1778-83
Worthington & Co Ltd, General Rules & Regulations to be observed by Servants employed on the Railways of Worthington & Co Ltd and the Sidings of the British Railways
Worthington Engine Log & Repair Books 1934-60

Also extracts from local newspapers, brewery journals, published and working timetables, brewery handbooks and various directories for Burton and Staffordshire

APPENDIX 6

INDEX

The Index covers pages 1 to 292 but does not include the maps or individual streets or buildings.

Great Central Railway 205
Great Central Railway (preserved) 128
Great Eastern Railway 41, 157
Great Northern Railway 26-29, 39, 40, 45, 51, 52,
    60, 72, 86, 88, 95, 112, 136, 192, 200
Great Western Railway 99, 117, 119
Great Western Society 266
Great Yarmouth 41
Greaves, Bull & Lakin 93
Green & Clarkson 35, 190
Gresford Colliery 170
Gresley 38, 109, 242
Gretna Munitions Factory 175
Gretton, John and Fred 14, 69, 70, 117, 190, 240,
    255, 266, 292
Griff Colliery 168
Grinling, J. Church 203
Gripper & Bayliss 134
Grout & Co 36, 138, 140, 203
Guild Street Branch 18-26, 37, 45, 47, 69-87, 105,
    107, 187, 197, 199, 201, 205, 208, 224, 234-
    39, 261, 267, 268, 279, 292
Gwaun cae Gurwen 117
Gwendraeth 117

Halbard, P.F. 199
Hall, John Bockett 23
Hall's Colliery 112, 279, 280
Hallam & Sons 138, 140
Hallfield Colliery 280
Hampton in Arden 10-13
Harbury Cement Works 93
Harringay Contract 95
Harrison, Mr 22, 148
Hawthorn & Co 175
Hawthorn Leslie & Co 123-26, 165, 183, 207, 211-
    20, 228, 258
Hawthorn Ltd, R. & W. (see Hawthorn Leslie)
Hay Branch 18-28, 45, 48, 51, 57, 66, 81, 82-95,
    100-109, 227, 233, 267
Haynes, F. 267-69
Haywood, Len 74, 233, 265, 268, 289
Heape, F. 35
Hemingways Ltd 250
Herbertson & Sons Ltd, A. 123
Hexham 123
Hibberd & Co, F.C. 134, 194, 229, 230, 264
Hill, Alfred 102, 229
Hill, Charles 8, 17, 35, 59, 142, 144, 169
Hill, John 15
Hill & Sons, Isaac 207, 251
Hill Ltd, David 190
Hill (Rotherham) Ltd, Thomas 222, 261, 262, 266
Hitchin 26
Hodges, George 80, 183
Hollington 108
Holwell Iron Co 203
Holyhead 45
Honeywill Brothers 131, 171, 208, 229

Horninglow Branch 25, 187-92
Horwich Works 161
Hoult & Son, J. 190
Hudson 194
Hudson, George 12, 13, 16
Hudswell Clarke & Co 88-93, 101, 102, 146, 170,
    171, 175, 200-08, 225-34, 253, 262
Hudswell Clarke & Rodgers (see Hudswell Clarke)
Hughes-Fowler 62
Hull 6, 51, 134, 149
Hunsbury Iron Co 291
Hunslet Engine Co 168, 176-78, 193, 194, 244-58,
    291
Hunt & Stephenson 197
Hurst Nelson 205, 284

Ibstock Colliery 165
Ind Coope (see Ind Coope & Allsopp)
Ind Coope & Allsopp 6, 8, 10, 15-32, 35, 36, 41,
    44-52, 55, 58-67, 72, 80-86, 95, 101, 118,
    123, 127, 134, 136-42, 146, 155, 156, 161,
    162, 170, 171, 181, 184-88, 196-223, 234,
    251, 267, 274
Ind Coope, Tetley & Ansells (see Ind Coope &
    Allsopp)
India 8, 41
India Rubber & Gutta Percha Co 131, 192
Infirmary, Burton 144, 145
Ireland 45, 48, 63

Jackson 191
Johnson, Samuel 39, 40, 198, 163, 247, 248
Jones & Broadbent Ltd 138, 140
Jones & Co, Frederick 138

Kay & Co, James C. 134
Keeling, H. 188
Kegworth 28
Kent Construction & Engineering Co Ltd 229, 230,
    264
Kenyon Junction 134
Kilgetty 117
Kilmarnock 209
Kind Ltd, J.B. 36, 134, 137-40, 282
Kirkby 139
Kirtley, Matthew 39, 55
Kitson & Co 161, 162
Knowles of Woodville 71, 112, 280
Körking Bros 246

Lacombe & Blindman Valley Electric Railway 91,
    133
Lancashire & Yorkshire Railway 157, 161, 195, 216
Lathbury 191
Leeds 37, 61, 68, 88, 89, 94, 118, 119, 201, 232,
    246-48
Leicester 10, 13-15, 40, 54, 65, 66, 68, 109, 155,
    163, 181
Leicester & Swannington Railway 13, 14

PHOTOGRAPHS

Every effort has been made to track down the various sources of the photographs. These are indicated in the captions and I am grateful for the support that everyone has given. Apologies are offered if a credit has been inadvertently omitted because of lack of information about the origin of a photograph. The Bass Museum at Burton on Trent has an interesting collection of over 3,000 prints, negatives and slides depicting the town and its breweries. Hugh Davies of Chalcot House, 32 Charterhouse Road, Godalming, Surrey GU7 2AQ offers railway photographs for sale, of which a number depict brewery scenes at Burton on Trent. Finally I should especially mention that Dick Riley and Bernard Mettam have been very helpful in providing photographs from their collections.

Industrial Railway Society

The Industrial Railway Society was formed in 1949 as the Industrial Locomotive Information Section of the Birmingham Locomotive Club. The Society is the leading organisation in the United Kingdom devoted to the study of all aspects of industrial and privately owned locomotives and railways, both at home and abroad. Members receive a quarterly magazine called the 'Industrial Railway Record', in addition to a bi-monthly bulletin containing topical news and amendments to the Society's Handbook Series, access to a well-stocked library, discounts on Society publications and visits to and rail tours of industrial railway systems. Further details are available by sending two first class stamps to Bernard Mettam, 27 Glenfield Crescent, Newbold, Chesterfield S41 8SF.

The Society is a major publisher of works devoted to industrial locomotives and railways. Books available for sale (as at April 1996) include:-

Industrial Locomotives (including preserved and Minor Railway Locomotives) 11EL Compiled by George Morton   **Hardback** **£21.00**   **Softback** **£17.00**
A new book listing all industrial, preserved and minor railway locomotives in the British Isles as at 1st January 1996.

Industrial Railways of Seaham
by Adrian Booth   **Hardback** **£12.95**   **Softback** **£9.95**

Locomotives and Railcars of the Spanish Narrow Gauge Public Railways
by John Morley and Paul Spencer   **Softback** **£9.99**

Industrial Locomotives of Dyfed and Powys
Compiled by John de Havilland   **Hardback** **£19.95**   **Softback** **£16.95**

Industrial Locomotives of South Staffordshire
Compiled by Ray Shill   **Hardback** **£17.95**   **Softback** **£14.95**

Industrial Locomotives of East Anglia
Compiled by Chris Fisher   **Hardback** **£19.95**   **Softback** **£16.95**

Industrial Locomotives of West Midlands
Compiled by Ray Shill   **Softback** **£16.95**

Small Mines of South Wales
by Adrian Booth   **Hardback** **£12.95**   **Softback** **£9.95**

Ministry of Defence Locomotives
Compiled by Roger Hateley   **Softback** **£9.95**

A Railway History of Denaby & Cadeby Collieries
by Adrian Booth   **Softback** **£7.95**

Industrial Locomotives of West Germany - Book 3 (Nordrheim-Westfalen)
by Brian Rumary   **Softback** **£10.00**

A new major work due to be published in June, 1996:-

Industrial Locomotives of West Glamorgan
by Martin Potts and Gordon Green   **Hardback** **£20.00**   **Softback** **£17.00**

All prices are inclusive of postage and packing.

Copies of these publications can be purchased from Mr S. Geeson, IRS Publications, 1 Clifton Court, Oakham, Rutland LE15 6LT.